Urban Politics
and Public Policy

Urban Politics and Public Policy

The City in Crisis

SECOND EDITION

EDITED BY

Stephen M. David AND Paul E. Peterson

Fordham University   *University of Chicago*

PRAEGER PUBLISHERS
New York

Published in the United States of America in 1976 by Praeger Publishers, Inc.
111 Fourth Avenue, New York, N.Y. 10003

Second printing, 1977

© 1976 by Praeger Publishers, Inc.

Library of Congress Cataloging in Publication Data
David, Stephen M   1934-   comp.
  Urban politics and public policy.
  Includes bibliographical references.
    1. Cities and towns—United States. I. Peterson, Paul E., joint comp.
II. Title.
HT123.D38   1976   309.2′62′0973   75-45450
ISBN 0-275-64290-9

Printed in the United States of America

Contents

Acknowledgments

This type of reader owes its greatest debt to the numerous scholars who have begun to probe the relations between urban politics and public policy. Our own interest in such matters was stimulated by the late Wallace Sayre and by Grant McConnell; those familiar with the works of these men will notice the many ways in which their ideas influenced the construction of these essays. We owe a more particular debt to J. David Greenstone, who generously permitted us to use material that he and one of the editors worked out for their study *Race and Authority in Urban Politics*.

Finally, we are especially grateful that Janet and Carol are as patient and indulgent as they are.

Introduction: Power, Policy, and the Urban Crisis

This collection of essays focuses on the relation between the processes of urban politics and the substance of public policy. In so doing, it seeks to build upon the major studies of urban politics that have, in the last two decades, transformed the study of local government into a heated but fascinating series of debates over the nature of urban political systems. At one time, the study of local government was confined to examination of variations in formal and legal structures. In more recent years, debate has raged over broad questions concerning the less formal but more important power relationships that "really" affect what happens in a community. A variety of approaches have been developed by sociologists and political scientists to provide answers to these questions. Some researchers have identified the individuals holding major formal positions of responsibility, others have tried to determine which persons have the greatest reputation for influence, and still others have tried to locate the people making decisions. Although all these approaches have their value, this reader argues that the distribution of power in cities cannot be known without focusing—at least in part—on the policy consequences of urban politics. A review of the "power structure" debate, as the controversy over community power has come to be known, helps to illuminate the importance of the study of urban public policy.

Floyd Hunter and a number of other sociologists advanced what has become known as the *elitist* interpretation of the structure of power in American cities.[1] These "elitists" have claimed that a small number of individuals, consisting primarily of high-ranking business executives, have enormous influence in local communities. They determine the issues that will receive public attention, and their informal connections with local governments give them an inordinate degree of influence over a broad range of urban policies. It is further argued that this influence is used to protect business interests.

The data supporting this elitist interpretation have been typically obtained by asking reasonably well-informed local community activists for the names of the individuals who seemed to have a great deal of influence in their community. One of Floyd Hunter's questions, for example, ran as follows: "If a project were before the community that required *decision* by a group of leaders —leaders that nearly everyone would accept—which [leaders] . . . would you choose?"[2] Even though the question did not directly ask, "Who's got clout around here?" the answer would seem to give a pretty good estimate of who people *thought* had a good deal of influence. And, when it comes to influence, what people *think* becomes crucial—as anyone can discover if he tries to promote an idea in a setting where he is little known or poorly regarded. Thus, Hunter and other sociologists believed they had quite good evidence for their elitist interpretation when those with the greatest reputation for influence usually turned out to be businessmen.

Their approach to the study of power was seriously criticized, however, by a number of political scientists, who have become known as *pluralists*.[3] These pluralists argued that elitists like Floyd Hunter had only studied people's reputation for power, not the actual exercise of power. Even those with great resources for influencing governmental action often do not have much impact on public policy—simply because they do not care enough about particular issues to mobilize their resources and coordinate their efforts with like-minded leaders. According to pluralists, the study of power, therefore, needs to focus not on reputations but on the actual decisions taken in the course of governing a city. Thus, in their analyses, they have attributed power to an individual only when he successfully initiates or vetoes a proposal.[4]

When pluralists applied this approach to the study of community power, they discovered a far more elusive set of power relationships than the elitists had found. As Robert Dahl argues in his seminal study of New Haven, no single group of individuals dominates decision-making in all areas of public policy.[5] A person who has influence in one area may be totally without influence in any other; and the influence that any group or individual wields fluctuates rapidly over time. Dahl admits that elected officials have considerably more influence over policy than other citizens have, but he stresses that politicians cannot hold office without the support of a majority of the voters. In fact, Dahl suggests that it hardly makes sense to talk about a power "structure," for that word implies something permanent, enduring, persisting over some substantial period of time. Instead, pluralists speak of political "processes," political activities that change so rapidly that it is hard to find any "structure" to them. Businessmen have influence in local politics, particularly on those matters of concern to them. But so do labor unions, ethnic groups, homeowners, taxpayers, PTA members, and almost every other group of individuals who care deeply enough about some aspect of public affairs to do something about it.

The pluralist argument is a powerful rebuttal to the elitist position. Although the reputational method probably does identify people of considerable political influence, any interpretation of urban politics that sees policy as merely the product of the decisions of a small elite overlooks the complexity of urban politics. The pluralists are also certainly correct in stressing the variation in power relations from issue to issue, the host of groups, organizations, and individual participants involved in the process, the conflicts *within* the business community, and the critical role that elections can play in shaping power relationships. Above all, the pluralists are able to show that power is fragmented into separate, functionally specific policy areas, such as housing, education, and transportation, each of which usually activates a distinct set of political groups.

If the pluralists rightly see complexity and multiplicity of forces in urban politics, serious questions about power relations in American cities still remain. Although it is unlikely that any one small group controls all policy decisions, the over-all pattern of power relationships can still be biased in favor of the rich, the well organized, and a host of specialized business and commercial interests. The elected politician may make many of the policy decisions; but as he makes these decisions, he may more carefully consider the interests of those who can finance his campaign, have good access to the news media, and can mount effective propaganda campaigns, than the interests of a poorly informed voter majority. The influence of specific individuals may vary from issue to issue, but in almost every specific functional policy arena, biases may be found that advantage the better-off at the expense of the less well-off or some special interests at the expense of consumers or the public at large. A variety of groups may be involved in the policy-making process, but the policies that are the result of these decisions may not benefit all groups in any roughly equal manner.

One of the major problems with the pluralists' analyses is that, in studying who was making the decisions, they paid no attention to *what* decisions were being made. Dahl's study of New Haven, for example, discusses the politics of urban renewal without ever focusing on the groups that benefited and the groups that lost as a result of urban-renewal policy. This ignores one of the very best ways of obtaining information about power relations in a city, for it is not unreasonable to conclude that groups that gain a good deal from governmental policies probably had something to say about their enactment. Looking at public policy in order to reach conclusions about political power is looking at who controls the field at the end of the battle. Although it cannot tell you all the factors that affected the outcome of the struggle, it gives you a fairly good idea of who in the end mustered the greatest force behind their position. On the other hand, if one looks at only the ongoing struggle without keeping in mind the eventual outcome, one may find such a wide variety of competing forces and ephemeral, changing power relationships that one concludes that power was widely shared—even when in the end one side was decisively defeated.

The study of urban public policy can thus make an important contribution to our understanding of power relations in American cities. By looking at how specific urban policies are made and the consequences these policies have for the lives of different groups living in a metropolitan area, we can see whether government responds to the needs and aspirations of unorganized and poorer groups in our society, or whether it listens primarily to the demands of the affluent and/or narrowly focused special interests. In the selections that follow, the reader will not find any simple or uniform answer to this question. Indeed, he will have to draw his own conclusions from the array of viewpoints and evidence that is presented. But, in our introductory essays, we shall not disguise our own conclusion that policy analysis reveals a far less open political process, a policy-making structure far more in the service of specialized and already advantaged interests, than is desirable in a society committed to democratic traditions and ideals. Indeed, the biases in our urban political structures are so great that American cities, even in a period of great national wealth and prosperity, are undergoing severe crises. Government seems incapable of responding to widely recognized problems, and citizens feel they are unable to influence its direction. These dual but interrelated problems of urban governance and citizen participation lie at the political heart of the urban crisis. They cannot be understood without an examination of the close relations between political power and public policy.

In order to develop this argument, we have divided this reader into three parts. Part I sets forth the two major political problems —urban governance and citizen participation—facing our cities. Urban areas have become ungovernable because power is so fragmented that political leaders are ill-equipped to respond creatively to centrifugal socioeconomic forces responsible for the twin problems of suburban sprawl and central-city decay. Because metropolitan areas are fragmented into a host of suburban communities and special districts, leaders are precluded from formulating any coherent plan controlling the pace and shape of urban growth. Within central cities themselves, power has shifted to municipal agencies which, as islands of functional power, concentrate on maintaining themselves and enhancing their status within the government at the expense of the consumer of their services and of the increasingly beseiged central-city taxpayer. Governmental efforts to improve the quality of services in the central city seem only to produce a worsening fiscal crisis.

But areal and functional fragmentation have not only sharply limited the capacities of urban political leaders; this maze of political jurisdictions has also discouraged all but narrowly focused producer groups from participating in the political life of the city. Although minority groups and consumer and other apparently public-spirited organizations have protested against the entrenched, specialized interests that dominate urban policy systems, the role of these groups has been extremely marginal.

Part II examines these two crises of governance and participation in the context of four specific policy areas—housing, transportation, education, and police. Data in this portion of the book may be used to evaluate the overarching arguments about governance and participation developed in its first section. The evidence is not always unequivocal, and the reader may wish to draw his own interpretation on the basis of the material presented. But the editors have concluded that the preponderance of information concerning each of these four policy areas suggests that power in the metropolitan area is fragmented among competing territorial jurisdictions and, within the central city, delegated to professionalized bureaucracies and specialized, narrowly focused group interests.

To be sure, the groups exercising power vary from area to area. In that sense, there is no single power elite that dominates American urban politics. Indeed, the urban crisis is in part due to the inability of any set of political leaders with any coherent vision of the needs of our metropolitan areas effectively to rein in the powerful socioeconomic forces laying waste once valuable central-city territory. On the other hand, if power has been decentralized areally and functionally to specialized interests that shape programs at the expense of consumers, taxpayers, minorities, and the poor, this hardly adds up to a pluralistic structure of power where the whole range of interests in the community is fairly represented.

The concluding section examines prospects for urban governance and participation in the late 1970s. On the positive side, it seems that some progress is being made toward incorporating at least the political leadership of black and other minority communities into the urban policy-making system. But however much this may mitigate conflict and stabilize intergroup relations, it has thus far hardly altered the crisis of urban governance from escalating to a point where the fiscal bankruptcy of cities must now be accepted as a genuine possibility. Without state and federal intervention on a scale not presently conceived, the processes of disinvestment and decay at the center of our metropolitan area will continue unabated.

NOTES

1. Floyd Hunter, *Community Power Structure* (Garden City, N.Y.: Doubleday, 1963). For other essays, see Willis D. Hawley and Frederick M. Wirt (eds.), *The Search for Community Power* (Englewood Cliffs, N.J.: Prentice Hall, 1968).
2. Hunter, *op. cit.*, p. 63.
3. Robert Dahl, *Who Governs?* (New Haven: Yale University Press, 1961); Aaron Wildavsky, *Leadership in a Small Town* (Totawa, N.J.: Bedminster Press, 1964); Edward Banfield, *Political Influence* (New York: Free Press, 1961); and Nelson Polsby, *Community Power and Political Theory* (New Haven: Yale University Press, 1963).
4. Dahl, *op. cit.*, pp. 332–33.
5. *Ibid., passim.* Dahl's generalizations about power in America more generally, which are largely based on his New Haven study, are presented in the selection by Dahl reprinted in this reader.

I
Governments Without Purposes; Citizens Without Power

I

Governments Without Purposes; Citizens Without Power

American cities face two equally fundamental, though apparently contradictory, political problems. One has to do with governance; the other, with citizen representation. According to some perspectives, the first problem is paramount. Governments in urban areas are so fragmented, power is so dispersed, authority is so decentralized among a host of competing agencies and jurisdictions that political institutions lack the capability to solve the common problems of the community.[1] A second perspective sees citizen representation as the critical issue. Ordinary citizens, particularly the less financially able and the more dependent upon governmental services, are unable to influence public policy. Power is concentrated in the hands of political, bureaucratic, and business elites to such an extent that it makes a mockery of the democratic formalities that legitimize local government.[2]

At first glance, urban governance and citizen representation may appear to be mutually exclusive objectives. If power is centralized so that decisions can be made and executed with efficiency and dispatch, most people would seem to have little opportunity to influence the outcome. On the other hand, if power is widely dispersed so that many individuals and groups can influence decisions, government's capacity to resolve common problems would seem to be sharply limited. Accordingly, one goal could be achieved only at considerable cost to the other. In the case of American urban politics, however, the problem is not that these are two horns of a political dilemma. The problem in American cities is *not* that power is so centralized in the hands of a small, controlling elite that citizens cannot participate in policy formation. Nor is the failure to resolve the dual problems of metropolitan areas due to the fact that opportunities to participate in decision-making are so widespread.

What is distinctive about the political crisis of American cities

3

is that neither effective government nor citizen participation is being achieved. Instead, the structure of government is so fragmented that those in authority seem incapable of effectively governing the metropolitan community. And, at the same time, many citizens seem—and certainly feel—powerless to influence the positions that governments take.

Political leaders of metropolitan areas in the seventies operate within a socioeconomic context raising problems that only in the past two decades have become matters of critical concern. At least until the end of World War II central cities were the dynamic center of American economic, social, and cultural life. Immigrants from abroad and the children of farmers and small-town shopkeepers flocked to the big city in search of a better, or at least a more prosperous, life. Industry and commerce settled near transportation crossroads in order to be proximate to a large labor force and to facilitate numerous face-to-face market transactions. Because the great cities invariably located themselves at key intersections in the nation's fixed transportation system, the dependence of business on ship and railroad reinforced the growth of cities as the economic wealth of the nation continued to spiral. Boston, New York, and Philadelphia were great Eastern seaports; Chicago, Detroit, and Cleveland's dominance in the Middle West was a function of their position on the inland waterway provided by the Great Lakes; Denver was at the crossroads through the mountain passes of the West; and the great Pacific seaports of Los Angeles, San Francisco, and Seattle all prospered because of their favored waterfront locations. Because railroad lines, once placed, remained fixed, they reinforced the pattern determined by the shape of the nation's geography.

By introducing new flexibility in transportation and communication patterns, the automobile and telephone dramatically altered the fate of central cities. Their monopolistic control over the most valuable territory in the region gave way to a highly competitive relationship among territorial units, each of which had some resources to attract commerce, industry, residents, and taxpayers. Whereas in earlier decades, city transportation centers could dominate the socioeconomic and therefore the political life of the surrounding territory, in the more competitive automobile age, which did not reach its full fruition until after World War II, their power over the hinterland rapidly decreased.

Indeed, cities found their competitive position marred by prior successes. Although they were still valuable nexus points in the sea and rail transportation network and although the skylines and prestigious addresses of the largest cities proved attractive locations for home offices of the nation's biggest corporations, many Americans found cities too dirty and congested for comfortable residence. City streets and apartments that were convenient in an age dependent on street cars and subways were perceived as overcrowded, dingy, and polluted with the arrival of trucks and automobiles. Moreover, residents could readily move to greener, more spacious suburban homes and live with neighbors sharing similar life styles because the automobile enabled them to migrate quickly back and forth from home to workplace. Even more, commerce and industry, now increasingly reliant on telephones, trucks, airplanes, and cars, had many more options when searching for desirable locations.

As a result suburbs are now the area of economic dominance and expansion. While the economies of the central cities are stagnant or in decline, the suburban growth rate has been exceedingly rapid. During the decade of the sixties, in the fifteen largest metropolitan areas, the total number of persons employed in the central cities declined nearly 7 percent, while those employed in the suburbs rose by nearly 45 percent. The suburbs are no longer merely a residential area for central cities' workers; they now employ fully three-fourths of their working population. By 1975, more than 50 percent of the jobs in metropolitan areas were located in the suburbs.

With the passing of the socioeconomic dominance of the central city, its political decline was perhaps inevitable. Whereas at one time central cities regularly annexed surrounding territory to expand in size, in modern times this has proved politically impossible. As the suburbs became economically prosperous, they demanded political independence both from one another and from the central city responsible for their development. Metropolitan areas have thus become split into cities and suburbs, and only the most haphazard arrangements link them together for the resolution of common metropolitan problems. As a result, leaders in the central city can no longer direct the development of the metropolitan community as a whole. And since the suburbs themselves are so fractionated, each specialized interest focuses on its own problems. Only a few planners, some altruistic citizen groups like the League of Women Voters, and perhaps a newspaper editor are concerned about the larger community. In short, although decisions are made in metropolitan areas, Norton Long can convincingly argue (in the article reprinted below) that no one makes decisions for metropolitan areas.[3]

Not everyone sees the fragmentation of the metropolitan area as a problem, of course. As some political scientists have pointed out, a large number of distinctive suburbs do give people opportunities to live in communities that suit their particular life style.[4] Jews, Catholics, and Episcopalians each tend to group together, older people look for a low-tax suburb, young families want good schools, some people prefer zoning laws that require large lots and huge lawns, and others prefer to live close to the metropolitan center. Clearly, one should not equate the metropolitan problem with a variety of distinctive communities within a metropolitan area.

On the other hand, fragmentation does create problems for public policies that do require coordinated planning throughout the metropolitan area. Some general planning is necessary to build a transportation system that connects workers with their jobs, links homes and recreation areas, and does not quickly clog with even moderate increases in usage. Moreover, geographical fragmentation rigidifies inequalities in urban areas. An educational system that has lavish facilities in one community and inadequate schools in another close by does provide citizens with a choice. But since the cost of land in the two communities is likely to vary accordingly, this choice may be open only to the well-to-do. Housing opportunities for low income groups can also become severely restricted when no agency has the metropolitan-wide authority necessary to build the facilities. Each local community is likely to oppose low income housing within its jurisdiction, fearing that such housing would generate a variety of social problems for the community. As a result, either the housing is concentrated in central cities that are already suffering a decline in their tax bases and job opportunities, or it is not built at all. In sum, the multiplicity of governmental jurisdictions in metropolitan areas makes coordinated, equitable public policies almost impossible to obtain.

If the coherence in the metropolitan area once provided by central city leaders has been dissipated by the fragmentation of the area into competitive, self-concerned territorial units, the problem is no less great within the central city itself. If at one time central cities could rely on their monopolistic control of valuable land, they must now compete with other territories for industry, commerce, and high-quality residents. In this context, competition is more than just a metaphor. The central cities' very fiscal viability, as determined by their credit in the nation's bond markets, depends on each central city's remaining sufficiently attractive to generate adequate revenue to support the large array of public services that its previously monopolistic territorial position traditionally enabled it to distribute.

In this regard, the functional fragmentation, i.e., the autonomous power of municipal bureaucracies, within central cities further complicates urban governance. As Lowi points out in his analysis of "Machine Politics—Old and New," public bureaucracies have developed a base of power in big-city politics that almost forecloses any close centralized supervision. Bureaucracies have a number of techniques by which they sustain their autonomy. First of all, the professionals directing the bureaucracy have an advantage in terms of experience, expertise, and control over information. They quietly carry out their business—in the manner that best suits them—while public attention is diverted elsewhere. Adaptations may be necessary when a storm of public concern is immediately threatening, but, with patience, such turbulences can be weathered by hardy bureaucrats. Secondly, bureaucracies develop a coterie of producer and employee organizations to which they turn for advice and information, backing for their plans of expansion, and general political support. To shield the bureaucrats themselves from public controversies, these interest groups often carry on the battle for them. As Sayre and Kaufman note, policemen's associations thus can become informal spokesmen for police departments, especially when the latter prefer to remain nominally neutral. And, as Michael Lipsky points out, the long-standing groups in the housing policy arena play a key policy-formation role when protest groups focus attention on housing problems. As a result, only unusually strong mayors can develop the resources to do much more than "disturb," to say nothing of directly control, the workings of these islands of functional power.[5]

Although bureaucracies should not be blamed for every problem, the autonomy of urban bureaucracies has had two significant policy consequences. First, bureaucracies have often been able to forestall, undermine, and sabotage reform proposals— whenever they disturb the organizational routines of the bureaucracy. For example, police have successfully resisted civilian review boards, fearing they would lessen the discretion of policemen. Highway departments have resisted systematic consideration of aesthetic or environmental values that are too far removed from their overriding concern with traffic flow to be easily included within the departments' routine mechanisms for defining problems and developing solutions. Secondly, the needs and preferences of the providers of government services typically take precedence over the needs of both consumers and taxpayers. As Frances Piven shows in the third part of this reader, in the midst of the political turmoil of the sixties, municipal agencies and their employees demanded increases in salaries and fringe benefits that pushed city budgets so rapidly upward that the very fiscal viability of large American cities is now in doubt. According to Piven, the primary beneficiaries were not poor minorities but the service-providers themselves, whose combined salaries and benefits in many cities now exceed those provided in the private sector. When cities held a monopolistic territorial position, they could live with such indulgences. Today, faced with attractive competitors in the hinterland, central city leaders seem unable to govern within the resource limits demanded by their declining position in the nation.

In maintaining their autonomous position vis-a-vis the political leadership of the central city, urban bureaucracies typically find *producer groups* among their most valuable allies. Producer groups represent the interests of industries and professionals engaged in the production and distribution of goods and services. In effect, they represent people in their occupational roles. Thus, specific producer groups represent such interests as those of truckers, policemen, teachers, bankers, and other comparable occupational groups. Because highway policies have a major consequence for truckers, educational policies a major impact on teachers, and so forth, producer groups pay a great deal of attention to the specific policy area in which they have a major stake. They usually support stable organizations with sophisticated leaders, who develop close associations with elected or appointed officials responsible for the policies affecting them. Oftentimes, they are consulted before officials are selected to serve in the agencies that most directly affect the group's livelihood. In this way, close, enduring relationships are built between certain producer groups and specific governmental agencies. The agency watches out for the group interest, and the producer group supports agency plans for institutional survival and expansion.

The concern that producer groups have for policies affecting them is quite understandable. The problem arises when their interests compete with consumer interests, which are not represented by any comparably sophisticated organizations. Consumer organizations find it far more difficult to build a stable, enduring relationship with public bureaucracies, because they tend to represent diffuse interests—those widely shared "public" interests that everyone has to some extent but that no one in particular has to any considerable extent. An illustration may help to clarify the point. The billboard industry has a great stake in obtaining permission to place signs along the highway; each traveler has a small but widely diffused stake in being able to see the countryside instead of a continuous parade of huge signs. Yet, countryside lovers have no organization comparable to that of the billboard industry, which has struggled to keep roads free of any government ban on signs. The fragmentation of policy-making into functional arenas, where organized interests and bureaucratic elites join to make policy, makes the representation of diffuse, consumer interests far more difficult. When the consumers are the poor, their particular lack of political resources accentuates the problem. For example, as we shall see in our discussion of housing policy, housing agencies consider more carefully the problems of the construction industry and financial institutions than the needs of low-income potential homeowners.

CITIZEN PARTICIPATION

While the fragmentation of the urban political structure has limited the "governing" capacities of urban authorities, this has in no way been offset by an increase in citizen participation. If the price paid in terms of coordination, efficiency, and equity throughout the metropolitan area were redeemed by a concomitant increment in the level of citizen participation in public affairs, the trade-off in goals might possibly be acceptable. But, for all the fragmentation of urban areas, citizens still seem to have limited chances to shape governmental action.

One should, of course, avoid unrealistic expectations as to the level of citizen participation that is in any way feasible. Participation clearly cannot consist of direct involvement by every adult in each of the various decisions made in the metropolitan area. In a modern, industrial, highly specialized society, people neither have the time, nor the financial resources, nor the inclination to participate in most policy decisions. On the other hand, people would like government to be responsive to their problems and complaints when they do become interested and involved. And they do expect that their interests will be represented by their officeholders even when citizens themselves do not become directly involved.

In his analysis of political leadership reprinted in this volume, Dahl makes the argument that governments do in fact respond to the pressure activities of groups of ordinary citizens, particularly when these groups feel strongly about a matter. He argues further that politicians cannot in general depart too significantly from what most people expect of their government; to do so would lead to imminent political defeat. From this perspective, the "problem" of participation, if indeed it is a problem, involves the apathy of citizens concerning the processes of government rather than any unresponsiveness on the part of the political order.

Although Dahl's argument carries considerable weight, too exclusive a dependence on this interpretation, we believe, overlooks the way in which the structural arrangements of our urban governments positively discourage citizens from participation. The fragmentation of governmental authority into sanitation boards, pollution-control boards, metropolitan water districts, school districts, counties, villages, housing authorities, and so forth, leaves the citizen baffled as to which jurisdiction he is living in, to say nothing of the way in which he can go about influencing its operations. Moreover, so many officials are elected for such obscure offices that the voters, unaware of their activities, can hardly instill in these officeholders any fear that their policies could lead to political defeat. And those few elected officials with some public visibility, such as the mayor of the central city, may not have enough control over most public agencies to be able to substantially alter their policies. Given the low probability of success, why should the citizen even try to influence government activity?

The problem runs even deeper. Most citizens simply do not receive quickly and conveniently the information that is necessary to induce them to take action on a policy question. Agencies develop their longer-range plans quietly, holding off public meetings until the plans are on the verge of being implemented. Press, radio, and television, by focusing on immediate, newsworthy topics, too often fail to arouse the public until it is too late to alter a policy. In their constant search for *new* news, they constantly move to fresh issues before the old ones are resolved, leaving the latter in the hands, once again, of the full-time paid professionals specializing in the policy area.

Given the high costs of acquiring the information needed to influence policy and the low probability of having any impact if one does participate, what is surprising is not citizen apathy but the frequency with which citizen groups do in fact try to shape local policy. If only sporadically, groups of consumers, community organizations, and representatives of the poor sometimes engage in almost "heroic" efforts to influence policy. Michael Lipsky's study of protest in this volume analyzes one such attempt. Yet, the typical pattern is for public policy-making to be dominated by a few entrenched, specialized, usually producer interests. The limited nature of citizen representation and the fragmentation of urban governments are not opposed but complementary problems. Each feeds upon and perpetuates the other. Power is fragmented in part because of the high costs of influencing decisions. Because most citizens are not willing to pay these costs, decisions are taken by the professionals and producers who have great stakes in the matter. More-diffuse, less-organized interests are squeezed out of the decision-making process. If fragmentation occurs because few people participate, fragmentation in turn retards participation. Once established relationships have developed among powerful interests in particular policy areas, they make it difficult for new groups to penetrate the policy-making process. Producer-bureaucratic control of policy further increases the cost of participation to outsiders, thereby further reducing the incentives to participate in urban politics. As a result, adequate representation of diffuse, unorganized interests, and particularly the interests of minority groups and the poor, whose political resources are even more limited, is not often achieved within the framework of a highly fragmented, decentralized urban political order.

A HISTORICAL PERSPECTIVE ON THE URBAN CRISIS

The roots of these interrelated urban problems are deeply embedded in American history and culture, which created two distinctive political forces and sets of institutions in American cities: the political machine and the reform movement. Both developed because America has always been a liberal society that knew neither a feudal aristocracy nor a class-conscious socialist movement.[6] Without an aristocratic legacy, the American rich had little sense of civic responsibility. Whereas, in Britain, distinguished public service was the mark of a gentleman, well-to-do Americans, after the first days of the Republic, avoided dirtying their hands in politics. As an astute English observer of nineteenth-century American politics commented, "[America has] no class with a hereditary prescription to public office, no great families whose names are known to the people, and who, bound together by class sympathy and ties of relationship, help one another by keeping offices in the hands of their own numbers."[7] At the same time, the working masses in America were quite confident of their own ability to govern and did not "defer" to their "betters" in the same way that European workers at one time did. Thus, uneducated, rough-tongued, tobacco-spitting politicians could grab political office. Or, as Max Weber, another European analyst of this period in American politics, reported, Americans claimed to "prefer having people in office whom we can spit upon, rather than a caste of officials who spit upon us as is the case with you [Europeans]."[8]

If American workers did not defer to their wealthier neighbors, neither did they hate them with the passion that inspired a great socialist movement in Europe. Indeed, the capitalist values which encouraged individual initiatives were accepted as legitimate by the workers themselves. Realistically or not, the great majority of nineteenth-century white Americans hoped that they or their children would achieve material success either in urban trade or in farming on the frontier. Any version of class politics which sought collective rather than individual betterment accordingly had limited and sporadic allure at best. However, Americans responded quickly to the prospect of engaging in politics in order to secure direct, personal economic gain. Because Americans seemed to believe in salvation through material success, public life became simply another arena where financial rewards could be secured, and the public treasury offered still another opportunity for the individual to better himself.

In this context, machine politics grew and flourished. If the rich had little sense of civic responsibility, and the poor had little common identity as members of one class, politics could be organized by the economically ambitious, who used public goods to their private advantage. And the rapidly expanding number of urban immigrants who spoke strange tongues, knew little about American political institutions, and were usually unfamiliar with democratic procedures, provided the votes that the machine politicians could so efficiently organize.

This seamy side of machine politics should not hide a signal contribution that political organizations made to the functioning of the urban community: They provided some semblance of order in otherwise chaotic urban conditions. As Mandelbaum points out in his account of *Boss Tweed's New York*, the communication and transportation problems in the nineteenth century were enormous.[9] The post office was incredibly inefficient; some twenty-five newspapers each had their own parochial audience; many residents were entirely illiterate; and streets were clogged with traffic, jammed with market stalls, and filled with dangerous potholes.

Unable to provide for all the city's children, the schools ignored compulsory attendance laws despite absenteeism which regularly ran above 50 percent. Welfare services were left to small private agencies, and private entrepreneurs provided such essential services as shipping docks, mass transit, and even fire control. One of the few major but seemingly simple public services the government did undertake, garbage collection, was notoriously bad. But, as Mandelbaum persuasively argues, "the failure to clear the streets properly could not entirely be laid at the door of the politicians." Rather, "precisely because street cleaning under the conditions of that time was doomed to failure . . . the cleaners . . . took their prestige from an outside organization, the political party."[10]

By privatizing politics, by appealing to the narrower interests of ethnic neighborhoods or even the individual and his family, the machine politicians, in effect, made up some of the deficit of political support for the government which administrative laxity created. They distributed administrative positions according to partisan criteria and bought support directly from voters through corruption, graft, and patronage, rather than acquiring it through popular public policies. In pursuit of this goal, they shaped urban institutions in a congenial fashion. The civil-service merit system was opposed, except to "blanket in" party supporters when the leadership feared an imminent defeat. Aldermen were selected from small wards so that men who knew their neighborhoods could assign patronage most advantageously. Many public officials were elected on partisan ballots, increasing direct party control over a large number of governmental positions. And the machine appealed to neighborhood and ethnic loyalties through careful balancing of the lengthy electoral ticket.

As Greenstone and Peterson argue in *Race and Authority in Urban Politics: A Study of Community Participation in the War on Poverty*, this appeal to particularistic interests did help secure public order by diffusing and privatizing conflict.[11] Business and labor, blacks and whites, Italians and Germans, Catholics and Jews were all successfully appealed to in ways that minimized the potential conflicts among them. Indeed, political conflict was so well controlled that in many American cities a one-party system emerged. Once in office, the dominant party used available patronage and contracts to solidify its base of power. In certain "inner city" wards, whose low-income residents were especially receptive to the precinct captain's favors, the opposition became co-opted. In exchange for cooperation on vital matters, including

only token opposition in general elections, the ruling party distributed some of its patronage to the minority party, whose leaders
used these resources to insure control over their own primaries.[12]
Thus, as James Bryce noted seventy years ago at the height of the
machine's power: "In many cities the party majority inclines so
decidedly one way or the other (e.g., New York City is steadily
Democratic, Philadelphia, Republican) that nomination is in the
case of the dominant party equivalent to election."[13]

If the machine relied on individual corruptibility to organize
urban politics, the reformers, outraged at the inefficiencies and
manipulative activities of these politicians, developed a contrasting theory that was based on a belief in the potential honesty and
decency of the urban American. The reformers believed both in
widespread citizen participation in politics and in efficient, honest,
even scientific management of public affairs by technically trained
experts. They could link these two goals, because they believed,
with John Stuart Mill, that the workers' participation in politics
would enhance the quality of the workers' own lives and make
them better citizens. In order to secure such participation, however, the reformers had to rid the community of the vested
interests, the corrupt politicians, and the vote buying and vote
stealing of the political machine. With the elimination of these
pernicious influences and the spread of universal education, it was
expected that citizens would vote freely and rationally in choosing
their leaders.

The reformers consequently promoted numerous devices to increase what they regarded as free, open, and public-spirited voting.
They suggested nonpartisan elections, where the partisan affiliations of candidates would be deleted from the ballot, weakening
the influence of the corrupt parties. They sought at-large rather
than ward elections to the city council, so that candidates would
have to campaign in terms of what was best for the city as a
whole rather than for what was best for any particular ward. They
advocated the initiative, which allowed voters to place on the
ballot proposed laws that could not be passed in the state legislature; the referendum, which allowed the voters to repeal legislative action; and the recall, which allowed voters to petition for
a special election to remove from office men who blatantly defied
the public will. In all these proposals, reformers expressed their
faith in free, unfettered, direct voter participation in political life.

But, if rational voters were expected to choose wise leaders,
these leaders were expected to rely on the advice of experts in the
science of government to implement their policies. Reformers ad-

vocated the city-manager form of government, in which an expert was hired to coordinate and administer local services. Police superintendents, highway engineers, urban planners, housing experts, and school superintendents were all to be selected for the specialized training and technical skill they could bring to their administrative tasks. With such professional competence in key positions, the efficiency of public services would rise, rewarding the citizens for their wise choice of leaders. With a civil-service system, there would no longer be a corrupt patronage system to tempt the voters. The perfectibility of government and citizens would replace the corruptibility of both under the urban machine. In this way, majority rule and good government could become not mutually exclusive but highly interdependent goals.

Future developments at best gave such reform optimists only sporadic encouragement, however. American voters did not always recognize the talents of the reformers who claimed to be sacrificing their private lives to serve the city. In part, this was due to the lack of deference working men and women had for their betters. As Ostrogorski observed, "The men of higher rank who come down as it were from the moon to exhort the people to vote for honest candidates opposed to the Machine, are strangers to them, and the people have no confidence in them because they belong to another social sphere."[14] Unless there was an especially earth-shaking scandal, the reformers had difficulty in sustaining political support. In the words of that Tammany Hall machine politician, George Washington Plunkitt, reformers tended to be "mornin' glories." They "looked lovely in the mornin' and withered up in a short time, while the regular machines went on flourishin' forever, like fine old oaks."[15] Consequently, in order to win elections, reformers at times had to stoop to such machine-style devices as slating ethnic candidates. In 1933, for example, New York reformers reluctantly nominated Fiorello La Guardia, the one reformer likely to capture the Italian vote.[16]

Yet, the reformers used their mornings of triumph, including La Guardia's administration, to eliminate much of the patronage and graft upon which the machine had depended. Meanwhile, certain secular trends (increasing income, more formal education, the advent of radio and television) made many citizens unwilling to sell their votes at a price the machine could afford to pay, or to rely for political information entirely on the friendly precinct captain. And the increased bureaucratization of welfare programs, especially since the 1930s, reduced the importance of the machine politicians' informal assistance to their neighbors.

As the machine weakened, the reform movement could no longer avoid explicit recognition of the tension between its dual commitment to both expertise and democratic participation. On one side, citizens did not always fulfill the reformers' hopes concerning rational voting behavior. Denied partisan cues, voters chose candidates on racial, religious, and ethnic criteria rather than for reasons having to do with their fitness for office. In the face of such behavior, some reform groups became increasingly suspicious of the voting public and sought less democratic mechanisms for protecting the city from corruption. For example, in order to satisfy reform demands in such cities as New York, Philadelphia, and Chicago, blue-ribbon panels of experts and prestigious citizens were given the power to prepare lists of school board nominees from which the mayors were expected to make their selection.

In the end, the reformers did little to increase participation in urban politics. In fact, many of their schemes had exactly the opposite effect. Fewer citizens, and particularly fewer working-class citizens, voted in nonpartisan elections than in partisan ones.[17] The initiative and the referendum were used by special interests who could at times pass more self-serving legislation by securing the backing of small groups of supporters among an apathetic public than they could through the state legislature. At-large elections created a much greater distance between the citizen and his representative than that provided by the old ward elections favored by the machine. The destruction of the machine did not necessarily pave the way for participatory democracy.

The fundamental problem was rooted in the reformers' own political theory. They believed that the destruction of the corrupt politicians would eliminate the hidden power of special interests. They thought the voter, freed from the enticements of patronage and special favors, would actively pursue goals that were in the public interest. But voters, even after the decline of the machine, have proven to be more concerned about their ethnic, class, racial, or other group interests than with some vague formulation of the public interest. Moreover, even if citizens were more concerned with the welfare of the community as a whole, it is not clear whether their individual efforts would have much effect. Because political participation is a costly activity, citizens need simplifying mechanisms that help them to influence policies without spending days and weeks in political action. If, instead of trying to reform the electoral process, the reformers had developed strong political organizations that would have assisted the voters in this way, their impact on citizen participation might have been much greater.

The reformers also came to discover that the increasing influence of experts in city government did not necessarily produce rationalized policies in the public interest. For one thing, administrative expertise and a theory of scientific management proved of little use in choosing among general policy alternatives. Rather than faithfully executing policy, officials in administrative bureaus and agencies developed specific organizational interests of their own, which they vigorously defended in bargaining with other administrators. Ironically, the reformers' own innovations encouraged such developments. In order to preclude the influence of machine politics, civil-service reforms often protected the job of every member of a bureau except its chief. But this arrangement made it virtually impossible to reshuffle key personnel in order to change policies. In some cases, the mayor did not even choose the heads of important bureaus. In other cases, reform rules forced him to make his selection from among officials who had already served for many years in the agency they were supposed to change. And, no matter how the administrator was chosen, the mayor risked accusations of political interference if he then tried to control his subordinates' activities. Urban bureaucracies had become free to operate in their spheres with little regard for either outside pressures or the conflicting goals of other agencies with overlapping jurisdictions.

The twin legacies of reform efforts are the crises of participation and fragmentation. The problem is, to be sure, deeply embedded in the structure of American government and politics, and it would be unfair and inaccurate to attribute all of our present discontent to the mistakes of reformers. For one thing, they have not had enough power to achieve all their goals. Reform efforts to achieve metropolitan government, for example, have had little success, because many other interests, created and protected by existing governmental institutions (not the least of which being suburban and central city officeholders), have been potent defenders of the *status quo*. Nonetheless, after a half-century of reform attempts to democratize and rationalize our cities' governing structures, these goals seem as far from reality as they ever have been. Political and social equality in urban America is still a distant goal. If the urban crisis is to be resolved, more is needed than simply the good will that many reformers undoubtedly had. Needed as well is an understanding of the social and political forces whose influence affects the actual operations of our political institutions and, eventually, the shape of urban public policy. The readings included below hopefully provide at least a beginning in this direction.

NOTES

1. For this argument, see Wallace Sayre and Herbert Kaufman, *Governing New York City* (New York: Norton, 1965); David Riesman, *The Lonely Crowd* (Garden City, N.Y.: Doubleday, 1953).
2. This view is expressed by Floyd Hunter, *Community Power Structure* (Garden City, N.Y.: Doubleday, 1963).
3. All references in the text to works that are not footnoted refer to articles reprinted in this reader.
4. Edward Banfield and Morton Grodzins, *Government and Housing in Metropolitan Areas* (New York: McGraw-Hill, 1958), pp. 30–43.
5. The point is well documented in Sayre and Kaufman, *op. cit.*, Chs. 8 and 9.
6. Louis Hartz, *The Liberal Tradition in America* (New York: Harcourt, Brace and World, 1955).
7. James Bryce, *The American Commonwealth II* (New York: Macmillan, 1895), p. 54.
8. H. H. Gerth and C. Wright Mills (eds.), *From Max Weber: Essays in Sociology* (New York: Oxford University Press, 1946), p. 110.
9. Seymour J. Mandelbaum, *Boss Tweed's New York* (New York: John Wiley and Sons, 1965).
10. *Ibid.*, p. 168.
11. Some passages in this section closely follow material in J. David Greenstone and Paul E. Peterson, *Race and Authority in Urban Politics: A Study of the War on Poverty* (New York: Russell Sage Foundation, 1973). We thank David Greenstone for granting us permission to draw upon this material.
12. Harold Gosnell, *Machine Politics: Chicago Model* (Chicago: University of Chicago Press, 1968), p. 44; Leo Snowiss, "The Metropolitan Congressman" (Ph.D. dissertation, Department of Political Science, University of Chicago, 1965), p. 92.
13. Bryce, *op. cit.*, p. 97.
14. M. Ostrogorski, *Democracy and the Organization of Political Parties: The United States* (Garden City, N.Y.: Doubleday, 1964), p. 221.
15. William Riordan, *Plunkitt of Tammany Hall* (New York: E. P. Dutton, 1963), p. 17.
16. Arthur Mann, *LaGuardia Comes to Power, 1933* (Philadelphia: J. B. Lippincott Co., 1965), Ch. 3.
17. Oliver P. Williams and Charles Adrian, "The Insulation of Local Politics under the Non-Partisan Ballot," *American Political Science Review* LIII (December, 1959), 1058–61; and Robert Salisbury and Gordon Black, "Class and Party in Partisan and Nonpartisan Elections: The Case of Des Moines," *American Political Science Review* LVIII (September, 1963), 589–90.

BIBLIOGRAPHY

AGGER, ROBERT, et al. *The Ruler and the Ruled*. New York: John Wiley and Sons, 1964.

BANFIELD, EDWARD. *Political Influence*. New York: Free Press, 1961.

————. *The Unheavenly City Revisited*. Boston: Little, Brown, 1974.

————, and JAMES WILSON. *City Politics*. Cambridge, Mass.: Harvard University Press, 1963.

BELLUSH, JEWEL, and STEPHEN DAVID, eds. *Race and Politics in New York City*. New York: Praeger, 1971.

CRENSON, MATTHEW. *The Un-politics of Air Pollution: A Study of Non-Decisionmaking in the Cities*. Baltimore: Johns Hopkins University Press, 1971.

DAHL, ROBERT. *Who Governs?* New Haven: Yale University Press, 1961.

DOWNS, ANTHONY. *Opening up the Suburbs*. New Haven: Yale University Press, 1973.

ELAZAR, DANIEL. *Cities of the Prairie*. New York: Basic Books, 1970.

GREENSTONE, J. DAVID, and PAUL E. PETERSON. *Race and Authority in Urban Politics: A Study of the War on Poverty*. New York: Russell Sage Foundation, 1973.

HUNTER, FLOYD. *Community Power Structure*. Garden City, N.Y.: Doubleday, 1963.

LONG, NORTON. *The Unwalled City*. New York: Basic Books, 1972.

LOWI, THEODORE. *At the Pleasure of the Mayor*. New York: Free Press, 1964.

MARRIS, PETER, and MARTIN REIN. *Dilemmas of Social Reform*. New York: Atherton, 1967.

ORREN, KAREN. *Corporate Power and Social Change*. Baltimore: Johns Hopkins University Press, 1974.

SAYRE, WALLACE, and HERBERT KAUFMAN. *Governing New York City*. New York: Norton, 1965.

WOOD, ROBERT. *Suburbia*. Boston: Houghton Mifflin, 1968.

Can Cities Be Governed?

THE CITY AS SANDBOX

GEORGE STERNLIEB

How is one to write about a Newark or a Youngstown? All the adjectives have been used up, as have all the warnings of disaster and dire happenings in the streets if "they" don't come across, all the stories of soaring syphilis rates, TB gone uncared for, children made vegetables by lead poisoning, rats running rampant, high infant mortality, increasing numbers of unwed mothers, schools and hospitals and garbage departments that don't work, or won't, etc. The cries of "wolf" have become so plentiful that we no longer listen and may even have begun to lose our fear of the beast itself. Yet there is something to be learned from a reshuffling of these dying embers of old rhetorical fires. For the Newarks of America are a foretaste of things to come, and if we want to understand the probable future that faces many of our older cities, then we will first have to get clear on what is happening—has already happened—in a place like Newark.

The bitterness of political conflict in such cities, and the intensity of their citizens' demand for an expansion of public services and public funding, provide a major clue. Of all the things people are prepared to fight over, their property interests are perhaps the most important, or at any rate the first; and of all a man's property interests, that in his job is usually the most important. Especially in cities like Newark, where the public sector has grown immensely while the private sector has decreased, the property interest which people possess—or seek—in their jobs

"The City as Sandbox" first appeared in *The Public Interest*, No. 25 (Fall 1971): 14–21. © 1971 by National Affairs, Inc., and reprinted with permission.

gives local politics a peculiar importance. At one level, of course, such politics is precisely what it appears to be—an effort to promote the public interest. Thus, a housing program is an effort to provide housing for the poor; school reform aims at improving the achievement of pupils; a health program may be measured by its effect in raising the level of health and care. But beneath this there is another level of reality—that of who gets the action. Who will get (or keep) the job, the patronage? Who is going to build the new school? Who is going to make those sandwiches for the lunch program? Who is going to give out the contracts? As the size of the public sector grows, such questions become increasingly important and therefore increasingly divisive, for they engage the property interests of more and more people. Why should there be a fight for community control in Ocean Hill-Brownsville or Newark? There are many reasons, but one of the simplest and most important is that, for more and more people, new government programs are the only game in town; there is little else worth fighting for. Thus, for those who remain in the central city, fighting for such new programs is the only realistic response to the economic sterility of their environment.

Exploited—or Merely Defunct?

It is often said that our older central cities are essentially colonies—areas rich in resources which are systematically exploited by the suburban hinterlands. The residents of the latter drive into the city in the morning, use its services all day, and then creep out at night, taking with them much of the city's income and wealth. In one or another variant, this is the vision subscribed to by most city leaders, and they find it a satisfying one. For it implies that the Golden Return is at hand if only the city is given justice. The city's lack of such equity, which creates all its problems, is the result of a shortsighted plot by "outside" interests. Let there be a reallocation of wealth, and all will be well again.

The only problem with this notion is that it is untrue. The size of the constituency which lives outside the cities but still wants to preserve them at any cost grows smaller day by day. It is not exploitation that the core areas must fear; it is indifference and abandonment. The crisis of the cities is a crisis of function. *The major problem of the core areas of our cities is simply their lack of economic value.*

For a long time, the principal role of our inner cities was as a staging area for the floods of immigrants who came from Europe and elsewhere. Cities provided jobs, schools, and an infrastructure which helped earlier groups of immigrants move upward and outward. Although each of these groups left a residue of those who didn't make it, on the whole the city was an extremely successful processing center. Now that these great migrant flows have been reduced to a comparative trickle, the city has lost its *raison d'être.* Formerly the focal point for cheap labor, uniquely amassable there in great volume, it now finds that competition from welfare payments keeps its labor far from cheap and that its traditional jobs have been taken over by Puerto Rico, Formosa, Hong Kong, Singapore, and the like. As its current group of immigrants begins to make it, they too are moving out; but because no new groups are moving in, the city emigrés leave behind a vacuum.

America's major cities are unique in that *they are losing population.* Everywhere else—in Moscow or Buenos Aires or Calcutta —the flow of the agrarian poor off the land to the big city is at its flood stage. We have already gone through that phase; we are now on uncharted territory. To be sure, the Puerto Rican migration may from time to time increase, depending on relative economic conditions, and small pockets of surplus population remain in the south. But for the most part, large-scale immigration to the city is a thing of the past, and much of the migration which does take place bypasses the older population centers for more promising areas.

The absence of replacements for the new emigrés from the city means that some of the first rungs in the nation's traditional ladder of upward mobility have been eliminated. The consequences of this development are already making themselves felt. One of the most common ways for earlier immigrant groups to accumulate capital was as slum landlords. They bought, as they could afford to buy, only the poorest and weakest of structures, which they would rent, at whatever they could get, to their immigrant successors. By trading up the real estate ladder to bigger and better properties, these slumlords became prominent sources of capital for the business-oriented among their own ethnic group. But today, there is no new immigrant group to exploit. Slum tenement ownership has become a dead end, instead of an avenue to wealth—a fact symbolized by the abandoned slum dwelling.

Another way for earlier ethnic groups to move upward and outward was the exploitation of their own countrymen. Members of the immigrant group could rise as brokers between their ethnic labor pool and the external economy. If one wanted to build a sidewalk a generation or two ago, the cheapest labor available was

Italian. Because the people who wanted sidewalks built rarely spoke Italian themselves, they dealt with bilingual Italian brokers, who would assemble and supervise the strong backs that were needed for the job. That was the stuff general contractors were made of. Or, to take another case, two generations ago the cheapest needle workers available were non-English-speaking Jews. Their labor was exploited by Jewish sweatshop owners, who served as go-betweens with the department stores of Grand Street. Of course the needle workers themselves had no chance to become rich; but the go-betweens did.

The need for strong backs and 15-hour-a-day sweated labor has been reduced to almost nothing by the transportation revolution, which has had the effect of homogenizing time and distance. Much of our labor-intensive work is now imported from abroad. Welfare legislation, minimum wages, maximum work hours, and the like have minimized the economic function of the conglomerations of poor-but-willing people in our cities. Similarly, the goad of hunger has been mitigated by the rising level of welfare payments. In Newark a woman with three children lives very badly on welfare payments, but these nevertheless average somewhere around $300 to $350 per month. To live at that same level, a man with a wife and three children would have to make about $5,500 a year. For unskilled labor, that sort of money just isn't available.

A New "Function"

Given that the older central cities have lost their capacity to serve as effective staging areas for newcomers, the question inevitably poses itself: What *is* the function of these cities? Permit me to suggest that it has become essentially that of a sandbox.

A sandbox is a place where adults park their children in order to converse, play, or work with a minimum of interference. The adults, having found a distraction for the children, can get on with the serious things of life. There is some reward for the children in all this. The sandbox is given to them as their own turf. Occasionally, fresh sand or toys are put in the sandbox, along with an implicit admonition that these things are furnished to minimize the level of noise and nuisance. If the children do become noisy and distract their parents, fresh toys may be brought. If the occupants of the sandbox choose up sides and start bashing each other over the head, the adults will come running, smack the juniors more or less indiscriminately, calm things down, and then, perhaps, in an act of semi-contrition, bring fresh sand and fresh toys, pat the occupants of the sandbox on the head, and disappear once again into their adult involvement and pursuits.

That is what the city has become—a sandbox. Government programs in the core city have increasingly taken on this cast. A glance at Sar Levitan's *The Great Society's Poor Law*, or the Marris and Rein work, or for that matter Tom Wolfe's *Mau-Mauing the Flack Catchers* is enough to make clear the lack of effective flow of much poverty money to its ostensible targets. Instead, this money has been used to create a growing bureaucracy which is sustained by the plight of the poor, the threat of the poor, the misery of the poor, but which yields little in the way of loaves and fishes to the poor. This is the height of sandboxism. When old programs begin to lose their credibility or become unfashionable, they are given new names—therefore, they are new programs. The act of repackaging or relabelling is equated with creativity.

This is not to belittle the importance of government programs. They do have trickle-down effects; they are creating, if not efficiently then certainly in bulk, some measure of leadership, and this leadership is highly cynical about the nature of the faucet from whence all goodies flow and, possibly as a result, is increasingly effective. Perhaps most significantly, these programs have become forms of symbolic action. In their ritualistic aspects they are of particular value. They give psychic satisfaction to the patrons of the poor, convince outsiders—especially the media—that "something is being done," and indicate to the urban poor that some one up there really cares. In a word, these programs are placebos, and they often produce all the authentic, positive results which placebos can have in medical practice. One of the greatest shortcomings of the present administration in Washington is its failure to recognize the salutary placebo-effects of social programs. The failure has been not so much in what it has done, as in what it has called what it has done—not so much in the substance of its programs, as in its rejection of the gamesmanship which does not merely accompany programs but is central to them.

The fact that so many programs are of only symbolic value is the result, not of Machiavellian scheming, but of simple incapacity. If the 1960's demonstrated anything, it was that the social sciences had not yet arrived at the point of being able to design programs that could be counted on actually to accomplish what they were supposed to accomplish. It is true that social scientists themselves were often quick to recognize the failure of a given program and would attempt to design a better one in light of that failure. But the new programs usually did not arise from any strong theory or experimentation; they were rather the complements of past failure. One simply took apparently salient parameters of the failed program and reversed them. The façade of intellectual rationalization was produced *post hoc*. Schools don't work because classes are too large and lack the personal touch? Make classes smaller. If smaller classes don't work, what is left? Ah! Skin color, the teacher's doesn't match that of the student; change the skin color. That doesn't seem to be working as well as one would have anticipated? It must be the supervisor's color—paint principal black. Principal black doesn't seem to provide the answer? Paint the board of education an appropriate hue. And when this entire mountain of stratagems brings forth nothing but mice, bring the parents in. Parents don't want to come in? Pay them, we'll call them paraprofessionals. And so it has gone. The rationalizers of these programs dutifully turn out Ph.D. theses and proposals without end to justify the programs.

In this kind of "social science," anecdotal accounts began to pass as consequential theories and models for the design of new institutions. A typical specimen of the genus is the account of how I, a young draft dodger, full of beans and aware of the fact that I wasn't going to spend my career there, came into a class of young sullens; in six months they loved me. This sort of recital became dignified both as an indictment of the flywheels of our institutions and also possibly as a model for new educational institutions of the future. The former may well have validity, but the latter defies rationality. The wonder is not the existence of a number of these anecdotal descriptions, but rather the childlike acceptance of them as a vision of a future that can be reproduced on a scale commensurate with the number of children and situations involved. The sordid fact that they enjoy such acceptance is but another indication of the extent to which we have begun to escape into fantasy.

THE FUTURE OF THE CENTRAL CITY

Jobs are leaving the central city. Except for insurance companies, banks, and other institutions which juridically find it difficult to leave, business institutions are virtually deserting the central cities. All major department store chains now do the bulk of their business in the suburbs; the efforts of urban renewal to retain major retail facilities in the core areas have died and are mourned by few. Smaller retailers in secondary urban shopping areas on the "trolley car streets" are also leaving or going out of business. The old mom and pop stores, candy stores, grocery stores on every block, fish stores, neighborhood bakeries, etc., are things of the far past. There has also been a flight of professionals. In the last ten years, Newark has lost half its physicians, and many of those who remain have one foot in the suburbs and are just waiting for their practices to take hold before moving out. As for cultural activities, it is the first-run movie theaters rather than opera houses or symphony halls which have been of especially great economic importance to the vitality of the core city. In Newark, *there is not a single first-run theater left in the entire city of 400,000,* while in the suburbs one of the most desirable pieces of realty available is a site for a movie theater and shopping center. True, the museum and public library still exist downtown, but their wealthy patrons become fewer, galleries must be closed off for lack of money to pay guards, and book acquisition budgets and opening hours must be reduced as the city's budget crisis makes its impact felt.

Meanwhile, the suburbs have achieved critical mass, a scale of population and buying power which permits them to sustain amenities of a type and at a level which once only the central city was capable of sustaining. The shopping center which had at best a single department store branch now has three and soon will have four. The suburban music calendar is evolving from a marginal summer collection of odds and ends to a year-round independent activity. Small suburban hospitals have grown to thousand-bed monsters which can supply all the services and specialists available in the biggest central city hospitals.

Who is left in the central city? Ride down the Central Avenues and Main Streets of our older cities and you will see that the new tenants are offshoots of the poverty program: pseudo-training programs for the poor, enlarged offices of the Welfare Department, and the like. These are the focal points of the new central-city entrepreneurs, the people who, in the absence of a booming private economy, are trying to make it with government money. The predominance of these public-sector entrepreneurs is an index of the degree to which the central city—its inhabitants' training irrelevant to the needs of the larger society—has become a forgotten back alley in a nation whose principal business still is business.

This process of the "defunctioning" of the central city would have occurred even if there had not been a problem of race. It would have been considerably slower in that case, and the capacity of society to adjust to it would have been greater, for the pace of change in our central cities has unquestionably been speeded up by racial tensions and fears. But serious though that cost has been, perhaps the greatest cost of the race factor is that it has obscured the real nature of what is going on in the central city. Even if there were no racial difference in our society, there would probably still be as many people on welfare and as many under- or unemployed, and they would still be unwelcome among their more affluent fellow citizens.

What, then, of the future? The first point to be made is that there is no going back in time. The city as we have known it, and the forms of economic and social organization which character- ized it, are simply irrecoverable. The folkways of our society have changed; they have also become homogeneous and monolithically dominant as no fashion has ever before been. The thin mist of eloquence emanating from upper-middle-class occupants of high- rise apartments cannot hide the fact that the dominant ethos today is a suburban one. It is as pervasive among minority groups as it is in the society as a whole. Thus, if we define the problems of the city as the gap between the reality of the cities as they exist today and a romanticized fantasy of cities as they used to be—as the economic center of the nation, as the font of civility and graciousness, as the source of everything that warms the hearts of social critics—then those problems are simply unsolvable and always will be unsolvable, at least for many of our older central cities.

Yet there is another way of defining the problems of the cities that does permit some real choice: Are they to become sandboxes entirely, or will we permit them to regain some useful economic function? Shall we optimize the machine, maximize capital in- vestment and capital returns at the cost of human involvement, and then take the largesse so provided and redistribute it in the form of welfare or subsidized, irrelevant, unproductive make-work? Or should we reject the sandbox on the ground that useful, pro- ductive work is essential to human well-being, and design our policies to insure that everyone has an opportunity for such work, even if this involves cost to overall economic growth and wealth?

The plight of the inhabitants of our central cities, and the strategy we seem to be adopting to meet that plight, indicate that we are opting for the sandbox. What this will mean for our society in the future we do not fully know; but that the conse- quences are likely to be cruel and disagreeable has become only too clear.

GOSNELL'S CHICAGO REVISITED
VIA LINDSAY'S NEW YORK

THEODORE J. LOWI

We can begin to introduce perspective by immediately setting
aside Gosnell's opening claim . . . to the representativeness of
the Chicago experience. It is the very uniqueness of Chicago's experience with the machine that gives the study value. New York
is the representative big city, not Chicago. In 1967, political
power in Chicago has an extremely strong machine base; political
power in New York has an entirely new and different base. As
New York was being revolutionized by the New Deal and its successors, Chicago politics was being reaffirmed. When New York
was losing its last machine and entering into the new era of
permanent Reform, Chicago's machine politics was just beginning
to consolidate. New York became a loose, multiparty system with
wide-open processes of nomination, election, and participation;
Chicago became a tight, one-party system. New York sought to
strengthen a weak mayor already operating under a strong-mayor
government; Chicago has had the opposite problem of an already
strong mayor in a weak-mayor government.

To evaluate the machine we must ask whether, by surviving,
machine politics, Chicago model, in any way distorted Chicago's
growth and development. How much change would there have
been in Chicago's history if the nationalization of politics had
made possible in Chicago, as it did in virtually every other big
American city, ways of "licking the ward boss" and altering precinct organization, means of loosening the hold of the county
organization on city hall, power for freeing the personnel and
policies of the professional agencies of government? We cannot
answer these questions for Chicago because the basis of machine

From Theodore J. Lowi, "Gosnell's Chicago Revisited Via Lindsay's New
York: Foreword to the Second Edition," in Harold F. Gosnell, *Machine
Politics: Chicago Model*, pp. 7–16. Reprinted by permission of the author
and The University of Chicago Press. Introduction © 1968 by The University
of Chicago Press.

strength still exists, and the conditions for its continuity, as Gosnell so accurately captures them, may continue through the remainder of the century. We might be able to answer them, however, at least better than before, by looking at Gosnell's Chicago through the contemporary experience of New York.

New York city government, like government in almost all large American cities except Chicago, is a product of Reform. It is difficult to understand these cities without understanding the two strains of ideology that guided local Reform movements throughout the past three-quarters of a century. *Populism* and *efficiency*, once the foundations of most local insurgency, are now, except in rare holdout cases like Chicago, triumphant. These two tenets are now the orthodoxy in local practice.

Populism was originally a statement of the evils of every form of bigness and scale in the city, including big business, big churches, and big labor as well as big political organizations. Decentralization was an ultimate goal. In modern form it has tended to come down to the charge to eliminate political parties, partisanship, and, if possible, politics itself.

Efficiency provided the positive program to replace what populist surgery excised. The doctrine calls essentially for a new form of centralization; that is, centralization and rationalization of government activities and services to accompany the decentralization of power. Some assumed that services do not constitute power. Others assumed the problem away altogether by defining a neutral civil servant who would not abuse centralized government but could use it professionally to reap the economies of scale and specialization. That was the secret of the business system; and, after all, the city is rather like a business. ("There is no Republican or Democratic way to clean a street.")

While there are many inconsistent assumptions and goals between these two doctrines, they lived well together. Their coexistence was supported by the fact that different wings of this large, progressive movement were responsible for each. Populism was largely the province of the working-class, "progressive" wing. Doctrines of efficiency were very much the responsibility of the upper-class wing. Populism resided with the politician-activists. Efficiency was developed by the intellectuals, including several distinguished university presidents, such as Seth Low, Andrew Dickson White, Harold Dodd, and, preeminently, Woodrow Wilson, who wrote a classic essay while still a professor of political science proclaiming the virtues of applying Prussian principles of administration in the United States.

These two great ideas were, by a strange and wonderful chemistry, combined into a movement whose influence is a major chapter of American history. Charters and laws have consistently insulated government from politics (meaning party politics). It became increasingly necessary with each passing decade to grant each bureaucratic agency autonomy to do the job as its professional commissioner saw fit.

On into the 1960's the merit system extends itself "upward, outward and downward," to use the Reformers' own dialectic. Recruitment to the top posts comes more and more often from the ranks of lifetime careerists in the agencies, party backgrounds increasingly signifying automatic disqualification. Reform has succeeded in raising the level of public morality and in making politics a dirty word. "Good press" for mayors consists of a determination to avoid intervening in the affairs of one department after another. The typical modern mayor is probably eager to cooperate, because this is a release from responsibility. Absolution-before-the-fact has become part of the swearing-in ceremony.

Reform has triumphed, and the cities are better run than ever before. But that, unfortunately, is not the end of the story, nor would it have been even without a Negro revolution. The triumph of Reform really ends in paradox: Cities like New York are now *well run but ungoverned*.

Politics under Reform is not abolished. Only its form is altered. *The legacy of Reform is the bureaucratic state*. Destruction of the party foundation of the mayoralty cleaned up many cities but also destroyed the basis for sustained, central, popularly based action. This capacity, with all its faults, was replaced by professionalized agencies. But this has meant creation of new bases of power. Bureaucratic agencies are not neutral, they are only independent. The bureaucrat may be more efficient and rational and honest than the old amateur. But he is no less political. If anything, he is more political because of the enormously important decisions so willingly entrusted to his making.

Modernization in New York and other modern cities has meant replacement of Old Machines with New Machines. The bureaucracies—that is, the professionally organized, autonomous career agencies—are the New Machines.

Sociologically, the Old Machine was a combination of rational goals and fraternal loyalty. The cement of the organization was trust and discipline created out of long years of service, probation and testing, slow promotion through the ranks, and centralized control over the means of reward. Its power in the community was based upon services rendered.

Sociologically, the New Machine is almost exactly the same sort of organization. There are more New Machines in any given city. They are functional rather than geographic in their scope. They rely on formal authority rather than upon majority acquiescence. And they probably work with a minimum of graft and corruption. But these differences do not alter their definition; they only help to explain why the New Machine is such a successful form of organization.

The New Machines are machines because they are relatively irresponsible structures of power. That is, each agency shapes important public policies, yet the leadership of each is relatively self-perpetuating and not readily subject to the controls of any higher authority.

The New Machines are machines in that the power of each, while resting ultimately upon services rendered to the community, depends upon its cohesiveness as a small minority in the midst of the vast dispersion of the multitude.

The modern city is now well run but ungoverned because it now comprises islands of functional power before which the modern mayor stands impoverished.[1] No mayor of a modern city has predictable means of determining whether the bosses of the New Machines—the bureau chiefs and the career commissioners—will be loyal to anything but their agency, its work, and related professional norms. Our modern mayor has been turned into the likeness of a French Fourth Republic premier facing an array of intransigent parties in the National Assembly. The plight of the mayor, however, is worse: at least the premier could resign. These modern machines, more monolithic by far than their ancient brethren, are entrenched by law and are supported by tradition, the slavish loyalty of the newspapers, the educated masses, the dedicated civic groups, and, most of all, by the organized clientele groups enjoying access under existing arrangements.

The Reform response to the possibility of an inconsistency between running a city and governing it would be based upon the assumption of the Neutral Specialist, the bureaucratic equivalent to law's Rational Man. The assumption is that if men know their own specialties well enough they are capable of reasoning out solutions to problems they share with men of equal but different technical competencies. That is a very shaky assumption indeed. Charles Frankel's analysis of such an assumption in Europe provides an appropriate setting for a closer look at it in modern New York: "[D]ifferent [technical] elites disagree with each other; the questions with which specialists deal spill over into areas where they are *not* specialists, and they must either hazard amateur opinions or ignore such larger issues, which is no better. . . ."[2]

During the 1950's government experts began to recognize that, despite vast increases in efficiency flowing from defeat of the machine, New York City government was somehow lacking. These concerns culminated in the 1961 Charter, in which the Office of Mayor was strengthened in many impressive ways. But it was quickly discovered that no amount of formal centralization could definitively overcome the real decentralization around the mayor. It was an organized decentralization, and it was making a mockery of the new Charter. The following examples, although drawn from New York, are virtually universal in their applicability:

(1) Welfare problems always involve several of any city's largest agencies, including Health, Welfare, Hospitals, etc. Yet, for more than forty years, successive mayors of New York failed to reorient the Department of Health away from a regulative toward more of a service concept of organization.[3] And many new aspects of welfare must be set up in new agencies if they are to be set up at all. The new poverty programs were very slowly organized in all the big cities—except Chicago.[4]

(2) Water pollution control has been "shared" by such city agencies as the Departments of Health, Parks, Public Works, Sanitation, Water Supply, and so on. No large city, least of all New York, has an effective program to combat even the local contributions to pollution. The same is true of air pollution control, although for some years New York has had a separate department for such purposes.

(3) Land-use patterns are influenced in one way or another by a large variety of highly professional agencies. It has proved virtually impossible in any city for any one of these agencies to impose its criteria on the others. In New York the opening of Staten Island by the Narrows Bridge, in what may be the last large urban frontier, found the city with no plan for the revolution of property values and land uses in that Borough.

(4) Transportation is also the province of agencies too numerous to list. Strong mayors throughout the country have been unable to prevent each agency from going its separate way. For just one example, New York pursued a vast off-street parking program, at a cost of nearly $4,000 per parking space, at the very moment when local rail lines were going bankrupt.

(5) Enforcement of civil rights is imposed upon almost all city agencies by virtue of federal, state, and local legislation. Efforts to set up public, then City Council review of police processes in New York have been successfully opposed by professional police officials. Efforts to try pairing and busing of school children on a very marginal, experimental basis have failed. The police commissioner resigned at the very suggestion that values other than professional police values be imposed upon the Department, even when the imposition came via the respected tradition of "legislative oversight." The superintendent of education, an outsider, was forced out. He was replaced by a career administrator. One education journalist at that time said: "Often . . . a policy proclaimed by the Board [of Education], without the advice and consent of the professionals, is quickly turned into mere paper policy. . . . The veto power through passive resistance by professional administrators is virtually unbeatable. . . ."

The decentralization of city government toward its career bureaucracies has resulted in great efficiency for the activities around which each bureaucracy was organized. The city is indeed well run. But what of those activities around which bureaucracies are not organized, or those which fall between or among agencies' jurisdictions? For these, as suggested by the cases above, the cities are suffering either stalemate or elephantitis—an affliction whereby a particular activity, say urban renewal or parkways, gets pushed to its ultimate success totally without regard to its balance against the missions of other agencies. In these as well as in other senses, the cities are ungoverned.

Mayors have tried a variety of strategies to cope with these situations. But the 1961 mayoral election in New York is the ultimate dramatization of their plight. This election was confirmation of the New York system in the same way the 1936 election was confirmation of Gosnell's Chicago. The 1961 New York election will some day be seen as one of the most significant elections in American urban history. For New York it was the culmination of many long-run developments. For the country it may be the first of many to usher in the bureaucratic state.

The primary significance of the election can be found in the spectacle of a mayor attempting to establish a base of power for himself in the bureaucracies. The mayor's "organization" included the following persons: his running mate for president of the City Council had been commissioner of sanitation, a position which culminated virtually a lifetime career in the Department of Sanitation. He had an impressive following among the sanitation workers, who, it should be added, are organized along precinct lines. The mayor's running mate for comptroller had been for many years the city budget director. As a budget official he had survived several administrations and two vicious primaries pitting factions of the Democratic Party against one another. Before becoming director he had served a number of years as a professional employee in the Bureau. The leaders of the campaign organization included a former, very popular fire commissioner who retired from his commissionership to accept campaign leadership and later to serve as deputy mayor; it also included a former police commissioner who had enjoyed a strong following among professional cops as well as in the local Reform movement. Added to this was a new and vigorous party, the Brotherhood Party, which was composed in large part of unions with broad bases of membership among city employees. Before the end of the election most of the larger city bureaucracies had political representation in the inner core of the new Administration.

For the 1961 election Mayor Wagner had put his ticket and his organization together just as the bosses of old had put theirs together. In the old days the problem was to mobilize all the clubhouses, districts, and counties in the city by putting together a balanced ticket about which all adherents could be enthusiastic. The same seems true for 1961, except that by then the clubhouses and districts had been replaced almost altogether by new types of units.

The main point is that destruction of the machine did not, in New York or elsewhere, elevate the city into some sort of political heaven. Reform did not eliminate the need for political power. It simply altered what one had to do to get it. In the aftermath of twenty or more years of modern government it is beginning to appear that the lack of power can corrupt city hall almost as much as the possession of power. Bureaucracy is, in the United States, a relatively new basis of collective action. As yet none of us knows quite what to do about it.

These observations and cases are not supposed to indict Reform cities and acquit Chicago. They are intended only to put Chicago in a proper light and to provide some experimental means of assessing the functions of the machine form of collective action. Review of Reform government shows simply and unfortunately that the problems of cities, and the irrational and ineffectual ways city fathers go about their business, seem to be universally distributed without regard to form of government or type of power base.

All cities have traffic congestion, crime, juvenile delinquency, galloping pollution, ghettoes, ugliness, deterioration, and degeneracy. All cities seem to be suffering about equally with the quite recent problems of the weakening legitimacy of public objects, resulting in collective violence and pressures for direct solution to problems. All cities seem equally hemmed in by their suburbs and equally prevented from getting at the roots of many of their most fundamental problems. Nonpartisan approaches, even approaches of New York's Republican mayor to Republican suburbs and a Republican governor, have failed to prevent rail bankruptcy in the vast Eastern megalopolis, to abate air or water pollution, to reduce automobile pressure, or to ease the pain of the middle-class Negro in search of escape.

The problems of the city seem to go beyond any of the known arrangements for self-government. However, low morality and lack of what Banfield and Wilson call "public-regardingness" may be a function simply of mass pressure, poor education, and ethnic maladjustment. The old machine and its abuses may have been just another reflection of the same phenomena. If that is so, then the passage of more time and the mounting of one sociocultural improvement after another might have reformed the machines into public-regarding organs, if they had not been first too much weakened to be repaired.

NOTES

1. Compare Wallace Sayre and Herbert Kaufman, *Governing New York City* (New York: Russell Sage, 1960), pp. 710 ff.
2. Charles Frankel, "Bureaucracy and Democracy in the New Europe," *Daedalus* (Winter, 1964), p. 487.
3. Sayre and Kaufman, *op. cit.*, p. 274.
4. Compare Paul Peterson, unpublished doctoral dissertation, University of Chicago, 1967.

WHO MAKES DECISIONS IN
METROPOLITAN AREAS?

NORTON E. LONG

The peculiarity of "the metropolitan problem" is that it is characteristically felt to be a problem requiring a governmental solution for which there is no readily available appropriate governmental machinery. This means that there is no structured decision-making process that has been developed for dealing with this order of problem. The lack of such a structured process means further that there is little institutional support for decision-makers envisioning their primary role as representing a "metropolitan public interest" rather than the interest of their particular group, organization or local government. The most likely role to be called into play in a territory without common political loyalty and institutions is that of the special interest ambassador.

The term, metropolitan problem, almost seems to assume that there is a metropolitan common interest, and the assumption that there is a metropolitan common interest leads easily to the notion that there is a metropolitan community. Many earnest souls have thought that the European problems should follow this same logic, to say nothing of the even more ambitious World Federalists. Common problems may create a community among those who share them. However, much history, especially where people have become accustomed to living under different governments, with different values and resources, underscores the painful fact that common problems may do little more than produce common quarrels.

What this adds up to is that the term decision in our title may be optimistic. One makes a decision in a business, a government, a conference of ambassadors, maybe even sometimes at the summit, but these are structured decision-making institutions. What is characteristic of metropolitan areas is the lack of overall decision-

From Norton E. Long, *The Polity*, © 1962 by Rand McNally & Company, Chicago, pp. 156–64.

making institutions. This does not mean that there are not institutions with power in metropolitan areas. It does mean that there are not institutions with sufficient power and overall responsibility to make decisions settling metropolitan issues and solving metropolitan problems. As a consequence, it is rare that we can speak of who makes metropolitan decisions. What we can speak about is who make decisions that have a significant effect on metropolitan problems.

Characteristically, metropolitan issues do not relate to problems that are solved by decisions in the sense we would use that term in a business or governmental organization, and naturally so, since the metropolitan area is not organized so as to be capable of making decisions. What does happen is that issues and problems have a career and over time processes of interaction develop through which interested and powerful parties exercise influence over the outcome.

We might then concern ourselves with who make decisions that influence the processes by which metropolitan problems and issues get handled. As in a business, one hates to admit that the concern just drifts along by guess and by god, so we are reluctant to admit that this is the way that a metropolitan area runs. This is especially true if one has little faith in an unseen hand guiding the selfish interests of the particular groups and local governments to an unintended but beneficent metropolitan result. Yet in large measure, the metropolitan area is a kind of natural governmental ecology in which institutions, groups and governments have developed a system of largely unintended cooperation through which things get done and the area considered as a system functions. The owls and the field mice, the oaks and the acorns, the flora and fauna of the woodlot have worked out over time a most effective system of unintended cooperation that, barring catastrophe, preserves and maintains a systemic balance, though one that evolves over time.

By and large, we accept a similar system of unintended cooperation for running our economy. The complex task of supplying the city of Philadelphia occurs without any central planning machinery. The fact is we are used to a largely unplanned economy producing functional results. It's a little difficult for us to accept this of an unplanned polity, but to a considerable degree this is just what happens in a metropolitan area. To be sure, the analogy to the economy may be closer to oligopoly than free market competition. What we have is a number of institutions, public and private, sharing a common territory, making demands on each other, cooperating, hindering, damaging and helping in an interdependent set of relations with no overall government exercising control.

The relationships among the governments, government departments, Federal, State and Local, businesses, associations, newspapers, and the myriad groups whose activities intersect and interact have grown up over time. They have a history, they have created habits and customs, use and want, ways that are accepted for handling problems that arise. The metropolitan area as a system for handling common problems is a going concern. The rather considerable problems of very large populations living under great diversity of governments have been managed.

If we look at the who, who make decisions in the metropolitan areas, we will be most interested in the actors, individual and institutional, that play the major roles in the process by which the metropolitan system handles the issues that confront it. We can best appreciate these actors if we see them as dealing with metropolitan problems from the limited point of view of a particular institutional base. This particular institutional base determines the point of view of the actor and how he scores his own success or failure. Much of the blame that is heaped on the heads of actors in the metropolitan scene for their lack of a sense of overall responsibility stems from the failure to recognize the constraints of their institutional reality. It is idle to blame a downtown store for behaving like a downtown store or the Port of New York Authority for behaving like the rubber based, toll fed, revenue bond undertaking that it is. There are very few actors whose particular institutionalized interests parallel in any complete way the metropolitan area. Just as there are almost no institutions, private or public, whose interests and organization cover the metropolitan territory, so there are few, if any, whose interests extend to any considerable number of the problems of the metropolitan area.

By and large, actors and institutions in the metropolitan area, civic ritual apart, are confined in their interests to particular areas and particular problems. Highways, schools, sewer and water, housing, parks and recreation, these problems have their peculiar clientele just as the diseases that afflict the human body have their special funds. Thus, in the highway area you may have a Port of New York Authority, a Bob Moses and the Triborough Bridge Authority, a New York City Transit Authority, Commuter Railways and Buses, two or more state governments and their assorted departments, a variety of political communities, businesses, trade associations, civic organizations, newspapers, all involved. Quite probably, the issues in the transportation field will be agitated with little effective concern for overall problems of coordination and none whatever for the implication of highway resource allocation for other claimants in the metropolitan area.

If we were to make a typology of the key actors in the typical metropolitan area, it might run as follows. First, we would have the metropolitan dailies. In almost all cases, they would exhibit a commitment to the preservation of downtown real estate, a consequent concern for mass transit, extending frequently to the advocacy of subsidy, a belief in planning and a disposition to favor some form of metropolitan integration. These newspapers are in a position to agitate the issues they favor, reward with publicity the politicians and civic leaders who agree with them and by appropriate news selection determine to a large extent what most people will be thinking are the hot issues. Rarely, except in a place like Miami, can the metropolitan press carry a general proposal for governmental change. On piecemeal bond issues and administrative matters, however, it can do much. Beginning to enter the field as a competitor in some areas are television and radio. Just how the structure of their interests will differ from that of the metropolitan press is not clear.

Frequently opposing the metropolitan dailies and following a particularist line is the community press. Usually, they support the interests of small business threatened by planning and the parochialism of suburban city governments.

Of equal importance with the media are, of course, the public officials concerned with the production of public services that cut across political boundaries or require resources that must be allocated among a number of claimants. These officials run the gamut from village to state and nation. They embrace such disparate undertakings as schools, watersheds, airports and a host of other things. Quite often it is the service departments of the governments badgered by their clientele that press the metropolitan issues with still other government officials in their budgetary capacity playing the role of reluctant Solomons.

Downtown stores, real estate interests concerned with central city property values, commuter railways, central city banks, central city and even other politicians concerned with the implications of the worsening of the central city tax base frequently make

common cause with the press, university professors, the foundations and the civic leaders in a crusade to save downtown. A subsidy at the expense of the highway user for mass transit, a massive
urban renewal program, a new layer of metropolitan government,
at the very least, a metropolitan planning agency, all or some combination of these, comprise a set of symbolic and frequently more
than symbolic acts by which a multitude of parties with the most
varied concerns express their feeling about the dynamic changes
that are transforming urban America.

However, these overall actions have all too often bogged down
in the quagmire of divisive local interests and electoral conservatism. Given the circumstances of local public life it is usually easy
to mount a campaign of metropolitan reform. The electoral consultation which our home rule tradition insists on forces such proposals to run the gauntlet of the antagonism of suburban voters
to the central city, vested interests of all kinds in the status quo,
central city ethnic and minority groups who fear any dilution of
their achieved central city power and a host of public officials and
employees who may fear the unsettling of their empires and jobs.
Certainly, high among the list of the who that make metropolitan
decisions, if no more than negatively, are the varied active elec-
torates called into play by referenda and the officials who have a
stake in the existing system.

The revolutionaries who wish to overturn the status quo are
most often university professors, foundations, Leagues of Women
Voters, Chambers of Commerce, civic leader businessmen especially those with a stake in downtown, those with a concern in
the planning of major metropolitan highways and utilities, suburban residents, officials and real estate promoters needing sewer
and water facilities, the media people seeking a cause and the
intellectuals of local government who follow the thinking of
Fortune, The National Municipal League and "the authorities."

The attempts at revolution have mobilized financial support
from elements of the business community such as Civic Progress,
Inc., in St. Louis, and the Cleveland Development Foundation.
They have usually enjoyed the support of the metropolitan dailies,
the League of Women Voters, the professors and most of the
do-gooders. The opposition the campaigns have mobilized, especially where general metropolitan integration has been sought, has
been sufficient to insure defeat at the polls. These defeats have
usually been as much due to the political ineptitude and lack of

energy of the proponents of change as to the power of the opposition.

It must be remembered that the existing metropolitan areas are going concerns—going systems—as systems we can expect them to react vigorously to attempts to seriously alter them. If the existing system of local government could be easily changed it would be intolerably unstable. If no powerful interests were vested in the status quo, the existing order would have so little allegiance it could scarcely run, much less endure. Some such situation obtained in Miami, the one successful case of metropolitan integration and a case where change won by an eyelash and the decision could have gone either way.

If we turn from overall decisions such as those that are embodied in researching county charters, studying metropolitan regions, writing new local constitutions and campaigning to the piecemeal decisions that are by their sheer cumulative weight determining the future of the metropolitan areas, a different order of actions emerged. Clearly among the most significant decisions affecting our metropolitan areas are those which determine the importation of cheap rural labor from the South, Puerto Rico and Mexico, without any provision for adequately housing it in standard housing. The demand for labor insures no equivalent demand for standard housing; it is in fact a demand for slums. Given the desire of the average low income rural immigrant to the city for television, the automobile and the other gadgets of the affluent society, plus his habitation to a very low housing standard in his place of origin, it is not surprising that expensive standard housing should be low on his list of priorities.[1] Doubtless, we could force urban immigrants to buy housing rather than other consumer goods by outlawing substandard housing. We probably won't and this is a key decision in metropolitan areas. The central city has a vested interest in slums as do those employers of cheap labor and those sellers of consumer goods which compete with housing for the slum dwellers' dollar.

Another key decision made by real estate people, bankers, building and loans, suburban neighborhoods and the rest, is whether the new minorities, Negroes, Puerto Ricans and Mexicans, but especially Negroes, will be able to follow the earlier ethnics into the melting pot of middle-class America or whether the color bar will prevent assimilation. This decision which will be made by a myriad of individual decisions will determine whether or not we create our own version of Algeria in our larger cities with an alienated group of second-class citizens led by an unassimilated, rejected but educated elite.

The decisions by our businesses on the location of industry, of manufacturing, retail trade and office buildings will over time critically determine the fate of downtown, the relation of residence and place of work and the future of our system of metropolitan transportation. While we may talk bravely of a pattern of land use control and a massive rehabilitation of the central city, the odds are probably with Professor Raymond Vernon of Harvard that our public expenditures and our controls are unlikely to be sufficiently massive or powerful to offset the natural locational forces. This seems the more likely if dozens of communities scramble to beef up their tax base in a competition for industry to meet mounting municipal costs. With the property tax still a major reliance of central city and suburbs, the struggle for tax base will conflict with and in all probability override efforts at a general plan of metropolitan land use.

While it is unpopular to say it, one of the crucial decisions in the metropolitan area will relate to the preservation of the middle-class values of American culture. Despite all its clumsiness the separate but not watertight compartments of the suburban communities prevent the flooding of schools and neighborhoods by an undigestable mass of immigrants of a different culture. In all probability, despite an uneasy conscience, there will be efforts by middle-class neighborhoods to preserve the political dikes that protect their values. However unsatisfactory, and it is clearly unsatisfactory, the present system of social absenteeism in the massive change in the central city has probably rendered impossible a desirable balance between the social classes. The recolonization of the central city by disenchanted suburbanites is probably little more than the utopia of the builders of luxury high rise apartments.

We can confidently expect that as the incomes of the mass of central city residents rise they will make the same key metropolitan decisions that the earlier middle-class ethnics made—to cross the tracks into suburbia.

Since the positions of power in our society can be expected to fight for survival, it can be expected that the vested interests in downtown should fight as hard for the preservation of outmoded central city land values as the embattled farmers have to preserve an outgrown pattern of agriculture. When one looks at the vested stake in central city real estate it is hard to imagine that the fight to achieve public subsidies to resist its obsolescence will be less than that put up by agriculture. Certainly, there might seem to be a greater appeal for spending the massive sums that now go into subsidizing an unproductive agriculture on the maintenance of our obsolescing central city plant. The sentimental appeal that persuades us to save the family farm can and has been raised to save "downtown." As yet the appeal goes no further than the appeal for urban renewal, and the subsidization of commuter railways and mass transit. If this does not work, we can expect the ante will be raised rather than the end abandoned.

An older generation accustomed to what Mumford has called the eotechnic city, the city of steam and mass transit can be frightened by a specter, the specter of the city of the automobile, Los Angeles. Lord Marple, the British Minister of Transport, said recently, "I saw Los Angeles, the city of the future, a fate we must avoid." Perhaps one day we will cease to regard Los Angeles as a monstrosity and accept the technological obsolescence of the older city. Our agricultural experience indicates the old will die hard.

One last decision, the greatest, I think, in our lifetime and the one nobody made but that has changed everything. In 1929 the shape of the American income was a pyramid with a broad base of the bulk of society close to the means of subsistence living at a family income of below $2,000. In the twenty-five years that *Business Week* once said remade America, 1929 to 1954, the income structure changed from a pyramid to a diamond—America had become a middle-class country. Even in 1929, the middle-class values led to a family centered suburban standard of life. This has been the dynamic. As the lower half of the present diamond of our income structure shrinks with the growth in its income we can expect the new middle classes to continue the trek and the pressure of their movement to continue to tax the public sector of our local economies.

Beyond the dynamic of the growth of the new middle class is the growing market orientation of industry and the new pattern of settlement of business in the metropolitan areas. How the community earns its living will, as always, be a vital determinant of the structure of metropolitan areas.

Ours, however, is an affluent society and the increasing desire to consume public goods will press constantly on our governments. Thus, the rush to the week-end especially with the four-day work week may mean that the peak loads for play will outweigh the peak loads for work on our highways.

The decisions then that may be most important in our metropolitan areas are economic, piecemeal, harmonized if at all by market forces. This is not to say we could not generate enough political power to make effective public metropolitan decision-making possible; it is to express a doubt that we will, in more than a piecemeal way, substitute government action for the forces of the economy. I suspect that as long as the existing system functions even tolerably well, we will tinker with it getting rid of the worst annoyances but putting up with what we know rather than venturing on untried seas. Should Miami and other areas provide an attractive imitable lesson, however, we can expect new civic fashions to spread. The unresolved problem of local government remains the desire for sharply increased amounts of public goods but at the same time stable or decreased taxes, the desire for the fruits of planning and control and the desire for the energy and enterprise of unregimented economic individualism.

Perhaps it is our successful capacity to live with and entertain these contradictory desires that is the genius of our tradition. As an Englishman once told an exasperated French colleague, "England is governed by parliament, not logic."

NOTE

1. I wish to credit Anthony Downs of the University of Chicago with the forceful development of this point.

Can Citizens Be Represented?

EQUALITY AND POWER
IN AMERICAN SOCIETY

ROBERT A. DAHL

. . . let me turn now to another interpretation of certain problems of American communities—problems created by their failure to measure up to the exacting demands of democratic ideals.

My emphasis, however, will be on *appraisal* rather than on description or explanation. What I want to evaluate are the distribution and patterns of influence over political decisions in American life. I shall lean heavily on New Haven for information on the distribution and patterns of influence, but I do so in the belief that New Haven is similar to many other communities and strikingly similar in many ways to the United States as a whole. Where there are differences, I shall try to take these into account.

To appraise, one needs standards of appraisal, criteria of performance, values. Many different criteria are relevant to the task of arriving at an appraisal of the distribution and patterns of influence. I propose, however, to concern myself with only one, the criterion of political equality. Obviously, other criteria might also be invoked. I will not attempt here to justify my choice of equal-

From Robert Dahl, "Equality and Power in American Society," in William D'Antonio and Howard J. Erlich (eds.) *Power and Democracy in America*, pp. 77–89. Copyright © 1961 by University of Notre Dame Press. Reprinted with permission of University of Notre Dame Press.

ity, except to say that it is a value that has always been a salient aspect of democratic beliefs.

When one examines a political decision—that is, a decision determining the policies enforced by governmental officials—or what persons become officials—one usually finds that for any particular sector of policy only a small number of persons ever initiate alternatives or veto the proposals of others. These individuals are leaders or policy-makers. One may say that they have the greatest *direct* influence on decisions. A larger number of persons, subleaders, generally have moderate influence. But most citizens usually have little or no *direct* influence in this sense: they never initiate or veto any alternatives.

One is also likely to find, however, that some leaders are extremely sensitive to the attitudes and preferences of individuals and groups who do not directly initiate or veto alternatives. Often this indirect influence is *anticipatory*: a leader initiates or vetoes a particular alternative because he anticipates rewards for choosing from one set of alternatives, or sanctions if he chooses from a different set. In this way, persons or groups who are not leaders may exert great indirect influence on the choice of alternatives even though they never directly initiate or veto.

In New Haven, for example, the present mayor has not until this present year ever advocated an increase in taxes, although he has done almost everything else to raise money. Why has he not tried to increase taxes? It was not, I think, because someone said, "Mayor Lee, don't you dare raise taxes!" For the mayor grew up in New Haven; he knows enough about the city to know that raising taxes is politically risky. He *anticipated* what might happen to him in the next election if he should raise taxes. If the decision to take the risk is made, at least it is a fact that the risk involved has been anticipated.

Indirect influence, which is often anticipatory in character, is very important for some kinds of leaders, particularly those who have to win elections. Yet even when indirect influence of this sort is taken into account, the distribution of influence in most sectors of policy is very far indeed from the perfect equality that some democratic theorists would regard as ideal.

One of the main reasons why the system does not very closely approximate political equality is the unequal distribution of access to political resources—that is, to inducements of all kinds. One's influence is partly a function of the political resources to which one has access—labor time, money and credit, jobs, information, popularity, wealth, social standing, legality, and the like. An examination of any one of these political resources will show that some persons have much greater access to it than others. So long as this is the case, political equality is not likely to be approximated. This is hardly a novel conclusion, for a great many writers on politics have said in one way or another that a high degree of equality in the distribution of political resources is a necessary—though by no means a sufficient—condition for a high degree of equality of control over political decisions. This was, for example, one of Tocqueville's key propositions in his analysis of democracy in America.

In appraising inequality in political resources, it is important not to make the mistake of assuming that what we are trying to judge is a ruling elite masquerading in the name of democracy. For if citizens do not rule the system as political equals neither does a unified elite control decisions, at least not in New Haven. There may be exceptions in specific communities, but I am inclined to think that most cities and states, and certainly the national government, are in this respect rather like New Haven.

To condemn our political system for inequality is one thing; to condemn it for being dominated by a ruling elite is another. In my view, appraisal is infinitely more complicated, precisely because the political system is neither a democracy in which citizens share equally in all important decisions nor an oligarchy ruled by an elite. Rather, it combines elements of both.

In the American system (insofar as New Haven is a fair prototype), though political equality is certainly not attained and political resources are unequally distributed, democracy is not wholly subverted into oligarchy because the growth of oligarchy is inhibited both by the *patterns* according to which political resources are allocated and by the ways in which resources are actually *used*.

Let me try to make my point clearer first by some abstract considerations on the nature of power and influence. Abstractly, there is no reason to assume that the relative influence different individuals or groups exert on the decisions of one another is simply and solely a function of the "size" of their resources, that is, of the inducements they have at their disposal.

In the first place, an individual need not *use* his political resources to gain direct or indirect influence over officials of government. To be sure, the extent to which one is willing to use his political resources for political ends, depends *in part* on the magnitude of his resources; for example a millionaire who contributed $100 to a political campaign gives up fewer alternative opportunities than a poor man. But the extent to which a person uses his political resources will depend on other factors as well, including his confidence in the success of his effort, the extent to which he has alternative ways of gaining his ends other than through politics, and the extent to which he expects he will be benefited or injured by government policies. In New Haven, we have found variations attributable to each of these factors.

For example, Negroes in New Haven, a minority of probably 10 or 12 per cent of the population, operate at a much higher level of political participation than any other single isolated group in the community. What is the reason for this? The political arena is one area where Negroes are not thwarted and blocked by substantial discrimination. They can get jobs, patronage, and city contracts; they have their votes; their votes are legitimate, and they are counted; and so it has been for a century. This isn't true in the other sectors of community life; so Negroes work harder in the political arena to compensate for their disadvantages.

In the second place, one individual may use his political resources more *skillfully* than another—a variation known to students of politics for several centuries. By a skillful use of limited resources, in fact, a political entrepreneur—Machiavelli's Prince—can increase his resources and thus his influence.

In the third place, the relative influence of different potential coalitions will depend in part on the extent to which individuals and groups actually *combine* their resources. The combined political resources of a very numerous group of individuals who are not very well off may easily exceed the combined political resources of a small elite, each member of which is, individually, very well off. The extent to which people in a group actually combine their resources depends, of course, on the degree of political unity among them. There is no a priori reason for supposing that the rich will display more unity than the poor; and even if they do, it does not follow that the combined resources of the well-off strata will inevitably exceed the combined resources of the badly-off strata of a society.

Now, when we turn from these abstract considerations to the way in which different kinds of inducements—political resources —are actually distributed in New Haven we discover that a most significant change seems to have taken place during the last century and a half. In 1800, the citizens of New Haven were not only very unequal in access to political resources of all kinds but their inequalities were *cumulative*. That is, the same tiny elite possessed the highest social standing, wealth, dominance in economic affairs, superior education, control over educational and religious institutions, a monopoly of public offices, evidently a large measure of legitimacy, and perhaps (though this is more doubtful) even popularity. Today, however, inequalities that exist with respect to all these resources tend to be noncumulative or *dispersed*. I can find no single elite at the top of the heap; instead there are many different varieties of political resources, with a somewhat different elite at the top of each. I am inclined to think that this pattern is not peculiar to New Haven but is common throughout the United States, though one would doubtless find exceptions to it here and there.

Moreover, I am tempted toward the hypothesis that the pattern of dispersed inequalities is a likely product of an advanced industrial society, at least if it operates with the kinds of political institutions that most of us would call democratic. The impact of Marx and Weber on habits of thought about industrial society has been very great, even among non-Marxists and non-Weberians, and both men lead us to expect that an advanced industrial society will be rather neatly and consistently stratified along lines shaped by economic class or bureaucratic position. I believe we should entertain the hypothesis that any industrial society in an advanced stage enters on a profound change that can be held back, if at all, only by a most vigorous and oppressive centralized regime. In a moderately free political system, at this stage, increasing affluence, widespread education, impersonal standards of recruitment, incredible specialization of functions and skills, the varieties of popularity, prestige, and achievement, standardization of consumer goods, social and geographical mobility, and probably many other factors, all tend to produce a pattern of dispersed rather than cumulative inequalities. The advance of industrial society may somewhat reduce inequalities in political resources; it does not, however, erase them. Nonetheless, in New Haven, and I think in American society generally, these inequalities are no longer cumulative.

To the extent that inequalities persist, tendencies toward oligarchy also exist in advanced industrial societies. But to the extent that inequalities are dispersed rather than cumulative—as I am suggesting they are in the United States—the growth of a unified oligarchy is inhibited. For the pattern of dispersed inequalities means that an individual or a group at a disadvantage with respect to one resource may compensate for his handicap by exploiting his superior access to a different resource. In New Haven, for example, for the past half century men whose main political resources were popularity and ethnic solidarity have been able to win elections. Very few individuals or groups in New Haven, and I believe this to be true in the United States, are totally lacking in political resources *of some kind.*

The possibility of turning to alternative kinds of resources would be less significant if one kind of resource—say wealth or social standing—dominated all the others, in the sense that a person or group superior in the one resource would invariably exert superior influence in a conflict with persons who drew on other political resources. Yet—and this is the second great limit on the growth of oligarchy—this is simply not the case, despite a tradition of economic determinism that runs in a straight line from Madison to Veblen, Beard, the Lynds, and C. Wright Mills. Surely if the New Deal demonstrated anything, it proved that leaders with popularity and votes can—even if they do not always do so—carry out their policies despite the opposition of leaders supported by men of wealth and social standing. This is a point that was perfectly obvious to both Aristotle and Tocqueville, who considered the problem in the light of observations made on radically different sorts of political systems.

In the third place, individuals or groups who are at a disadvantage in their access to resources can sometimes compensate by using their resources at a relatively high level. In New Haven, Negroes who, as I said before, are more active politically than any other identifiable ethnic group in the city, have overcome some of the disadvantages imposed by their incomes, status, and occupations.

Fourth, an individual or group at a disadvantage in resources may compensate by developing a high level of political skill. Fortunately the skills required in electioneering and party politics are by no means a monopoly of any stratum in the community; one might even conclude that leaders drawn from the well-to-do tend to be somewhat less likely to develop these skills to a high peak of proficiency than leaders drawn from the less-well-off strata of the community. In fact, many sorts of politicking run more sharply counter to the norms of the upper strata than of the lower or lower-middle strata.

Fifth, a group of citizens each of whom is weak in political resources may compensate by combining resources so that in the aggregate these are formidable. One resource that can be most easily aggregated by the less-well-off strata is the ballot. In New Haven, historically the least well-off citizens in the community have been Negroes and members of various immigrant groups whose circumstances produce a unity at the polls that declines as assimilation progresses. This unity among the poor has enabled them—or more accurately, perhaps, their leaders—to influence nominations, elections, and policies (often, to be sure, covert rather than overt policies) despite their lowly status, their low incomes, and their poverty in many other political resources.

Sixth, competitive elections insure that elected officials attempt to shape their covert and overt policies so as to win elections, hence to maximize votes, or at any rate to gain more votes than any rival. Consequently, whenever the many are believed to hold views on government policies at odds with the views held among the few, there exists one set of persons, elected politicians, who are strongly impelled to win votes by shaping or seeming to shape governmental policies according to the views of the many.

The system would be easier to judge either if it did not fall so far short of the goal of political equality—or, ironically, if it fell much shorter than it does. In the first case one might conclude that we possess a reasonable approximation of political equality, and approve the fact; in the other, one might conclude that we have an oligarchy, and condemn it roundly. But in my view the facts do not permit either judgment.

Some of you might draw comfort from the belief that the American system, if I have described it rightly, comes close to the mixture of democracy and oligarchy that Aristotle concluded was "the best constitution and the best way of life for the *majority* of states and men," and which he called a polity. I cannot forbear quoting here a few lines from Barker's translation of *The Politics.*

> It is a good criterion of a proper mixture of democracy and oligarchy that a mixed constitution should be able to be described indifferently as either. . . . A properly mixed 'polity' should look as if it contained both democratic and oligarchical elements—and as if it contained neither. It should owe its stability to its own intrinsic strength, and not to external support; and its intrinsic strength should be derived from the fact, not that a majority are in favor of its continuance . . . , but rather that there is no single section in all the state which would favor a change to a different constitution. . . . It is clear from our argument, first, that the best

form of political society is one where power is vested in the middle class, and secondly, that good government is attainable in those states where there is a large middle class—large enough, if possible, to be stronger than both of the other classes, but at any rate large enough to be stronger than either of them singly. (*pp. 177, 178, 180*)

You will recall also Aristotle's observation that polities of this kind were in fact rather rare, because in most states the middle class was small, and both the masses and the rich sought to install the constitution most favorable to them, either democracy or oligarchy.

For those who do not want to yield up the marvelous Utopian objective that animated the Declaration of Independence and the Gettysburg address, Aristotle's words will scarcely give complete comfort. Unless we abandon the ideal of political equality, and with it the American Dream, I do not see how we can live comfortably with the inequalities of power and political resources that we find around us. Can anyone who holds democratic beliefs remain satisfied with the American political system simply because it is not an oligarchy?

Unfortunately, however, solutions to the problem of political inequality are not as simple as they may have seemed to many hopeful democrats a century or more ago. In order to eliminate large inequalities in direct influence on governmental policies we should have to make far-reaching, indeed revolutionary, alterations in the character of modern society, such as the destruction of the national state and the elimination of all forms of bureaucratic organization including the business corporation. It would also require a world at peace. Even then, so long as individuals had different motives, interests, and skills, sizable differences in direct influence undoubtedly would appear. I do not believe that enough people are interested in these changes—which would generate their own train of uncertainties and impose great costs to other values we all hold—to make it worth the effort to explore them here, even though attempts to think through these problems realistically should continue.

Nor should one be misled by glib solutions. It might be argued, for example, that if inequalities in direct influence are inevitable, at least we should insure that there is equal opportunity to *gain* influence. Many persons are handicapped in the contest for office and influence by inequalities in resources that can be reduced, such as handicaps stemming from gross differences in income and inherited wealth, handicaps arising from inadequate opportunities for education, and handicaps arising from discriminatory practices based on race, ethnic group, religion, or social class. To the extent that these are remediable, surely we should not rest on our oars until the race is won.

But we must not be beguiled into assuming that equality of opportunity to *gain* influence will produce equality of *influence*. In fact, we are reducing and probably in the future will reduce even more many old inequalities in opportunities. But this merely insures that individuals will start out more or less even in a race for unequal influence. Even a modern dictatorship can achieve that. In fact some dictatorships seem to do a tolerably good job of it. It might be thought, too, that inequalities in direct influence over government policies could be reduced solely to *legitimate* differences in the relative influence of government officials, particularly elected officials, and ordinary citizens. No one, I suppose, would quarrel with the proposition that the President or the Secretary of State should have much greater influence over foreign policies, because of official position, than any other citizen. Yet it would be misleading to suppose that we are likely to reach a state of affairs in which reality corresponds to the simple model of democratic representation whereby appointive officials are merely the agents of elected officials, and elected officials are merely the agents of the majority. For in many sectors of policy, including most of the highly critical ones, elected and appointive officials have enormous leeway; public opinion and voting often provide only the vaguest sort of guide as to what is preferred by or even acceptable to a majority of voters. Views are often highly plastic: it is not so much the elected officials who are the agents of a majority as the other way round—voters wait for their trusted leaders to indicate what lines of policy should be followed.

If we are not likely—at least in the present state of national and world organization—to reduce very greatly the enormous differences that now exist with respect to direct influences on government policies, the problem of indirect influence is somewhat more manageable. The most promising means for providing an equal though indirect influence on policies is, surely, through participation in nominations, campaigns, and elections. Here the situation strikes me as a very hopeful one, for political self-confidence and participation are so much a function of education that the wide diffusion of educational opportunities is likely to reduce to insignificance many of the differences in political participation that stem from socioeconomic position rather than differences in personality. (Perhaps it is just as well that the differences in personality still elude control.)

Even in the case of campaigns and elections, however, wide participation is no cure-all. A formidable problem arises because of the enormous differences in opportunities for influencing the voters themselves. The problem is much more serious at the national than at the local level, for it is incomparably more expensive and more difficult to obtain a national hearing than a local one. Political theory has barely been extended to cover this problem; in particular, liberal democratic theory has often started with the assumption that the preferences of individuals, whether voters or consumers, should be taken as given, as autonomous to the individual rather than socially determined. To be sure, Tocqueville, Mill, and Bryce all looked beyond the individual to the towering influence of majority opinion on the views of the individual; and critics at the right and left have looked beyond the majority to the influence on its opinions wielded by key minorities of wealth, status and skill. There have been some innovations, like equal time, and more recently the famous TV debates between the presidential candidates. But clearly we have barely begun to grapple with this problem.

There can be no doubt, then, that our political system falls far short of the high standards of performance indicated by the criterion of political equality. No one who places a high value on political equality can afford to be complacent about the achievements of the American political system.

Nonetheless, it is misleading in the extreme to interpret the inequalities of power that mark our political life as signs of oligarchy. For in our system of dispersed inequalities, almost every group, as said before, has access to some resources that it can exploit to gain influence. Consequently, any group that feels itself badly abused is likely to possess both the resources it needs to halt the abuse and the incentive to use these resources at a high enough level to bring about changes. Nearly every group has enough potential influence to mitigate harsh injustice to its members, though not necessarily enough influence to attain a full measure of justice. The system thus tends to be self-corrective, at least in a limited fashion. If equality and justice are rarely attained, harsh and persistent oppression is almost always avoided. To this extent, the system attains one of the important ends of political equality without the means.

PLURALISM, RACE, AND THE URBAN POLITICAL SYSTEM

STEPHEN M. DAVID AND JEWEL BELLUSH

It was not until the late 1950's that political scientists began to give serious attention to the study of community power and influence. Up to that time, sociologists had held a monopoly of the field, while political scientists had been preoccupied with promoting "good government" prescriptions for city management and writing dry texts. By and large, those early sociological studies had concluded that a power elite, representing an upper class (whose definition varied from study to study), governed American communities. Party officials and civic and labor leaders were said to hold places subordinate to this upper-class elite.[1] These conclusions were arrived at by a variety of approaches. The best known placed primary reliance either on analysis of the resource bases (sources of power) of the elite or on identifying reputed influentials in the community.[2]

Political scientists, almost en bloc, attacked such findings, complaining that sociologists had failed to verify these conclusions about the role and character of a "power elite." The major thrust of this attack was that the studies had not proved elites used their power to rule local communities; instead, sociologists had relied on potential sources of power or reputed influence, rather than on actual acts of power.[3] To avoid this error, political scientists set to work to study actual decisions made by local government officials. In this way, they hoped to determine the most influential actors and to reveal what constituted the patterns of power in American cities. Concentrating on the "case study approach" (as their method of reconstructing government decisions came to be known), they hoped to uncover the loci of power in various urban centers.[4]

Most of these studies arrived at a conclusion sharply different from that reached by the sociologists: A pluralistic, rather than hierarchical, pattern of decision-making was the real shape of urban power. Political scientists, perceiving urban political systems to be made up of a myriad of small special-interest groups having widely differing power bases and undertaking a multitude of strategies on decisions salient to them, were able to conclude that no single power elite dominated the full spectrum of decision-making; instead, there existed a relatively wide sharing of power among leaders and groups tending to specialize in one or a few issue areas. Believing these multiple centers of power to be the norm, they argued that no single group constituted an all-encompassing power elite. The various centers, or clusters, of power provided the political system with discrete, functional arenas, each public activity operating separately with a different constellation of interests. While accepting the sociological claim that the active, interested, affected groups (always a minority of citizens) dominated the policy process, the advocates of pluralism contended that what eventually evolved into public policies was the result of bargaining and compromise; participants were constrained, checked, and balanced either by other leaders or by those they led.[5]

Thus, as the 1960's began, political scientists had designed a new pattern of urban decision-making that challenged the prevailing power elite model. The pluralists, as this group of political scientists came to be called, were initially widely praised for their studies. Their reliance on the case method to test the validity of their conclusions was considered a major improvement upon the methodology used by the sociologists. Moreover, their findings fitted the optimistic mood of the country during those years, when the process of accommodation and compromise in an open system seemed to be confirmed by daily events.

The events of the 1960's, however, forced many academics to take a closer look at the works of these political scientists. The black revolution, student rebellions, the peace movement, mounting concern for the plight of such groups as the Indians, migrant laborers, and the poor whites of Appalachia—these events raised fundamental questions about the ability of our political systems to function in an open, democratic, and responsive manner. Problems such as these could not be denied or ignored, and the prevailing political theory that could not explain them came into question.

The earliest major critique came from a group of scholars disturbed by the pluralists' sole reliance upon the case study technique, which they believed to be inadequate in the determination of the distribution of power in a given locality. These critics, holding that there were limitations inherent in the very methodology of the pluralists, described three types of situations in which a would-be participant could fail to act (though affected by the policy) and hence would not be represented in a case study reconstruction of the governmental decision.

In each of these situations, groups fail either to initiate a controversy or to promote certain positions that are in their self-interest. The first occurs when a group feels it lacks sufficient influence to affect governmental policy and thus takes no action to promote its interests. In the second, a group fails to initiate or participate in political controversies because it fears the use of sanctions were it to choose to get involved; the history of America is replete with examples of actions—such as lynchings of Southern blacks or police raids on "extremist" groups—taken to discourage political involvement. The last occurs when community norms, which are supportive of the interests of particular groups, lead either to the failure of a group to initiate a controversy or to the exclusion of a whole range of alternatives during the course of a conflict. In this last type of situation, the norms are accepted by government officials and nongovernmental groups alike. In all three cases, those groups that are advantaged by the nonoccurrence of the controversy or by the failure to consider certain alternatives have exercised influence on government officials without any action on their part. Yet, such use of power never comes within the purview of the case study approach.[6]

Criticisms of the pluralist school have not been limited to attacks on their methodology. On the contrary some of their most significant conclusions concerning the nature of urban political systems have been questioned. These pluralist findings can be broadly categorized thus: (1) Urban political systems are open and responsive; (2) there exists a workable model for decision-making; and (3) functional islands of decisions can be perceived. It is to these categories that the remainder of this essay is devoted.

OPENNESS AND RESPONSIVENESS OF THE POLITICAL SYSTEM

Although the pluralists have conceded that differential influence exists within the American political system, they have also maintained that no significant groups are left out of the system.

This view has been expressed in a variety of ways: Robert Dahl has written that any active and legitimate group can usually "make itself heard at some crucial stage in the process of decision";[7] Nelson Polsby expresses the same view, when he states that, in our pluralistic systems, "the claims of small, intense minorities are usually attended to";[8] in summing up New York City's political system, Wallace Sayre and Herbert Kaufman found it to be open and responsive, available "to all the inhabitants of the city and particularly to the active participants in the contest for the stakes of politics."[9]

The pluralists, generally drawing these conclusions from their analyses of the processes and the policy outcomes of decision-making, have maintained that most citizens most of the time are politically apathetic, getting involved and organizing themselves effectively only when their "primary goals" would be affected by political activity. The classic exposition of this pluralist view appears in Dahl's description of the metal-houses controversy in *Who Governs?*[10] In that case, a working-class, poorly educated, politically apathetic Italian community in New Haven organized itself and succeeded in preventing the construction of metal houses, which were intended as residences for blacks, in the neighborhood. These otherwise apolitical people quickly formed a civic association and were able to muster large numbers to appear at meetings of the Board of Aldermen and the Board of Zoning Appeals. At the conclusion of his description of the controversy, Dahl wrote that it illustrated several durable characteristics of the political system—most especially, that involvement in political activities occurs when there is a threat to the primary goals of an individual or group; at such times, the affected citizens will quickly and effectively organize themselves. Sayre and Kaufman wrote in a similar vein about New York:

> Some inhabitants of the city have been slower than others to make use of the weapons the political system places within their grasp, but most—even immigrants from lands with altogether different traditions—have learned quickly, and there are not many who accept passively whatever the system deals out. They have learned that governmental decisions of every kind in the city are responsive to the demands upon the decision centers.[11]

Pluralists have also maintained that each participant in a political controversy almost invariably receives some satisfaction from its outcome. Thus, Sayre and Kaufman wrote that "if there is any single feature of the system of government and politics . . . that may be called ubiquitous and invariant, it would seem to be the prevalence of mutual accommodation. Every program and policy represents a compromise among the interested participants."[12]

The validity of the pluralists' views can be challenged at a number of points. To begin with, in their analysis and conclusions concerning political activation the pluralists argued that political involvement is conditioned upon a threat (be it government action or inaction) to primary goals. When such a threat does not exist, citizens are apathetic, the assumption being that their greatest desires (for example, security, sex, love, food, self-esteem) are best attained by channeling their efforts into nonpolitical activities.[13] This view of the cause of political activation led the pluralists to describe the apathetic state of the general populace in our cities as indicating satisfaction with the prevailing political system. According to pluralist reasoning, since the system was open for those groups of citizens who felt threatened, their failure to become politically involved signified their general approval of the actions of public officials.[14] Such reasoning is, however, simplistic. The pluralists failed to consider a crucial question: How does the citizen become informed of governmental action (or inaction) that would threaten his primary goals? Nor did they consider the processes involved in informing the citizen that public action could actually help in dealing with his daily problems. Put another way, the pluralists used an individual, rather than a societal, perspective to analyze the hindrances to activation; they failed to realize that changes in the *political system* could affect the chances of the citizen's being informed of potential or actual governmental action. In short, the pluralists failed to see the complexity of the political processes involved in activation.

These processes—which involve informing the citizen about political issues, interpreting these issues to him, relating the problems in his daily life (of which he is very aware) to the potential or actual activities of government—must be understood before one can begin to generalize about political activation. When one reflects upon these processes, one is struck by the role that society's institutional structure plays in communicating political issues to the citizen and in shaping his frame of reference for interpreting these issues as well as the events in his everyday life. He depends upon a number of institutional factors for these functions: the existence (or absence) of groups that share interests and concerns similar to his and are able to reach him; the activities of those participants in the political system that may threaten or use sanctions against the activities of said groups; the role of television and the newspapers in informing the citizen and shaping his perceptions; and the role of various institutions—such as the school system, the police, the political party, or charitable organizations —that seek to impose their definitions of the situation upon the citizen. In short, when one begins to speculate on the processes involved in activating the citizen, one becomes aware that these processes do not resemble the simplistic model of the pluralists; instead, they are highly complex and have biases built into them. Without an analysis of these processes and built-in biases, one cannot assume, as the pluralists did, a one-to-one relationship between citizen involvement and government threats, by action or inaction, to primary goals. . . .

More, however, is at stake than activation. Even if a group of citizens is politically activated, can we accept the pluralist assumptions about the spontaneous and inevitable emergence of group action and leadership skilled in the selection of strategies necessary for success?[15] The pluralists were aware that political resources and skills were differentially distributed throughout the system; yet they never seemed to have analyzed whether particular groups were *systematically* disadvantaged in their ability to organize because they lacked the requisite resources and skills. Pluralists seemed to feel that, if such communities as New Haven's Italians could rouse themselves from their usual lethargic state and organize effectively in a short period of time, any group of urban residents were similarly capable of so performing.

It appears, nonetheless, that groups initially entering the political process are at a distinct disadvantage in this regard. Such groups are usually short on funds, and material resources have been known to be among the best inducements for getting people to work for an organization, particularly if they are low income with little leisure time.[16] The best-known example of a successful organization among the low-income urban poor is the political machine, and it depended upon such material resources. But, in addition, the leaders of these organizations are often political neophytes, and the acquisition of political skills stems, in large part, from experience in the political process. If these groups come from the poorer and less well-educated sectors of the population, as is often the case, their leaders will often lack the technical and professional expertise needed to engage successfully in combat in today's urban political system.

Blacks, in particular, have encountered difficulties in their efforts to organize on their own behalf. For example, New York City black residents experienced considerable difficulty in becoming an organized force capable of challenging the relatively cohesive power alliance of Columbia University and the traditional voluntary health organizations in control of the Community Mental Health Board. On the other hand, the war on poverty's community-action program illustrates how a government program helped promote the organization and development of leadership skills among certain segments of the black community.[17] These two cases suggest that resources such as money, technical and professional expertise, and group cohesion and the skillful use of these resources are scarce commodities among New York blacks. The reality these case studies describe is a long way from the assumption that activated citizens can easily organize and become influential in politics at any time. Once again, findings of the pluralists, upon which they based their conclusion that our urban political systems are open, come into question.

Not only are there doubts about the validity of pluralist conclusions concerning the activation and organization of the citizenry, but also about their conclusion that public decisions almost invariably reflect an accommodation or compromise among the contending parties. Pluralists have claimed that the interests of all the contending parties will somehow be represented in the final outcome, even if only partially. Such a conclusion is open to attack on several grounds. Surprisingly, the pluralists have generally failed to analyze the outcomes of their case studies systematically in order to determine who gained from the final decision. They have limited their efforts instead to analyzing the extent to which the participants obtained what they asked for.[18] Pluralists have argued that an index that documents the extent to which a participant gains what he demanded during the course of a controversy is preferable to one that focuses on the outcome and ascertains who gained from that decision.[19] As a result of this choice, the outcomes the pluralists analyze represent an accommodation and compromise only for those groups that participated in the controversy; only their demands, made in the course of the conflict, are included. Yet, Nelson Polsby, who has made the best-known defense of this methodological approach, has readily admitted that these factors reflect the power realities of the community.[20] In other words, when the pluralists argue that accommodation is the rule, they are, in effect, saying compromise occurs if we limit our analysis to those who had been activated and organized and to the demands they made, which were shaped by their perceptions of what was politically attainable. By so narrowing the definition of the political system we are seeking to characterize, the pluralists have provided us with a conclusion about the distribution of rewards that is of limited value. One wonders whether any political system, as defined by the pluralists, could not be said to accommodate the demands of its various participants.

Before any conclusion concerning the responsiveness of a political system can be drawn, it would seem necessary to study those conflicts that have been suppressed (whether such suppression be due to a decision of the potential initiator that his demands stand no chance of recognition or to threatened or actual use of sanctions against the initiator) and those conflicts that involve "significant" challenges to the values held by the politically dominant groups in the community.[21] There is no gainsaying the methodological problems involved in studying such events (or nonevents); yet without this kind of data, it seems premature to draw any conclusions as to the responsiveness of a political system.

Even if the pluralist approach to ascertaining responsiveness were to be used for the cases in this volume, the limited extent to which the city's political system has accommodated the demands of the black community would become apparent. Before discussing this question, it is necessary to raise a logically prior problem; namely, the value bias inherent in making any judgment about the responsiveness of a political system. The determination of whether a decision has accommodated the demands of a particular participant is a judgment based upon empirical fact *and* upon one's value preferences. It is not enough to validate empirically that a participant received something he had sought from the decision. To conclude that the participant has been accommodated by the outcome, one must make a judgment that the benefits received were, in some sense, satisfactory. This judgment should be made by the participants, not by the researcher; yet the pluralists, after verifying that the actors in their controversies achieved some measure of success, drew the conclusion that urban political systems accommodated the varying demands and pressures put upon them.[22] That conclusion reflected the beliefs of the pluralists as to what the participants in a controversy should reasonably expect. These beliefs, of course, can be very different from the expectations of the actors. Although it is always hazardous to generalize about the biases of a group of scholars, it does appear that the pluralists as a group placed a high value upon stability and upon change that comes about incrementally.[23] As a result, a political system that rewarded all participants, both those who supported the *status quo* and those who sought change, was considered responsive. It was the pluralists, not necessarily the participants (or the potential claimants) in political controversies, who were satisfied with the outcomes of urban political systems. . . .

The Model of Decision-Making

Throughout the pluralist writings, a certain model of political decision-making emerges. The actors are usually individuals who represent organizations, agencies, and organized groups, but not broad social classes. Almost invariably, there are coalitions representing the various contending parties. Participation is confined almost exclusively to those activists who represent organized interests. These actors communicate among themselves in a covert manner, avoiding public notice. The conflict is resolved through bargaining, and the resolution is usually an accommodation among the interests of all contending parties.[24]

Questions concerning a number of these characteristics of the pluralistic model can be raised. The pluralists expected participation to be limited to the leaders of organized groups; little consideration was given to participation by the membership. This was in accord with the pluralist belief that most citizens most of the time were not involved in political activities.[25] The activation and organization of the Italian community in Dahl's metal-houses case was considered a deviation from the normal processes of decision-making. Sayre and Kaufman, listing political participants, refer to the leaders of groups—for example, public officials, both elected and appointed; the leaders of the political parties; the organized public bureaucracies; nongovernmental groups; and officials and bureaucrats of other governments—with only a passing reference to the mass of the citizenry.[26] . . .

However, during the 1960's, we find larger communities of people becoming involved in the racial conflicts of the period. Controversies involving attempts at school or housing integration mobilized nearly all segments of the affected white community. Other issues perceived by the white community as having racial implications witnessed similar patterns. For example, the more massive style is exemplified in the well-known conflicts in New York City over the establishment of a Civilian Review Board and over the attempt to initiate community control of the schools in Ocean Hill–Brownsville.

This larger number of participants also cast doubt on the pluralist finding that conflicts almost invariably take place between small, well-organized groups. Instead, the character of race politics appears to be more and more a social-class or social-group phenomenon. In the controversy over community control of education, the Ocean Hill–Brownsville conflict was not merely a clash between an experimental school district and the United Federation of Teachers (UFT); it became a clash between large segments of the black community and large segments of the white community, particularly its Jewish grouping. The controversy over the establishment of a Civilian Review Board exhibited similar tendencies, with the Catholic, rather than the Jewish, community in the forefront of the white population group opposed to the black community.

The pluralist model also stressed a covert process of communication. This means of communication among the participants allowed for and promoted compromise among them. One effect of such a strategy of secrecy is to limit the number of participants. Groups (often promoting different ends from the ones being pressed by those already participating) that might have become involved are never informed of the decision process in time. This type of communication process also enables leaders to avoid public commitments to their constituents, thereby allowing greater latitude for maneuver and compromise in the negotiations.[27]

In the 1960's, however, racial controversies had a high, rather than a low, visibility, and it was therefore much more difficult for the city's bargaining process to proceed in the traditional manner described by the pluralists. Thus, in the decentralization case, the conflict was resolved, not through quiet bargaining between representatives of the union and the community but only through a highly publicized citywide strike. In effect, this conflict was fought out in the communications media. . . .

Another aspect of the pluralist decision-making model is the existence of coalitions representing the various sets of participants. Again, the pluralists assumed that alliances were an invariant characteristic of the process and that no significant groups would encounter any particular difficulties in obtaining allies. The importance of coalitions to the pluralists is stated by Polsby: One of his five conditions for success in influencing public officials is the "capacity to form coalitions with other participants in order to achieve one's goals."[28] Yet, throughout the decade, black groups encountered growing difficulty in obtaining white allies. White groups which sought to unite with blacks often found their membership resisting such moves. White elites who identified with black demands found that the risks to their leadership position increased.

In short, the pluralists appear to have believed that, in describing a covert process of decision-making with limited participation, they were dealing with universal tendencies that were not likely to change: Almost all urban controversies would be marked by participation limited to the leaders of organized groups, by the absence of involvement of the mass of the citizenry, and by the use of covert processes of communication.[29] Ironically, the pluralists, who criticized the sociologists for assuming that power distributions were permanently related to the social structure, appear to have made similar assumptions about the permanence of the processes involved in decision-making.

To understand this belief of the pluralists in the universal tendencies of the model, one needs to know their perception of American society and its political systems at all levels of government. Nelson Polsby nicely summarized much of what they believe when he wrote:

> Pluralists, who see American society as fractured into a congeries of hundreds of small special interest groups, with incompletely overlapping memberships, widely differing power bases, and a multitude of techniques for exercising influence on decisions salient to them, are not surprised at the low priority Americans give to their class memberships as bases of social action. In the decision-making of fragmented governments—and American national, state, and local governments are nothing if not fragmented—the claims of small, intense minorities are usually attended to. Hence it is not only inefficient but usually unnecessary for entire classes to mobilize when the preferences of class members are pressed and often satisfied in piecemeal fashion. The empirical evidence supporting this pluralist doctrine is overwhelming, however stratification theorists may have missed its significance for them; the fragmentation of American governmental decision-making and of American society makes class consciousness inefficient and, in most cases, makes the political interests of members of the same class different.[30]

The pluralists assumed that the fragmented nature of American society and its political system would continue indefinitely. The basis of this assumption was their belief that the claims of all of these significant small competing groups would continue to be accommodated. The responsiveness of the political system would make it unnecessary, in the words of Polsby, "for entire classes to mobilize when the preferences of class members are pressed and often satisfied in piecemeal fashion."[31]

Yet, within a decade of the pluralist writings, broad social classes did appear on the political scene. While this is not the place to work out the complex causal chain that accounts for the changes described in this section, the inability of urban political systems—as well as of political systems at other levels of government—to respond to the demands of black groups is probably of major importance.

The failure to respond to the integrationist demands of the civil rights organizations in the early 1960's presumably led to increased dissatisfaction within the black community.

This dissatisfaction, in turn, led to the organization of new black groups promoting different goals (for example, community control), to attempts by the older, more established groups to broaden their support, and, most importantly, to a growing sense within the black community that they shared a common fate in the political arena. The movement toward a unified black community has, in turn, led to a mobilization of its opponents and to the kind of political controversy unforeseen by the pluralists.[32]

FUNCTIONAL ISLANDS OF DECISIONS

The pluralists argued that there were different political arenas whose boundaries were determined by functional policy areas. Each of these arenas involved different public officials who were influenced by different nongovernmental interest groups. What little overlap existed among these functional areas was provided by city-wide officials and a few interest groups whose concerns spread over a number of functional areas, but the dominant characteristic of the political system was the relative autonomy of each functional area. Herbert Kaufman neatly presents the core of the argument:

> Each consists of a complex of decision-making "islands." From each such island emanates a flow of decisions and actions embodying the stakes and prizes of politics. The flow from any given island is only loosely related to the flow from all the others; all are, by the same token, relatively autonomous. Every island is composed of a cluster of participants especially concerned with the types of decision that issue from it.[33]

Based upon these findings concerning the degree of autonomy of the functional areas and the minimal overlap of the areas by city-wide officials and nongovernmental actors, these political scientists concluded that the system was pluralistic because there was no single power elite dominating decision-making. Instead, political influence was spread among the actors in the various functional areas. The pluralists, however, never made any attempt to determine the distribution of influence *within* these policy areas. By reconstructing only "important" decisions in each functional area surveyed rather than "representative" controversies, they ruled out such a possible determination.[34] Their choice made sense in light of their goal of determining whether a power elite existed in a particular community. Presumably, if such elite existed, it would more likely appear in "important" rather than in "trivial" issues. By limiting their focus to the "big," rather than the "representative," decisions, the pluralists could not obtain the data necessary to draw any conclusions concerning the patterns of influence within the functional areas.

Several consequences flow from this failure. One of the most important is that we cannot assume that the system is responsive to all groups merely because a power elite fails to exist. The pluralists, by spreading their net over the entire framework of urban decisions, felt satisfied that enough groups, enough pressures, enough interests, enough actors were absorbed by the subsystems to guarantee responsiveness. But how can the responsiveness of the system be judged without considering the possible controlling influence of particular groups over each functional area? What guarantee does one have that there is, for all participants, adequate access to those making official decisions in each functional island?

It may be suggested that, in various functional areas, there are elites who are capable of placing severe constraints on—or preventing public officials from accommodating—the demands of groups promoting antagonistic goals. The school bureaucracy and teachers were highly effective against the proponents of community control, as was the police officialdom in its conflict with groups concerned about police brutality. Although no generalized conclusions can be drawn about the patterns of influence in the various functional islands covered by the case studies, the controversies do uncover the existence of a number of potential elite groupings that are able to determine the responsiveness of the system in their area.

Finally, the existence of functional islands of decision has a built-in bias against those who desire to change the *status quo*. In the current urban political system, there is an obvious fragmentation of authority and power. This fragmentation, as many

pluralists have pointed out, provides participants, both those favoring and those opposing change, with a variety of points of
access. Because, however, any demand for change almost invariably requires the approval of a number of public officials, it is
necessary for those who wish to alter the *status quo* to achieve
access to all these officials. On the other hand, the supporters of
the *status quo* can prevent or limit the scope of change by achieving access to one or, at most, a few of the officials involved in the
controversy. In short, our fragmented urban political systems make
reform more difficult to obtain. As Sayre and Kaufman concluded
in their description of New York's political system: "One consequence of this ordering of the city's political relationships is that
every proposal for change must run a gauntlet that is often fatal.
The system is more favorable to defenders of the *status quo* than
to innovators. It is inherently conservative."[35]

In summary, while the pluralists made a significant contribution when they discovered the existence of these functional islands
of decisions, their assumption that such areas promoted the responsiveness of urban political systems is open to question. The
pluralists made little or no attempt to ascertain the patterns of
influence within the areas they surveyed. Finally, it is hard to
ignore the possibility that the very existence of this dispersion of
authority and power serves those who support the *status quo*,
thereby making the system less responsive to those promoting
change. . . . .

A number of significant questions concerning some of the conclusions reached by the pluralist school have been raised by this
essay: The optimism of the pluralists in regard to the system's
openness and responsiveness; their belief in the primacy, if not
universality, of a particular decision-making process that promoted
the accommodation of conflicting interests; and their conclusions
about the pluralist nature of the system based on their findings
that a power elite fails to exist. All such aspects of pluralist
thought are subject to challenge.

This essay has stressed the inadequacies of the pluralist school;
its members can expect better treatment from those who will
look at their contributions from the perspective of intellectual
history. The role pluralists played in redirecting the orientation of
urban political scientists, away from the sterile efforts of the
"good government" prescriptionists who preceded them and toward
the direction of describing and explaining urban political systems,
will be applauded. They will also be praised for their concern for

methodology and empirical theory and for their writings on elite activity during a particular period in the history of our cities. At the same time, they can expect to be criticized for universalizing their conclusions and limiting their concern to the activities of political elites. We can only hope that future political scientists will both appreciate the contributions of the pluralists and transcend their limitations.

NOTES

1. This conclusion was reached in an excellent analysis of their literature by Nelson W. Polsby, *Community Power and Political Theory* (New Haven, Conn.: Yale University Press, 1963), pp. 8–10.
2. *Ibid., passim.*
3. *Ibid.,* particularly ch. 6.
4. Among the best known of these studies were Robert A. Dahl, *Who Governs?* (New Haven, Conn.: Yale University Press, 1961); Wallace Sayre and Herbert Kaufman, *Governing New York City* (New York: Russell Sage Foundation, 1960); Edward Banfield, *Political Influence* (Glencoe, Ill.: The Free Press, 1961)—although Banfield didn't primarily use the case study method for this purpose so much as for showing the workings of influence; and Frank J. Munger, *Decisions in Syracuse* (Bloomington: Indiana University Press, 1961).
5. Lewis Froman, Jr., *People and Politics* (Englewood Cliffs, N.J.: Prentice-Hall, 1962), pp. 49 ff. The pluralist approach has also attracted the attention of European scholars, and, in fact, several have applied it to community studies abroad. See for example, *The New Atlantis*, No. 2 (Winter, 1970), which is devoted to current work on community power in several European countries.
6. Peter Bachrach and Morton S. Baratz, "Two Faces of Power," *American Political Science Review*, LVI, 4, pp. 947–52; Shin'ya Ono, "The Limits of Bourgeois Pluralism," in Charles A. McCoy and John Playford, eds., *Apolitical Politics* (New York: Thomas Y. Crowell, 1967), pp. 99–123; Todd Gitlin, "Local Pluralism as Theory and Ideology," *ibid.,* pp. 124–45. For a critique of this school of thought, see Richard M. Merelman, "On the Neo-Elitist Critique of Community Power," *American Political Science Review*, LXII (June, 1968), pp. 451–60.
7. Robert A. Dahl, *A Preface to Democratic Theory* (Chicago: University of Chicago Press, 1956), p. 145. See also Dahl, *op. cit.* (note 4), p. 228.
8. Polsby, *op. cit.* (note 1), p. 118.
9. Sayre and Kaufman, *op. cit.* (note 4), p. 720.
10. Dahl, *op. cit.* (note 4), pp. 192–98.
11. Sayre and Kaufman, *op. cit.* (note 4), p. 721.
12. *Ibid.,* p. 714.
13. Dahl, *op. cit.* (note 4), ch. 19.
14. *Ibid.,* pp. 309–10.
15. Dahl, *op. cit.* (note 4), pp. 197–98.
16. This argument is persuasively made by Peter B. Clark and James Q. Wilson, "Incentive Systems: A Theory of Organization," *Administra-*

tive Science Quarterly, (September, 1961), pp. 129–66. This same analysis is made by Bellush and Hausknecht in their analysis of urban renewal politics. See Jewel Bellush & Murray Hausknecht, eds., *Urban Renewal: People, Politics and Planning* (Garden City, N.Y.: Doubleday, 1967), pp. 278–86.

17. Jewel Bellush and Stephen David, *Race and Politics in New York City* (New York: Praeger, 1971), chs. 2 and 6.

18. This methodology was followed by Dahl in *Who Governs?* See his description on pages 332–36 of the appendix of that volume. The rationale for this approach is found in Polsby, *op. cit.* (note 1), pp. 132–36.

19. Polsby, *op. cit.* (note 1), pp. 132–36.

20. *Ibid.,* pp. 134–35.

21. This argument is covered more extensively by Peter Bachrach and Morton S. Baratz, *Power and Poverty* (New York: Oxford University Press, 1970), part one.

22. Sayre and Kaufman, *op. cit.* (note 4), pp. 712–14.

23. Polsby, *op. cit.* (note 1), p. 134; Dahl, *op. cit.* (note 4), ch. 28; Sayre and Kaufman, *op. cit.* (note 4), pp. 736–38.

24. For a description of some of the aspects of this model, see Sayre and Kaufman, *op. cit.* (note 4), pp. 712–14. See also J. David Greenstone and Paul E. Peterson, *Race and Authority in Urban Politics* (New York: Russell Sage, 1973), ch. IX.

25. See the discussion is this chapter on the pluralist views toward citizen apathy.

26. Sayre and Kaufman, *op. cit.* (note 4), ch. 3.

27. For an illustration of this point, see the description of how secrecy aided the promoters of urban renewal, by Jewel Bellush and Murray Hausknecht, "Entrepreneurs and Urban Renewal: The New Men of Power," in Bellush and Hausknecht, *op. cit.,* p. 221.

28. Polsby, *op. cit.* (note 1), p. 137.

29. After describing this controversy, Dahl wrote that "conflict of this intensity is a rarity. Ordinarily, political decisions move along in an atmosphere of apathy, indifference, and general agreement." *Op cit.* (note 4), p. 198.

30. Polsby, *op. cit.* (note 1), p. 118.

31. *Ibid.*

32. Much of the difficulty of the pluralists on this point is perhaps explained by Jacobs and Lipsky, when they criticized the pluralists for their almost exclusive focus on elite activity rather than on other strata in local politics. Attention to this latter realm might have forewarned the pluralists of possible changes in the political system. See Herbert Jacobs and Michael Lipsky, "Outputs, Structure, and Power: An Assessment of Changes in the Study of State and Local Politics," in M. D. Irish, ed., *Political Science: Advance of the Discipline* (Englewood Cliffs, N.J.: Prentice-Hall, 1968), pp. 236–38.

33. Herbert Kaufman, *Politics and Policies in State and Local Governments* (Englewood Cliffs, N.J.: Prentice-Hall, 1963), p. 110.

34. For a discussion of the reasons the pluralists chose to reconstruct "important" decisions, see Polsby, *op. cit.* (note 1), pp. 95–96.

35. Sayre and Kaufman, *op. cit.* (note 4), p. 716.

PROTEST AS A POLITICAL RESOURCE*

MICHAEL LIPSKY

The frequent resort to protest activity by relatively powerless groups in recent American politics suggests that protest represents an important aspect of minority group and low income group politics.[1] At the same time that Negro civil rights strategists have recognized the problem of using protest as a meaningful political instrument,[2] groups associated with the "war on poverty" have increasingly received publicity for protest activity. Saul Alinsky's Industrial Areas Foundation, for example, continues to receive invitations to help organize low income communities because of its ability to mobilize poor people around the tactic of protest.[3] The riots which dominated urban affairs in the summer of 1967 appear not to have diminished the dependence of some groups on protest as a mode of political activity.

This article provides a theoretical perspective on protest activity as a political resource. The discussion is concentrated on the limitations inherent in protest which occur because of the need of protest leaders to appeal to four constituencies at the same time. As the concept of protest is developed here, it will be argued that protest leaders must nurture and sustain an organization comprised of people with whom they may or may not share common

* This article is an attempt to develop and explore the implications of a conceptual scheme for analyzing protest activity. It is based upon my studies of protest organizations in New York City, Washington, D.C., Chicago, San Francisco, and Mississippi, as well as extensive examination of written accounts of protest among low-income and Negro civil rights groups. I am grateful to Kenneth Dolbeare, Murray Edelman, and Rodney Stiefbold for their insightful comments on an earlier draft. This paper was developed while the author was a Staff Associate of the Institute for Research on Poverty at the University of Wisconsin. I appreciate the assistance obtained during various phases of my research from the Rabinowitz Foundation, the New York State Legislative Internship Program, and the Brookings Institution.

From Michael Lipsky, "Protest as a Political Resource," *American Political Science Review* LXII, No. 4 (December, 1968), pp. 1144–58. Copyright © 1968 by the American Political Science Association. Reprinted with permission.

values. They must articulate goals and choose strategies so as to maximize their public exposure through communications media. They must maximize the impact of third parties in the political conflict. Finally, they must try to maximize chances of success among those capable of granting goals. The tensions inherent in manipulating these four constituencies at the same time form the basis of this discussion of protest as a political process. It is intended to place aspects of the civil rights movement in a framework which suggests links between protest organizations and the general political processes in which such organizations operate.

I. "Protest" Conceptualized

Protest activity as it has been adopted by elements of the civil rights movement and others has not been studied extensively by social scientists. Some of the most suggestive writings have been done as case studies of protest movements in single southern cities.[4] These works generally lack a framework or theoretical focus which would encourage generalization from the cases. More systematic efforts have been attempted in approaching the dynamics of biracial committees in the South,[5] and comprehensively assessing the efficacy of Negro political involvement in Durham, N.C. and Philadelphia, Pa.[6] In their excellent assessment of Negro politics in the South, Matthews and Prothro have presented a thorough profile of Southern Negro students and their participation in civil rights activities.[7] Protest is also discussed in passing in recent explorations of the social-psychological dimensions of Negro ghetto politics[8] and the still highly suggestive, although pre-1960's, work on Negro political leadership by James Q. Wilson.[9] These and other less systematic works on contemporary Negro politics,[10] for all of their intuitive insights and valuable documentation, offer no theoretical formulations which encourage conceptualization about the interaction between recent Negro political activity and the political process.

Heretofore the best attempt to place Negro protest activity in a framework which would generate additional insights has been that of James Q. Wilson.[11] Wilson has suggested that protest activity be conceived as a problem of bargaining in which the basic problem is that Negro groups lack political resources to exchange. Wilson called this "the problem of the powerless."[12]

While many of Wilson's insights remain valid, his approach is limited in applicability because it defines protest in terms of mass action or response and as utilizing exclusively negative inducements in the bargaining process. Negative inducements are defined as inducements which are not absolutely preferred but are preferred over alternative possibilities.[13] Yet it might be argued that protest designed to appeal to groups which oppose suffering and exploitation, for example, might be offering positive inducements in bargaining. A few Negro students sitting at a lunch counter might be engaged in what would be called protest, and by their actions might be trying to appeal to other groups in the system with positive inducements. Additionally, Wilson's concentration on Negro civic action, and his exclusive interest in exploring the protest process to explain Negro civic action, tend to obscure comparison with protest activity which does not necessarily arise within the Negro community.

Assuming a somewhat different focus, protest activity is defined as a mode of political action oriented toward objection to one or more policies or conditions, characterized by showmanship or display of an unconventional nature, and undertaken to obtain rewards from political or economic systems while working within the systems. The "problem of the powerless" in protest activity is to activate "third parties" to enter the implicit or explicit bargaining arena in ways favorable to the protesters. This is one of the few ways in which they can "create" bargaining resources. It is intuitively unconvincing to suggest that fifteen people sitting uninvited in the Mayor's office have the power to move City Hall. A better formulation would suggest that the people sitting in may be able to appeal to a wider public to which the city administration is sensitive. Thus in successful protest activity the *reference publics* of protest *targets* may be conceived as explicitly or implicitly reacting to protest in such a way that target groups or individuals respond in ways favorable to the protesters.[14]

It should be emphasized that the focus here is on protest by relatively powerless groups. Illustrations can be summoned, for example, of activity designated as "protest" involving high status pressure groups or hundreds of thousands of people. While such instances may share some of the characteristics of protest activity, they may not represent examples of developing political resources by relatively powerless groups because the protesting groups may already command political resources by virtue of status, numbers or cohesion.

It is appropriate also to distinguish between the relatively restricted use of the concept of protest adopted here and closely related political strategies which are often designated as "protest" in popular usage. Where groups already possess sufficient resources with which to bargain, as in the case of some economic boycotts and labor strikes, they may be said to engage in "direct confrontation."[15] Similarly, protest which represents efforts to "activate reference publics" should be distinguished from "alliance formation," where third parties are induced to join the conflict, but where the value orientations of third parties are sufficiently similar to those of the protesting group that concerted or coordinated action is possible. Alliance formation is particularly desirable for relatively powerless groups if they seek to join the decision-making process as participants.

The distinction between activating reference publics and alliance formation is made on the assumption that where goal orientations among protest groups and the reference publics of target groups are similar, the political dynamics of petitioning target groups are different than when such goal orientations are relatively divergent. Clearly the more similar the goal orientations, the greater the likelihood of protest success, other things being equal. This discussion is intended to highlight, however, those instances where goal orientations of reference publics depart significantly, in direction or intensity, from the goals of protest groups.

Say that to protest some situation, A would like to enter a bargaining situation with B. But A has nothing B wants, and thus cannot bargain. A then attempts to create political resources by activating other groups to enter the conflict. A then organizes to take action against B with respect to certain goals. *Information concerning these goals must be conveyed through communications media (C, D, and E) to F, G, and H, which are B's reference publics.* In response to the reactions of F, G, and H, or in anticipation of their reactions, B responds, *in some way,* to the protesters' demands. This formulation requires the conceptualization of protest activity when undertaken to create bargaining resources as a political process which requires communication and is characterized by a multiplicity of constituencies for protest leadership.

A schematic representation of the process of protest as utilized by relatively powerless groups is presented in Figure 1. In contrast to a simplistic pressure group model which would posit a direct relationship between pressure group and pressured, the following discussion is guided by the assumption (derived from observation) that protest is a highly indirect process in which communications media and the reference publics of protest targets play critical roles. It is also a process characterized by reciprocal relations, in which protest leaders frame strategies according to their perception of the need of (many) other actors.

In this view protest constituents limit the options of protest leaders at the same time that the protest leader influences their perception of the strategies and rhetoric which they will support. Protest activity is filtered through the communications media in influencing the perceptions of the reference publics of protest targets. To the extent that the influence of reference publics is supportive of protest goals, target groups will dispense symbolic or material rewards. Material rewards are communicated directly to protest constituents. Symbolic rewards are communicated in part

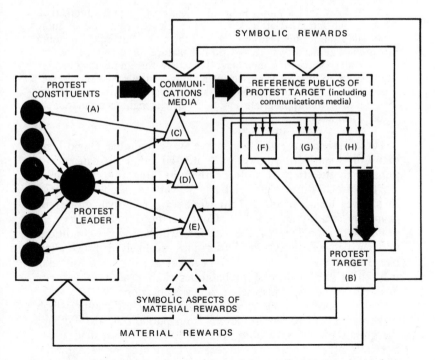

FIG. 1. Schematic representation of the process of protest by relatively powerless groups.

to protest constituents, but primarily are communicated to the reference publics of target groups, who provide the major stimuli for public policy pronouncements.

The study of protest as adopted by relatively powerless groups should provide insights into the structure and behavior of groups involved in civil rights politics and associated with the "war on poverty." It should direct attention toward the ways in which administrative agencies respond to "crises." Additionally, the study of protest as a political resource should influence some general conceptualizations of American political pluralism. Robert Dahl, for example, describes the "normal American political process" as one in which there is a high probability that an active and legitimate group in the population can make itself heard effectively at some crucial stage in the process of decision.[16]

Although he agrees that control over decisions is unevenly divided in the population, Dahl writes:

> When I say that a group is heard "effectively" I mean more than the simple fact that it makes a noise; I mean that one or more officials are not only ready to listen to the noise, but expect to suffer in some significant way if they do not placate the group, its leaders, or its most vociferous members. To satisfy the group may require one or more of a great variety of actions by the responsive leader: pressure for substantive policies, appointments, graft, respect, expression of the appropriate emotions, or the right combination of reciprocal noises.[17]

These statements, which in some ways resemble David Truman's discussion of the power of "potential groups,"[18] can be illuminated by the study of protest activity in three ways. First, what are the probabilities that relatively powerless groups can make themselves heard effectively? In what ways will such groups be heard or "steadily appeased"?[19] Concentration on the process of protest activity may reveal the extent to which, and the conditions under which, relatively powerless groups are likely to prove effective. Protest undertaken to obstruct policy decisions, for example, may enjoy greater success probabilities than protest undertaken in an effort to evoke constructive policy innovations.[20]

Second, does it make sense to suggest that all groups which make noises will receive responses from public officials? Perhaps the groups which make noises do not have to be satisfied at all, but it is other groups which receive assurances or recognition. Third, what are the probabilities that groups which make noises will receive tangible rewards, rather than symbolic assurances?[21] Dahl lumps these rewards together in the same paragraph, but dispensation of tangible rewards clearly has a different impact upon groups than the dispensation of symbolic rewards. Dahl is undoubtedly correct when he suggests that the relative fluidity of American politics is a critical characteristic of the American political system.[22] But he is less precise and less convincing when it comes to analyzing the extent to which the system is indeed responsive to the relatively powerless groups of the "average citizen."[23]

The following sections are an attempt to demonstrate the utility of the conceptualization of the protest process presented above. This will be done by exploring the problems encountered and the strains generated by protest leaders in interacting with four constituencies. It will be useful to concentrate attention on the maintenance and enhancement needs not only of the large formal organizations which dominate city politics,[24] but also of the ad hoc protest groups which engage them in civic controversy. It will also prove rewarding to examine the role requirements of individuals in leadership positions as they perceive the problems of constituency manipulation. In concluding remarks some implications of the study of protest for the pluralist description of American politics will be suggested.[25]

II. Protest Leadership and Organizational Base

The organizational maintenance needs of relatively powerless, low income, ad hoc protest groups center around the tension generated by the need for leadership to offer symbolic and intangible inducements to protest participation when immediate, material rewards cannot be anticipated, and the need to provide at least the promise of material rewards. Protest leaders must try to evoke responses from other actors in the political process, at the same time that they pay attention to participant organizational needs. Thus relatively deprived groups in the political system not only receive symbolic reassurance while material rewards from the system are withheld,[26] but protest leaders have a stake in perpetuating the notion that relatively powerless groups retain political efficacy despite what in many cases is obvious evidence to the contrary.

The tension embraced by protest leaders over the nature of inducements toward protest participation accounts in part for the style adopted and goals selected by protest leaders. Groups which seek psychological gratification from politics, but cannot or do not anticipate material political rewards, may be attracted to militant protest leaders. To these groups, angry rhetoric may prove a desirable quality in the short run. Where groups depend upon the political system for tangible benefits, or where participation in the system provides intangible benefits, moderate leadership is likely to prevail. Wilson has observed similar tendencies among Negro leaders of large, formal organizations.[27] It is no less true for leadership of protest groups. Groups whose members derive tangible satisfactions from political participation will not condone leaders who are stubborn in compromise or appear to question the foundations of the system. This coincides with Truman's observation: "Violation of the rules of the game normally will weaken a group's cohesion, reduce its status in the community, and expose it to the claims of other groups."[28] On the other hand, the cohesion of relatively powerless groups may be strengthened by militant, ideological leadership which questions the rules of the game and challenges their legitimacy.

Cohesion is particularly important when protest leaders bargain directly with target groups. In that situation, leaders' ability to control protest constituents and guarantee their behavior represents a bargaining strength.[29] For this reason Wilson stressed the bargaining difficulties of Negro leaders who cannot guarantee constituent behavior, and pointed out the significance of the strategy of projecting the image of group solidarity when the reality of cohesion is a fiction.[30] Cohesion is less significant at other times. Divided leadership may prove productive by bargaining in tandem,[31] or by minimizing strain among groups in the protest process. Further, community divisions may prove less detrimental to protest aims when strong third parties have entered the dispute originally generated by protest organizations.

The intangible rewards of assuming certain postures toward the political system may not be sufficient to sustain an organizational base. It may be necessary to renew constantly the intangible rewards of participation. And to the extent that people participate in order to achieve tangible benefits, their interest in a protest organization may depend upon the organization's relative material success. Protest leaders may have to tailor their style to present participants with tangible successes, or with the appearance of success. Leaders may have to define the issues with concern for increasing their ability to sustain organization. The potential for protest among protest group members may have to be manipulated by leadership if the group is to be sustained.[32]

The participants in protest organizations limit the flexibility of protest leadership. This obtains for two reasons. They restrict public actions by leaders who must continue to solicit active participant support, and they place restraints on the kinds of activities which can be considered appropriate for protest purposes. Poor participants cannot commonly be asked to engage in protest requiring air transportation. Participants may have anxieties related to their environment or historical situation which discourages engagement in some activities. They may be afraid of job losses, beatings by the police, or summary evictions. Negro protest in the Deep South has been inhibited by realistic expectations of retribution.[33] Protests over slum housing conditions are undermined by tenants who expect landlord retaliation for engaging in tenant organizing activity.[34] Political or ethical mores may conflict with a proposed course of action, diminishing participation.[35]

On the other hand, to the extent that fears are real, or that the larger community perceives protest participants as subject to these fears, protest may actually be strengthened. Communications media and potential allies will consider more soberly the complaints of people who are understood to be placing themselves in jeopardy. When young children and their parents made the arduous bus trip from Mississippi to Washington, D.C. to protest the jeopardizing of Head Start funds, the courage and expense represented by their effort created a respect and visibility for their position which might not have been achieved by local protest efforts.[36]

Protest activity may be undertaken by organizations with established relationship patterns, behavior norms, and role expectations. These organizations are likely to have greater access to other groups in the political system, and a demonstrated capacity to maintain themselves. Other protest groups, however, may be ad hoc arrangements without demonstrated internal or external relationship patterns. These groups will have different organizational problems, in response to which it is necessary to engage in different kinds of protest activity.

The scarcity of organizational resources also places limits upon the ability of relatively powerless groups to maintain the foundations upon which protest organizations develop. Relatively powerless groups, to engage in political activity of any kind, must command at least some resources. This is not tautological. Referring again to a continuum on which political groups are placed according to their relative command of resources, one may draw a line somewhere along the continuum representing a "threshold of civic group political participation." Clearly some groups along the continuum will possess some political resources (enough, say, to emerge for inspection) but not enough to exercise influence in civic affairs. Relatively powerless groups, to be influential, must cross the "threshold" to engage in politics. Although the availability of group resources is a critical consideration at all stages of the protest process, it is particularly important in explaining why some groups seem to "surface" with sufficient strength to command attention. The following discussion of some critical organizational resources should illuminate this point.

Skilled professionals frequently must be available to protest organizations. Lawyers, for example, play extremely important roles in enabling protest groups to utilize the judicial process and avail themselves of adequate preparation of court cases. Organizational reputation may depend upon a combination of ability to threaten the conventional political system and of exercising statutory rights in court. Availability of lawyers depends upon ability to pay fees and/or the attractiveness to lawyers of participation in protest group activity. Volunteer professional assistance may not prove adequate. One night a week volunteered by an aspiring politician in a housing clinic cannot satisfy the needs of a chaotic political movement.[37] The need for skilled professionals is not restricted to lawyers. For example, a group seeking to protest an urban renewal policy might require the services of architects and city planners in order to present a viable alternative to a city proposal.

Financial resources not only purchase legal assistance, but enable relatively powerless groups to conduct minimum programs of political activities. To the extent that constituents are unable or unwilling to pay even small membership dues, then financing the cost of mimeographing flyers, purchasing supplies, maintaining telephone service, paying rent, and meeting a modest payroll become major organizational problems. And to the extent that group finances are supplied by outside individual contributions or government or foundation grants, the long-term options of the group are sharply constrained by the necessity of orienting group goals and tactics to anticipate the potential objections of financial supporters.

Some dependence upon even minimal financial resources can

be waived if organizations evoke passionate support from constituents. Secretarial help and block organizers will come forward to work without compensation if they support the cause of neighborhood organizations or gain intangible benefits based upon association with the group. Protest organizations may also depend upon skilled non-professionals, such as college students, whose access to people and political and economic institutions often assist protest groups in cutting across income lines to seek support. Experience with ad hoc political groups, however, suggests that this assistance is sporadic and undependable. Transient assistance is particularly typical of skilled, educated, and employable volunteers whose abilities can be applied widely. The die-hards of ad hoc political groups are often those people who have no place else to go, nothing else to do.

Constituent support will be affected by the nature of the protest target and whether protest activity is directed toward defensive or assertive goals. Obstructing specific public policies may be easier than successfully recommending constructive policy changes. Orientations toward defensive goals may require less constituent energy, and less command over resources of money, expertise and status.[38]

III. Protest Leadership and Communications Media

The communications media are extremely powerful in city politics. In granting or withholding publicity, in determining what information most people will have on most issues, and what alternatives they will consider in response to issues, the media truly, as Norton Long has put it, "set . . . the civic agenda."[39] To the extent that successful protest activity depends upon appealing to, and/or threatening, other groups in the community, the communications media set the limits of protest action. If protest tactics are not considered significant by the media, or if newspapers and television reporters or editors decide to overlook protest tactics, protest organizations will not succeed. Like the tree falling unheard in the forest, there is no protest unless protest is perceived and projected.

A number of writers have noticed that the success of protest activity seems directly related to the amount of publicity it receives outside the immediate arena in which protest takes place. This view has not been stated systematically, but hints can be found in many sources. In the literature on civil rights politics, the relevance of publicity represents one of the few hypotheses available concerning the dynamics of successful protest activity.[40]

When protest tactics do receive coverage in the communications media, the way in which they are presented will influence all other actors in the system, including the protesters themselves. Conformity to standards of newsworthiness in political style, and knowledge of the prejudices and desires of the individuals who determine media coverage in political skills, represent crucial determinants of leadership effectiveness.

The organizational behavior of newspapers can partly be understood by examining the maintenance and enhancement needs which direct them toward projects of civic betterment and impressions of accomplishment.[41] But insight may also be gained by analyzing the role requirements of reporters, editors, and others who determine newspaper policy. Reporters, for example, are frequently motivated by the desire to contribute to civic affairs by their "objective" reporting of significant events; by the premium they place on accuracy; and by the credit which they receive for sensationalism and "scoops."

These requirements may be difficult to accommodate at the same time. Reporters demand newsworthiness of their subjects in the short run, but also require reliability and verifiability in the longer run. Factual accuracy may dampen newsworthiness. Sensationalism, attractive to some newspaper editors, may be inconsistent with reliable, verifiable narration of events. Newspapers at first may be attracted to sensationalism, and later demand verifiability in the interests of community harmony (and adherence to professional journalistic standards).

Most big city newspapers have reporters whose assignments permit them to cover aspects of city politics with some regularity. These reporters, whose "beats" may consist of "civil rights" or "poverty," sometimes develop close relationships with their news subjects. These relationships may develop symbiotic overtones because of the mutuality of interest between the reporter and the news subject. Reporters require fresh information on protest developments, while protest leaders have a vital interest in obtaining as much press coverage as possible.

Inflated reports of protest success may be understood in part by examining this relationship between reporter and protest leader. Both have role-oriented interests in projecting images of protest strength and threat. In circumstances of great excitement, when competition from other news media representatives is high, a reporter may find that he is less governed by the role requirement of verification and reliability than he is by his editor's demand for "scoops" and news with high audience appeal.[42]

On the other hand, the demands of the media may conflict with the needs of protest group maintenance. Consider the leader whose constituents are attracted solely by pragmatic statements not exceeding what they consider political "good taste." He is constrained from making militant demands which would isolate him from constituents. This constraint may cost him appeal in the press.[43] However, the leader whose organizing appeal requires militant rhetoric may obtain eager press coverage only to find that his inflammatory statements lead to alienation of potential allies and exclusion from the explicit bargaining process.[44]

News media do not report events in the same way. Television may select for broadcast only thirty seconds of a half-hour news conference. This coverage will probably focus on immediate events, without background or explanatory material. Newspapers may give more complete accounts of the same event. The most complete account may appear in the weekly edition of a neighborhood or ethnic newspaper. Differential coverage by news media, and differential news media habits in the general population,[45] are significant factors in permitting protest leaders to juggle conflicting demands of groups in the protest process.

Similar tensions exist in the leader''s relationships with protest targets. Ideological postures may gain press coverage and constituency approval, but may alienate target groups with whom it would be desirable to bargain explicitly. Exclusion from the councils of decision-making may have important consequences, since the results of target group deliberations may satisfy activated reference publics without responding to protest goals. If activated reference public are required to increase the bargaining position of the protest group, protest efforts thereafter will have diminished chances of success.

IV. Protest Leadership and "Third Parties"

I have argued that the essence of political protest consists of activating third parties to participate in controversy in ways favorable to protest goals. In previous sections I have attempted to analyze some of the tensions which result from protest leaders' attempts to activate reference publics of protest targets at the same time that they must retain the interest and support of protest organization participants. This phenomenon is in evidence when Negro leaders, recognized as such by public officials, find their support eroded in the Negro community because they have engaged in explicit bargaining situations with politicians. Negro leaders are thus faced with the dilemma that when they behave like other ethnic group representatives they are faced with loss of support from those whose intense activism has been aroused in the Negro community, yet whose support is vital if they are to remain credible as leaders to public officials.

The tensions resulting from conflicting maintenance needs of protest organizations and activated third parties present difficulties for protest leaders. One way in which these tensions can be minimized is by dividing leadership responsibilities. If more than one group is engaged in protest activity, protest leaders can, in effect, divide up public roles so as to reduce as much as possible the gap between the implicit demands of different groups for appropriate rhetoric, and what in fact is said. Thus divided leadership may perform the latent function of minimizing tensions among elements in the protest process by permitting different groups to listen selectively to protest spokesmen.[46]

Another way in which strain among different groups can be minimized is through successful public relations. Minimization of strain may depend upon ambiguity of action or statement, deception, or upon effective inter-group communication. Failure to clarify meaning, or falsification, may increase protest effectiveness. Effective intragroup communication may increase the likelihood that protest constituents will "understand" that ambiguous or false public statements have "special meaning" and need not be taken seriously. The Machiavellian circle is complete when we observe that although lying may be prudent, the appearance of integrity and forthrightness is desirable for public relations, since these values are widely shared.

It has been observed that "[t]he militant displays an unwillingness to perform those administrative tasks which are necessary to operate an organization. Probably the skills of the agitator and the skills of the administrator . . . are not incompatible, but few men can do both well."[47] These skills may or may not be incompatible as personality traits, but they indeed represent conflicting role demands on protest leadership. When a protest leader exhausts time and energy conducting frequent press conferences, arranging for politicians and celebrities to appear at rallies, delivering speeches to sympathetic local groups, college symposia and other forums, constantly picketing for publicity and generally making "contacts," he is unable to pursue the direction of office routine, clerical tasks, research and analysis, and other chores.

The difficulties of delegating routine tasks are probably directly related to the skill levels and previous administrative experiences of group members. In addition, to the extent that involvement in protest organizations is a function of rewards received or expected by individuals because of the excitement or entertainment value of participation, then the difficulties of delegating routine, relatively uninteresting chores to group members will be increased. Yet attention to such details affects the perception of protest groups by organizations whose support or assistance may be desired in the future. These considerations add to the protest leader's problem of risking alienation of protest participants because of potentially unpopular cooperation with the "power structure."

In the protest paradigm developed here, "third parties" refers both to the reference publics of target groups and, more narrowly, to the interest groups whose regular interaction with protest targets tends to develop into patterns of influence.[48] We have already discussed some of the problems associated with activating the reference publics of target groups. In discussing the constraints placed upon protest, attention may be focused upon the likelihood that groups seeking to create political resources through protest will be included in the explicit bargaining process with other pressure groups. For protest groups, these constraints are those which occur because of class and political style, status, and organizational resources.

The established civic groups most likely to be concerned with the problems raised by relatively powerless groups are those devoted to service in the public welfare and those "liberally" oriented groups whose potential constituents are either drawn from the same class as the protest groups (such as some trade unions), or whose potential constituents are attracted to policies which appear to serve the interest of the lower class or minority groups (such as some reform political clubs).[49] These civic groups have frequently cultivated clientele relationships with city agencies over long periods. Their efforts have been reciprocated by agency officials anxious to develop constituencies to support and defend agency administrative and budgetary policies. In addition, clientele groups are expected to endorse and legitimize agency aggrandizement. These relationships have been developed by agency officials and civic groups for mutual benefit, and cannot be destroyed, abridged or avoided without cost.

Protest groups may well be able to raise the saliency of issues on the civic agenda through utilization of communications media and successful appeals or threats to wider publics, but admission to policy-making councils is frequently barred because of the angry, militant rhetorical style adopted by protest leaders. People in power do not like to sit down with rogues. Protest leaders are likely to have phrased demands in ways unacceptable to lawyers and other civic activists whose cautious attitude toward public policy may reflect not only their good intentions but their concern for property rights, due process, pragmatic legislating or judicial precedent.

Relatively powerless groups lack participation of individuals with high status whose endorsement of specific proposals lend them increased legitimacy. Good causes may always attract the support of high status individuals. But such individuals' willingness to devote time to the promotion of specific proposals is less likely than the one-shot endorsements which these people distribute more readily.

Similarly, protest organizations often lack the resources on which entry into the policy-making process depends. These resources include maintenance of a staff with expertise and experience in the policy area. This expertise may be in the areas of the law, planning and architecture, proposal writing, accounting, educational policy, federal grantsmanship or publicity. Combining experience with expertise is one way to create status in issue areas. The dispensing of information by interest groups has been widely noted as a major source of influence. Over time the experts develop status in their areas of competence somewhat independent of the influence which adheres to them as information-providers. Groups which cannot or do not engage lawyers to assist in proposing legislation, and do not engage in collecting reliable data, cannot participate in policy deliberations or consult in these matters. Protest oriented groups, whose primary talents are in dramatizing issues, cannot credibly attempt to present data considered "objective" or suggestions considered "responsible" by public officials. Few can be convincing as both advocate and arbiter at the same time.

V. PROTEST LEADERSHIP AND TARGET GROUPS

The probability of protest success may be approached by examining the maintenance needs of organizations likely to be designated as target groups.[50] For the sake of clarity, and because protest activity increasingly is directed toward government, I shall refer in the following paragraphs exclusively to government agencies at the municipal level. The assumption is retained, however, that the following generalizations are applicable to other potential target groups.

Some of the constraints placed on protest leadership in influencing target groups have already been mentioned in preceding sections. The lack of status and resources that inhibit protest groups from participating in policy-making conferences, for example, also helps prevent explicit bargaining between protest leaders and city officials. The strain between rhetoric which appeals to protest participants and public statements to which communications media and "third parties" respond favorably also exists with reference to target groups.

Yet there is a distinguishable feature of the maintenance needs and strategies of city agencies which specifically constrains protest organizations. This is the agency director's need to protect "the jurisdiction and income of his organization [by] . . . [m]anipulation of the external environment."[51] In so doing he may satisfy his reference groups without responding to protest group demands. At least six tactics are available to protest targets who are motivated to respond in some way to protest activity but seek primarily to satisfy their reference publics. These tactics may be employed whether or not target groups are "sincere" in responding to protest demands.

1. Target groups may dispense symbolic satisfactions. Appearances of activity and commitment to problems substitute for, or supplement, resource allocation and policy innovations which would constitute tangible responses to protest activity. If symbolic responses supplement tangible pay-offs, they are frequently coincidental, rather than intimately linked, to projection of response by protest targets. Typical in city politics of the symbolic response is the ribbon cutting, street corner ceremony or the walking tour press conference. These occasions are utilized not only to build agency constituencies,[52] but to satisfy agency reference publics that attention is being directed to problems of civic concern. In

this sense publicist tactics may be seen as defensive maneuvers. Symbolic aspects of the actions of public officials can also be recognized in the commissioning of expensive studies and the rhetorical flourishes with which "massive attacks," "comprehensive programs," and "coordinated planning" are frequently promoted.

City agencies establish distinct apparatus and procedures for dealing with crises which may be provoked by protest groups. Housing-related departments in New York City may be cited for illustrations. It is usually the case in these agencies that the Commissioner or a chief deputy, a press secretary and one or two other officials devote whatever time is necessary to collect information, determine policy and respond quickly to reports of "crises." This is functional for tenants, who, if they can generate enough concern, may be able to obtain shortcuts through lengthy agency procedures. It is also functional for officials who want to project images of action rather than merely receiving complaints. Concentrating attention on the maintenance needs of city politicians during protest crises suggests that pronouncements of public officials serve purposes independent of their dedication to alleviation of slum conditions.[53]

Independent of dispensation of tangible benefits to protest groups, public officials continue to respond primarily to their own reference publics. Murray Edelman has suggested that: "Tangible resources and benefits are frequently not distributed to unorganized political group interests as promised in regulatory statutes and the propaganda attending their enactment."[54] His analysis may be supplemented by suggesting that symbolic dispensations may not only serve to reassure unorganized political group interests, but may also contribute to reducing the anxiety level of organized interests and wider publics which are only tangentially involved in the issues.

2. Target groups may dispense token material satisfactions. When city agencies respond, with much publicity, to cases brought to their attention representing examples of the needs dramatized by protest organizations, they may appear to respond to protest demands while in fact only responding on a case basis, instead of a general basis. For the protesters served by agencies in this fashion it is of considerable advantage that agencies can be influenced by protest action. Yet it should not be ignored that in handling the "crisis" cases, public officials give the appearance of response to their reference publics, while mitigating demands for an expensive, complex *general* assault on problems represented by

the cases to which responses are given. Token responses, whether or not accompanied by more general responses, are particularly attractive to reporters and television news directors, who are able to dramatize individual cases convincingly, but who may be unable to "capture" the essence of general deprivation or of general efforts to alleviate conditions of deprivation.

3. Target groups may organize and innovate internally in order to blunt the impetus of protest efforts. This tactic is closely related to No. 2 (above). If target groups can act constructively in the worst cases, they will then be able to pre-empt protest efforts by responding to the cases which best dramatize protest demands. Alternatively, they may designate all efforts which jeopardize agency reputations as "worst" cases, and devote extensive resources to these cases. In some ways extraordinary city efforts are precisely consistent with protest goals. At the same time extraordinary efforts in the most heavily dramatized cases or the most extreme cases effectively wear down the "cutting-edges" of protest efforts.

Many New York City agencies develop informal "crisis" arrangements not only to project publicity, as previously indicated, but to mobilize energies toward solving "crisis" cases. They may also develop policy innovations which allow them to respond more quickly to "crisis" situations. These innovations may be important to some city residents, for whom the problems of dealing with city bureaucracies can prove insurmountable. It might be said, indeed, that the goals of protest are to influence city agencies to handle every case with the same resources that characterize their dispatch of "crisis" cases.[55]

But such policies would demand major revenue inputs. This kind of qualitative policy change is difficult to achieve. Meanwhile, internal reallocation of resources only means that routine services must be neglected so that the "crisis" programs can be enhanced. If all cases are expedited, as in a typical "crisis" response, then none can be. Thus for purposes of general solutions, "crisis" resolving can be self-defeating unless accompanied by significantly greater resource allocation. It is not self-defeating, however, to the extent that the organizational goals of city agencies are to serve a clientele while minimizing negative publicity concerning agency vigilance and responsiveness.

4. Target groups may appear to be constrained in their ability to grant protest goals.[56] This may be directed toward making the protesters appear to be unreasonable in their demands, or to be well-meaning individuals who "just don't understand how com-

plex running a city really is." Target groups may extend sympathy but claim that they lack resources, a mandate from constituents, and/or authority to respond to protest demands. Target groups may also evade protest demands by arguing that "If-I-give-it-to-you-I-have-to-give-it-to-everyone."

The tactic of appearing constrained is particularly effective with established civic groups because there is an undeniable element of truth to it. Everyone knows that cities are financially undernourished. Established civic groups expend great energies lobbying for higher levels of funding for their pet city agencies. Thus they recognize the validity of this constraint when posed by city officials. But it is not inconsistent to point out that funds for specific, relatively inexpensive programs, or for the expansion of existing programs, can often be found if pressure is increased. While constraints on city government flexibility may be extensive, they are not absolute. Protest targets nonetheless attempt to diminish the impact of protest demands by claiming relative impotence.

5. Target groups may use their extensive resources to discredit protest leaders and organizations. Utilizing their excellent access to the press, public officials may state or imply that leaders are unreliable, ineffective as leaders ("they don't really have the people behind them"), guilty of criminal behavior, potentially guilty of such behavior, or are some shade of "left-wing." Any of these allegations may serve to diminish the appeal of protest groups to potentially sympathetic third parties. City officials, in their frequent social and informal business interaction with leaders of established civic groups, may also communicate derogatory information concerning protest groups. Discrediting of protest groups may be undertaken by some city officials while others appear (perhaps authentically) to remain sympathetic to protest demands. These tactics may be engaged in by public officials whether or not there is any validity to the allegations.

6. Target groups may postpone action. The effect of postponement, if accompanied by symbolic assurances, is to remove immediate pressure and delay specific commitments to a future date. This familiar tactic is particularly effective in dealing with protest groups because of their inherent instability. Protest groups are usually comprised of individuals whose intense political activity cannot be sustained except in rare circumstances. Further, to the extent that protest depends upon activating reference publics through strategies which have some "shock" value, it becomes

increasingly difficult to activate these groups. Additionally, protest activity is inherently unstable becaues of the strains placed upon protest leaders who must attempt to manage four constituencies (as described herein).

The most frequent method of postponing action is to commit a subject to "study." For the many reasons elaborated in these paragraphs, it is not likely that ad hoc protest groups will be around to review the recommendations which emerge from study. The greater the expertise and the greater the status of the group making the study, the less will protest groups be able to influence whatever policy emerges. Protest groups lack the skills and re-source personnel to challenge expert recommendations effectively.

Sometimes surveys and special research are undertaken in part to evade immediate pressures. Sometimes not. Research efforts are particularly necessary to secure the support of established civic groups, which place high priority on orderly procedure and policy emerging from independent analysis. Yet it must be recognized that postponing policy commitments has a distinct impact on the nature of the pressures focused on policy-makers.

VI. Conclusion

In this analysis I have agreed with James Q. Wilson that pro-test is correctly conceived as a strategy utilized by relatively pow-erless groups in order to increase their bargaining ability. As such, I have argued, it is successful to the extent that the reference publics of protest targets can be activated to enter the conflict in ways favorable to protest goals. I have suggested a model of the protest process which may assist in ordering data and indicating the salience for research of a number of aspects of protest. These include the critical role of communications media, the differential impact of material and symbolic rewards on "feedback" in protest activity, and the reciprocal relationships of actors in the protest process.

An estimation of the limits to protest efficacy, I have argued further, can be gained by recognizing the problems encountered by protest leaders who somehow must balance the conflicting maintenance needs of four groups in the protest process. This approach transcends a focus devoted primarily to characterization of group goals and targets, by suggesting that even in an environment which is relatively favorable to specific protest goals, the tensions which must be embraced by protest leadership may ultimately overwhelm protest activity.

At the outset of this essay, it was held that conceptualizing the American political system as "slack" or "fluid," in the manner of Robert Dahl, appears inadequate because of (1) a vagueness centering on the likelihood that any group can make itself heard; (2) a possible confusion as to which groups tend to receive satisfaction from the rewards dispensed by public officials; and (3) a lumping together as equally relevant rewards which are tangible and those which are symbolic. To the extent that protest is engaged in by relatively powerless groups which must create resources with which to bargain, the analysis here suggests a number of reservations concerning the pluralist conceptualization of the "fluidity" of the American political system.

Relatively powerless groups cannot use protest with a high probability of success. They lack organizational resources, by definition. But even to create bargaining resources through activating third parties, some resources are necessary to sustain organization. More importantly, relatively powerless protest groups are constrained by the unresolvable conflicts which are forced upon protest leaders who must appeal simultaneously to four constituencies which place upon them antithetical demands.

When public officials recognize the legitimacy of protest activity, they may not direct public policy toward protest groups at all. Rather, public officials are likely to aim responses at the reference publics from which they originally take their cues. Edelman has suggested that regulatory policy in practice often consists of reassuring mass publics while at the same time dispensing specific, tangible values to narrow interest groups. It is suggested here that symbolic reassurances are dispensed as much to wide, potentially concerned publics which are not directly affected by regulatory policy, as they are to wide publics comprised of the downtrodden and the deprived, in whose name policy is often written.

Complementing Edelman, it is proposed here that in the process of protest symbolic reassurances are dispensed in large measure because these are the public policy outcomes and actions desired by the constituencies to which public officials are most responsive. Satisfying these wider publics, city officials can avoid pressures toward other policies placed upon them by protest organizations.

Not only should there be some doubt as to which groups receive the symbolic recognitions which Dahl describes, but in failing to distinguish between the kinds of rewards dispensed to groups in the political system, Dahl avoids a fundamental question. It is literally fundamental because the kinds of rewards which can be obtained from politics, one might hypothesize, will have an impact upon the realistic appraisal of the efficacy of political activity. If among the groups least capable of organizing for political activity there is a history of organizing for protest, and if that activity, once engaged in, is rewarded primarily by the dispensation of symbolic gestures without perceptible changes in material conditions, then rational behavior might lead to expressions of apathy and lack of interest in politics or a rejection of conventional political channels as a meaningful arena of activity. In this sense this discussion of protest politics is consistent with Kenneth Clark's observations that the image of power, unaccompanied by material and observable rewards, leads to impressions of helplessness and reinforces political apathy in the ghetto.[57]

Recent commentary by political scientists and others regarding riots in American cities seems to focus in part on the extent to which relatively deprived groups may seek redress of legitimate grievances. Future research should continue assessment of the relationship between riots and the conditions under which access to the political system has been limited. In such research assessment of the ways in which access to public officials is obtained by relatively powerless groups through the protest process might be one important research focus.

The instability of protest activity outlined in this article also should inform contemporary political strategies. If the arguments presented here are persuasive, civil rights leaders who insist that protest activity is a shallow foundation on which to seek long-term, concrete gains may be judged essentially correct. But the arguments concerning the fickleness of the white liberal, or the ease of changing discriminatory laws relative to changing discriminatory institutions, only in part explain the instability of protest movements. An explanation which derives its strength from analysis of the political process suggests concentration on the problems of managing protest constituencies. Accordingly, Alinsky is probably on the soundest ground when he prescribes protest for the purpose of building organization. Ultimately, relatively powerless groups in most instances cannot depend upon activating other actors in the political process. Long-run success will depend upon the acquisition of stable political resources which do not rely for their use on third parties.

NOTES

1. "Relatively powerless groups" may be defined as those groups which, relatively speaking, are lacking in conventional political resources. For the purpose of community studies, Robert Dahl has compiled a useful comprehensive list. See Dahl, "The Analysis of Influence in Local Communities," *Social Science and Community Action*, Charles R. Adrian, ed. (East Lansing, Michigan, 1960), p. 32. The difficulty in studying such groups is that relative powerlessness only becomes apparent under certain conditions. Extremely powerless groups not only lack political resources, but are also characterized by a minimal sense of political efficacy, upon which in part successful political organization depends. For reviews of the literature linking orientations of political efficacy to socioeconomic status, see Robert Lane, *Political Life* (New York, 1959), ch. 16; and Lester Milbrath, *Political Participation* (Chicago, 1965), ch. 5. Further, to the extent that group cohesion is recognized as a necessary requisite for organized political action, then extremely powerless groups, lacking cohesion, will not even appear for observation. Hence the necessity of selecting for intensive study a protest movement where there can be some confidence that observable processes and results can be analyzed. Thus, if one conceives of a continuum on which political groups are placed according to their relative command of resources, the focus of this essay is on those groups which are near, but not at, the pole of powerlessness.

2. See, e.g., Bayard Rustin, "From Protest to Politics: The Future of the Civil Rights Movement," *Commentary* (February, 1965), 25–31; and Stokely Carmichael, "Toward Black Liberation," *The Massachusetts Review* (Autumn, 1966).

3. On Alinsky's philosophy of community organization, see his *Reveille for Radicals* (Chicago, 1945); and Charles Silberman, *Crisis in Black and White* (New York, 1964), ch. 10.

4. See, e.g., Jack L. Walker, "Protest and Negotiation: A Case Study of Negro Leadership in Atlanta, Georgia," *Midwest Journal of Political Science*, 7 (May, 1963), 99–124; Jack L. Walker, *Sit-Ins in Atlanta: A Study in the Negro Protest*, Eagleton Institute Case Studies, No. 34 (New York, 1964); John Ehle, *The Free Men* (New York, 1965) [Chapel Hill]; Daniel C. Thompson, *The Negro Leadership Class* (Englewood Cliffs, N.J., 1963) [New Orleans]; M. Elaine Burgess, *Negro Leadership in a Southern City* (Chapel Hill, N.C., 1962) [Durham].

5. Lewis Killian and Charles Grigg, *Racial Crisis in America: Leadership in Conflict* (Englewood Cliffs, N.J., 1964).

6. William Keech, "The Negro Vote as a Political Resource: The Case of Durham," (unpublished Ph.D. Dissertation, University of Wisconsin, 1966); John H. Strange, "The Negro in Philadelphia Politics 1963–65," (unpublished Ph.D. Dissertation, Princeton University, 1966).

7. Donald Matthews and James Prothro, *Negroes and the New Southern Politics* (New York, 1966). Considerable insight on these data is provided in John Orbell, "Protest Participation among Southern Negro College Students," this REVIEW, 61 (June, 1967), 446–456.

8. Kenneth Clark, *Dark Ghetto* (New York, 1965).

9. *Negro Politics* (New York, 1960).

10. A complete list would be voluminous. See, e.g., Nat Hentoff, *The New Equality* (New York, 1964); Arthur Waskow, *From Race Riot to Sit-in* (New York, 1966).

11. "The Strategy of Protest: Problems of Negro Civic Action," *Journal of Conflict Resolution*, 3 (September, 1961), 291–303. The reader will recognize the author's debt to this highly suggestive article, not least Wilson's recognition of the utility of the bargaining framework for examining protest activity.

12. *Ibid.*, p. 291.

13. *Ibid.*, pp. 291–292.

14. See E. E. Schattschneider's discussion of expanding the scope of the conflict, *The Semisovereign People* (New York, 1960). Another way in which bargaining resources may be "created" is to increase the relative cohesion of groups, or to increase the perception of group solidarity as a precondition to greater cohesion. This appears to be the primary goal of political activity which is generally designated "community organization." Negro activists appear to recognize the utility of this strategy in their advocacy of "black power." In some instances protest activity may be designed in part to accomplish this goal in addition to activating reference publics.

15. For an example of "direct confrontation," one might study the three-month Negro boycott of white merchants in Natchez, Miss., which resulted in capitulation to boycott demands by city government leaders. See *The New York Times*, December 4, 1965, p. 1.

16. *A Preface to Democratic Theory* (Chicago, 1956), pp. 145–46.

17. *Ibid.*

18. *The Governmental Process* (New York, 1951), p. 104.

19. See Dahl, *A Preface to Democratic Theory*, p. 146.

20. Observations that all groups can influence public policy at some stage of the political process are frequently made about the role of "veto groups" in American politics. See *Ibid.*, pp. 104 ff. See also David Reisman, *The Lonely Crowd* (New Haven, 1950), pp. 211 ff., for an earlier discussion of veto-group politics. Yet protest should be evaluated when it is adopted to obtain assertive as well as defensive goals.

21. See Murray Edelman, *The Symbolic Uses of Politics* (Urbana, Ill., 1964), ch. 2.

22. See Dahl, *Who Governs?* (New Haven, 1961). pp. 305 ff.

23. In a recent formulation, Dahl reiterates the theme of wide dispersion of influence. "More than other systems, [democracies] . . . try to disperse influence widely to their citizens by means of the suffrage, elections, freedom of speech, press, and assembly, the right of opponents to criticize the conduct of government, the right to organize political parties, and in other ways." *Pluralist Democracy in the United States* (Chicago, 1967), p. 373. Here, however, he concentrates more on the availability of options to all groups in the system, rather than on the relative probabilities that all groups in fact have access to the political process. See pp. 372 ff.

24. See Edward Banfield, *Political Influence* (New York, 1961), p. 263. The analysis of organizational incentive structure which heavily influences

Banfield's formulation is Chester Barnard, *The Functions of the Executive* (Cambridge, Mass., 1938).

25. In the following attempt to develop the implications of this conceptualization of protest activity, I have drawn upon extensive field observations and bibliographical research. Undoubtedly, however, individual assertions, while representing my best judgment concerning the available evidence, in the future may require modification as the result of further empirical research.

26. As Edelman suggests, cited previously.

27. *Negro Politics*, p. 290.

28. *The Governmental Process*, p. 513.

29. But cf. Thomas Schelling's discussion of "binding oneself," *The Strategy of Conflict* (Cambridge, Mass., 1960), pp. 22 ff.

30. "The Strategy of Protests," p. 297.

31. This is suggested by Wilson, "The Strategy of Protest," p. 298; St. Clair Drake and Horace Cayton, *Black Metropolis* (New York, 1962, rev. ed.), p. 731; Walker, "Protest and Negotiation," p. 122. Authors who argue that divided leadership is dysfunctional have been Clark, p. 156; and Tilman Cothran, "The Negro Protest Against Segregation in the South," *The Annals*, 357 (January, 1965), p. 72.

32. This observation is confirmed by a student of the Southern civil rights movement:

> Negroes demand of protest leaders constant progress. The combination of long-standing discontent and a new-found belief in the possibility of change produces a constant state of tension and aggressiveness in the Negro community. But this discontent is vague and diffuse, not specific; the masses do not define the issues around which action shall revolve. This the leader must do.

Lewis Killian, "Leadership in the Desegregation Crises: An Institutional Analysis," in Muzafer Sherif (ed.), *Intergroup Relations and Leadership* (New York; 1962), p. 159.

33. Significantly, southern Negro students who actively participated in the early phases of the sit-in movement "tended to be unusually optimistic about race relations and tolerant of whites [when compared with inactive Negro students]. They not only *were* better off, objectively speaking, than other Negroes but *felt* better off." Matthews and Prothro, *op. cit.*, p. 424.

34. This is particularly the case in cities such as Washington, D. C., where landlord-tenant laws offer little protection against retaliatory eviction. See, e.g., Robert Schoshinski, "Remedies of the Indigent Tenant: Proposal for Change," *Georgetown Law Journal*, 54 (Winter, 1966), 541 ff.

35. Wilson regarded this as a chief reason for lack of protest activity in 1961. He wrote: ". . . some of the goals now being sought by Negroes are least applicable to those groups of Negroes most suited to protest action. Protest action involving such tactics as mass meetings, picketing, boycotts, and strikes rarely find enthusiastic participants among upper-income and higher status individuals": "The Strategy of Protest," p. 296.

36. See *The New York Times*, February 12, 1966, p. 56.

37. On housing clinic services provided by political clubs, see James Q. Wilson, *The Amateur Democrat: Club Politics in Three Cities* (Chicago, 1962), pp. 63–64, 176. On the need for lawyers among low income people, see e.g., *The Extension of Legal Services to the Poor*, Conference

Proceedings (Washington, D.C., n.d.), esp. pp. 51–60; and "Neighborhood Law Offices: The New Wave in Legal Services for the Poor," *Harvard Law Review*, 80 (February, 1967), 805–850.

38. An illustration of low income group protest organization mobilized for veto purposes is provided by Dahl in "The Case of the Metal Houses." See *Who Governs?*, pp. 192 ff.

39. Norton Long, "The Local Community as an Ecology of Games," in Long, *The Polity*, Charles Press, ed. (Chicago, 1962), p. 153. See pp. 152–154. See also Roscoe C. Martin, Frank J. Munger, *et al.*, *Decisions in Syracuse: A Metropolitan Action Study* (Garden City, N.Y., 1965) (originally published: 1961), pp. 326–327.

40. See, e.g., Thompson, *op. cit.*, p. 134, and *passim*; Martin Oppenheimer, "The Southern Student Movement: Year I," *Journal of Negro Education*, 33 (Fall, 1964), p. 397; Cothran, *op. cit.*, p. 72; Pauli Murray, "Protest Against the Legal Status of the Negro," *The Annals*, 357 (January, 1965), p. 63; Allan P. Sindler, "Protest Against the Political Status of the Negroes," *The Annals*, 357 (January, 1965), p. 50.

41. See Banfield, *op. cit.*, p. 275.

42. For a case study of the interaction between protest leaders and newspaper reporters, see Michael Lipsky, "Rent Strikes in New York City: Protest Politics and the Power of the Poor" (unpublished Ph.D. dissertation, Princeton University, 1967), pp. 139–49. Bernard Cohen has analyzed the impact of the press on foreign policy from the perspective of reporters' role requirements: see his *The Press and Foreign Policy* (Princeton, N.J., 1963), esp. chs. 2–3.

43. An example of a protest conducted by middle-class women engaged in pragmatic protest over salvaging park space is provided in John B. Keeley, *Moses on the Green*, Inter-University Case Program, No. 45 (University, Ala., 1959).

44. This was the complaint of Floyd McKissick, National Director of the Congress of Racial Equality, when he charged that ". . . there are only two kinds of statements a black man can make and expect that the white press will report. . . . First . . . is an attack on another black man. . . . The second is a statement that sounds radical, violent, extreme—the verbal equivalent of a riot. . . . [T]he Negro is being rewarded by the public media only if he turns on another Negro and uses his tongue as a switchblade, or only if he sounds outlandish, extremist or psychotic." Statement at the Convention of the American Society of Newspaper Editors, April 20, 1967, Washington, D.C., as reported in *The New York Times*, April 21, 1967, p. 22. See also the remarks of journalist Ted Poston, *ibid.*, April 26, 1965, p. 26.

45. Matthews and Prothro found, for example, that in their south-wide Negro population sample, 38 percent read Negro-oriented magazines and 17 percent read newspapers written for Negroes. These media treat news of interest to Negroes more completely and sympathetically than do the general media. See pp. 248 ff.

46. See footnote 31 above.

47. Wilson, *Negro Politics*, p. 225.

48. See Wallace Sayre and Herbert Kaufman, *Governing New York City* (New York, 1960), pp. 257 ff. Also see Banfield, *op. cit.*, p. 267.

49. See Wilson, *The Amateur Democrats*, previously cited. These groups are

most likely to be characterized by broad scope of political interest and frequent intervention in politics. See Sayre and Kaufman, *op. cit.*, p. 79.

50. Another approach, persuasively presented by Wilson, concentrates on protest success as a function of the relative unity and vulnerability of targets. See "The Strategy of Protest," pp. 293 ff. This insight helps explain, for example, why protest against housing segregation commonly takes the form of action directed against government (a unified target) rather than against individual homeowners (who present a dispersed target). One problem with this approach is that it tends to obscure the possibility that targets, as collections of individuals, may be divided in evaluation of and sympathy for protest demands. Indeed, city agency administrators under some circumstances act as partisans in protest conflicts. As such, they frequently appear ambivalent toward protest goals: sympathetic to the ends while concerned that the means employed in protest reflect negatively on their agencies.

51. Sayre and Kaufman, *op. cit.*, p. 253.

52. See *ibid.*, pp. 253 ff.

53. See Lipsky, *op. cit.*, chs. 5–6. The appearance of responsiveness may be given by city officials *in anticipation* of protest activity. This seems to have been the strategy of Mayor Richard Daley in his reaction to the announcement of Martin Luther King's plans to focus civil rights efforts on Chicago. See *The New York Times*, February 1, 1966, p. 11.

54. See Edelman, *op. cit.*, p. 23.

55. See Lipsky, *op. cit.*, pp. 156, 249 ff.

56. On the strategy of appearing constrained, see Schelling, *op. cit.*, pp. 22 ff.

57. Clark, *op. cit.*, pp. 154 ff.

II
Government, Citizens, and Public Policy

The Politics of Housing

The provision of adequate living quarters for all Americans is the central problem for housing policy-makers. It is difficult to determine the number of individuals and families who live in unsatisfactory housing. The most often used criteria are those of the U.S. Bureau of Census. The Bureau, which relies on physical structural standards, defines "substandard housing units" as units that are physically dilapidated and that do not have hot water and plumbing within the unit. Based on that standard, United States housing stock has improved over the years and, by 1970, only about 10 percent of all housing units were substandard. However, definitions of substandard housing are not fixed, but vary according to judgments as to what constitutes adequate housing. Thus, the Census Bureau does not consider deteriorating housing (as distinguished from dilapidated housing) with inadequate plumbing facilities to be "substandard" housing. Nor does it consider overcrowding as a factor in its definition. Lastly, it fails to take into account a related problem: the proportion of family income spent for rent or ownership costs. If all these factors are considered, then estimates of the proportion of the population living in inadequate housing vary from 15 percent to 25 percent (10 to 17 million households),[1] and a disproportionate number of these households are made up of poor nonwhites.

More than 50 percent of these substandard houses are located in urban areas, and most of them are to be found in the central cities. They are the eventual result of the "trickle-down" process that shapes the urban housing supply. Most new, high-quality housing is built in suburbia and occupied by households with considerable income. The housing formerly occupied by these households is taken over by those with somewhat less income. As this filtering process runs its course, the deteriorating housing that eventually becomes available is that located in the inner-city slums. Governmental programs have not simply failed to alleviate the impact of these private market forces; they have, we shall see, contributed to the physical deterioration of the core city.

In the United States, governmental intervention in the housing market did not begin until the turn of the century. During the nineteenth century, slum properties were considered good investments. The continuous supply of immigrants to the cities provided sufficient demand for such housing. And, because of this heavy demand for low-rental housing, the maintenance costs on the properties were minimal. As a result, slum housing was a good business for the builder, the lender, and the owner.

The initial pressures for government action against slum housing came, not from the poor, but from middle-class groups associated with the late nineteenth-century Progressive movement. These groups were generally composed of Protestant, native Americans opposed to the activities and ethos of the immigrant and his political machine. They sought better housing for the poor out of a belief that the slum environment caused the undesirable vices they associated with the immigrant. Better housing was intended as an instrument for socializing the ethnic population into more middle-class values. This pattern, whereby groups with superior status and higher incomes purport to represent the interests of the poor in the housing arena, has continued to the present time. In the discussion to follow, these groups will be referred to as *surrogate groups.*

Around the turn of the century, these surrogate groups began to obtain the passage of building codes by municipal governments. These codes specified standards of lighting, ventilation, sanitation, and fire prevention. The effect of these codes on the private-housing sector during the following half century was to make the low-rental housing market less attractive. The additional building and maintenance costs required by the codes became one of the factors that led to significant changes within the private sector regarding this housing market. The construction of such housing solely by private enterprise all but disappeared. Large financial institutions ceased accepting such properties as securities for loans, and large property owners sold their holdings to small-scale, speculative operators. These operators, in order to keep down maintenance costs, have tried to prevent the enforcement of the building codes, and city governments, anxious to prevent the abandonment of slum properties, have succumbed to their demands. As a result, slum residents have found these codes to be of little help when they seek to improve the quality of their housing or maintenance services.[2]

The next significant intervention by government into the housing market occurred at the time of the Great Depression in the

1930s. The two most important New Deal housing programs involved federal legislation; they were a mortgage-insurance program (the Federal Housing Administration—FHA) and a public-housing program. Unlike municipal building codes, these programs were responses to pressures for public aid to increase the supply of housing rather than attempts to prevent the construction of inferior housing.

The FHA mortgage-insurance program, enacted in 1935, insured mortgages extended by lending institutions. The FHA set regulations determining the interest charge, the amount of down-payment required, and the maximum time period for the mortgages. Over the years, these regulations have been liberalized; home buyers are now required to make both smaller down-payments and smaller monthly payments as the result of the lengthened time period permitted for the mortgages. It was not until 1967 that the FHA would guarantee loans when there seemed to be substantial risks concerning repayment.

From the time it was enacted, and to the present day, the program has served the interests of the private sector exceedingly well. Pressures from the private-housing market were primarily responsible for the passage of the legislation. The construction of homes had all but ceased; the real-estate market had collapsed; and lending institutions were holding sour mortgages and foreclosing on property which had sharply depreciated in value. The result of the FHA mortgage-insurance program, reports the National Commission on Urban Problems in the reading found in this section, has been to permit financial institutions "to make practically risk-free loans on new and old homes." Home builders and realtors, too, have profited from the expansion of the potential market for their services. In short, the FHA mortgage-insurance program, from the point of view of the financiers, real estate brokers and contracting industry, has increased their profits and protected them against loss.

The chief consumer beneficiaries of the FHA program have been suburban middle-income home buyers rather than working-class or poor families residing in the central cities. By insuring well over 90 percent of the appraised value of new homes, the FHA program has enabled millions of Americans to become homeowners in suburbia. The FHA, until recently, has been generally unwilling to insure mortgages to poor and working-class members (particularly blacks), because they have been regarded as bad credit risks. Related to this decision by the FHA has been its reluctance to insure homes in the central city. Not only was the FHA insurance program never intended as a program to aid the poor, but its effect has also been to increase the disparities between the haves and have-nots.

On the other hand, the public-housing program, also initiated during the New Deal era, was intended to benefit the poor. However, the poor have only benefited from the program to a limited extent. The major enabling legislation was the Low Rent Housing Bill of 1937. The law established the United States Housing Authority (USHA), which was to regulate the activities of municipal public-housing authorities. These authorities would construct, own, and control public-housing projects. Two provisions in the legislation enabled these authorities to maintain low rents for the residents. The local authorities were eligible to obtain long-term loans from the USHA for clearing the land and constructing the project. The long-term nature of the loan meant that the local authorities would be paying a lower debt charge, thereby lowering its costs. In addition, the USHA was authorized to make grants to the local authorities to cover the difference between the rents necessary to cover the costs of the projects and the actual rental income; the rents were required to be at a level which the low-income tenants could afford. As laudatory as these features were, they were offset by a number of regulations issued by USHA that resulted in inferior housing, including limitations on the physical structure of the project (maximum size of rooms, maximum costs per room) and income limitations on tenants (both maximum and minimum). And these were not substantially altered when the continuation of the public-housing program was authorized by the Taft-Ellender-Wagner Housing Act of 1949.

From the outset, private-housing interests viewed public housing as competitive to their market and damaging to the demand for older homes and apartments.[3] Moreover, they have always been concerned about the possible extension of this type of governmental intervention into other housing markets. Unlike the FHA mortgage-insurance program, in which governmental backing expands their potential market, public housing is potentially competitive to their efforts. The effectiveness of their opposition to the program increased over the years. The initial legislation contained provisions that limited the proportion of the housing market that could and would make use of public housing. These provisions included the above-mentioned maximum income limitations on residents and inferior standards for the physical structure of the project. Other triumphs of private producer interests in the post–World War II era are described in the Freedman reading. At the present time, appropriations for the program have all but ceased. Public housing currently constitutes only 1 percent of the nation's housing stock.

As Freedman's data reveal, the surrogate groups promoting public housing encompassed a wider scope of participants than earlier housing-reform efforts. In addition to such middle-class groups as social workers, charitable organizations, and "good government" groups, support for the program came from organized labor and minority groups representing middle-class blacks (for example, the NAACP and the Urban League). However, no organizations that could be said to represent the poor—the potential tenants in the projects—were major actors in the political arena of public housing. Without the direct, personal stake in the issue that the poor themselves had, the surrogate groups were all too willing to reach an accommodation that severely limited the number of public-housing units to be constructed.

This pattern is unfortunately all too clear in the case of the urban-renewal program, which was the major urban housing legislation in the post–World War II era. Urban renewal, initiated in 1949, provided first for slum clearance by the local government and then for sale of the cleared land to a private developer who would build residential housing on the site. The federal government paid two-thirds of the cost of the city's loss in buying and preparing the land for the private developer. The legislation was amended in 1954 and subsequent years to provide that increasingly larger percentages of the cleared land could be developed for nonresidential uses. As a result, a significant portion of urban-renewal developments came to be used for more profitable commercial purposes.

The urban-renewal program is a classic example of the use of government incentives to aid the private housing market. Under the public-housing program, slums had been razed and replaced with locally owned low-rental housing. Under urban renewal, the slum-cleared sites were turned over to private developers at a price invariably less than the costs incurred by the city. The private interests then owned the land and could retain all profits achieved from their investments. These investments generally involved commercial buildings and high-rise, upper-middle-income housing.

Aside from the private sector, the major participants in the politics of urban renewal were the mayors of central cities, businessmen with central city investments, "good government" groups, the press, and urban planners. All of these groups saw urban renewal as a means of expanding the city's tax base, improving its aesthetic appearance, and making the central city more attractive to middle- and upper-middle-income groups.

The interests of the poor, again, were not represented by their own organizations, but by other participants in the system. The poor were expected to benefit from the program by the relocation into public housing of those whose slum housing was torn down. The same 1949 legislation that authorized the urban-renewal program also authorized the construction of public housing for the families uprooted by slum clearance. However, the relocation aspects of the program have never been successful. As mentioned above, the public-housing program has been underfinanced, and a sufficient number of units have never been built. The poor have had to undergo the difficult process of relocation to make way for the more expensive housing constructed on the sites of their former homes. They have generally settled in other areas of the city, resulting in either an expansion of the slums or increased rents for ghetto residents.

The 1960s witnessed a new approach in dealing with the housing problems of the poor. Because the public-housing program was stalled by the opposition of the private housing groups, this new direction sought to merge the interests of the private sector with those of the poor. The federal government, increasingly represented by the FHA, began providing financial subsidies in order to induce the private sector to build for this previously unrewarding market. Typical of this genre are two FHA-administered programs enacted in 1968. The first, seeking to enable the low- and moderate-income family to possess their own home, provides a mortgage subsidy that in some cases leaves the buyer with only 1 percent interest to pay (Section 235 of the Housing Act of 1968). The financial institution lending the money receives the subsidy and FHA insurance of the mortgage. The other legislation is intended to lower the rents for low- and moderate-income tenants. The Rental Housing Assistance program (Section 236 of the Housing Act of 1968), which also relies on a mortgage subsidy and loan guarantee to the lending institution, is intended to lower the amortization costs of the landlord, enabling him to charge lower rents. By 1971, 25 percent of all new housing was financed through these two programs or other subsidy programs following this pattern.[4]

Even though these new housing programs are intended specifically for low-income groups, the major participants in the political arena involved in their enactment and administration have been the private sector and surrogate groups.[5] Most private interests viewed these programs as in the tradition of previous government intervention that enlarged the potential market for their services. The surrogate groups, which included almost the very same groups that supported public housing, saw this approach as an acceptable compromise between their concern to enlarge and improve the housing supply for these income groups and the business interests of the private sector.

Ironically, one of the consequences of these subsidy programs has been to spur housing abandonment, a phenomenon already seriously contributing to the deterioration of ghetto neighborhoods. Housing abandonment is presently a widespread phenomenon in the core cities of the Northeast and Midwest. In their essay, George Sternlieb, et al., conclude, on the basis of their studies of the Newark experience, that abandonment appears to be related to the withdrawal of private investment from nonwhite neighborhoods, even though housing shortages and physically sound structures existed in such areas.

The same conclusion is arrived at by James Vitarello, in his short discussion of the impact of "redlining" by traditional lending institutions. In the past, buildings were abandoned when they became structurally unsound; now, they are being given up even though in good physical condition and needed by ghetto residents. Another study, which analyzed the home loan decisions made by Chicago banks, found that they discontinue such investments whenever a neighborhood changes racially, regardless of the income status of the residents.[6]

The FHA subsidy programs succeeded in inducing the private real estate sector to enter this market. However, the interest of lending institutions, housing developers, and real estate brokers in maximizing their profits led them to construct and repair poor quality housing that they could acquire cheaply. They were able to sell such properties at substantial profits to unsophisticated minority buyers who had limited housing choices. When many of the owners and renters of these properties found their homes or apartments uninhabitable or too costly to maintain, they simply abandoned them. The defaults have left the housing in the hands of the mortgage insurer, FHA, or technically, the Department of Housing and Urban Development (HUD). By 1974, defaults in these two programs were costing HUD two billion annually.[7] Even more important than these fiscal consequences, FHA-abandoned houses spurred neighborhood deterioration. The subsidy programs that were intended to provide homes for the central city turned out to be a major factor promoting the deterioration of minority neighborhoods.

In still other ways, these subsidy programs have failed to improve the housing of the central city poor. It appears that their primary beneficiaries have been moderate-income working-class families rather than the low-income group; those families whose income is too high for public housing, but too low for conventional housing. Moreover, it was not until this date that governmental efforts first began to assist this working-class group. The FHA also, in administering these programs, has left undisturbed the present patterns of housing segregation by, on the one hand, limiting its aid to nonwhites solely to financing central city residences while, on the other hand, helping white families to obtain homes in suburbia. These two subsidy programs were suspended in January, 1972. In 1974, special revenue sharing legislation was passed—the Housing and Community Development Act of 1974 —and it now devolves upon the local governments to play a role in shaping future housing policy.

Lastly, governmental efforts to end segregation in housing have been extremely limited. Prior to the 1960s, the FHA, responding to pressures generated by the private sector, refused to approve mortgages to blacks seeking to live in white neighborhoods. The enactment of a fair-housing law by Congress in 1968 has had little impact. The selection in this volume by the National Commission on Urban Problems describes how the fragmentation of suburbia has promoted segregated housing.

The limited success of governmental efforts to provide adequate housing for the poor is explained, in part, by the political system that has developed around housing. The major participants in the system have been groups representing the interests of the private-housing sector and surrogate groups claiming to represent the urban poor. The private market has been represented by associations speaking for builders of housing, financial institutions that provide credit for the construction and purchase of homes, and realtors who trade in property and housing. These groups have sought to ensure that governmental intervention would increase the number of potential customers for their services. For example, banks that deal in housing mortgages have approved of the government insuring their mortgages, but have opposed direct government loans to home buyers. Builders have supported government subsidies that enable them to construct homes for income groups that otherwise could not afford such housing, but they oppose the government itself constructing homes for these groups.

The surrogate groups that have pressed for governmental involvement in the housing field have included organized labor, social workers, church groups, professional organizations, and local governmental officials. These groups have tried to increase the quantity and quality of housing available to low- and moderate-income groups and, to achieve this, have been willing to enter into partnership with the private sector. By these accommodations, they have sought to encourage the private sector to serve as large a percentage of the market as possible, with government intervention intended to aid and expand these private efforts. However, groups whose membership is largely urban poor—the potential beneficiaries of these programs—seldom, if ever, have achieved much access and cannot be considered participants in the political system that evolves housing policy. It is ironic that the middle-class "do-good" organizations, whose surrogate activities ostensibly were on behalf of the poor, have only legitimized the latter's exclusion.

The cooperation between the private interests and the surrogate groups has prevented any serious consideration of housing proposals that might disturb the market of the private sector. There are no groups in the arena to propose alternatives such as massive federal efforts to construct housing for low-income residents, direct income grants to the poor themselves rather than subsidies to the private sector, or serious attempts to house the nonwhite poor in suburbia. Whatever the merits of these programs, they share the common characteristic of threatening the private-housing market. Federal construction of low-income housing would remove this group as potential customers for private housing. Direct grants to the poor might not be spent on housing. Programs aimed at housing integration disturb the "normal" workings of a housing market that segregates homeowners by race.

It has been argued that the private sector has been meeting the housing needs of the poor as a result of a "filtering" process in which residences become available to the poor as each successively lower-income group is able to move into better housing. Apologists for the housing policies followed since the 1930s have used this argument to maintain that public programs that aided higher-income groups eventually redounded to the benefit of the poor.[7] However, it is questionable whether the poor are indeed receiving adequate housing as a result of this filtering process. As noted at the beginning of this essay, millions of American families can be considered "ill-housed." The slums of our cities are replete with deteriorating and discarded buildings. Moreover, the racial restrictions of the housing market limit the volume and quality of housing available to blacks as a result of filtering.

The net result of the political system that has developed around housing is that we have government programs for almost all income groups except the poor. The newly enacted FHA subsidy programs, the traditional FHA-insured mortgages, and the urban-renewal program aid all but the very rich and the poor, particularly the black poor. These patterns can be expected to continue as long as the private-housing sector continues to play a dominant role in the politics of housing, and as long as groups representative of ghetto residents are denied an effective voice in the making of housing policy.

Notes

1. Robert Lineberry and Ira Sharkansky, *Urban Politics and Public Policy* (New York: Harper and Row, 1971), p. 320; Anthony Downs, *Urban Problems and Prospects* (Chicago: Markham, 1971), pp. 115–20.
2. Harold Wolman, *Politics of Federal Housing* (New York: Dodd, Mead, 1971), p. 25.
3. Thomas R. Dye, *Politics in States and Communities* (Englewood Cliffs, N.J.: Prentice-Hall, 1969), p. 436.
4. "DHA—From Suburb to Ghetto," *New York Times*, III, May 7, 1972, p. 1.
5. Wolman, *op. cit.*, chap. 3.
6. The study's conclusion was that the financial institutions "redline" areas rather than making their credit decisions based on individual criteria such as job security of home owner and soundness of physical structure. See Metropolitan Area Housing Alliance, "Redlining and FHA: New Research Proves Dual Home Financing in Chicago Neighborhoods," (Chicago, Ill.: 1975).
7. Chester W. Hartman, *Housing and Social Policy* (Englewood Cliffs, N.J.: Prentice-Hall, 1975), pp. 136–45.
8. For example, see Bernard J. Frieden, "Housing and National Urban Goals: Old Policies and New Realities," in James Q. Wilson, ed., *The Metropolitan Enigma; Inquiries into the Nature and Dimensions of America's "Urban Crisis"* (Garden City, N.Y.: Doubleday, 1970), pp. 170–225.

Bibliography

Abrams, Charles. *The City Is the Frontier*. New York: Harper and Row, 1965.

Bellush, Jewel, and Murray Hausknecht, eds. *Urban Renewal: People, Politics and Planning*. Garden City, N.Y.: Doubleday, 1967.

Davies, J. Clarence, III. *Neighborhood Groups and Urban Renewal*. New York: Columbia University Press, 1966.

Downs, Anthony. *Federal Housing Subsidies*, Lexington, Mass.: Heath, 1973.

FREEDMAN, LEONARD. *Public Housing*. New York: Holt, Rinehart and Winston, 1969.

GANS, HERBERT. "The Failure of Urban Renewal." *Commentary* (April, 1965), pp. 29–37.

HARTMAN, CHESTER. *Housing and Social Policy*, Englewood Cliffs, N.J.: Prentice-Hall, 1975.

KAPLAN, HAROLD. *Urban Renewal Politics*. New York: Columbia University Press, 1963.

MEYERSON, MARTIN, and EDWARD BANFIELD. *Politics, Planning, and the Public Interest*. New York: Free Press, 1955.

MEYERSON, MARTIN, et al. *Housing, People, and Cities*. New York: McGraw-Hill, 1962.

PYNOOS, JON, et al., eds. *Housing Urban America*, Chicago: Aldine, 1973.

WILSON, JAMES Q. "Planning and Politics: Citizen Participation in Urban Renewal." *Journal of the American Institute of Planners* XXIX (November, 1963), pp. 242–49.

WOLMAN, HAROLD. *Politics of Federal Housing*. New York: Dodd, Mead, 1971.

FINANCING OF HOUSING: FHA

NATIONAL COMMISSION ON URBAN PROBLEMS

Few Americans can afford to pay cash for a house. Most people must go into debt to buy a home. Despite a traditional conservative bias against personal indebtedness, an exception has almost always been made for home purchase.

Homeownership is not a new goal. Everyone pays for shelter in some form. The form of purchasing by borrowing enables young families to pay off their debt in lieu of rent when their earning power is steady or growing, and promises security to those who complete payments and achieve full ownership before their earning power dwindles.

To provide the necessary credit and enable a family to have its own home when the need for it is greatest, an elaborate financing system has developed. The various institutions that serve the credit needs of home buyers are:

Governmental institutions:
>Federal Housing Administration (FHA).
>Veterans' Administration (VA).
>Federal National Mortgage Association (FNMA).

Private and conventional credit institutions:
>Mutual savings banks.
>Savings and loan associations.
>Commercial banks.
>Life insurance companies.

During the century preceding the Depression of the 1930's, home loans, or mortgages, were handled entirely by private money lenders. They charged high interest, required large downpayments, and required rapid repayment, typically in 7 to 10 years. Buyers short of cash to meet approximately 35 percent of purchase price as downpayment had to borrow further from a

From the National Commission on Urban Problems, *Building the American City* (Washington, D.C.: U.S. Government Printing Office, 1969), pp. 94–107.

second mortgage at still higher interest rates. Periodic payments often covered only the interest, with the full principal due at the expiration date. Buyers who could not meet payments because of illness or loss of jobs were in a precarious position, in danger of losing their homes and all the savings invested in them. Understandably, money lenders often were painted as villains in plays and novels, and the term "mortgage" was surrounded with an aura of fear.

The optimism of the 1920's tended to hide these risks, however. Home buying increased greatly at the same time that values became highly inflated. When the economy collapsed in 1929, millions lost their homes in foreclosures and other millions were about to lose them. One measure of the severity of the crash is that new housing units were being built at an annual rate of 900,000 a year in the years before the Depression and only one-tenth of this amount, or 90,000 housing units, were built in 1934.

This disaster brought the Federal Government into the picture. First, under the Hoover administration, the Federal Home Loan Banks were set up to supply capital advances to home loan institutions. Under the Roosevelt administration, to stem the continuing defaults, the Home Owners Loan Corporation was created to put Federal funds behind distressed mortgages; first interest, and then both interest and principal, were insured.

Also in the mid-1930's, the Government invested about $275 million in federally chartered savings and loan associations, insuring depositors against loss. The whole structure of home financing was purified. The "balloon payments" at the end of the mortgage term (which posed such an unmanageable financial burden on the poor purchaser) were eliminated by amortizing the principal in regular payments over the life of the loan. Interest rates were reduced.

Both homeowners and lenders who held the mortgages were substantially aided by these Government measures, and hence by the taxpayers. Strangely the same economic middle class which then received these benefits, and in large measure still does, often forgets its debt to society; many of its members are frequently in the forefront of opposition to housing programs designed to help less fortunate Americans.

While the Government kept a significant number of Americans from losing their homes through the policies described, the hoped-for recovery of the housing market did not occur. Financial institutions handling the mortgages were stabilized, but they were still fearful of making home loans for which they might not be repaid. In 1935, to stimulate construction and homeownership, the Federal Housing Administration was created to provide more direct support for those wishing to acquire homes by insuring their mortgages under certain circumstances.

Despite rising building costs and interest rates, the pattern of FHA mortgage financing has enabled many more families, and many with lower incomes than formerly would have been in the market, to become homeowners. They have become debt-encumbered, to be sure, but homeowners nevertheless. The chief means of achieving this end have been (1) reduced downpayment requirements, and (2) extended mortgage life.

Mortgage financing has grown to vast proportions. As table 1 shows, there was a doubling of mortgage debt in the 9 years noted.

TABLE 1.—Total Mortgage Debt in Nonfarm
1- to 4-Family Houses

	Billion
1958	$118
1964	198
1967	236

While there are still some individual lenders, the bulk of the mortgage business is institutionalized. The FHA does not make direct loans to borrowers, but rather insures the mortgages extended by institutions. The same is primarily true of mortgages insured by the Veterans' Administration. Mortgages extended by private lending institutions without recourse to either FHA or VA are called "conventional financing."

Interest Rates, Length of Term, Downpayments—
Some Relationships

The discussion of housing costs [described] how the total and monthly costs of housing vary with changes in interest rates, length of the mortgage term, etc.

Table 2 shows that while the average cost of homes rose 52 percent in the 13 years from 1952 to 1965, the downpayment to the average buyer decreased by about $1,800 because FHA was insuring a larger percentage of the mortgage.

TABLE 2.—Average Home Costs and Downpayments

Year	Average cost of home	Down payment required (percentage)	Cash outlay for down-payment (rounded)
1952	$11,300	27.0	$3,100
1965	17,200	7.4	1,300

Monthly payments were reduced by extending the life of the mortgage from 20 to 35 years.

Rising interest rates tended to offset these reductions to the home buyers. They added to the initial cash outlay, insofar as points had to be paid to the lender to compensate for his acceptance of an FHA loan at a legally set interest rate below the market rate. Rising interest rates also added, of course, to monthly charges and to total interest charges.

Successful attempts to lower downpayments and monthly charges were thus accomplished through Government programs by saddling the buyer with more future debt and higher total interest payments. The interest payments were rationalized as (1) compensation to the lender for the owner's inability to make a 100 percent cash outlay for the house at the purchase time, or as (2) the owner's charge for the privilege of using the house on credit, while he is earning and saving to pay the full cost.

Conventional, FHA and VA Financing: How They Share the Mortgage Market

Conventional financing provided for 23 million, or 65 percent, of the 30.6 million new housing units built from 1946 through 1967. Mortgages insured by the Federal Housing Administration have financed 4.4 million new units, or approximately 15 percent of the total, since World War II, while Veterans' Administration guarantees have helped to provide nearly 2.9 million new housing units for veterans, or a little more than 9 percent of the total. The two together have assisted in the building of 7.3 million new housing units, or 24 percent of the total.

Government guarantees in one form or another, therefore, helped to stimulate nearly a quarter of the new housing units during the period of 1946 through 1967. The same three methods—

FHA, VA, and conventional financing—also operated in the purchase and the improvement of existing housing.

THE FEDERAL HOUSING ADMINISTRATION

Capsule Summary

In essence, the FHA has been a mortgage guarantee program.

The guarantee does not go to the home buyer. If he fails to meet his payments, the FHA does not bail him out. He loses his home. The guarantee is given to the lender, assuring him of repayment even if the borrower defaults.

FHA thus bolsters the lending institutions, permitting them to make practically risk-free loans on new and old homes, and on home repair work.

FHA helps home buyers indirectly; first, by encouraging lenders to make mortgage loans; second, by helping to bring about lower downpayments; and third, by inducing lower monthly payments. These benefits to borrowers have been accomplished over the years as FHA has insured or guaranteed an increasing portion of the cost of the home and has applied this guarantee to mortgages for which payments could be stretched out over an increasing period of years.

FHA thus, also indirectly, supports the homebuilding industry by providing a credit instrument that greatly expands housing production and consumption.

The FHA pattern of benefits stems from (1) the depression era from which it emerged; (2) the various changes over the years, such as the congressional mandates, the housing desires of the public, the suburbanization of the metropolis; and (3) the administrative policies within FHA itself.

The chief beneficiaries of FHA have been the middle-income home buyers, the suburban areas of the cities, the well-to-do insofar as they are among the lenders and builders, and a sparse number of the poor and near-poor. . . .

A GENERAL APPRAISAL OF FHA

Within its limits, FHA has performed well. By insuring a large portion of the appraised value, it greatly diminished the amount of down payment required. Recourse to costly second mortgages in this field was reduced. It made first mortgages more attractive and increased the amount of capital invested in them.

As the proportion of the appraised value which is insured has risen to well over 90 percent, the amount of the down payment has, of course, been correspondingly reduced. With risks reduced and payments lower, millions of young families have enjoyed homeownership at a much earlier age, and have been able to bring their children up in what we like to think of as the conventional American manner.

An increasing proportion of home purchase money was being financed on credit. Financial institutions in effect were possessing a larger share of the value of the house. Homeownership was expanded by letting the "owner" become more of a renter.

FHA has also been a vital factor in financing and promoting the exodus from the central cities and in helping to build up the suburbs. That is where the vast majority of FHA-insured homes have been built. The suburbs could not have expanded as they have during the postwar years without FHA. Superhighways constructed at Government expense have also opened up the areas outside the cities and supported the exodus of a large proportion of the white middle class.

By prescribing minimum standards of construction, including toilet and hot water facilities, and by discouraging the use of shoddy building materials, FHA has lessened the possibility that the new suburbs would soon turn into slums. At the same time, while it did not enthusiastically embrace new methods of construction and materials, it has been more receptive to them than have most of the building code writers and officials of the central cities. For example, FHA permitted Romex and plastic pipe when these new products were effectively forbidden by most codes. FHA actions in this respect have been beneficial.

Taking all factors into consideration, it is difficult to see how any institution could have served the emerging middle class more effectively than has the FHA and its counterpart, the Federal home loan bank systems. Most important, FHA helped to end the practice of letting the big final payment of principal come due at the end of the mortgage term, supplanting this with amortization of this amount over the life of the mortgage. It has brought consumer protection into the entire mortgage field, with conventional lenders following FHA's lead. For example, interest is only computed on the amounts actually owed. Many investors and lenders have been influenced by FHA to moderate their terms as regards interest, down payments, and length of mortgages. All of these steps have brought in more purchasers among the lower and middle sections of the middle class.

The Decline in the Relative Volume of FHA Insurance

Yet, despite its constructive services, it became apparent that FHA was becoming relatively less important.

During the 20 years from 1935 to 1954, FHA insured 3.76 million homes, or almost 23 percent of the 16.57 million that were built. The proportion dropped to 14 percent in 1957, but revived to 22.5 percent in 1958. By 1963, it had fallen to 14 percent, and remained below that proportion through 1967.

No one has given a fully satisfactory reason for this decline, but it was probably due to the fact that such lending institutions as savings and loan associations, savings banks, and insurance companies were being given more money to invest by depositors and were themselves moving more aggressively into the real estate field. Savings deposits in commercial banks were also rising rapidly. All these institutions were increasingly willing to make mortgage loans without being insured against loss. In this way, the borrower saved the yearly insurance premium of one-half percent a year of the outstanding value of the mortgage.

What FHA Has Not Done

The main weakness of FHA from a social point of view has not been in what it has done, but in what it has failed to do—in its relative neglect of the inner cities and of the poor, and especially Negro poor. Believing firmly that the poor were bad credit risks and that the presence of Negroes tended to lower real estate values, FHA has generally regarded loans to such groups as "economically unsound." Until recently, therefore, FHA benefits have been confined almost exclusively to the middle class, and primarily only to the middle section of the middle class. The poor and those on the fringes of poverty have been almost completely excluded. These and the lower middle class, together constituting the 40 percent of the population whose housing needs are greatest, received only 11 percent of FHA mortgages. [See Table 3.]

Redlining

This tendency to neglect the poor has been reinforced and partially extended by the FHA tendency to shun the central cities and concentrate on the suburbs. The experience of members of

TABLE 3.—PURCHASERS OF FHA HOMES IN 1965, BY INCOME CLASS

Income class	Income range	Percent of FHA mortgages
Poor and near poor	$4,000 and under	0.5
	4,000 to 5,000	2.9
Total		3.4
Lower middle class	$5,000 to $6,000	7.6
Middle and upper middle	$6,000 to $8,000	30.0
	$8,000 to $10,000	26.0
	$10,000 to $15,000	27.0
Total		83.0
Well to do	$15,000 and over	6.0

the Commission and others convinced us that up until the summer of 1967, FHA almost never insured mortgages on homes in slum districts, and did so very seldom in the "gray areas" which surrounded them. Even middle class residential districts in the central cities were suspect, since there was always the prospect that they, too, might turn as Negroes and poor whites continued to pour into the cities, and as middle and upper-middle income whites continued to move out.

The result was a general, even if unwritten, agreement between lending institutions and FHA that most of the areas inside the central cities did not have a favorable economic future, and that their property values were likely to decline. Each group blamed the other for the failure to help the cities. Apologists for FHA asked how could they be expected to insure mortgages if the lending institutions would not lend. The lending institutions asked how could they be expected to lend if the FHA would not insure the mortgages. Each passed the buck to the other.

A third set of institutions, the fire insurance companies, was drawn into the circle of mutual alibis, for there were certain sections of the cities, notably the Negro slums, where insurance companies would not insure against fires. The sad experience of the last 2 years of burnings may be seen by some as proving that this refusal had a solid basis. But the years of neglect of these districts by FHA, by lenders, by insurers, and often by local governments (especially in terms of low levels of community services and facilities), must be listed among the causes for the eventual urban conflagrations. Redlining by insurers weakened still further the ability of the slums to obtain loan capital with which to improve existing housing or to construct new units.

There was evidence of a tacit agreement among all groups— lending institutions, fire insurance companies, and FHA—to block off certain areas of cities within "red lines," and not to loan or insure within them. The net result, of course, was that the slums and the areas surrounding them went downhill farther and faster than before.

Segregated Housing

For many years FHA operated with the conventional racial prejudice characteristics of many middle class real estate men. The agency's original personnel was primarily recruited from this group in the 1930's. Until 1948, when restrictive covenants or written agreements not to sell to Negroes were declared unconstitutional by the Supreme Court, FHA actually encouraged its borrowers to give such guarantees and was a powerful enforcer of the covenants. The FHA definition of a sound neighborhood was a "homogeneous" one—one that was racially segregated.

FHA's segregation position cannot be defended by any current standard of what is right for the home, the neighborhood, the city, or the Nation (although it may be understood in the context of the Nation's overall backwardness in race matters at the time FHA policies were forged).

Yet the FHA had a strong case for its economic conservatism which, in all fairness, needs to be stated and understood. Defaults by homeowners on mortgage obligations prior to 1960 were, as we have seen, originally very low. By 1950, out of 2.5 million home mortgages, 15,300 had gone into what is known as termination default, the step just prior to foreclosure, and these losses were amply covered by the insurance reserve. In the next 10 years, up to 1960, 35,600 more went to default out of an additional 3 million insured mortgages. While the cumulative defaults had increased to a total of nearly 51,000, the number of total mortgages insured had also increased to about 5.6 million. The overall default rate had risen slightly to 0.9 percent, still relatively low. Financially, FHA remained in a very sound and solid position.

Meanwhile FHA was failing to reach lower income families, central city residents and Negroes. It had not, in fact, been designed especially to help these groups. Also, the suburban trend originally had not been clearly foreseen. FHA managers could, therefore, claim that they were following both the letter and the intent of the original 1934 act. As restrictive FHA policies were subjected to the pressure of increasing public and congressional criticism, the standard for some lending was changed from economic soundness to reasonable risk. As a result, FHA did relax its policies to some extent. It did not venture into the slums and gray areas of the central cities, but it did insure the mortgages of some of the weaker suburban subdivisions and of financially dubious individual homes in the suburbs. Unfortunately, the number of terminal defaults rose more rapidly than the number of insured mortgages.

By computing defaults as a percentage of the cumulative total of insured mortgages, FHA was able to show that the total record was still not alarming. But this understated the risks inherent in the new mortgages, since it included the full volume of the past mortgages which had been made to stable income elements. Thus, the cumulative default average rose from 0.9 percent in 1960 to 3.7 percent in 1967. But on the basis of the *rate* at which additional defaults occurred from year to year as compared with the increase in the number of insured mortgages, the increase was much more startling. It went from 2.16 percent in 1960 to 8.1 in 1965. These figures, of course, overstate the risk factor in new loans since a considerable, although unknown, proportion of defaults occurred on mortgages which had been previously insured. The truth about the relative safety of the new loans, therefore, lay somewhere between the cumulative average and the incremental. But by either standard, a great increase in risk showed up at the same time that the insurance criteria were being liberalized. . . .

A group of financially conservative Members of Congress, though unaware of the full extent of the losses, was frightened by the increased number of foreclosures. This group, therefore, demanded greater caution in insuring. On the other hand, congressional liberals, seeing the deterioration of the central cities, and also unaware of FHA losses, wanted FHA to take more chances and to help rebuild at least the gray fringes of the central cities. FHA was caught between two fires. It was damned if it did and damned if it didn't. . . .

Its new losses, however, were not really in the central cities. There was little insuring going on there. It was rather in the so-called inferior subdivisions in the suburbs, where the loans were going sour. After the Watts riots and again during the widespread riots of 1967, FHA was again accused of being too conservative, and once again those who felt FHA should have a social as well as a business purpose urged it to insure in the gray and slum areas of the inner cities. In the summer of 1967, the regional directors of FHA and important local representatives were summoned to Washington and told by the head of FHA that they should be more receptive to such mortgages and should look favorably on the various special assistance programs. There has not been time enough to determine how the new program is working out, but there seems to be evidence that FHA has, on the whole, tried to meet the criticisms leveled against it and to follow the instructions of its chief. Whatever its sins in the past, there is little one can criticize about its recent national leadership. Whether this will continue in the future is an open question. It depends on public opinion and on Congress. Certainly there remain deep pockets of resistance to liberalizing policies within regional and local staffs.

PUBLIC HOUSING AND GROUP PRESSURES

LEONARD FREEDMAN

Each of the innumerable stages in the making of decisions governing the public housing program provided a "point of access" for a wide array of private and public housing groups. These groups used the abundant opportunities the system offered to influence the outcome significantly.

The extent of this influence was not as great as claimed by some critics. Public policy, after all, is rarely the simple resultant of group pressures. Legislators respond not only to special interests, but also to presidential leadership, party loyalties, other legislators, their own consciences, and the tides of opinion in their constituencies. Nonetheless, in the public housing case there was an extraordinary amount of activity by interest groups. There is no way to calculate precisely the impact of their pressure on the decisions that were made. Yet, it is unlikely that public housing would have suffered such severe punishment had it not been for the sustained and furious attack on the program by national and local organizations.

THE OPPOSITION GROUPS

National Groups

Both nationally and locally, opposition groups included most of the trade associations directly and indirectly engaged in the building, selling, or financing of housing. At the national level, three of these associations carried the major part of the campaign:

The National Association of Real Estate Boards (NAREB) is a trade association of "realtors"—real estate brokers who are accepted into membership on local real estate boards. When the

From Leonard Freedman, *Public Housing: The Politics of Housing*, pp. 58–91. Copyright © 1969 by Holt, Rinehart and Winston, Inc. Reprinted by permission of Holt, Rinehart and Winston, Inc.

Taft-Ellender-Wagner program was enacted in 1949, the association included approximately 44,000 realtors in over 1100 real estate boards in communities encompassing most of the nation's urban areas. By the time the 1965 housing act was law, the membership was approaching 75,000 individuals in nearly 1500 local boards. The association describes itself as "a trade and professional organization, to improve the real estate business, to exchange information, and, incidentally, to seek to protect the commodity in which we deal, which is real property, and to make home ownership and the ownership of property both desirable and secure."[1] The headquarters of NAREB is in Chicago, but the association maintains a Washington office, which houses the Realtors' Washington Committee, the organization's legislative arm. Executive vice-president of the association for thirty-two years until his retirement in 1955 was Herbert U. Nelson, a well-known figure on Capitol Hill for most of those years.

The National Association of Home Builders (NAHB) grew out of one of the specialized institutes of NAREB—the Home Builders Institute—and became an autonomous organization in 1943. In 1949 there were 16,500 member home-building companies, mostly small-scale operations typically constructing about fifteen houses a year.[2] By 1965 membership had grown to 40,000, close to 80 percent of the total number of house builders in the country. During the period of the struggle against public housing, the organization's executive vice-president was Frank W. Cortwright, whose offices were in the impressive Washington headquarters of the association.

The United States Savings and Loan League (USSLL) had close to 3700 members in 1949, including most of the savings and loan associations in every state in the country. The number had reached 5000 by 1965. The primary business of the league is to make long-term loans for the purchase and construction of homes, originally for lower-income groups, but in recent years mainly for those of middle and upper incomes. The league's headquarters is in Chicago, and there is a Washington office. The chairman of the executive committee for many years, Morton Bodfish, lived in Chicago, but he was active and influential in Washington.

These three groups and their leaders—Nelson, Cortwright, and Bodfish—were the major spokesmen for the opposition to public housing in the decisive years after 1949. They were closely backed by other powerful organizations. The United States Chamber of Commerce, with 2600 local chambers in 1949 (2900 in 1965), worked against public housing through its construction division. Then there were the Mortgage Bankers Association of America, the American Bankers Association, the National Apartment Owners Association, the Producers' Council, and a number of specialized associations of building-material manufacturers and subcontractors, including the National Association of Retail Lumber Dealers, the National Association of Lumber Manufacturers, the Associated General Contractors of America, and the Building Products Institute.[3]

Each week in Washington, twenty-three of the private housing organizations met for lunch as the "National Homes Foundation," for which NAREB provided the secretariat. The foundation did not constitute a close-knit general staff, and there were many issues on which the component organizations disagreed fundamentally. But during the period of greatest controversy over public housing, they were united in their dislike of the proposed program. It was, they declared, a threat by government to the well-being and integrity of the private industry that they represented.

Their efforts to counter this threat from the late 1940s through the mid-1950s were brilliantly executed. Most of the private housing groups had able and experienced representatives in Washington, professionals at their craft of lobbying. In their campaigns against public housing, they neglected none of the techniques described in many case studies of pressure-group operations.

Working in the approved tradition, they helped to write speeches for congressmen; provided them with searching questions to fire at administration officials;[4] and drafted bills and amendments, either at the request of a legislator or for submission to any one of several legislators known to agree with their policies.[5] They advised congressmen as to which legislative procedures would best obstruct public housing proposals.[6] They stood ready, as the lobbyist always does, to "give the facts" to congressional committees. While the entertainment they offered members of Congress was rarely on the lavish scale of an earlier and cruder era, they did discuss business with them over lunch and dinner. Sometimes handsomely paid speaking engagements were arranged for friendly legislators, and the private housing leaders sought ways to be of personal service to congressmen and their families.[7]

All of these tactics have been used at one time or another by every effective lobby in Washington. The private housing groups practiced them with at least as much skill as any other congerie of lobbyists. But there was another technique deployed by the housing groups more effectively than by almost anyone else: This was the application of grass-roots pressure from all around the country at strategic times and places in the Washington legislative process. The use of this device is a natural consequence of the fact that most of the power sources of the American national legislature are back home in the states and districts. The private housing organizations were especially well equipped to take advantage of this condition. Savings and loan leagues and units of the NAHB were widely distributed throughout the country and were frequently important forces in their communities. To an even greater extent, the NAREB had its roots in the local situation, for there was a real estate board in almost every sizeable community. It is not surprising that the Buchanan Committee's investigation of lobbying in 1950 should have found that "the National Association of Real Estate Boards . . . has systematized all means of direct contact between its members and legislators more completely than any other group appearing before this committee."[8] Perhaps the American Medical Association has an even greater advantage in this respect, since every member of Congress has his own doctor, and doctors are even more widely distributed (and have much greater prestige) than realtors. Nonetheless, during the struggle over public housing, NAREB developed a machinery for the application of local pressures on the national scene which no other organization could match. . . .

The Communities

As soon as the Taft-Ellender-Wagner Bill was passed, the Washington offices of several of the national housing associations sent appeals to their local units to mount campaigns against the implementation of public housing in the communities. The response in several cities was enthusiastic. Coalitions quickly formed, usually led by organizations affiliated with the national associations. The composition of the alliances varied from place to place (the lumber industry, for example, played a more prominent role in the Northwest than elsewhere), but in most cases the real estate board was very much involved; and often the local chamber of commerce played an active part.

The fact that these groups were related to national organizations was generally helpful to the opposition campaigns. NAHB and the USSLL supplied their members with packages of material providing arguments and techniques for attacking public housing.[9] The national offices also facilitated the flow of suggestions from city to city. The best of the locally prepared materials came from the Seattle Master Builders, who commissioned and made generally available a kit of materials giving a detailed description of their successful campaign, with copies of radio and TV spots, newspaper and billboard ads, and day-by-day news stories.

These processes brought a considerable measure of uniformity to the local campaigns. The same slogans appeared all over the country. Newspapers in various cities carried accounts of identical speeches made on the same day by local organization leaders.[10] Identical editorials on "socialized housing" appeared in Hearst newspapers in four of the cities where public housing was under attack.[11] In addition, staff members from the Washington offices showed up from time to time to lobby before city councils.

These various kinds of national intervention were pointed to by defenders of public housing as proof that the battles in the communities were merely part of a carefully planned and coordinated campaign that was controlled and directed from Washington, the local units of the associations acting without volition of their own. This assessment was not accurate. . . .

A number of community groups with no national affiliations were also involved in the battles against public housing. There were the owners, for example, of small rental properties (many of them dilapidated) which might be pulled down to make way for public housing or whose tenants might move into public housing. Thus, in Los Angeles "the dirty work in the fight was done by . . . the Small Property Owners League . . . which furnished the mass base which the other organizations lacked."[12] But there was an even broader mass base to be found in the associations of property owners who lived and worked in the vicinity of proposed housing projects. In Los Angeles, three such groups, two of them created for this purpose, engaged in a fierce attack on a projected public housing site close to their own neighborhoods.[13] In Chicago, about 200 neighborhood associations provided the bulk of the opposition, supported by the State Street Council, "a powerful group of merchants who were able to act in concert."[14] National leadership in the Chicago case was discounted by Meyerson and Banfield in their study of the controversy there: "Elaborate and ramified as it undoubtedly was, the national real estate lobby and its Chicago affiliates would have little direct influence in the struggle over sites in Chicago. . . . The organizations themselves would stay somewhat aloof from the struggle."[15]

Clearly, even had there been no national opposition to public housing, the program would have had its troubles in some communities. It was an element for change in residential areas; and whenever changes in the "character of the neighborhood" are proposed, the antipathies of local communities tend to be aroused.

Still, if it is necessary to refute the charge that the local campaigns were totally controlled from Washington, it does not follow that the story in the cities would have been much the same had there been no intervention from the national associations. Without that intervention, the local opposition might have been bitter, but it would have been spontaneous and sporadic. While it certainly would have prevented the selection of a number of specific sites, it might not have been sufficient to bring about the total rejection of the program in a number of major cities.

In fact, the combination of local initiative on the one hand and national guidance, encouragement, and coordination on the other, happened to be the most effective possible combination for the conduct of the local campaigns. Without the national involvement, local rejections of individual sites would have had only isolated significance. Without the locally based organizations the intensity and fury of the opposition could never have been provoked. Moreover, the financing of the campaigns was essentially local, for the national organizations did not command the resources to underwrite battles in so many communities. . . .

THE PRO–PUBLIC HOUSING GROUPS

In public policy disputes in America, the organized group pressures are never on one side only. The public housing issue was no exception. The program would never have existed in the first place but for the initiative provided by a combination of labor unions, local housing officials, and various religious, racial, ethnic, and political groups who formed themselves into the National Public Housing Conference. In 1934 the conference issued "A Housing Program for the United States," acclaimed as "the first long-range and carefully considered program to be formulated in the United States."[16] It was this coalition that Senator Wagner relied on to do most of the work of drafting the public housing provisions of the 1937 housing act.

The component units of the coalition had grown considerably by the time they entered into the struggle over the Taft-Ellender-Wagner proposal. By 1949 there were well over 3000 members in the National Association of Housing Officials; by 1965 the organization, now the National Association of Housing and Redevelopment Officials (NAHRO), included 5000 individual members, working for 1000 local agencies. NAHRO's excellent monthly publication, the *Journal of Housing*, contains a great deal of information that has been invaluable over the years to the groups supporting public housing. Organizations of local government officials, such as the National League of Cities and the National Institute of Law Officers, expressed support for the program. Consistently fighting for public housing during its period of greatest duress was the United States Conference of Mayors. Social workers, organizing as the American Association of Social Workers and the National Federation of Settlements, were vocal supporters, too.

Labor was a prime mover in the coalition. Until their merger in 1955, both the AFL and the CIO had housing committees, the AFL's directed by Boris Shishkin since 1935, the CIO's by Leo Goodman. In addition, an assortment of organizations usually numbered among the backers of welfare legislation were included in the pro-public housing coalition. There were church groups, Protestant, Catholic, and Jewish; women's organizations, such as the American Association of University Women and the League of Women Voters; Negro organizations, including the NAACP and the National Urban League; veterans' groups, including the American Legion and the American Veterans of World War II, both of which were at first hostile to the plan but changed their minds in time to support the 1949 act; and various others, including the National Association of Parents and Teachers, the American Council on Human Rights, and the National Association of Consumers.

Providing coordination between the pro-public housing groups was the National Public Housing Conference (later the National Housing Conference), which worked for both the Wagner-Steagall and the Taft-Ellender-Wagner Acts. During the struggles of the 1940s and 1950s, the conference had an able leader in its vice-president, Lee F. Johnson, an experienced Washington hand.

While the housing conference included all the major organizations backing public housing, its membership and leadership were principally representative of officials of local housing authorities.[17] In addition, the Housing Legislative Information Service brought together informally about forty of the national organizations actively involved in the fight for public housing.

In the communities, too, large numbers of individuals and groups rallied to the defense of public housing, organizing themselves in coalitions under such titles as the Citizens League for Better Homes in Portland, the Citizens Housing Committee in Seattle, the Citizens Housing Council in Los Angeles, and the Citizens Committee for Slum Clearance in Miami.

By and large, these local coalitions paralleled closely the combinations of groups supporting the program in Washington. Labor waged a strong fight in Los Angeles, Seattle, and other communities. Usually there was representation from veterans' groups, church, women's, civic, and minority group organizations, and sometimes Democratic clubs. Local housing officials were inevitably participants in the defense of their programs. In most places their involvement could not be overt, and the degree to which they provided behind the scenes leadership varied from place to place. In Los Angeles, however, the Citizens Housing Council was actually nothing more than a "list of prominent names which had no budget or workers," a paper organization through which the city housing authority worked.[18] Other official backing came from the commissioners of the housing authorities, lay people charged with the responsibility of establishing policy for the projects and of representing the programs to the public and the local governmental structure.

It was part of the standard argument of the pro-public housing forces that the techniques used by the opposition, nationally and locally, were essentially undemocratic and manipulative. Yet, none of the tactics utilized by the opposition was neglected in the defense of the program. Lee Johnson and Leo Goodman sent repeated appeals to their constituent units in the NPHC and the CIO for masses of communications from the grass roots. They cultivated their personal contacts with congressmen, and maintained a careful surveillance of legislative developments.

In the cities the public housing forces did all they could to match the opposition's tactics in influencing city-council decisions. Employees of the housing authorities sometimes turned out in force at the hearings.[19] Labor unions encouraged their members to attend, reminding them that public housing meant jobs for unemployed plumbers and other craftsmen. Nor were distortions and oversimplifications limited to the opposition side in the referendum campaigns. In Los Angeles, the brochures and other materials used by public housing's supporters were redolent with half-truths and high-pitched language. In California, officials of the housing authorities who spearheaded the attack on Proposition 10, quickly decided that the truth could not be left to speak for itself, and they hired a leading advertising agency. In Seattle, the Citizens Committee, which conducted the defense of the program, did so without recourse to the skills of the professional publicist but with subsequent regret: "We should have developed a counter slogan," said the secretary of the committee, "or, in the alternative, we should have concentrated much earlier on the 'real estate lobby.' "[20]

PLURALISM?

Any examination of the forces engaged on both sides of a public policy issue must lead to a test of the two rival theories concerning the group process in American politics. On the one hand, it is postulated that, by and large, there is a reasonable balance of interest groups and that no one, or combination, of them dominates the rest.[21] Against this, it has been argued that American politics reflects the fact that ours is essentially a business society, and that organizations representing business interests tend to prevail in the struggle over public policy.[22]

Both sides in this controversy can find evidence for their positions in the public housing case, as will be demonstrated here. In the view of the present writer, however, the group balance theory ultimately provides a less satisfactory interpretation of this case than the opposite thesis.

The Group-Balance Thesis

It is clear that the public housing program was by no means a helpless, motionless prey, waiting to be devoured by marauding private housing interests. Impressive coalitions, representing vast memberships, worked vigorously on behalf of the program, fighting back with all of the methods employed by the opposition. Moreover, the forces aligned on the public housing side did not consist only of private organizations. The federal bureaucracy helped them substantially. During the congressional campaigns on behalf of the Taft-Ellender-Wagner Bill, counsel for the federal housing agencies were made available as advisors to the Senate and House Banking and Currency Committees and "their knowledge of the legal problems involved and their judgments as to desirable courses of action doubtless exercised strong influence on the course of the legislation."[23] And, of course, the White House worked vigorously for the cause from the New Deal period through 1952, and again from 1961. In the local communities, the housing officials were fighting for their own programs, sometimes for their very jobs. Additional help was quietly given in a number of places by the field offices of the federal housing agencies.

Nor was there monolithic unity among private business interests on the public housing question. Nationally, it was true that the major business organizations testified against the program. But this antipathy was not always matched in the communities, especially in the older cities of the East and Midwest, where the major business concerns have often displayed a sense of civic responsibility and a willingness to support programs designed to help low-income people and minority groups.

To a considerable extent, the business hostility to public housing was a regional phenomenon, mostly evidenced in cities of the West and Southwest which were growing at a phenomenal pace.[24] Consequently, they were communities in which the real estate, home building, and home finance interests were flourishing and politically aggressive. . . .

Further support for the group-balance thesis can be found in the final outcome of the public housing controversy. The program still exists and continues to grow. While it was totally rejected in several communities, it was approved in many others. In the biggest local conflicts of all—those in Chicago and Los Angeles—the result was a compromise. The Chicago settlement provided for the construction of 12,500 units. In Los Angeles, almost half of the original program was salvaged. In large measure this happened because, while the opposition gained control of some of the decision points, it was unable to establish its hold on all of them. No sooner had the anti-public housing forces gained control of the mayor's office than their power in the city council slipped away. Of the three vacancies on the council which were in serious contention in the 1953 election, the *Los Angeles Times* endorsement bore fruit in only one, while the other two victors were backed by labor and could be relied on to support the housing authority. The public housing struggle provides yet one more illustration of the lack of a single, concentrated power structure in Los Angeles.

At the national level, both sides continued in their intractability for several years. But slowly a more conciliatory spirit began to emerge. While the private housing groups still told congressional committees that they disliked public housing, after 1954 other aspects of housing legislation commanded more of their attention. Urban renewal, for example, entailed higher stakes and bigger issues for the housing industry. Furthermore, once public housing had been reduced to minor proportions and provided shelter for people displaced by other programs favored by private housing groups, it hardly could continue to be regarded as a major threat to private housing interests. So, the home builders and the savings and loan leagues and most of the other organizations that had been so militant in the early years grew increasingly mellow in their attitude toward public housing. Only NAREB maintained the appearance, at least, of unyielding and total hostility; but even they were devoting much less time to the issue by the end of the 1950s.

By the time of the hearings on the 1965 housing legislation, group opposition to public housing had dwindled still further. The United States Savings and Loan League was now opposed only "to any public housing program beyond the rate of 35,000 units per year."[25] While the National Association of Home Builders continued to argue that private builders could do a better job than the PHA, a NAHB spokesman declared in 1965 that public housing needed "a thorough overhaul of its financing and construction requirements. New and existing projects should be revamped to provide much more effective housing relief for the poor and destitute families in our land."[26] This was hardly the unyielding language of the Taft-Ellender-Wagner days. This was a call for reform, not abolition. The United States Chamber of Commerce continued to invoke its research findings against public housing.[27] Yet, in clarifying comments on his House testimony, a chamber director was anxious to emphasize that his "wasn't a sweeping condemnation . . . at all"; that the program simply "left work undone" which might be better done by other government programs; and that a public housing program comprising, as it did, about 1 percent of the total housing inventory of the nation was no cause for alarm.[28] The National Lumber and Building Material Dealers Association argued against further authorizations, but went on to concede: "We also realize that Congress saw fit to approve this years ago and that the program will undoubtedly continue."[29] NAREB still inveighed against public housing, but its 1965 testimony on the subject was cursory and lacked the old self-confident ring.[30]

Moreover, as the provisions of the 1965 act went into effect, and as they were supplemented by new administrative rulings from the PHA, some of public housing's traditional foes saw new business opportunities for themselves in the program. Home builders, realtors, and apartment owners in several cities began to work closely with the local housing authorities in developing these opportunities. Thus, the opposition's drift, first apparent in the mid-1950s, toward acceptance of a limited public housing program was strongly in evidence by the mid-1960s.

This movement toward a more conciliatory posture was matched on the other side among the proponents of public housing. To some extent, their declining zeal was the product of sheer exhaustion. The battle to establish the program had been debilitating. The effort to keep it alive in the face of years of hostility in Washington and of a series of rejections in the communities was bound to sap the vitality of the movement sooner or later. But along with depleted energies went an emerging disappointment with the program.

Among the most disappointed was Catherine Bauer, whose credentials as a supporter of the program were unimpeachable. She had been one of the key people in the establishment of the original public housing program during the New Deal. She served as the U.S. Housing Authority's director of research and information. She had been deeply involved in the program as a leading member of housing organizations, as a government consultant, and as a writer and teacher. But in 1957 she wrote an article entitled "The Dreary Deadlock of Public Housing." She suggested that the reason the program "drags along in a kind of limbo, continuously controversial, not dead but never more than half alive" was partly the obstructionism of the real estate lobby and "the neuroses that come from chronic fright and insecurity" inflicted on housing officials by the incessant attacks on their program.[31] But there were also, she contended, certain "inner weaknesses" in the program itself that rendered it incapable of ever accomplishing its purposes.

Catherine Bauer's criticisms were echoed by a number of other people who hitherto had been among the most vigorous spokesmen for public housing, including Charles Abrams, one of the great figures of the movement. Like Miss Bauer, Abrams recognized that much of the problem was attributable to the opposition:

> By the time you get through all of this [lobbying for laws, fighting court cases, and pushing to get funds] it is too hard to start things all over again with a program that makes common sense.[32]

Yet, the essential point in Abrams' argument was that, in the light of experience, public housing in its existing form no longer seemed to make common sense.

Many housing officials resented this public airing of dissatisfaction; but privately there was a growing readiness in the housing agencies to recognize the weaknesses identified by the liberal critics.[33] These weaknesses were serious, and they grew worse as time passed. Most important, however, they compelled the emergence of a new empirical spirit among the public housing forces. Ideas that previously had been regarded as anathema (many of them notions first introduced by the opposition groups as substitutes for public housing) were now seriously considered as ways of modifying or supplementing the public housing program. It was this new resiliency that led to the changes in legislation and administration under President Kennedy and to the fresh approaches built into the 1965 act.

This willingness to accept modifications on the public housing side, combined with the granting of recognition to the program by the private housing industry, transformed the climate of relationships between the public and private housing forces. In the past there was little contact between them in Washington. Today, there are matters of mutual concern to discuss, and staff members from the various organizations are known to meet on occasion in a spirit of amicability.

So, in this perspective, the public housing case is an exemplification of pluralism triumphant. At the outset there had been rival alliances which, in the view of one group of scholars, were "evenly balanced."[34] They confronted each other intransigently, with no common ground and with no desire to establish any. But with the passage of time, continued pressures from both sides, changes in Congress and administrations, at last it was made clear that neither side could achieve total victory. Once this was recognized, the way was clear for that process of conciliation, compromise, and—ultimately—consensus which is the special genius of American politics. The result of this process was the 1965 housing act. The provisions of the act were not, of course, completely satisfactory to either of the contending parties. Nonetheless, the legislation gave all of the organized interests some part of their original demands, and the final product was at least tolerable to each of them. Indeed, the 1965 act ought to be seen not merely as a safe midpoint between competing claims. The public housing program under the new legislation was recognized on all sides to be a better, more imaginative and flexible instrument than it had been before. If it was a smaller program than had been provided for in 1949, it had gained in quality what it had lost in quantity. It was a compromise settlement but compromise at its most constructive and most creative.

The Group-Imbalance Thesis

The evidence just presented convincingly refutes allegations that the public housing conflict was completely one-sided and that the enemies of public housing had everything their own way. Yet, it does not necessarily contradict the view that there is a general bias in the American political system in favor of business groups. In fact, it would appear to this author that the public housing case provides more support for the group-imbalance thesis than it does for the group-balance, or pluralist, theory. Though there were strong coalitions on both sides, this does not mean they were evenly matched. If the private housing interests had to accept a compromise, it can still be argued that they got very much the best of the bargain.

First, then, the pro-public housing groups suffered from some important disadvantages. Unquestionably, both nationally and locally they had less money and staff at their disposal than the opposition, although few precise figures are available. Lobbying reports reveal only part of the story. Financial statements of the organizations are not very revealing, for most of the groups engaged in the struggle are not single-purpose organizations, and their statements do not make clear which of the items reported might have some relation to the public housing campaigns. Nonetheless, as the available information is pieced together, it reveals greater expenditures against the program than for it.[35] The difference is not of the proportions claimed by the public housing forces, who used traditional liberal rhetoric in insisting that they were heroic but puny defenders of the public welfare against the ravages of massively staffed and monied special interests. In fact, the funds committed to the attack in Congress on public housing were not unlimited, and the opposition staffs seem to have been remarkably effective in creating the impression of far greater numbers of men than were actually deployed. Just the same, the opposition groups obviously had substantial sums committed to the struggle and did not suffer from the chronic shortage of funds that afflicted the National Housing Conference, which lived in a perpetual state of financial crisis and periodically sent out emergency appeals for money simply to enable it to survive. In the communities, too, the sheer scale of some of the opposition campaigns, especially in the very expensive context of the referendum, was everywhere greater than the efforts to defend the program.[36]

Another factor favoring the opposition was the greater internal cohesion of the various opposition groups. None of them, of course, was single-minded. There is invariably a gap between leaders and many of the followers. It has already been noted that some of the local units of the private housing associations did not follow the lead of their national officers; and within the local organizations there were individuals who either acted against the positions taken by the organizations or did not care very much one way or the other. Still, the private housing groups were relatively homogeneous, and their primary interest was housing. On the public housing side, this could be said only of the housing officials. For social workers and mayors and veterans, housing was but one of many issues they must be concerned with. Furthermore, in the mass-membership organizations declaring their support for the program, the claims of the leadership to speak for their members were often dubious in the extreme. Church social action groups tend to be far more liberal than the general congregation; and in the local battles, clergy and prominent church laymen were often openly hostile to the official stands of their ministerial associations on behalf of public housing. Voting patterns in the local referenda made it obvious that not all members of labor unions agreed with their national leaders on this issue.[37] So, while the list of organizations declaring for public housing was always much longer than the opposition list, both nationally and locally, this was an illusory asset.

To some extent, the support of public housing by the federal and local bureaucracy redressed the balance of forces. Yet even this was not quite as solid a factor as the public housing side would have wished. During the critical years of the 1950s, the housing officials responsible for the program in Washington were so harassed that they could hardly be an effective force for their program. Moreover, after 1953, their top leadership pursued policies which, if not hostile to public housing, were cautious and austere.

In the communities, the officials responsible for the operation of the projects suffered from other liabilities. In the smaller cities, many of the housing officials had come into their jobs without prior public service experience. Some, indeed, came from the private housing industry and lacked a full commitment to the purposes of those who had created the public housing program. In the larger communities, on the other hand, the housing authority tended to be staffed by people with backgrounds in public administration, social work, community planning, law, and engineering. This helped to give them an understanding of the goals of public housing, but it did not always provide them with the political experience that was so necessary when the program was under attack. The problem was especially complicated because the local housing authorities were not part of the regular governmental framework. Partly because of the fear of municipal corruption, partly because most cities were close to or had reached the limits of their borrowing powers, the housing authorities had been established as semiautonomous agencies, financed through their own bond issues. They were not subject to the direct control of the local mayors and councils, although the housing commissioners were appointed by the mayors. This could be useful on occasion; but it meant that the program was denied a natural power base in the community. In some places—Los Angeles, for example —the housing authority staffs refused to be inhibited by the peculiarity of their situation. But in Chicago, as Meyerson and Banfield show, the housing authority's political rootlessness and the emphasis by the staff on professional and technical considerations to the neglect of political factors were damaging to the program's prospects.[38]

Of course, the housing commissioners were supposed to provide the link between the staffs of the housing authorities and the political community. Yet, preponderantly they represented the established local interests. Almost half of the national total of housing commissioners in 1948 came from business, banking, and industry, with a substantial number from the private housing field. Only 15 percent were wage earners or labor officials. A mere

6 percent were public officials and civic leaders.[39] This is not to say that in general the commissioners did not support public housing. Indeed, some worked with dedication in its behalf.[40] Yet, when the heat was on, when an ostensibly nonpolitical program became the focus of intense political controversy, the kind of people appointed to the housing commissions could not always be expected to supply the staunch defense so urgently needed. To enter the lists vigorously on behalf of public housing might not only alienate them from lifelong friends, but might also have continuing adverse political, personal, and professional effects. Thus, confronted with the ferocity of the attacks, many of the housing commissioners were, in fact, intimidated and failed to undertake the necessary counterattack.

Nor does a favorable interpretation necessarily emerge from the fact that the public housing forces managed to prevent the dismantling of the program, and that the struggle actually produced some improvements in the program between 1949 and 1965.

For one thing, the quantitative price that had to be paid was very high. The 1949 program, which was to have been completed in six years, has not been fully carried out in twenty. Second, while the process of group conflict has produced improvements in the program, the fact that this could only be accomplished by such an abrasive and prolonged confrontation does not reflect well on representative government. Conflict is an inevitable concomitant of democratic politics. But it can be questioned whether the conflict need be as harsh and unremitting as it was in this case. . . .

Finally, and most important, the terms of the conflict were biased from the outset against the interests of those who were most affected by the problem—that is to say, the poor themselves, who were the only ones who could qualify as tenants in the projects.

NOTES

1. U.S. Congress, House of Representatives, Select Committee on Lobbying Activities, *Housing Lobby, Hearings Pursuant to H.Res.* 298, 81st Cong., 2d sess., 1950, Exhibit 349, p. 11; hereinafter referred to as: House, *Hearings, Housing Lobby.*
2. House, *Hearings, Housing Lobby*, p. 234.
3. See *Congressional Quarterly Almanac*, V (1949), 286: House, *Hearings, Housing Lobby*, pp. 181–183.

4. House, *Hearings, Housing Lobby*, p. 400, and Exhibit 306, p. 868.
5. U.S. Congress, House of Representatives, Select Committee on Lobbying Activities, *United States Savings and Loan League*, H.R. *Rept.* 3139, Pursuant to H. Res. 298, 81st Cong., 2d sess., 1950, Exhibit 82, p. 92. (Hereinafter referred to as: House, H.R. *Rept. 3139, United States Savings and Loan League.*) This is an interoffice memorandum by Morton Bodfish in which he says: "I wonder if Monroney has seen the lobbying amendments that we developed in connection with Dirksen?"
6. See memorandum "To Harry" [Cain] headed: "Suggested Procedure for Action by the Senate Banking and Currency Committee on *S. 1459* and *H.R. 3492*," from the Realtors' Washington Committee, in House, *Hearings, Housing Lobby*, Exhibit 305-B, pp. 864–865.
7. House, H.R. *Rept. 3139, United States Savings and Loan League*, Exhibit 255, p. 213, and Exhibit 166, p. 150; House, *Hearings, Housing Lobby*, p. 54.
8. U.S. Congress, House of Representatives, *General Interim Report of the House Select Committee on Lobbying Activities*, H.R. *Rept. 3138*, 81st Cong., 2d sess., 1950, p. 24.
9. NAHB prepared a packaged kit called "Home Builders' Information Material to Oppose Socialized Public Housing," which contained a basic manual, various pieces of mimeographed information about the program, accounts of successful opposition campaigns around the country, and reprints of articles and congressional speeches, some made available from the Realtors' Washington Committee, which was also sending out large numbers of reprints. In 1950 the USSLL too, produced a substantial kit containing sample slogans, advertisements, editorials, news stories, speeches, pamphlets, and articles, as well as a detailed manual on "How to Prevent the Spread of Government Housing."
10. On April 1, 1951, the *Cincinnati Enquirer* and the *New Orleans Item* carried identical statements attacking public housing that were attributed to the president of the home builders association in each of those cities. Reprinted in "Home Builders' Information Material to Oppose Socialized Public Housing" kit.
11. "Hearst Papers Use Canned Editorial," *Journal of Housing*, IX, no. 1, (1952), 17.
12. Richard Norman Baisden, "Labor Unions in Los Angeles Politics," unpublished Ph.D. dissertation, Department of Political Science, University of Chicago, 1958, p. 308.
13. See Monterey Woods Improvement Association, *Rose Hills Report* (Los Angeles: Monterey Woods Improvement Association, 1953).
14. Martin Meyerson and Edward C. Banfield, *Politics, Planning, and the Public Interest* (New York: The Free Press, 1955), p. 116.
15. Meyerson and Banfield, *Politics, Planning, and the Public Interest*, p. 117.
16. Timothy L. McDonnell, *The Wagner Housing Act* (Chicago: Loyola University Press, 1957), pp. 80–81.
17. Twenty-three of the fifty-two members of the conference's legislative committee in 1948 to 1949 were public officials. (See House, *Hearings, Housing Lobby*, Exhibit N-2, pp. 1338–1339.)
18. Baisden, "Labor Unions in Los Angeles Politics," p. 369.
19. Monterey Woods Improvement Association, *Rose Hills Report*, p. 9.

20. Kenneth A. MacDonald, "Report on the Seattle Referendum Campaign," Seattle 1950, p. 11 (Mimeographed).

21. See John Fischer, "Unwritten Rules of American Politics," *Harper's Magazine* (November 1948), pp. 27–36; and Earl Latham, "The Group Basis of Politics: Notes for a Theory," *The American Political Science Review*, XLVI, no. 2 (1952), 376–397. See also David B. Truman, *The Governmental Process* (New York: Alfred A. Knopf, 1951).

22. Elmer Eric Schattschneider, *The Semi-Sovereign People* (New York: Holt, Rinehart and Winston, Inc., 1960).

23. Martin Meyerson, Barbara Terrett, and William L. C. Wheaton, *Housing, People, and Cities* (New York: McGraw-Hill, Inc., 1962), p. 277.

24. The trend in the 1950s was for cities to lose population to the surrounding suburban communities. But the big public housing defeats in Los Angeles, Houston, and Seattle (and later, in Dallas and San Antonio) occurred in cities whose populations increased substantially between 1950 and 1960.

25. U.S. Congress, Senate, Banking and Currency Subcommittee, *Housing Legislation of 1964, Hearings on S. 2468*, 88th Cong., 2d sess., 1964, p. 1165; hereinafter referred to as: Senate, *Hearings, Housing Legislation of 1964*.

26. U.S. Congress, House of Representatives, Banking and Currency Subcommittee, *Housing and Urban Development Act of 1965, Hearings on H.R. 5840 and Related Bills*, 89th Cong., 1st sess., 1965, Pt. I, p. 548; hereinafter referred to as: House, *Hearings, Housing and Urban Development Act of 1965*.

27. See *The Impact of Federal Urban Renewal and Public Housing Subsidies* (Washington, D.C.: Construction and Community Development Department, Chamber of Commerce of the United States, 1964).

28. House, *Hearings, Housing and Urban Development Act of 1965*, Pt. 2, pp. 1006–1007.

29. U.S. Congress, Senate, Banking and Currency Subcommittee, *Housing Legislation of 1965, Hearings on S. 1354*, 89th Cong., 1st sess., 1965, p. 518; hereinafter referred to as: Senate, *Hearings, Housing Legislation of 1965*.

30. Senate, *Hearings, Housing Legislation of 1965*, p. 608.

31. *Architectural Forum*, CVI, no. 5 (1957), 140.

32. *The Housing Yearbook, 1952* (Washington, D.C.: The National Housing Conference, 1952), pp. 10–11.

33. The nature of these weaknesses will be developed in the chapters which follow.

34. Meyerson, Terrett, and Wheaton, *Housing, People, and Cities*, p. 278.

35. From 1947 through 1950, $40,000 a year was allocated from the general budget of NAREB to the Realtors' Washington Committee, and an additional $90,000 a year came in from special contributions of $5 a member solicited through the local boards. The lobbying reports reveal that approximately $260,000 was spent in 1949 to influence legislation by NAREB, NAHB, USSLL, the Associated General Contractors of America, the Building Products Institute, the Producers' Council, the National Apartment Owners' Association, and the U.S. Chamber of Commerce. On the other side, the CIO and AFL housing committees and the National Housing Conference registered lobbying expenses of

over $112,000. These figures do not accurately reveal the scale of activity on both sides. On the one hand, all the organizations mentioned had concerns that went beyond public housing. On the other hand, a great deal of effort and money expended by both sides did not go into the records, including activities defined as "education" or "public relations" and the kind of grass-roots involvement, paid for by individuals, which was an especially strong feature of the realtors' campaigns.

36. In Los Angeles, the AFL alone spent $73,000 in the 1952 referendum campaign, mostly from the building trades workers. (See Baisden, "Labor Unions in Los Angeles Politics," p. 369.) But the scale of their opponents' campaign required resources very much larger than this. In Portland it was estimated that the proponents raised $8500, the opposition $15,000. (See Chester Rapkin, "Rent-Income Ratio–Should Formula for Public Housing Be Changed?" *Journal of Housing*, XIV, no. 1 [1957], 8.) The Seattle Citizens' Housing Committee could only raise about $6000. (See MacDonald, "Report on the Seattle Referendum Campaign," p. 3.)

37. Nor did all local unions follow the lead of their national organizations with enthusiasm. Even in Seattle, where labor was a mainstay of the defending alliance, the unions did not contribute much money, and some locals were uninvolved.

38. Meyerson and Banfield, *Politics, Planning, and the Public Interest*, pp. 260–267.

39. *Journal of Housing*, VI, no. 1 (1949), 9.

40. Thus, in New Jersey a pamphlet defending public housing against some proposed hostile legislation carried the note: "This brochure is published by the commissioners of local housing authorities in New Jersey, acting as citizens with a responsibility for answering misrepresentations and distortions" (New Jersey Association of Housing Authorities, *What's Wrong with the Hillery Bill?* [New Jersey Association of Housing Authorities, n.d.]).

THE STRUCTURE OF LAND USE CONTROL

NATIONAL COMMISSION ON URBAN PROBLEMS

Many of the most serious problems facing the Nation's cities are metropolitan in scope. Problems of air and water pollution, transportation, open space, solid waste disposal, housing, and employment do not end at municipal borders. At the same time, land-use controls, which are important factors in the creation and solution of such problems, are lodged in local governments with virtually no supervision by metropolitan or State agencies.

The constituency served by local officials making land-use decisions is quite different from that of the metropolitan area as a whole, whose concerns are affected by those decisions. It is hardly surprising that the interests and desires of one small jursidiction do not always conform to the needs of the larger area of which it is a part. It is understandable, for example, that local officials—and their constituents—may not want a regional waste disposal plant within their own borders. Indeed, many officials would prefer to have as little development as possible of any kind—to keep the community just as it is. The inevitability of regional development may be obvious; but, to local officials and their constituents, it may be equally obvious that much of it should be located somewhere else. Similarly, there may well be a recognition that low- and moderate-income families within the metropolitan area need to be housed somewhere; that they need to be housed within any given jurisdiction in the area is far less readily accepted.

The problem takes on momentous proportions when compounded by the reliance of local governments on the property tax as their major source of revenue. How land within their borders is used becomes not merely a question of esthetic and social sensitivity, it is a matter of governmental solvency. Land-use controls have become a major weapon in the battle for ratables.

From the National Commission on Urban Problems, *Building the American City* (Washington, D.C.: U.S. Government Printing Office, 1969), pp. 211–17.

The game of "fiscal zoning" requires the players—i.e., zoning jurisdictions—to attract uses which add more in property taxes or local sales taxes than they require in expensive public services and to exclude uses which do not pay their own way. In essence, this means that jurisdictions are influenced to seek industrial and commercial uses and luxury housing and discourage or prohibit such uses as housing for low- and moderate-income persons.[1] A further refinement is the desire to exclude housing which attracts families with many children in favor of housing with no children or as few as possible—all this because children require schools, the most significant expenditure item of local governments. Low-income housing is bad from a purely fiscal perspective because it does not add to the tax rolls the same amount of assessed value as luxury housing and because it often brings large families into a community. In addition, the families occupying such housing may require welfare and, it is widely believed, more of other services from the local government than higher income families require.

Of course, there are sometimes important nonfiscal policies behind certain types of exclusionary land-use decisions. "Undesirable" uses such as junkyards are not very attractive. "Undesirable" people—minority groups and the poor—would not "fit in." Indeed, for many suburban dwellers it was just such "undesirable" aspects of the city that drove them out; and for central city dwellers who have managed to find neighborhoods which satisfy them, it may well be the absence of such "undesirables" that keeps them in.

Attracting industry and commerce in competition with neighboring jurisdictions is not new. Many localities have developed it into a fine art, using such magnetic devices as the issuance of municipal bonds to help private companies finance land acquisition and plant construction. The land-use control contribution is overzoning for such uses, which is common practice, or adoption of a permissive policy with respect to requests for rezonings and special exceptions for such uses. The exclusionary side of fiscal zoning takes a variety of forms which are considered below.

LARGE-LOT ZONING

The most widely discussed form of exclusion is large-lot zoning, by which a jurisdiction attempts to limit development in substantial portions of its territory to single-family residences on very large lots. The actual effects of this practice are not easy to isolate.

Many factors determine the price which a particular lot will command in the market. In a weak market, large-lot zoning may make little difference, with a 4-acre tract selling for little more than a 2-acre tract, and both sizes providing sites for shacks. In a strong market, a change from a 4-acre minimum to a 2-acre minimum may not lower the price per lot since potential developers are concerned primarily with the number of units that can be built on a given tract and will bid up the price of the rezoned tract. Comparisons of different properties are difficult. A 2-acre lot may be more valuable than a 4-acre lot because of factors unrelated to size—location, topography, etc. Broad comparisons thus become extremely suspect. Nevertheless, it does appear that land prices per lot do diminish as minimum lot size is reduced, though usually not commensurately with the change in size. That is to say, a half-acre lot will cost less than a 1-acre lot, but will cost more than half the price.

Even where prices per lot do not differ markedly from zone to zone, it does appear that large-lot zoning can have significant effects on the cost of housing. *First*, extensive large-lot zoning in a given area has the effect of substantially reducing the total amount of housing that can be accommodated. If demand for new housing is strong, this restriction of the supply of housing sites will increase residential land costs generally. Moreover, by limiting the amount of land for housing on smaller lots and multi-family units below that which the market demands, the prices for these sites may be increased.

Second, the increase in the total house-and-lot price may be greater than the increase in land price caused by large-lot zoning. Some builders will simply not build the same house on a large lot that they will on a smaller lot, believing that a larger house is necessary. Furthermore, many builders observe a rule of thumb that the price of a lot should be some specified percentage of the total price of house and lot, e.g., 20 percent. If such a rule is strictly observed, a $1,000 increase in lot cost will result in a $5,000 increase in the price of the finished house and lot.

Third, large-lot zoning generally results in added costs for land improvements. Depending on specific requirements in the zoning ordinance regarding lot width, the effect can be to increase significantly the required linear feet of streets, sidewalks, gutters, sewers and water lines.

In some instances the fiscal objectives behind large-lot zoning are quite clear. In St. Louis County, for example, the Parkway

School District has calculated that any home costing less than $26,274 does not pay its own way in educational costs. On this basis, district officials oppose any change in zoning to permit lots of less than a quarter-acre, below which they believe housing costing less than this amount can be built.

But the motives for large-lot zoning are generally not clear-cut. Rather they are a mixture of fiscal and non-fiscal factors. Where a community does not wish to bear the cost of extending water and sewer lines beyond present development, it may limit new development to large lots so that it can be served by septic tanks and wells. Some communities think of large-lot zoning as a means of retarding development or preserving rural character or open space. And, in some instances, it is clearly viewed as a technique for keeping out "incompatible" people—lower-income groups and minorities.

Large-lot zoning is a common and widespread practice in many major metropolitan areas. Data are scarce, however, since few metropolitan planning agencies or other regional groups have attempted to make consolidated area zoning maps or compile data on the total zoning pattern in the area. A Commission survey shows that 25 percent of metropolitan area municipalities of 5,000-plus permit *no* single-family houses on lots of less than one-half acre. Of these same governments, 11 percent have some two-acre zoning; 20 percent have some one-to-two-acre zoning; 33 percent have some one-half-to-one-acre zoning; and more than 50 percent have some one-fourth-to-one-half-acres zoning. . . .

EXCLUSION OF MULTIPLE DWELLINGS

Perhaps an even more important form of exclusionary zoning is the limitation of residential development to single-family houses. Again, motives are undoubtedly mixed. Apartments are viewed by many suburban dwellers as central city structures, having no place in the "pastoral" setting of suburbia. Apartment dwellers are sometimes stereotyped as transients who, not having the permanent ties to the community which homeownership provides, will not be sufficiently concerned about the community or their own residences. But fiscal motives are also present. There is a concern that apartments—especially those which have large units and thereby can accommodate large families—will not pay their way. Where low- or moderate-income units are involved, both fiscal and social concerns increase.

Multifamily housing units generally provide the best opportunities for housing persons of low and moderate incomes. The rental nature of such housing, and the savings produced by spreading land costs over a greater number of units, place such housing within the means of many who could not afford new single-family houses. Furthermore, many of the publicly assisted housing programs are multifamily programs and depend on the existence of zoning for multifamily structures.

Most jurisdictions have some zoning for multifamily structures, and it appears that more suburban zoning jurisdictions are permitting them than in the past. A Commission survey shows that 87 percent of municipalities and New England-type townships of 5,000-plus have at least one district in which multifamily housing can be built. But the figure fails to reveal the way in which such zoning comes about. In many suburban jurisdictions zoning for multifamily housing occurs only through a piecemeal rezoning process. There is at any one time little undeveloped land available for multifamily construction. The price of land zoned for such purposes is thus inflated because of the uncertainty about the total amount of land that may become available. Of the undeveloped land zoned for residential purposes in the New York metropolitan area, for example, 99.2 percent is restricted to single-family dwellings.

MINIMUM HOUSE SIZE REQUIREMENTS

The most blatant, though not most extensive, exclusionary practice takes the form of excluding housing which fails to contain a minimum floor area as set out in the zoning ordinance.[2] Such requirements raise the lower limits of construction costs, and thus can be the most direct and effective exclusionary tool. An extreme application of the technique is found in Bloomington, Minn., an affluent suburb of the Twin Cities. Bloomington imposes a 1,700-square-foot minimum floor area. At a square foot construction cost of $15.82, the average for FHA Section 203 housing in the Minneapolis area in 1966, the smallest house permitted would require $26,894.00 in construction costs alone.

ADMINISTRATIVE PRACTICE

Some of the most effective devices for exclusion are not discoverable from a reading of zoning and subdivision ordinances.

Where rezoning is, in effect, necessary for many projects or where apartment development requires a special exception (as it does in some suburban communities), officials have an opportunity to determine the intentions of each developer with some precision. How many bedrooms will the units in his apartment house contain? What will be the rent levels? To whom does he plan to rent or sell? "Unfavorable" answers in terms of the fiscal and social objectives of such officials do not necessarily mean that permission will be denied outright. They may, however, mean long delays, attempts to impose requirements concerning dedications of land and provision of facilities over and above those which are properly required under the subdivision ordinance, and the like.

One witness heard by the Commission in Philadelphia stated the problem this way:

> Regulations are frequently written so that each apartment developer has to negotiate with the community in order to get in at all. He negotiates either to get a zoning amendment because there is no permitted area zoned for apartments in the community, or he negotiates in order to get a special exception because the zoning ordinance does not permit apartments outright. In both cases the negotiation process is one of trying to bid up the price or cost of the apartment structure in order to limit the number of people who can come in at lower cost.
>
> A subdivision ordinance was used as a club in Abington against a veterans' cooperative which had intended to build about 250 free-standing houses which conformed with the zoning ordinance. This was in the late 1950's. I was a member. . . . It was an outright question of refusing to give the approval, and keeping the matter in the courts until the veterans' group broke up because they couldn't wait for housing.[3]

INSTITUTIONS FOR ENDING METROPOLITAN GOAL DISTORTION

Agencies for resolving the conflicts of regional and local goals do not exist in most metropolitan areas at the present time. The rapid growth of regional planning suggests a recognition by States and metropolitan areas that many problems do not lend themselves to purely local decisions. But the agencies which do such planning rarely have any implementation powers other than persuasion. Popularly elected regional bodies, which might undertake supervision of certain types of local decisions, do not exist; and the States themselves have thus far done little to assume responsibility in this area. The courts, then, are the only existing decision-making institution which might resolve some of these goal conflicts. But such resolution requires policy decisions of a type the judiciary usually declines to make.

Questions of exclusion, as distinguished from more technical planning aspects of the problems of localism, would seem to involve basic constitutional issues of the sort that courts decide. Where public action—land-use control—is used to exclude large numbers of persons from certain areas on the basis of economic status, size of family, or race, fundamental questions arise for a democratic society. Generally, however, the courts have refused to consider such questions in the context of land-use control cases. They continue to view such cases as largely matters of police power vs. private property rights, with no consideration of broader social implications or the rights of the non-parties—those that are excluded.

The reasons for these are complex. *First*, property law is among the most venerable branches of the common law, and traditional notions about how to approach cases involving such rights have shown considerable staying power. *Second*, the nature and importance of these issues has only recently begun to emerge. *Third*, the Supreme Court has refused to hear any zoning case since *Nectow v. City of Cambridge*,[4] decided 40 years ago. Lower courts, lacking the leadership to see these cases in a broader perspective, often refuse to venture forth. *Fourth*, courts are reluctant to consider the motivations of public officials in arriving at particular decisions. This becomes especially important in the case of administrative practices aimed at exclusion. *Fifth*, the factual information needed to show significance of exclusionary practices simply does not exist in most areas, and the cost to a private litigant of obtaining it would prove prohibitive. As noted earlier, most metropolitan areas do not have consolidated zoning maps, showing the cumulative pattern of local zoning ordinances. More important, they do not have housing and site inventories showing the location, cost and types of housing which presently exist in the area and the sites (along with their zoning designations) which exist for future residential development. The litigant who seeks to challenge the zoning of a particular tract as exclusionary may encounter the argument that he has failed to show the absence of land zoned for the kind of development he wants elsewhere in the jurisdiction or the metropolitan area. The result of all these factors is that even some of the most outrageous exclusionary practices go unchecked by any institution outside the local government itself.

Directions

The problems of metropolitan goal distortion can be attacked by dealing with causes or with symptoms. In the long run, there is little doubt that the causes themselves must be faced and eliminated. Such an approach requires the restructuring of local governments within metropolitan areas to make them responsible to a broader cross section of the urban population and to make effective coordination possible. Such units of government must be made fiscally sound, with less reliance on property taxes and with a greater assumption of expenses by the States, regional governments, and the Federal Government. So long as new development means increased fiscal woes, the incentive to exclude will remain.

The treatment of symptoms must begin immediately. Local governments cannot continue to disregard their responsibilities toward the metropolitan area. It is essential that some institution, other than the courts, be established to reconcile local conflicts and to assure that attempts to solve regional problems are not thwarted by the parochialism of individual jurisdictions within a metropolitan area.

NOTES

1. The implications of this for job opportunities are obvious. In Part I [of *Building the American City*] there is a description of the growing disparity between new job locations, and especially blue-collar jobs, and the surplus labor force. Fiscal zoning would appear to contribute significantly to the problem.
2. Such provisions are to be distinguished from minimum floor area requirements in housing codes. Housing codes provisions, applying both to new and existing housing, plainly purport to deal with minimum health and safety requirements and not with maintaining neighborhood character or property values. They are stated in terms of minimum floor area per occupant, and typically they are lower than the minimum requirements in zoning ordinances. The American Public Health Association model housing code, for example, requires that a dwelling unit have a minimum floor space (limited to habitable room areas) of 150 square feet for the first occupant and 100 square feet for each additional occupant.
3. Testimony of Mr. Morton Lustig, *Hearings Before the National Commission on Urban Problems*, Volume 4, p. 343.
4. 277 U.S. 183 (1928).

HOUSING ABANDONMENT IN
THE URBAN CORE

GEORGE STERNLIEB, ROBERT W. BURCHELL,
JAMES W. HUGHES, AND FRANKLIN J. JAMES

Residential abandonment is the final symbol of all the urban ills of our society. Although it may have become an urban common-place, it is little known or understood. The very definition of abandonment is far from precise. It has been defined as a condition in which buildings are vacant of tenants; commonly this is coupled with the virtual disappearance of the owner either *de jure* or *de facto*. But this definition fails to recognize that abandonment appears to be a process, a reflection of a much more deeply-seated and extensive phenomenon—the disinvestment of private capital in core cities (Sternlieb and Burchell, 1973).[1]

An abandoned structure has been perceived as a positive token of housing betterment. Through the filtering-down process, the development of new and better housing has precipitated the successive shifting of families into increasingly better accommodations; the vacant buildings they have left behind are no longer competitive within the market. But the obvious anomaly is that abandonment occurs amidst substantial housing shortages. In a growing number of cities, abandonment has swept away both good housing and substantial shells which are much needed. There is no reason to believe that abandonment will not spread within the areas already experiencing it, or that it will not appear in several other metropolitan areas. The current abandonment process, then, may not be explained simply in terms of the "normal market" forces.

THE UNEVEN FIT OF THE THEORETICAL BASE

The reality of abandonment is challenging the theoretician's capacity to explain the phenomenon or predict its growth. Ana-

Reprinted from the *Journal of the American Institute of Planners* 40 (September 1974): 322–32. By permission.

lysts have brought their entire theoretical arsenal to bear on the subject but the dynamics are elusive. Intrametropolitan job dispersal; shifting transportation facilities; changes in the level and distribution of income and consequent change in housing and neighborhood demand; demographic and racial turnover; local government fiscal systems; housing obsolescence; and numerous other factors are inextricably interrelated.

The urban ecologists Park and Burgess (1925) saw neighborhood change in terms of population *invasions* of a neighborhood by lower-status *racial and ethnic groups* and by *nonresidential uses*. As such groups immigrated into the center of the metropolis and as the central business district (CBD) expanded, the city grew radially from its center, forming a series of concentric zones or annules. Each of the zones, five in total, represents a type of area differentiated in the growth process. The driving force of this concentric zone model is the expansion of the CBD—continual pulses of growth pushing out from the center. The inner rings of the model, already aging and obsolete, are not only invaded by business and industry, but also by newly arriving racial and ethnic groups to the city. The owners of inlying properties were assumed to be only interested in the long-term profits to be made from the expansion of the CBD and the short-term profits obtainable from subdivided residential units.

Thus, external causes of central city instability were seen as occasioned by growth—both of the commercial heart and of new immigrations to the city. While these forces caused decay of neighborhoods, they also created an economic rationale for the continued usage of inlying areas. With the decline of immigration and the decline of the CBD, the inner zones (the processing places for new migrants to the city) lose a portion of their justification for being. With need diminished the ultimate fate of the worst structures is abandonment.

The Sector Theory

Land economist Homer Hoyt (1939) recognized the existence of these forces of neighborhood evolution, but he also gave emphasis to their differential effects on different *sectors* of the metropolis, and to the existence of *pull* as well as *push* forces of change. His sector theory described how high-rent residential neighborhoods move slowly but predictably across the urban landscape, exerting a gravitational pull on the middle-class, leaving behind the structure by which slums are made. Added to the obsolescence and invasion-succession dynamics, a cluster of forces is thus isolated.

The effects of these changes vary according to the type of neighborhood or sectors of different types of housing. The deterioration of low-rent sectors leads to great change. Because the buildings in these sectors are occupied by the poorest unskilled or unemployed persons, collection losses and vacancies are highest. The worst structures are demolished. Unless subsequent waves of poor immigrants enter the city to create a demand, many obsolete structures are removed from the supply.

SUPPLY AND DEMAND APPROACH

Yet despite this early theory, the dynamics of neighborhood evolution continue to be poorly understood. Conventional economic concepts of supply and demand lose much of their defining power at this level. Nevertheless, some researchers have successfully used a *supply-demand* framework to illuminate the abandonment decision of individual landlords (Kain and Ingram, 1972; James, Burchell and Hughes, 1972). In these analyses, *supply* embraces those factors that affect the landlord's expenditures in servicing his property. Some examples of such factors are: 1) "problem tenants," often accused of wearing out housing faster than do normal tenants; problem tenants are usually assumed to be poor and unwilling or unable to recompense landlords sufficiently to allow adequate maintenance; 2) problem neighborhoods, where high rates of crime and vandalism increase both operating and maintenance costs; and 3) the widely disparate kinds of housing stock that prevail in different neighborhoods; this is perhaps the most important example of supply side variation in the cost of providing housing. Although some versions of this third argument are almost indistinguishable from demand factors, on the simplest level it is apparent that maintenance and operating costs differ with structure and unit design, that is to say, older structures typically require greater maintenance outlays.

Demand factors are those that affect the landlord's gross revenues. Examples are neighborhood quality, the level of public services, and the race of neighborhood residents. Some empirical evidence has been developed indicating that the segregation of black households in urban ghettos maintains these often obsolete neighborhoods beyond their normal limits. Another important demand factor is the location of housing within urban areas, especially as it affects accessibility to jobs and various services;

accessibility patterns have been markedly changed as a result of secular decentralization of metropolitan areas (James, Burchell, and Hughes, 1972).

Although this supply-demand approach to the analysis of abandonment offers potentially important insight, it is fundamentally limited by its omission of the factors producing neighborhood change. Such change is largely the result of individual landlord decisions producing further changes. Because this pattern can be quite complex and difficult to predict or understand, some analysts have chosen to make inductive generalizations about neighborhood evolution patterns. For example, the Federal Home Loan Bank Board in 1939 suggested the following simple and useful lifecycle model:

> In its life cycle, the residential area begins with the need of a growing city for additional homes and the consequent development of a new urban community. It then passes through a considerable and often comparatively long period of normal use, marked by reasonable maintenance. It next begins to suffer from advancing age, accelerating obsolescence, and structural neglect. As the process of decay continues, investment and rent values gradually fall; since these values no longer justify proper maintenance, repairs are progressively scaled down or are wholly neglected; one by one individual residential units—and presently the district as a whole—show marked evidence of important deterioration. And finally, the district emerges as a slum area, wherein depreciated property values reflect a tremendous investment loss and physical structures have become unfit for decent human habitation.

STAGE THEORIES

Edgar Hoover and Raymond Vernon offered a more explicit five-stage model of neighborhood evolution in the classic New York Metropolitan Region Study. Five evolutionary stages were hypothesized (Hoover and Vernon, 1959):

Stage 1: transforms undeveloped rural land to residential use. The building boom of the 1920s defined this stage for many northeastern cities—frame multidwelling units responsive to the needs of that era.

Stage 2: comprises a time of apartment construction. Many of the development sites are either patches of open space, bypassed in the first building wave for various reasons, or obtained through the demolition of the oldest single-family homes. This stage is most evident in the inner rings of metropolitan areas.

Stage 3: can occur several years later, and is a period of housing downgrading and conversion. Population and density increase through the crowding of existing structures by the newest immigrants to the region. The growth of young families generates additional strains on an aging infrastructure. This downgrading stage is often associated with the "slum invasions" by segregated ethnic and minority groups.

Stage 4: occurs after the immigrants have settled down. This "thinning out" stage, characteristic of long-established slum areas, is mainly a phenomenon of household size shrinkage as children and boarders move out. Large portions of Newark appear to be at this development stage.

Stage 5: is the renewal stage, where the obsolete areas of housing arriving at Stage 4 are replaced by new multifamily units. Most often this has either been subsidized moderate- or low-income housing, or luxury apartments. In almost every case, this stage is initiated through public intervention.

Hoover and Vernon optimistically assumed that some kind of renewal would follow the neighborhood collapse represented by stages three and four. But they suggested few specifics about the nature and implementation of these new land uses beyond their assumption that public intervention would probably take the form of community renewal programs. The role of private housing abandonment in their scheme is unclear. It has been suggested that so long as public and private demolition programs are adequate, abandonment may act as a sort of piecemeal land clearance program. On a sufficient scale, abandonment might facilitate the private renewal of slum neighborhoods. Moreover, it might supplement existing public renewal programs, and substitute for inadequacies in their scale.

Anthony Downs, in a preliminary report to the U.S. Department of Housing and Urban Development, was one of the few early researchers to acknowledge the stages of neighborhood decline and to recommend the introduction of counteractive measures at various points along the way. His description of neighborhood evolution includes five basic steps along with subsequent variations and repetitions (Public Affairs Counseling, 1973):

1. Racial transition—from white to black.
2. Decline in average income of residents as a result of the "filtering" process.

3. Declining levels of security accompanying increase in number of low-income households.
4. Increasing difficulty with tenants involving rent payment, maintenance of the parcel, and turnover.
5. Inability of landlords to obtain loans through normal mortgage channels.

The remaining steps in the process are essentially repetitions or combinations of 2 through 5 as they interact with each other to produce steadily worsening conditions:

6. Physical deterioration.
7. Declining tenant quality.
8. Psychological abandonment by the landlord.
9. Final tenancy decline and evacuation—the actual physical abandonment of the structure.

Downs regards abandonment as resulting from a dual process that involves both neighborhood and landlord. Decaying *neighborhoods* are unable to attract households with steady incomes and to reduce significantly the level of local insecurity. And the *landlord* contributes to the process through his inability to secure financing, his slackening off of property maintenance, and his worsening relationship with his tenants.

The Newark Data

In our detailed analysis of residential abandonment in Newark, New Jersey, we have attempted to cull existing theory on abandonment and to document the resulting hypotheses empirically. Our approach, which is largely exploratory, employs only a limited model of landlord behavior and housing demand. It is our hope that our research will serve as a guide to more precise hypothesis testing and to the ultimate isolation of early indicators of residential abandonment. . . .

Our most surprising finding was that the parcel's physical condition is relatively unimportant in contributing to the abandonment decision. The size of the parcel, its construction, the extent of commercial occupancy, the prevalence of adjacent nuisances, and its specific location within urban renewal zones are not related to its probability of abandonment. This finding is especially striking because a structure's physical condition has traditionally been considered as vital to the level of housing services it provides, and thus its value.

Only three physical features significantly relate to abandonment probability: the quality of maintenance, the level of neighborhood vacancy, and the condition of neighboring housing units. The quality of maintenance of these structures is in large part determined both by the demand for the housing services and the costs of meeting those demands. It is not in itself an independent variable affecting the abandonment decision. Its significance here undoubtedly reflects the number of structure and neighborhood characteristics impacting both on structure value and the costs of adequate maintenance. This is certainly true of neighborhood housing condition.

The second variable indicative of physical condition and significantly related to abandonment is neighborhood vacancy rate. Again we may have here something more of symptom than cause. Vacancy, like tax delinquency, may well be a way station enroute to ultimate structure loss, considerably after social and economic forces have rendered local neighborhoods no longer viable.[2]

The third significant physical variable—the deterioration of neighborhood housing—is highly correlated with poverty, crime and vandalism, housing crowding, and a number of other pathologies affecting the housing market. As in our first analysis, social events appear to be crucial to the understanding of housing abandonment.

The landlord's abandonment decision appears, then, to hinge upon his relationship with his tenants and the strength of his commitment to his property. Landlord dissatisfaction with tenants bears a particularly important relationship to abandonment, those who consider their tenants to be serious problems are much more likely to abandon. Landlords told interviewers of case after case of tenant vandalism and destruction. Although some of their complaints appeared well-founded, in other cases their unhappiness seemed to mirror their own social and racial prejudice.

RACE AND ABANDONMENT

The significance of landlord-tenant conflict is highlighted by the relationship of race and abandonment. Structures inhabited by black and Puerto Rican tenants were much more likely to be abandoned than those inhabited by whites alone; furthermore, white landlords (in most cases the popularized "slumlord") were more likely to abandon than were black, minority landlords. It appears, then, that the interaction of white landlords with nonwhite tenants may significantly affect the decision to abandon.

Undoubtedly, racial tensions are translated into both tenant vandalism and the erosion of the landlord's commitment to his property and to his abdication of responsibility. In many cases, landlords reported that they were afraid to visit their own structures. When fear and prejudice pervade the relationship between landlord and tenant, effective management is impossible.

MANAGEMENT AS A VARIABLE

The management techniques themselves are strongly related to abandonment. The probability of structure abandonment apparently increases with institutional ownership (variable 16); ownership by a large-scale landlord (variable 17); the owner's use of professional managers or rent collectors (variable 22); and absentee ownership (variable 21). All these techniques imply management at arms length; they remove the landlord from personal involvement in decisions about tenant choice, eviction, repairs, and frequently even rent collection. Because hired managers, superintendents, and rent collectors have less at stake than the owner, they tend to be less rigorous in fulfilling their duties.

Despite the welcome demise of the large-scale slumlord, it has been generally agreed that large-scale ownership offers distinct competitive advantages. For example, it provides economies in maintenance expense, by allowing for the hiring of plumbers, electricians, and so forth, on a reasonably continuous basis. It facilitates access to both internal and external financing, and the exploitation of tax shelters.

The disadvantages of large-scale ownership—lack of personal supervision and servicing, ineffective screening and control of tenants—can be irreversible, and in the case of the Newark housing market, apparently lethal.

The decision to manage his property from a distance may result from a landlord's justifiable fear for his health and safety. The crime and violence rampant in some neighborhoods often create dangerous situations for rent collectors, for instance. But landlord withdrawal is not an independent variable because it usually results from the demands imposed by an already deteriorating or pernicious situation.

MORTGAGE STATUS

The presence of a mortgage binding the landlord to the structure (variable 13) significantly *reduces* the probability of abandonment. This finding contradicts the traditionally held notion that abandoned structures are usually those with top-heavy financing. We found that in most instances of abandonment, the parcel was owned free and clear; those that were heavily mortgaged appeared to have secured their indentures *after* the decision to abandon had been made. This is suggested by the fact that many structures later to be abandoned were sold for only purchase money mortgages; no cash actually changed hands. If there is a later public taking of the parcel, the holder of these mortgages may be able to cash them in. If not, he can claim a bad debt loss.

Both these scenarios suggest that abandonment and mortgages should be directly related. That they bear an inverse relationship to one another may be attributable to the impact of "red-lining" by banks and other financial institutions. Abandoned structures with no mortgages may be structures for which mortgages were unavailable from lending institutions. Lending institutions in Newark, rapidly withdrawing financing from all but a few stable ethnic neighborhoods on the city's fringe, issue virtually no credit to city properties, except through some purchases at sub-par prices of insured mortgages (Sternlieb and Burchell, 1973). This withdrawal appears to have significantly increased housing abandonment in Newark.

In summary, then, abandonment is affected by a combination of neighborhood degradation, absentee ownership, racial antagonism, tenant vandalism, landlord abdication, and credit shortages.

CONCLUSIONS

Residential abandonment appears to be more a function of owner-tenant interplay and neighborhood change than of the physical characteristics of the building itself.

Where the landlord sees tenant behavior as obstructive to his operation, there exists a potentially volatile abandonment situation. Abandonment may be imminent if the situation is exacerbated by racial differences generating mistrust or noncooperation.

Locational factors suggest that abandonment is a function of poor areas, principally black and Puerto Rican. Yet, this finding, based on a one-shot appraisal in 1960, may be too outdated or too limited to afford an adequate explanation.

Residential abandonment appears not only to be a function of poor areas but also of changes occurring within these areas. The last remnants of European ethnic neighborhoods seem to resist abandonment. On the other hand, black penetration into neighborhoods seems to increase housing abandonment.

Black home ownership appears to promise stability for inner-city neighborhoods. The trend in Newark toward resident, minority ownership provided a brief ray of hope for the city. However, our subsequent interviews with these new owners tended to diminish the mood of optimism even though they were indeed providing better maintained structures than equivalent nonresident owners. Many minority owners, expressing doubts about their properties' future, cited the weakness of financing mechanisms and the decline in the municipal services, such as schools, sanitation, and the like.

Are the various stage/sector theories helpful in attempting to explain abandonment within this associational arena? The answer must be yes. Abandonment is largely a Park/Burgess inner ring phenomenon impacted by the push-pull forces detailed by Hoyt. The resulting obsolescent neighborhoods appear as Stage 4 in Vernon and Hoover's urban evolutionary process.

Yet, viability of these neighborhoods may have been preserved and their dysfunctional end state halted were it not for a variety of social factors. The fear of reduced public safety, the decline of public services, the emergence of a dominant new core population, and the change of the city's pace from vibrance to mere sustenance all impact upon an owner's decision to abandon.

This study has only attempted to deal with a narrow aspect of the abandonment process—its findings are neither startling nor revolutionary. Much more research needs to be performed in this area. Probably the most important thrust for future endeavors is the abandonment contagion phenomenon. Does the abandonment of one structure lead to a similar disposition of others? To date this frontier is virtually unresearched.

We have paid a high price for our overoptimism about the central city's future. Public policy directed toward merely cosmetic once-over-lightly efforts has failed to restore the city to its earlier preeminence.

The precursors of abandonment which have been isolated here are at work in most of the older industrial cities of the Northeast and Midwest. A glance at the 1970 Census indicates the prevalence of the advance indicators which were at work ten years earlier in the Newark experience.

Notes

1. A report recently completed for the U.S. Department of Housing and Urban Development summarizes the literature as a prelude to discussing the various stages of neighborhood evolution. These stages correspond almost exactly with Hoover and Vernon's except for the last stage. In this report abandonment is recognized as a legitimate end for urban core realty (Public Affairs Counseling, 1973).

2. The definition of abandoned structures does not include vacant structures as defined by the U.S. Census. A vacant structure, according to Census definition, is one which is unoccupied at the time of survey but physically *capable* of being occupied. According to this study's definition, an abandoned structure, if still standing, usually *cannot* be occupied due to structural deficiencies and/or housing services and the absence of interior fixturing. The reciprocal of occupancy, that is, vacancy, is thus *not* a surrogate for abandonment although the two may frequently occur in similar neighborhoods.

THE REDLINING ROUTE
TO URBAN DECAY

JAMES VITARELLO

To buy a house, you have to have credit. That's well known; even the very rich take out mortgages to pay for their homes.

But what if you're a black family of moderate means trying to buy a home in an older inner-city neighborhood that is becoming, or has already become, largely black? Chances are you'll have trouble getting a mortgage from many savings and loan associations or commercial banks.

The reason is in many cases "redlining," a form of discrimination that has existed for many years but is just recently receiving widespread attention.

Community organizations in cities around the country have documented the practice of redlining in their neighborhoods. Redlining exists when lending institutions, in effect, draw a "red line" around a particular geographic area, and impose artificial restrictions on the flow of housing loans to that area. The individual seeking a loan may have a good credit rating and the house the person seeks to buy may be in good condition, but still no loan is granted. The only thing that seems to distinguish neighborhoods that are the victims of redlining is that in such neighborhoods, minorities have started to move in, or there is the potential that they will.

The early stages of redlining are subtle: Higher down payments on mortgages are required, loans have higher interest rates, the loan must be paid back in a shorter time, older houses are excluded altogether. In the more advanced stages of redlining, loans are openly refused or an institution claims it has no money to lend.

As a result, homeowners are forced to borrow from mortgage banking firms which obtain their funds from out-of-town insurance companies or pension funds. These loans are usually insured by the Federal Housing Administration or the Veterans Administration. A lender who makes a large number of these 100 percent insured mortgages is less likely to remain concerned with the development of a neighborhood. Such lenders know that the federal government will pay off the balance of the mortgage in the event of default.

FHA loans also tend to attract real estate speculators and absentee landlords who are better prepared to cut through government red tape and regulations and to make the down payments, which are lower than those required for nonguaranteed loans. A housing market limited to noninstitutional financing will have to choose from fewer sources of funds on more difficult terms.

As some housing deteriorates, the remainder of the neighborhood soon follows in a self-perpetuating cycle of decay. Lack of concern on the part of absentee owners and speculators, coupled with the scarcity of home improvement loans and conventional mortgages, results in poor maintenance and eventually leads to slum conditions and abandoned housing.

As conditions worsen, insurance becomes difficult or too costly to obtain. Neighborhood businesses, already pressed by a lack of credit, begin to leave, taking essential services and important sources of cash flow out of the area.

Those who can move elsewhere do so. However, low or middle-income families who live in redlined neighborhoods have trouble getting out or improving their property. They cannot obtain loans to purchase homes in neighborhoods where the price of property is within their budget, and they cannot get money to renovate their existing property. They must remain static while their property values decrease and years of accumulated savings are devalued.

Declining property values undermine the tax base of the neighborhood, causing the city to lose revenue in redlined areas. At the same time, the city must provide greater public service in the form of public housing, urban renewal, and welfare and social services. The city must also deal with all the problems of crime, drug use and disease that are associated with poor living conditions. In the meantime, the tax rate for the city as a whole rises to compensate for the loss of revenue.

Savings and loan associations (S&L) have dominated the home finance market since the end of World War II.

This domination of the mortgage market by S&Ls is not a coincidence. The Federal Home Loan Bank (FHLB) Board, created by Congress in 1932, was intended to ensure the financial soundness and continuity of "local mutual thrift" associations designed to provide financing to individual home buyers. The FHLB Board has effectively protected the savings and loan associations from many of the risks of the financial marketplace through a variety of financial assistance activities such as deposit insurance, direct loans (advances) from the FHL Bank, and the purchase of first mortgages from savings and loans. The Board, however, has failed to exercise the same degree of diligence in protecting the public interest.

Studies in Washington, D.C., Oakland, St. Louis, Philadelphia, Chicago, and the Bronx, N.Y., show that savings and loans associations are no longer serving as a "pool" of local funds to provide loans to local residents on an equitable basis.

In Washington, for example, the D.C. Public Interest Research Group found that of all real estate loans made by S&Ls with offices in the city between 1972 and 1974, only 7.4 percent went to people in the city likely to be buying single-family houses, i.e., loans of less than $100,000 for non-condominium property. In fact, only 11.6 percent of real estate loans went for any property in the city.

This shift away from local lending has occurred because the FHLB Board allows S&Ls to lend anywhere within the state where they are located and permits them to lend up to 15 percent of their funds outside the state. In the District of Columbia, savings and loans may lend up to 100 miles away from their central office.

The original intent of the FHLB System, to provide money for home finance, has been further subverted as S&Ls make large individual loans for commercial development. For example, DC PIRG found more than 30 loans totalling more than $34 million had been made for mortgages of $250,000 or more between 1972 and 1974. One of the loans was for $6.5 million! This is not home finance.

Poor as its record is in carrying out its original congressional mandate, the FHLB Board has been even less effective in enforcing Section 805 of the 1968 Civil Rights Act, which prohibits lenders of real estate loans from discriminating by either denying the loan or fixing the amount, interest rate, duration or other terms of the loan.

Although the board has done little to enforce the Civil Rights Act, it does have a stated policy which, if implemented, could have considerable effect. In December 1973 it issued a regulation which stated: "Refusal to lend in a particular area solely because of the age of the homes or the income level in a neighborhood may be discriminatory in effect since minority group persons are more likely to purchase used housing and to live in low-income neighborhoods."

In March 1974, the board's general counsel interpreted this to mean that "redlining that is discriminatory in effect . . . is unlawful." He said that to justify such a practice, a lender would have to show "some reasonable genuine business purpose for redlining," not just "an unsubstantiated belief that no profitable loans could be made in a given area." The burden of proof is now on the lender—it is time to hold S&Ls and other lenders to these ground rules.

It is becoming increasingly apparent to many community organizations across the country that their neighborhoods are the victims of redlining. Since the early 1970s, several community groups have moved beyond filing individual complaints of home finance discrimination, and have attempted to document the existence of redlining in their cities.

Organizations such as DC PIRG in Washington, D.C., the Metropolitan Area Housing Alliance (MAHA) in Chicago and the Westside Action Coalition in Milwaukee have inspected thousands of pages of recorded mortgages to determine the lending patterns of local financial institutions. This is a time-consuming and difficult process and the information obtained does not include such crucial facts as how many people applied for loans, how many were turned down, and why.

Community groups have been pressing Congress to act on a mandatory disclosure law for all federally insured lending institutions. Last May the Senate Banking and Urban Affairs Committee approved a bill titled the Mortgage Disclosure Act of 1975 (S. 1281), introduced by Chairman William Proxmire (D-Wis.). If enacted, the bill would require all federally insured lenders to disclose all residential mortgage loans by census tract and make it publicly available at all branch offices of each lending institution.

The House Banking and Currency Committee has held one day of hearings on an even tougher disclosure bill, but has yet to approve the measure.

Other efforts to combat redlining have been made on the state and local levels. Several community organizations across the country have led "greenlining" campaigns to pressure lenders into disclosing vital information and making sizeable commitments toward neighborhood investment.

The greenlining tactic involves collecting pledges from individuals and institutions to deposit their savings only in those institutions which agree to put money back into city neighborhoods. The Chicago campaign alone received more than $100 million in pledges, and five local lenders signed "greenlining" agreements committing them to make substantial loans in specific Chicago neighborhoods.

Political pressure on local and state governments has also proved to be a successful weapon against redlining. The Chicago City Council required all banks and savings and loans bidding for deposits of city funds to sign anti-redlining pledges and to disclose all consumer, commercial and housing loans by zip code (by census tract in future years). The Illinois legislature is considering legislation that would permit applicants victimized by redlining to seek damages, court costs and attorney fees.

The city council of the District of Columbia is studying a city depository and tax incentive measure. In addition to requiring disclosure similar to that required by the Chicago ordinance, the proposed system would award "points" or credits for loans which help meet major policy objectives, such as increased home ownership and small business development in certain neighborhoods in the city. A lender who builds up points by making home loans in such neighborhoods would be eligible for more deposits of city funds and would enjoy a lower city tax rate.

The Politics of Transportation

The coordination of transportation objectives with other goals desired by groups living in the metropolis is the major transportation-policy issue. Historically, most transportation decisions, especially those involving road construction, have been based exclusively on projected consumer demand for a particular facility, and the impact of these decisions on other sought-after goals has not been taken into account.

Yet, transportation judgments do have numerous by-products. Most importantly, they play a prominent role in shaping the development of the metropolitan area. Transportation decisions vitally influence the way land will be put to use. A metropolis that emphasizes the use of roads is promoting the dispersal of its population, thereby encouraging a suburban pattern of living. The promotion of mass-transit facilities permits a more concentrated use of land, thereby aiding the development of the central city and its central business district. Recent conflicts have also highlighted the impact of transportation decisions on other seemingly unrelated goals. For example, groups have objected to the construction of roads and mass-transit facilities because these projects imperiled homes, neighborhoods, and historic quarters and threatened to destroy open land used for recreational purposes or to blight aesthetically pleasing landscapes.

Prior to World War II, most important transportation decisions involved mass transit. The subway, elevated train, commuter rail line, streetcar, and bus were the common means of movement. Use of the automobile, particularly for getting to work, was fairly limited. The tremendous growth of suburbia was yet to take place. There was no federal financial aid nor, in most states, state funding for the construction of city streets and highways.

The post-World War II era (1945–60) witnessed the emergence of the automobile as the dominant mode of transportation in urban areas. It is estimated that, in most cities during this fifteen-year period, half of those who had previously used public transit facilities to get to work switched to the car. Present national estimates (which include nonurban areas) are that 80 percent of all work trips are made by car. Moreover, travel during nonrush hours is overwhelmingly by automobile. The link between automobile usage and suburbanization is illustrated by the fact that over 95 percent of all work trips in suburbia involve the car.

The effect on mass transit of this loss of patronage has been financial deficits and deteriorating service. While the number of passengers has severely declined, expenses have risen because of inflation, higher labor costs, and government requirements that service be provided for the few customers during nonrush hours. As a result, most cities have had to establish public-transit authorities to "bail out" private operators. Commuter rail lines, undergoing similar financial difficulties, have obtained state subsidies and cut costs by reducing and discontinuing service. The financial straits of mass-transit companies have forced them to continue to use obsolete equipment that has made their rides more uncomfortable and dangerous, further discouraging potential users.

While these changes in transportation use were occurring, decisions determining the financing, construction, and operation of all forms of transportation were taking place in an uncoordinated fashion. According to Lupo, Colcord, and Fowler's study of transportation decision-making, there were separate decisional arenas around highways, commuter railroads, and local mass transit. The resulting functional fragmentation within our metropolitan transportation systems helped road interests promote their claims in this policy area.

Highway decisions involved participants on the federal, state, and local levels. The federal Bureau of Public Roads administered the interstate highway system. Under the provisions of the Federal Aid Highway Act of 1956, these roads were 90 percent federally financed, with 25 percent of the total funds to be spent in urban areas. The Bureau of Public Roads was also responsible for state highways systems for which the federal government provided a 50 percent matching grant. Both programs were financed by payments by highway users, such as tolls and excise taxes on gasoline. State highway departments, which typically were autonomous of elected officials, played the major role in planning the routes of these highways.[1] The localities were usually represented by their public works, traffic, or streets department.

All of these agencies shared common values and a common

frame of reference in making decisions concerning the use of the roads. They were automobile-oriented in their approach. If they perceived a demand for their product (roads), and if the potential consumers were willing to pay for the product (through various user charges), then they promoted its construction and usage. They did not take into account the impact of building the road upon any other desired values.[2] During this post–World War II era, most decisions concerning urban roadways were made within this closed system.

The arena for decisions on mass transit resembled the political system involving the highways, although it encompassed a somewhat wider range of participants. Transit facilities within cities increasingly came under the control of public authorities during the 1950s. Although these transit authorities, like other special districts of the same genre, were relatively independent of control from elected officials, the growing need for public subsidies enabled local governmental officials to exercise some influence on transit policy. Decisions concerning commuter lines were generally made by the private operator and the state public service or utility commission (which had to approve all reduction in service). Only New York State provided financial aid to commuter lines.

The outlook of these transit authorities and the commuter rail lines was also primarily consumer-oriented. They, like the highway department, made judgments on transit service based on projected use of facilities and estimated revenue. As a result, no attempt was made to coordinate the decisions of the highway and mass-transit policy-making agencies. While the consequences of decisions made by highway and mass-transit interests affected each other (for example, increased use of the roads worsened the financial outlook for mass-transit facilities), there were few, if any, instances where the different transportation interests made their decisions jointly.

It was not until the 1960s that groups unfavorably affected by this mode of transportation decision-making were able to bring about some changes. As the interstate highway system entered urban areas, opposition developed to the plans drawn up by the highway and road interests. Most of the opposition came from groups located in the central city, such as the downtown business community, residents of neighborhoods affected by the proposed plans, and professional groups concerned with the quality of life within the city. These groups succeeded, in 1962, in amending the Federal Aid Highway Act to require that the federal government not fund highway programs that had not been coordinated with mass-transit plans and that had not evaluated all aspects of their impact upon urban areas. This amendment, however, did not begin to be seriously implemented until the latter part of the decade.[3] Since that date, federal aid, at times, has been withheld when highway agencies have not given due consideration to such values as maintaining stable neighborhoods, preserving recreational areas, and conserving historical districts.

Since the mid-1960s, there have been a series of actions in the direction of a more "balanced" transportation system. In 1964 and 1970, federal legislation was enacted authorizing expenditures for capital improvements for the financially ailing urban mass-transit systems. In 1973, Congress authorized the use of some of the monies in the Highway Trust Fund (the large sums of money raised by user charges for the interstate system) for mass transportation purposes. For the first time, the Urban Mass Transportation Act of 1974 authorized the use of federal monies for the operating expenses of public transit carriers. Administratively, the establishment of the Department of Transportation (DOT) was a step in the direction of promoting greater coordination among transportation interests. The bureau responsible for the federal highway program (the Bureau of Public Roads) was removed from the Department of Commerce and placed under the Federal Highway Administration in DOT, and the Urban Mass Transportation Administration was transferred to DOT from the Department of Housing and Urban Development. DOT has used its authority over the various modes of transit to promote greater equality of treatment.

Despite these recent trends toward greater coordination in this policy area, urban transportation systems are, and will remain, unbalanced. For the past thirty years, the highways have been built while mass-transit facilities have languished. From 1947 through 1970, the federal government spent $58 billion for highways and less than $1 billion on mass transit. Looking at transportation expenditures by all levels of government, over 80 percent of the $25 billion spent in 1970 was for roads and streets. The highway coalition—composed of, among others, the automobile, oil, rubber, construction, asphalt, and limestone industries; car dealers and renters; bus lines; trucking concerns; and motel owners—has dominated this policy arena. Moreover, the construction of roads has created a whole new set of interests in suburbia—gas-station owners, store owners located in suburban shopping centers, homeowners, and land developers—who have major stakes in the continued and expanded use of the road. The growing forces for change—central-city interests and environmentalists—may achieve some incremental gains, but these groups cannot be expected to, exert the influence necessary to redress the imbalances that have already developed from the heavily road-oriented policies of the past.

These past policies have many defenders who have generally argued that they reflect the preferences of most Americans for the automobile as their desired mode of transportation. However, when public expenditures (at the federal level) have been nearly sixty times greater for road-building than mass transit and when private investment in mass-transit facilities has been almost nil, has the American consumer been confronted with a *real* choice between these two modes of transportation? Matthew Edel's essay below addresses this question. He argues that the consumer has not been confronted with a real choice between the car and mass transit. The dispersion of the population of our cities has made it nearly impossible to establish and maintain public transit systems on any significant scale. The few new systems, such as San Francisco's BART and Washington D.C.'s METRO, that seek to connect the core city and the surrounding suburbs, have incurred, or are projected to incur, large financial deficits. Without concentrated settlement patterns, public transportation cannot meet user needs for time-saving work trips and personalized transport for nonwork trips. Since land-development goals were never coordinated with transportation decisions, the consequence is the modern metropolis, with the inextricable linkage between suburbanization and the utilization of the automobile.

NOTES

1. Robert Friedman, "State Politics and Highways," in Herbert Jacob and Kenneth Vines (eds.), *Politics in the American States* (Boston: Little, Brown, 1965), pp. 411–18.
2. Wilfred Owen, *The Metropolitan Transportation Problem* (Garden City, N.Y.: Doubleday, 1966), ch. 8.
3. Thomas A. Morehouse, "The 1962 Highway Act: A Study in Artful Interpretation," *Journal of the American Institute of Planners* (May, 1969), pp. 160–68.

BIBLIOGRAPHY

COLCORD, FRANK C., JR. "Decision-Making and Transportation Policy: A Comparative Analysis." *The Southwestern Social Science Quarterly* XLVIII (December, 1967), pp. 383–97.

Doig, Jameson W. *Metropolitan Transportation Politics in the New York Region*. New York: Columbia University Press, 1966.

Friedman, Robert S. "State Politics and Highways." In *Politics in the American States*, edited by Herbert Jacob and Kenneth Vines. Boston: Little, Brown, 1965.

Lupo, Alan, *et al. Rites of Way: The Politics of Transportation in Boston and the U.S. City*. Boston: Little, Brown, 1971.

Morehouse, Thomas A. "The 1962 Highway Act: A Study in Artful Interpretation." *Journal of the American Institute of Planners* (May, 1969), pp. 160–68.

Owen, Wilfred. *The Accessible City*, Washington, D.C.: Brookings Institution, 1972.

————. *The Metropolitan Transportation Problem*. Garden City, N.Y.: Doubleday, 1966.

Shannon, William V. "The Untrustworthy Highway Fund." *New York Times Magazine* (October 15, 1972), p. 31.

Smerk, George M. *Urban Transportation: The Federal Role*, Bloomington, Ind.: Indiana University Press, 1965.

TRANSPORTATION DECISIONMAKING
IN U.S. URBAN AREAS

ALAN LUPO, FRANK COLCORD,
AND EDMUND P. FOWLER

The story of Boston's problems with transportation planning dramatically illustrates several points. The first is that the planning and construction of transportation facilities are far more than an engineer's technical problems: it presents important political decisions that affect, directly and indirectly, the lives of millions of people, both users and persons impacted upon by the construction. In fact, those impacted upon by construction are often far more deeply influenced than the users. All decisions must be approved, or at least accepted, by political leaders. Almost all major transportation decisions are the direct responsibility of government, although a few still remain the prerogative of privately owned firms, such as railroads, business, and airlines.

The second key point is that although transportation decisions are unquestionably political, there is strong doubt that the political process has been working well to make them. A perfectly functioning democratic system should be open to the inputs of all significant groups and individuals in the affected communities; it should provide for open debate of all policy alternatives and reach decisions in an open and credible manner, so that those who "lose" know why and know that their views have been heard as well as considered. And, in such a perfect democracy, those responsible for making decisions should be obliged to confront their constituencies from time to time through the election process.

Transportation is not alone in failing to live up to these high ideals—our system, like all others, is imperfect—but this policy area is peculiarly vulnerable to the charge of consistently giving certain groups greater opportunity than others to influence decisionmaking. . . .

From Alan Lupo, Frank Colcord, and Edmund P. Fowler, *Rites of Way: The Politics of Transportation*, pp. 171–87. Reprinted by permission of Little, Brown and Co. Copyright © 1971 by Little, Brown and Company (Inc.).

Most of the material comes from over five hundred interviews conducted in seven metropolitan areas as well as from secondary sources relating to these cities and others. Besides Boston, the cities are Baltimore, St. Louis, Kansas City, Houston, San Francisco, and Seattle. Additional information from Los Angeles, America's automobile city par excellence, was introduced from a separate research project. These eight cities represent a sample of over one-third of the twenty-one independent urban areas of the United States with a population over the one million mark. The one million cut-off point, although quite arbitrary, was selected because cities with smaller populations are not likely to be seriously considering rapid transit, a matter that generates ample controversy, as an alternative to freeways. . . .

To understand the policies and programs relating to urban transportation in the United States, it is necessary to know how decisions are made. This extraordinarily complex process involves all levels of government and many private institutions as well.

Urban transportation, by definition, refers to movement within the metropolitan area, not between major urban centers. It includes automobiles, trucks, taxis, buses, streetcars, subways, rapid transit lines, and commuter railroads, as well as ferry boats, hydrofoils, monorails, helicopters, and other more modern devices. Of the major kinds, buses, streetcars, and rapid transit lines (for example, subways) are all encompassed by the term "transit"; "rapid transit" is a more restricted term, meaning public transit with its own right-of-way.* While typically it is on rails (below, on, or above ground), rapid transit could include buses on exclusive highway lanes, a much talked of but still rare phenomenon, and even "air-cushion vehicles."[1] All forms of transit, plus the commuter railroads, fall within the general term "public transportation," as opposed to "private transportation," which refers primarily to the automobile.

In the United States, only six cities currently have any significant form of public transportation besides buses. New York, Chicago, Philadelphia, and Boston all have rapid transit and commuter railroads. Cleveland has rapid transit, and San Francisco

---

* "Transit" is defined as a system of urban public transportation (either publicly or privately owned) for passengers; however, the term does not ordinarily apply to commuter railroads. The distinction is arbitrary, but this is the common usage. The basis of the distinction is in the type of car used and in the closeness of stations: train cars are typically larger and more comfortable than subway cars, and subway stations are typically closer together than train stations.

has one commuter rail line in operation. And although the first four have fairly complete rail systems, even these leave many outlying communities unserved. Both Washington, D.C., and San Francisco have approved and are now building rapid transit systems.

Deteriorating service, steadily dropping patronage, and fiscal crisis have been the near universals of public transportation since World War II. Transit now primarily serves the ever decreasing percentage of the total number of commuters who travel during rush hour to and from the core city. Otherwise, during the rest of the day and on the weekends the systems are severely underutilized but must operate to serve the few who need them. With few exceptions, the larger U.S. urban areas are now served by public transit authorities, which had to be established to "bail out" the private carriers. As of 1967, fifteen of the principal transit organizations in the twenty-one metropolitan areas of over one million were publicly owned. The responsibilities of these agencies, their organizational structures, and sources of political control vary considerably. Some, like those in Boston and St. Louis, have regional jurisdictions, full operating responsibilities, and are basically state agencies run by a board appointed by the governors. In New York City, Chicago, and Los Angeles, they are subregional. Some are directed by locally appointed officials, as in Seattle, or are county agencies, as in Pittsburgh. A few public transit agencies have only planning and regulating but not operating duties, as in Baltimore and Seattle.[2]

With a few exceptions, these organizational differences are not very significant. Regardless of whether transit is run by a state, region, or city, costs ordinarily are the responsibility of the local community. Only three states—New York, Pennsylvania, and Massachusetts—provide significant financial support for urban transit systems.[3] Elsewhere, subsidies—where they are authorized at all—are provided by the municipalities served.

Only a few states have a statewide administrative agency responsible for public transit; the best developed of these are the departments of transportation of New York and New Jersey. A number of other states (for example, California and Wisconsin) have established agencies with that name, but they do not have responsibility for transit. Thus with few exceptions, governors of urban states do not have any regular means of receiving advice on total urban transportation problems or on transit in particular.[4]

At the local level, transit authorities have advantages and disadvantages common to other autonomous regional authorities.[5] They are generally freed of traditional civil service, purchasing, and contracting restrictions, so they can operate more like a "private business." They are also freed of meaningful political control. At best, these transit authorities are strong, effective fighters for the transit-riding public. At worst, they become so oriented toward their own internal objectives (economy, labor relations, budget) that they tend to be unresponsive to other community objectives that may impinge on theirs. And, even more serious, they may be obliged to accept unqualified political appointees in order to achieve their objectives in the political decisionmaking bodies.

The transit authorities studied in this research covered the whole spectrum of problems. Boston's had almost all the above-mentioned ailments. Its top management in recent years has been of high quality, but competence beneath that level has been low. It is expansionist-minded but tends neither to work well with other planning bodies nor with the cities it serves.[6] Baltimore's transit authority was so lacking in vision that it was replaced after only a few years of existence, its planning powers effectively transferred to the Regional Planning Council. San Francisco's efficient regional transit agency is narrowly self-protective and has a history of difficulties in its local working relationships. The city transit agencies of San Francisco and Seattle are frequently criticized for a lack of imagination. The transit authorities of St. Louis and Kansas City are too new to have developed a clear-cut style.

The restriction on the powers of these agencies needs reemphasis. The lack of authority to raise needed funds for expansion and improvements tends to make them cautious in outlook. Politicians and the public often seem to expect them to perform the impossible, to operate cheaper and better service within an ever tightening revenue situation. The cities, which in many instances have provided some subsidies for transit, have been experiencing severe financial problems of their own and can ill afford to support public transit at adequate levels. The states view the transit problem as a local one.

The picture has been brighter since 1964, when Congress approved the Urban Mass Transportation Act.[7] Since that time, limited federal aid has been available for capital improvements by urban transit operations, with the federal government providing up to two-thirds of the cost of such projects. While this has stimulated significant local improvements in some cities, funds have been so limited that they have not altered the generally depressing picture. Under the 1964 act, $150 million was authorized to be appropriated annually for the grants program; this was increased to $190 million in fiscal year 1970. A maximum of 12.5 percent of the total was allowed to any one state, although the Secretary of Transportation was authorized discretionary funds of $12.5 million, which he could use to exceed this state limitation. Considering the enormous estimated costs of modernizing and expanding the existing rapid transit systems (for example, over $1 billion for Boston's "master plan," over $1 billion for New York City's current projects) and the vast expenditures needed to create new ones such as those proposed for Los Angeles ($2.5 billion), clearly these amounts could hardly make a dent in the problem.

It appears that in the 1970's federal financial assistance for transit will be vastly larger. On September 29, 1970, the House of Representatives passed H.R. 18185, Urban Mass Transportation Assistance Act, which had already been approved by the Senate. This act provides for long-term five-year financing commitments to a total of $3.1 billion. This is about four times the previous level and thus substantially brightens the future picture for transit.

The transit authority, with its limited powers, can be pictured as being literally "in the middle," receiving frequently unanswerable pressures and at the same time being relatively immune from political retaliation by its opponents. It can meet these demands only through the receipt of local, state, or federal financial assistance. Demands are local, (mostly from municipal politicians, the public, and downtown businessmen), but the local jurisdiction is least capable of meeting requests for subsidy. Demands for subsidies have fallen on deaf ears in most state legislatures because the bulk of the state's population would receive no visible benefits. Given these circumstances, federal assistance is clearly the most attractive answer. And, since so many transit systems are now feeling the financial pinch, support for more extensive federal aid has now been sufficient to achieve victory in the Congress.

Transit controversies generally emerge from rapid transit plans proposing large expenditures of local funds. Pressures for such plans usually come from civic, political, and business groups associated with the central city. In the past decade major political campaigns for new rapid transit systems have been waged in the San Francisco. Washington, Atlanta, Los Angeles, and Seattle areas to invest hundreds of millions in local funds in new rapid transit lines, but only in the first two areas were the campaigns successful. Greater success has marked efforts to extend and improve the five existing rapid transit systems, but in all cases only after extensive and prolonged debates over financing. And in no case has financing been sufficient to meet the needs of a modernized, full-scale system. Opposition to new transit investments comes from poorly served neighborhoods and voters who do not expect to make much use of the facilities.

The plight of the rail commuter is a familiar story. With the exception of two lines in Chicago, no commuter railroad in the United States admits to anything but loss on commuter service. The reasons are similar to those for transit: rising cost, declining patronage, continuing decentralization and dispersion of the city. The response of most railroads has been to cut costs at every opportunity and to plead with regulatory bodies to grant reduction or discontinuance of passenger service.[8] In only one case, the Long Island Railroad, which is the only rail line in the United States almost totally dependent on commuter fares, has the problem of commuter service resulted in the same policy response as in transit, namely public ownership. The Long Island was taken over in 1965 by the Mertopolitan Commuter Transportation Authority.

The states have been more responsive to the rail commuter than to the transit rider, but few visible improvements have yet resulted from their subsidy programs. In the early 1950's, New York state acted to stabilize and improve the financial condition of the Long Island Railroad.[9] New Jersey accepted a similar responsibility in 1961 with respect to lines running to Manhattan,[10] as did Pennsylvania in the late 1950's for the Philadelphia lines. In the early 1960's, Massachusetts and Connecticut began providing subsidies for commuter service on the New Haven Railroad, and Massachusetts began aiding the Boston and Maine line. Neither Illinois nor California has resorted to subsidy for commuter railroads. In Illinois most of the lines are operating profitably.

Decisions affecting rail commutation have become a combination of state and private responsibility. As with transit, few states have any real staff capability in this field. The governor, unless aided by a railroad "expert," and the legislature are largely dependent for knowledge on the state public service or utility commission. With the exception of the two Chicago lines and the Long Island, railroads have little interest in working with public officials to improve commuter services.

Controversies over commuter services are similar to rapid

transit disputes in that they usually concern public financial aid. A second and related type of dispute concerns the discontinuance or reduction of service. Major differences from transit disputes are that first, the train operators' primary objective is to phase out rather than to enlarge or improve their operations; second, most of the pressure for subsidy comes from the suburbs; and third, pressure is directed at the state rather than at local governments.

The last and largest of the urban transportation programs is the highway program, whose key decisionmaking body is the state highway agency commonly known as the highway department or department of public works, the latter usually encompassing other construction programs. In most states, the highway program is headed by a commission, the members of which have long overlapping terms to keep them immune from "politics." In two states (Michigan and Mississippi) the desire for independence of the program has led to the practice of direct election of the highway commissioner(s). In other states recent reform for "efficiency" reasons has led to giving the governor appointive and removal power of a director, thus placing the program under the governor's control. Illinois and Pennsylvania are examples of this. Of the six states included in this study, all now have commissions, but in Maryland and Massachusetts, departments of transportation with multi-modal responsibilities have been approved to replace the more limited agencies. . . .

State highway agencies have tended to be a power unto themselves. In most instances, they are clearly responsible neither to the governor nor to the communities through which they build highways. This situation is beginning to change in some states.

The power of the cities and counties to influence highway decisions varies greatly, and the means of asserting that power also differs from place to place. In a few states—for example, California—every municipality has an effective veto over highway plans. Prior to final approval of a design, the California Division of Highways must negotiate a "freeway agreement" with the local authorities on the closing of streets affected by the new facility. If the city objects to the design or to the highway itself, it may refuse to sign the agreement. The San Francisco Board of Supervisors used this power to effectuate their famous "freeway revolt," which ended all highway construction in most sections of the city in 1959. Several similar cases have occurred or are being threatened in the Los Angeles area. In addition to this veto power, California cities may introduce legislation to delete an objectionable piece of planned highway from the state system established by law in 1959 and force discontinuation of studies by the state Division of Highways.

The city of Baltimore has a different kind of veto power. Because it occupies the unique position in Maryland of being a city and a county, Baltimore was long ago granted full control over a portion of the state's gasoline and auto excise tax revenue and full authority to build its own highways. In 1966 this was modified somewhat by an agreement to have the state assume responsibility for the interstate system, but the city retains its veto power through the requirement that it approve all condemnations of property to be taken in the path of the highway. . . .

Except for unusual cases like California cities and Baltimore, which receive large allocations from the state gas tax, the cities covered by this study are not responsible for the construction of major highways. The city's role has generally been limited to working with the state highway engineers in developing the master plan and working out adjustments and traffic patterns required by new freeways.

The natural local agencies to handle these negotiations have been the cities' streets (or public works or engineer's) departments and the traffic departments, if they are separate organizations. These agencies are staffed by the same kinds of people as those in the state agency, with the same viewpoints and jargon. They understand each other. In some cities with powerful planning agencies, they also play a significant role, but this is the exception rather than the rule. An example is Kansas City, where good city planning has been a tradition since early in this century. In Houston also city planners have had an important input. In smaller satellite or suburban cities, city planning agencies are as a rule insufficiently staffed to have a significant role.

Unless a major controversy develops over a new highway, local political officials have generally stayed out of highway planning except to give perfunctory formal approval. Where controversy does erupt, a number of city agencies may become involved, as well as the mayor and city council. The controversies, almost always the result of a highway's damaging something of high value in the community, are sometimes stimulated by one or another of these agencies or political leaders. When a controversy between the local public works director and other local agencies arises, the political leadership has little choice but to intervene and resolve the issue or ignore it and let it remain unresolved. If the municipality has no formal power over the road and lacks other informal political means of influencing the decision, the politicians may prefer to pretend the problem doesn't exist, at the risk of losing the support of the opponents. When this happens, of course, the highway planners "win," and the politician must explain his lack of authority. If formal power resides in the city, failure to settle a dispute is tantamount to a defeat for the highway planners, since they cannot proceed.

Urban highway systems are by definition metropolitan programs. So one might reasonably ask what role metropolitan planning agencies play in highway planning. The 1960's was the decade for the establishment of such agencies in large American urban centers. Unquestionably, highways are a major factor, perhaps *the* major factor, in determining the specific directions of metropolitan development. Although one might assume a major decisionmaking role for these metropolitan planning agencies, this has not been the case.

The eight urban areas studied established these agencies during the 1960's. In San Francisco, Seattle, St. Louis, and Los Angeles, they were created by previously established metropolitan councils of government.[11] In Boston, Baltimore, Kansas City, and Houston they were established by state statute as planning bodies.[12] All are governed by boards of elected officials or their designees, although two (in Boston and Baltimore) have some state representation on the governing body as well. Without exception, these metropolitan planning agencies are staffed with competent personnel. None has more than thirty professionals and some have fewer than ten. The agencies of Seattle, Baltimore, Kansas City, and Houston, the four smallest of the eight areas, appear to be the strongest.

The reasons for the relatively insignificant roles played by these bodies are several. They are weak politically because they lack any direct relationship to an existing government, in contrast to the state highway departments. They are relatively new and small, seeking to find an appropriate and useful niche, and reluctant to get involved in major controversies. Their only weapon has been often ineffective "sweet reason." These agencies came onto the scene only after the plans on which most current highway programs are based were developed. They do participate with varying effectiveness in long-range transportation planning and particularly in transit planning.

The final and, in many respects, most important participant in urban highway programs is the federal government. The responsible agency is the Bureau of Public Roads, now lodged under the Federal Highway Administration, an agency of the Department of Transportation, established in 1966. Formerly a part of the Department of Commerce, the Bureau of Public Roads was moved to the new DOT as part of the national effort to place all major federal transportation programs under one roof. Also in this Department are the Urban Mass Transportation Administration (shifted from the Department of Housing and Urban Development to DOT in 1968), the Federal Aviation Administration, and a number of smaller units.

The federal government's interest in highways has a long history. As early as 1916, when the first Federal Aid Road Act was passed, there has been federal financial assistance to the states for highway construction. The original objective was to ensure that the states coordinate their highway planning, so that the roads would meet at state borders. The program was continued and enlarged through the years, but not until 1944 were urban areas specifically included in federal aid programs.[13] In most states the cities were expected to finance their own highways without benefit of state aid, and some still do. Both state and federal programs were thus completely rurally oriented.

The federal aid program for cities did not become important until after the passage of the Federal Aid Highway Act of 1956, which provided 90 percent federal financing.[14] That act specified that 25 percent of the total funds would be spent in urban areas, the places experiencing the most severe traffic problems. The Clay Report, which recommended this program, dwelt at some length on the need for vast expenditures for urban and suburban roads.[15] It also assumed the superiority of suburban versus urban living and argued that the new freeway program would encourage the decentralization of American cities. It has had that effect and is approved or deplored depending upon one's viewpoint and interest.

Federal aid highways fall into several categories, the most expensive of which are the interstate roads. Federal aid to the extent of 50 percent matching grants is also extended to states for what have become secondary highways. Both programs are financed from excise taxes on gasoline and other automobile-related purchases. The interstate funds are also available for studies of highway needs, relevant research and development, and for traffic control programs. They are not intended for maintenance and construction of city streets, although limited funds for aid to cities to improve the capacity of local streets are now provided under a new program called TOPICS (Traffic Operations to Improve Capacity and Safety). Costs incident to relocation have been increasingly recognized as appropriate charges to the higway fund, and they have become more generous over the years.

Until recently, federal control over the operations of federally aided state highway programs was minimal. The Bureau of Public Roads has maintained a district office in each state capital and generally worked rather closely with the state highway agencies. Routes and designs were ordinarily accepted without much question after approval at the state level. Controversies began to develop as early as the late 1950's, and increased in the 1960's, as the new highways began to enter built-up urban areas. By the mid-1960's, it was becoming more and more difficult for the federal highways organization to remain outside these controversies, and by the late 1960's, Lowell Bridwell, the first federal highway administrator, began to change the character of federal involvement in local decisionmaking.

Bridwell accepted the view that where controversies existed, the federal agency was obligated to examine the pros and cons before granting the federal dollars. In San Francisco Bridwell took the side of the city in the Junipero Serra freeway dispute. In Boston he agreed to the restudy of the Inner Belt route. In Baltimore he played a significant role in developing a new approach to freeway planning, the "design concept team," the result of which was not only a new design but a new route.

Bridwell was instrumental in encouraging state highway departments to take other values besides traffic movement into account in the development of highway plans. The San Francisco case related to esthetic and recreational considerations. The Boston and Baltimore cases were instances of serious social impacts not adequately considered in the original designs. Baltimore's road also seriously affected parks and historic districts. Numerous other cases occurred in cities such as Louisville, New York, Chicago, Detroit, Cleveland, and Philadelphia.

Bridwell seems to have succeeded in establishing this as a permanent policy for the Federal Highway Administration. With the advent of the Nixon administration, John Volpe, Governor of Massachusetts, was appointed Secretary of Transportation. The general view was that Volpe would "pave the country," since as a former DPW Commissioner in Massachusetts he had adamantly demanded the completion of the Inner Belt. However, Volpe made an early and important decision reversing a state-approved plan in New Orleans that would have cut off Jackson Square in the Vieux Carré from the Mississippi, thus suggesting the continuance of the policy of direct involvement of the federal government in such decisions.

Three separate institutional and decisionmaking structures handle the planning and operation of the metropolitan transportation system. Planning, construction, and operation of the urban freeway system is largely centered in state roads agencies, which have strong ties with the federal Bureau of Public Roads and city and county public works departments. The commuter railroads in a few places like New York and New Jersey are accepted as a state transportation department responsibility; elsewhere their fate lies in the hands of public service commissioners and the primary leadership of the state (the governor and the legislature). In most large metropolitan areas transit has become the responsibility of a regional transit authority, financed mostly with local funds and enjoying a semi-autonomous status.

Each mode of transportation has had its own political arena, rarely overlapping that of another except at the edges. Political controversies about highways, public transit, and commuter railroads reflect the differing political makeup of the decisionmaking structure of each mode. Controversies over highways are primarily concerned with opposition to particular roads or to overall plans for the metropolitan highway system. They reflect the absence of local participation in planning and a sense that decisions are made with a narrow transportation orientation from which other urban values are excluded. These controversies often are local-state confrontations, with the Federal Highway Administration sometimes stepping in as mediator.

Disputes over public transit are different. Pressures to preserve or improve an old system or to create a new one are always local in origin. Debates on these questions usually revolve around cost, which places the issue in competition with other demands for the local tax dollar. Plans or guidelines for new or improved rapid transit systems are frequently the responsibility of the metropolitan planning agency. Controversies over commuter railroad service are state-centered, and generally arise from suburban opposition to cutbacks, usually supported by the central city.

The contrast between the politics of transit and the politics of highways, in particular, is striking and illustrates the major problem of achieving a unified and responsive political and planning process for urban transportation. Forces are at work to achieve this unification, primarily at the federal and local levels. Both modes, as well as railroads, are brought together at the federal level in the cluster of responsibilities assigned to the Department of Transportation. Through federal intervention, they have been forced to come together in the regional transportation planning process, and they come together with increasing frequency in the governor's office and in the central city, both of which have usually had only informal powers to deal with the decisionmaking agencies.

NOTES

1. The first of the exclusive highway lanes have been approved by DOT for Milwaukee and Los Angeles. DOT is working with the L.A. Airport Authority on an experimental "air-cushion" line from the airport to the San Fernando Valley.
2. Both of these are authorized to operate but do not as yet.
3. Michigan, Washington, and Florida all have limited mass transit assistance programs as well.
4. While traditional public service agencies generally have regulatory responsibilities regarding transit, their orientation is rarely such that they can serve this purpose.
5. For a general discussion of the characteristics of such authorities, see John C. Bollens, *Special District Governments in the United States* (Berkeley: University of California Press, 1957), esp. pp. 116–44. Also see Robert C. Wood, *1400 Governments* (Cambridge: Harvard University Press, 1961).
6. See part 2 of Governor's Task Force on Transportation, *Report to Governor Sargent* (Boston, June 1970), pp. 18–20.
7. P.L. 38–365, 88th Congress, 2nd Session.
8. George M. Smerk, *Urban Transportation: The Federal Role* (Bloomington: Indiana University Press, 1966), pp. 51–52.
9. Jameson W. Doig, *Metropolitan Transportation Politics in the New York Region* (New York: Columbia University Press, 1966), p. 45.
10. *Ibid.*, pp. 215–17, 297.
11. The Association of Bay Area Governments (ABAG), Puget Sound Government Council (PSGC), and East-West Gateway Coordinating Council (EWGCC), respectively.
12. The Metropolitan Area Planning Council (MAPC, Boston), Regional Planning Council (RPC, Baltimore), Metropolitan Planning Commission–Kansas City (MPC), and Houston-Galveston Area Council (HGAC).
13. The Federal Aid Highway Act of 1944 (P.L. 78–521).
14. The Federal Aid Highway Act of 1956 (P.L. 84–627).
15. U.S., Congress, House of Representatives, *Needs of the National Highway Systems, 1955–84*, House Document No. 120, 84th Congress, 1st Session

(1955). See also Daniel P. Moynihan, "New Roads and Urban Chaos," *The Reporter*, Vol. 22 (April 14, 1960), pp. 13–20. The Clay Report, quoted in the *Reporter* article, says in part, "We have been able to disperse our factories, our stores, our people; in short, to create a revolution in living habits. Our cities have spread into suburbs dependent on the automobile for their existence. The automobile has restored a way of life in which the individual may live in a friendly neighborhood, it has brought city and country closer together, it has made us one country and united people." Moynihan comments, "To undertake a vast program of urban highway construction with no thought for other forms of transportation seemed lunatic."

AUTOS, ENERGY, AND POLLUTION

MATTHEW EDEL

Many urban areas allow few alternatives to automobile use. Land use patterns have developed presuming the predominance of auto transport. Separation of cities and residential suburbs, the unavailability of mass transit, and lack of government support for alternative transit modes make the automobile a necessity of life. Taxing the automobile user would place a heavy fiscal burden on the public, without significantly reducing pollution. The economist must agree that unless the entire transportation system is reorganized, the benefits to each driver from access to work, shopping, and recreation may be greater than the individual automobile's addition to pollution costs.

Although each motorist may be justified in driving, given the available alternatives, the entire system may still be irrational. Indeed, a city with several million drivers rationally choosing to use their engines may become uninhabitable. Replacing the present organization of cities by a more compact settlement pattern with good public transit might allow an equivalent standard of living with less pollution. Analyzing automotive pollution requires considering not only the limits to present government economic policies, but also the social and economic organization of cities, transport systems, and energy supply. The principal question is what forces limit the options open to residents, giving them little alternative but to contribute pollutants to the air. This article examines the institutions of urban life and the political economy of the petroleum industry in light of this question.

Automotive exhausts are the largest source of air pollution in the United States. Household automobile use accounts for nearly one-third of all petroleum use.[1] Cars, trucks, and other transportation equipment account for 23.6 percent of all energy consump-

From Mathew Edel, *Economies and the Environment* (Englewood Cliffs, N.J.: Prentice-Hall, 1973), pp. 112–24. © 1973 by Prentice-Hall, Inc., and reprinted by permission.

tion (measured in British Thermal Units), and automotive engines represent 95 percent of all of the installed horsepower capacity of prime movers. Motor vehicles emit 60 percent of air pollution (measured by weight), including most of the carbon monoxide, half the hydrocarbons, and almost half of the nitrogen oxides in the air (see Table 1). The transport of petroleum to its consumers also causes ecological problems, including oil slicks from tanker accidents and damage to tundra environments from heat required to keep oil flowing in arctic pipelines.[2]

Cities are particularly affected. Normally, the atmosphere disperses pollutants, which are eventually recycled by natural processes. Emissions in congested areas, however, may accumulate more rapidly than natural dispersal can remove them. They form pollutant clouds within which chemicals combine to form new and dangerous gases. Large cities without public transit systems and with unfavorable wind conditions suffer most. Thus, Los Angeles has a worse air pollution problem than Chicago, although the two metropolitan areas have roughly equal populations. Los Angeles, with no rapid transit system, spreads over an area greater than that of Chicago. It burns 2,540 million gallons of gasoline daily, to 1,850 for Chicago. What is more, because of Chicago's wind, and California's frequent periods of stationary air, Los Angeles burned 231 gallons per cubic mile of air passing through the city, as against only 144 gallons for Chicago. Even in Chicago, or in cities with lower emission levels, air pollution is still a problem.[3]

Factory smoke, home heating, and garbage incineration add to auto exhausts to create pollution. These other sources can sometimes be controlled, as the cleanup of the air in Pittsburgh proved. Conversion from coal to natural gas, replacement of high sulfur

TABLE 1.—SOURCES AND TYPES OF AIR POLLUTION
(millions of tons annually, 1965)

	Carbon Monoxide	Sulfur Oxides	Nitrogen Oxides	Hydro-carbons	Particulate Matter	Totals
Motor vehicles	66	1	6	12	1	86
Industry	2	9	2	4	6	23
Power plants	1	12	3	1	3	20
Space heating	2	3	1	1	1	8
Refuse disposal	1	1	1	1	1	5

Source: The Economy, Energy and the Environment, Joint Economic Committee, U.S. Congress, 1970.

fuel oil by higher grades from which sulfur is removed, controls over specific industrial processes, scrubbing of smoke, and use of landfills for garbage can reduce pollution. These substitutions are costly, and individual firms or citizens will not make them unless compelled by law or induced by tax mechanisms. Using sulfur-free fuel for electric generation, for example, requires either that consumers pay higher rates or that electric companies' profits fall. Imposition of controls may be difficult, as when companies threaten to move or lay off workers if required to bear cleanup costs. However, if only a few sources of pollution are to blame, or if multiple sources (such as home incinerators) can easily be replaced by municipal services (such as garbage collection), control is easier than for automotive emissions.

PROBLEMS OF REGULATION

There are millions of automobile users. Most have no alternative to driving, at least some of the time. Regulating the amount of automotive travel is thus very difficult. Discussions of ways to induce drivers to switch to existing public transit systems show this. Replacement of automobile commuting by electrified mass transit would reduce emissions of hydrocarbons, carbon monoxide, lead, and nitrogen oxide. (Thermal electric generation may, however, cause some increase in sulfur oxide emission.) Economists have asked whether reducing fares or subsidizing free mass transit might tempt passengers to fill the trains. The estimates are not promising.

One study compared residents of Boston neighborhoods who face differing fares, riding times, and driving times to reach the central business district by subway and by automobile. It concluded that the number of trips to work made by public transit was not affected greatly by differences in fares. Cutting fares by half would increase transit use by less than 10 percent. Shopping trips are more responsive to fares. More people shop downtown when fares are lower, but this is not a shift from automobiles to subways. Use of public transit for commuting was more responsive to the relative times required to travel downtown by public and private modes of transit. Faster subways might lure a significant number of passengers away from their cars, but free transit alone would not.[4]

Another study compared commuting times by car and by elevated and commuter trains in Chicago. For most commuters, public modes took a longer time than driving. Evaluating each hour saved as worth an hour's wages to the commuter, the investigators found that for most commuters interviewed, it was cheaper to drive than to go by slower public transit systems. To make public modes equivalent in real cost, as long as they remained slower than roads, it would be necessary not only to make public transit free, but also to charge automobile users a dollar a day for entering the city.[5]

If public transit is fast and automobile use very expensive, commuters will use the trains. In New York, the subway is used for more than half of journeys to work. Public transit is used to a great extent in many European cities. But many commuters cannot be tempted, even by large subsidies, to switch from cars to public transit, because no public transit exists where they live and work. Although public transit may not be economical in small towns where few people travel between any two locations, there are still major cities, like Detroit and Los Angeles, that do not have rapid transit systems. Some parts of Los Angeles do not even have bus lines available to those who cannot drive. In other cities, public transit is often too slow to compete.

Economists often take this lack of rapid public transit as a given condition for their analyses and conclude, naturally, that driving cannot be eliminated. Even then, however, they may ask whether smaller, or cleaner, automobiles might reduce damage from pollution, and whether use of these less-polluting cars could be induced by feasible controls or effluent charges.

Reducing of horsepower might be one alternative. A more powerful car uses more gasoline per mile than one with smaller engine capacity and produces more pollution when forced to drive below its high cruising speed on a crowded expressway. However, once consumers must buy automobiles anyway, many prefer cars that can carry their entire families on weekends and that they can also drive rapidly when they are not in town. A six-cylinder compact car is the smallest that many find satisfactory. Comparison of demand for different automobiles at different price levels, and with different horsepower, has led one economist to argue that the price of an additional 1 percent of horsepower would have to rise more than 3 percent to induce a 1 percent reduction in power. Such small reductions would not have much effect on total emissions.[6] Fees for high-powered cars would have to be very great indeed to reduce pollution, and such high fees would be resisted for the hardship they would bring to people who must drive between cities given the lack of good rail transport in the United States.

Studies do not indicate that raising the prices of all automobiles would reduce auto use greatly. Nor would an increase in gasoline taxes have much effect. Per mile gas costs are a small part of total motoring expenses. Past imposition of gasoline taxes has not reduced motoring noticeably in the United States, although considerably higher taxes in other countries may have had that effect. Given present transport systems and settlement patterns, it would take very severe bribes or charges to induce people not to use automobiles.

Fine tuning methods [such as regulatory controls] have also been suggested to make combustion in cars of present sizes somewhat cleaner. Taxes on lead in gasoline have been proposed. Standards for engine construction and exhaust controls are scheduled to become more stringent. These can reduce pollution somewhat, although at a cost of up to several hundred dollars for each car. But they are limited in their effect and will not end many air pollution problems. Because none of the existing technologies can remove both hydrocarbons and nitrogen oxides completely, and because even a partial reduction is costly at existing horsepower levels, economists sometimes have doubted whether much net benefit improvement in the air will be possible from controls.[7]

THE WRONG CONCLUSION

It is sometimes concluded from this that nothing can be done to eliminate automotive air pollution. The consumer is said to have chosen the automobile consciously, and, in the process, to have accepted pollution as the price of keeping a big, fast, private car. Psychological theories have even been developed to explain this choice. They claim that the American—particularly the male American—is irrationally attached to his car. The automobile represents power, compensates for deep-seated fears of impotence, or allows avoidance of personal contact with other commuters. Among some people it is fashionable to consider their fellows as half-insane for driving.

Many people do enjoy driving, although most prefer it when roads are not crowded. Undoubtedly, some people do have their self-esteem lifted by ownership of a fancy car. However, in Manhattan, where automotive commuting is prohibitively expensive, people rent cars for pleasure outings, take subways to work, and find other ways to keep up with the Joneses. Psychological manipulation may help auto companies sell new model cars more often, but there is no need to assume the consumer is irrational,

to explain his driving. The lack of alternatives is sufficient explanation. If one must work to eat, and must drive to get to work,
then one must drive to eat. Even a person who hates driving cannot change highway patterns through individual actions, and most
have to commute by car. In the language of economics, this is
rational suboptimizing or making the best of a bad situation.

The relation of each driver to others can be described by what
game theorists call the prisoner's dilemma, after the case of two
suspects, each of whom is told separately by the district attorney
that the other is likely to confess to a crime. Confession will
bring a light sentence, but if both remain quiet, they will go free.
Because each must fear that the other will confess, in which case
his sentence may be harsh, each will confess to keep his risk small.
In any prisoner's dilemma situation, one course can yield everyone
the best result if everyone follows it. But if not everyone follows
it, then those who do make the attempt suffer a great loss. Unless
there is some mechanism for ensuring that others will make the
attempt, it is therefore rational to accept a suboptimal outcome
and not try for the best possible result. This is the case with the
automobile. For each individual it may be irrational not to drive,
unless enough others also stop driving and demand good public
transit.

In this situation, to seek a psychological explanation for why
individuals drive is to ask the wrong question. The problem is not
why individuals drive, given the options open to them. It is why
the options in American cities involve few alternatives to life in
residential neighborhoods that require automobiles be used for
work, shopping, and other necessary activities.

Asking why the options are limited involves questions that go
beyond estimating the costs and benefits of using any one automobile. It involves asking why cities are so big in the first place.[8]
It involves asking why more research is not directed to producing
alternatives to the internal-combustion engine.[9] It involves asking, too, why cities take the form they now have; why there is
not more public investment in rapid transit systems; and why
internal combustion, on the other hand, does receive so much
government support.

Ignoring these questions of why options are limited leads to
the wrong conclusion about the sources of pollution. To blame
the psychological problems of the individual who drives is "blaming the victim" of the problem.[10] To tax driving may be "penal-
izing the victim." An effluent charge might be more of a burden
to low income commuters than to the wealthy. Because most

workers in American cities (except New York) drive to work, a fee for commuting that costs each family the same amount of money would take a larger percentage of the earnings of low wage workers than of incomes of the more affluent. This is what is called a regressive tax. A tax geared to exact production of effluents might be even more regressive, because poorer commuters buy used cars that allow more pollutants to escape into the atmosphere. Such regressive taxes are not only considered socially undesirable by many economists; they would also be opposed by the majority of working commuters. Civil rights organizations and labor unions have complained that attacks on the automobile would place a burden on the poor, and that a commuter tax in the name of ecology might amount to taxing the poor to subsidize playgrounds for the rich. Even businesses which would not pay the taxes might oppose them because if workers could not drive to jobs, this would cause the businesses problems when they tried to hire workers.

URBAN SETTLEMENT AND TRANSPORT

Commuting first became a problem when cities grew after the industrial revolution. The growth of large factories, and of commercial districts from which the factories were managed, led to the concentration of many people into cities. The separation of residential and business areas became possible because of several interrelated inventions: the trolley car, the subway, and the automobile, on the one hand; the elevator and the skyscraper, on the other. More offices could crowd into business districts than was possible in walk-up buildings, more people could live within commuting range than was possible when only walking and horse-drawn vehicles could be used. However, inventions did not make urban sprawl and a dependence on the automobile inevitable. They only made it possible. Institutional reasons must be found for why the fearsome possibility was realized.

WHY SUBURBS SPRAWL

Even in large cities, compact settlement patterns might reduce automobile commuting, and people might live closer to business districts or in nodes close to rapid transit stations. This would require that more multifamily dwellings be built. Families may prefer to live in single-family homes than to live in apartments, at least if the price differential is not too great. However, they might accept change if they had to pay the full cost the present commuting pattern imposes on society, and if an alternative were really available. At present, however, alternatives are limited, and incentives reward, rather than charge, families for living in suburbs and driving to work. These are institutional biases in the organization of the urban economy. Society could change them, but the individual commuter cannot.

The theory of "externalities" explains one reason for urban sprawl. A service will be overused if each user, when making decisions, does not take into account the costs—"externalities"—he imposes on other users. Highway use creates several such external costs. In congested traffic, each driver slows down the other users of a road. The more cars that try to cover a stretch of road every minute, the fewer that may actually drive the entire distance in that time. Each commuter who buys a house at the end of a freeway takes congestion as given and does not consider what his presence will do to other drivers. When many commuters do this, all find they are slowed down. A commuter highway, in this sense, is like a common pasture or fishery. If not regulated, it will be overused.[11]

Commuters also impose external costs on those not using freeways. As cars drive downtown from suburbs, they pass other neighborhoods. New highways disrupt communities by taking land from some facilities and homes and leaving those that remain with fewer neighbors to support local services. Once in use, highways are a source of noise and air pollution.[12] There is little wonder that in neighborhoods through which highways are to be built, residents often oppose construction.[13]

These external costs, imposed by commuters on less suburban neighborhoods, are not reflected in the costs of commuting. The costs are hard to measure, and highway departments, which are supposed to compensate those dispossessed by construction, often fail to measure them. The costs thus give no disincentive to buying a home in the suburbs and driving to work. Rather, they are an incentive to people in the inner rings of a city to move further to the suburbs. By suburbanizing, they can escape these costs for which they will not be compensated by the drivers. External diseconomies without compensation thus are a cause for greater urban sprawl.

Externalities only distort incentives because of the specific institutions of an economy. Economists and highway engineers could set tolls that would charge road users for the congestion they impose on other drivers and for damage to neighborhoods disrupted by commuter roads. These institutions are not introduced. Suburban housing developers know they can only sell homes if good, toll-free roads are built. They can be counted on to lobby for roads. Those already living in suburbs, who have bought homes at high prices and have mortgages to pay off, also resist tolls. In the past, residents of the generally poorer neighborhoods closer to the centers of cities were not organized enough to meet this pressure. If they can achieve more power and demand compensation or block new construction, it would be a case in which equality improved the efficiency of resource use. Up to now, however, the prohighway forces have generally been stronger, and damages remain uncompensated.

A number of other institutions also reward those who move to the suburbs. One is the division of metropolitan areas into separate towns with distinct tax bases. Central city governments often must provide services used by the entire metropolitan area, as well as special services to poor people who live in the older neighborhoods. Those who live in suburbs often avoid the property taxes that support these services. Even when per capita government costs are equal in all neighborhoods, a wealthier community can keep its tax down to a smaller percentage rate on residents' wealth by becoming a separate town. When state laws allow suburbs to remain independent jurisdictions, as they do for most American metropolitan areas, the result is the separation of low-tax suburbs from high-tax central cities and inner ring towns. This in turn leads to a vicious circle of oversuburbanization. The wealthiest people left in the city at each round flee to the suburbs to reduce their tax burdens. Those left behind must either reduce the equality of public services or raise taxes. Either response leads to new incentives to suburbanization.

Another institution with similar effects is the availability of easier credit on some purchases than for others. Government supported mortgage credit to suburban homeownership encourages ownership of homes and automobiles rather than other consumer goods and services on which money might be spent by a person who chooses apartment life and a shorter commuting radius. The United States tax system also subsidizes private homes by allowing the deduction of interest and property tax payments. Subsidies on rental properties are less easily obtained and may not give rent reductions to the actual residents. Condominium arrangements allow apartments in high rise dwellings to receive single family tax treatment but are complicated to arrange. Real estate assessments are sometimes more lenient for single family dwellings than for rental apartment buildings; and the general property tax, by taxing buildings rather than just land, reduces tax costs for speculative holding of idle land. This speculation may force builders of new dwellings to choose sites farther from the central city.

PROBLEMS OF PUBLIC TRANSIT

These institutional biases and externalities give a strong incentive to American families to live in the suburbs. However, even with this settlement pattern, it might be possible to develop public transport systems. These systems would not be as efficient as those that would be possible given more concentrated settlement patterns. However, if they were provided, and roads for the commuters were not built as readily as they are now, suburbanites might reduce auto use.

In most American cities, this is not even attempted. Roads for commuters are built regularly; rapid transit systems are rarely constructed, and most of those in use are financial failures. From a peak of 23 billion rides per year at the end of World War II, total public transit use, including subways, trolleys, buses, and commuter trains, declined to 8 billion by 1967. Subway rides fell less drastically, from 2.7 billion to 1.9 billion. The high wartime figures may have been inflated because cars were unavailable and gasoline rationed, but the decline continued long after the emergency controls ended.

Why did use of public transit decline? In part, a movement of people from older neighborhoods served by transit systems to new suburbs reduced ridership. But this is not a full explanation. Subways were not built to follow the riders. Bus lines only partially replaced the trolley lines that were torn up. Use of remaining lines declined and complaints about fares and services increased. This occurred for several reasons.

One problem is a need for subsidy that stems from the difficulties of running an enterprise on a break-even basis in the presence of economies of scale. That additional customers can use a service with little cost to the system ought to be an advantage to the public. But it also involves problems familiar to economists. If a subway has empty seats, if new cars can be added to an existing train, or if trains can run more often on existing tracks, the marginal cost of adding passengers will be low. If the benefit of carrying an additional passenger covers marginal cost, the economist argues the passenger should be induced to ride the train. The principle that operation should expand until marginal cost equals marginal benefit is the same one used in evaluating pollution control. It can be presumed that marginal benefit is at least as great as what an added passenger would be willing to pay. Thus, if it costs five cents per additional passenger to double the number of riders on a subway system, and a nickel fare would lead to a doubling compared to the number riding with existing twenty-five cent fares, economists would approve the fare reduction. Even zero fare would be considered optimal if it were needed to fill the larger train, and if each passenger added reduced air pollution more than five cents worth by not using his car.

To break even, however, subways must not only pay the marginal costs of transporting extra passengers. They also must bear the fixed costs of maintaining their facilities and paying off the debts incurred for their original construction. These costs are particularly high because capacity must be great enough to handle rush hour crowds. If these fixed total costs are divided by the number of passengers on a system, the resulting fixed cost per rider must be added to the average operating cost per rider to compute the average cost per rider of the system. This average cost will be greater than the marginal cost added by an additional rider. If the fare, which is paid by all riders, is to attract enough riders to equalize marginal costs and benefits, it will be less than average cost. Thus, on every rider, the average revenue collected will be less than the average cost. If the line attracts the optimal number of passengers, it will suffer a loss.

To the economist, this is a normal and justifiable loss. The transit line should receive a subsidy so it can cover costs without driving away riders through high fares. The governments that have control over public transit have not seen it that way. They demand that transit systems break even, an institutional requirement that forces lines to raise their fares and drive away riders. Sometimes they have also saddled public transit systems, acquired from private owners, with heavy debt burdens. The private owners sold to the government because lines couldn't operate profitably, so that one might think that the government could have bought the lines cheaply. Often, however, cities borrowed money to pay high prices for the money-losing lines. Thereafter, the transit systems were burdened with annual fixed costs for interest payments that made the need for subsidy greater.

The result has been, for some subway systems, a spiral of increasing fares, decreased ridership, and growing deficits. High fares, however, are not the only problem. Poor facilities are even more serious. Declining numbers of passengers and rising deficits led city governments to think that new investments in subways and other transit facilities would prove unjustified. This was not necessarily a correct conclusion. The studies that show low or zero fares might not attract riders also show that faster or more frequent trains, by reducing trip times, might make a difference.[14] More comfortable trains, not considered in the studies, might make a difference. But cities did not spend the money for these improvements or even, in some cases, the money needed to subsidize adequate repair of their equipment. In the United States, no well-designed, well-operated and adequately subsidized public transit system has ever really been given the chance to attract riders.

THE SUBSIDIZED HIGHWAYS

The need for subsidies is no less for highways than for public transit. To cover the cost of highway building, maintenance, and policing, funds must be collected. However, if tolls are charged on uncongested roads to cover average costs, ridership might be discouraged excessively. Not surprisingly, tolls are almost never collected on rural roads and streets within residential districts. Even commuter routes, for which tolls are sometimes charged, have generally received subsidies in the United States. When suburbs build roads, inner cities are forced to expand facilities because of rising congestion levels. Repair, policing, and environmental costs are all borne by local communities or by the states, out of general tax revenues. For construction itself, there is also an abundant source of cheap money. This construction receives all of the proceeds of a national tax on gasoline. These funds are deposited in a Highway Trust Fund, and distributed to the states for construction of the Interstate Highway System. The states must pay only 10 percent of construction costs—through their own gasoline taxes. Between 1956, when it was created, and 1970, $40 billion had been invested in the interstate Highway System.

Financing highway construction out of a gasoline tax that is uniform throughout the country involves a large subsidy to urban highways. In cities, automobiles drive fewer miles to the gallon, than in rural areas; more automobiles also use each mile of road. So, gasoline revenues for each mile of road are greater than in the country. However, the construction cost of each mile of road is also much higher. More overpasses or underpasses for connecting streets are required, as are more entrances and exits. Land acquisition, demolition of buildings, and compensation of former landowners are also more expensive (although the highway system pays inadequate compensation). Construction costs in a city will often be five to ten million dollars per mile for a six-lane highway, although rural costs are often under one million dollars.[15] Travelers driving between cities or in some rural areas thus subsidize the highways for urban commuters. Of course, the intercity drivers themselves are often forced to drive and to pay the gas tax subsidy to urban highways because of institutions that have made good passenger trains for journeys of up to several hundred miles unavailable in the United States, although they operate effectively in Europe.[16]

The subsidization of highways is not the only benefit the automobile commuter receives. The oil depletion allowance, which allows producers of petroleum substantial tax savings, may reduce gasoline prices to the driver. Faced with heavily subsidized automotive commuting and with low-quality public transit that the government has generally refused to subsidize adequately, it is not surprising that most commuters take to the roads. This choice is not the result of psychological idiosyncrasies, but rather of the alternatives available. These alternatives, in turn, are the result of political decisions to subsidize highways much more than other modes of ground transport. At one level, the Highway Trust Fund appears to be the travelers' choice—the Congress and the state governments that allow it to continue are elected by the public, including the many travelers. Governmental officials, however, are not elected on the issue of highways alone. People select candidates for positions on foreign policy, wages and employment, or other issues. Elected officials and the voters themselves may also be limited by institutions from finding alternative transit systems to support.

NOTES

1. Edel, M., *Economies and the Environment*, pp. 70–71. Tables 4–3 and 4–4.
2. *The Economy, Energy and the Environment*, Joint Economic Committee, U.S. Congress, Washington, D.C., 1970.
3. Report to the Joint State Government Commission, Panel of Technical Advisers on Automotive Air Pollution, Pennsylvania, 1963.
4. Kraft, Gerald, and Thomas Domencich, "Free Transit," in M. Edel and J. Rothenberg, *Readings in Urban Economics*. New York: Macmillan, 1972, pp. 459–80.
5. Moses, L. N., and H. F. Williamson, "Value of Time, Choice of Mode, and the Subsidy Issue in Urban Transportation," *Journal of Political Economy*. 71 (June 1963):247–64.

6. Dewees, Donald N., "Costs and Effectiveness of Automobile Pollution Control Systems," unpublished paper, Harvard University, 1971.

7. Downing, Paul B., and Lytton W. Stoddard, "The Economics of Air Pollution Control for Used Cars," unpublished paper, University of California, Riverside, 1971.

8. The total population is not the answer because 85 percent of the U.S. inhabitants live on less than 2 percent of the land. The growth of big business, concentrating productive assets into fewer and fewer organizations, may be part of the answer because it draws people to cities where major factories and headquarters are located. A full answer remains to be discovered.

9. As long as the automobile is a necessity, auto companies know it cannot be banned and so have little incentive to look for alternatives. They are well off now. Those interested in transport research, however, can often get little funding elsewhere.

10. Ryan, William, Blaming the Victim, Random House, New York, 1971, shows a number of cases in which people are blamed for their own misfortune. Many of these involve misapplication of natural science, as well as economics, as when Darwinian theories of evolution or heredity are misapplied to claim that anyone who does not succeed is necessarily "unfit," rather than considering the structure of the economy.

11. Walters, A. A., "The Theory and Measurement of Private and Social Costs of Highway Congestion," in Edel and Rothenberg, op. cit., pp. 417–439.

12. A report of the California Department of Public Health, Lead in the Environment and Its Effects on Humans, showed persons living far from freeways had 16 micrograms of lead for each 100 grams of blood; those living near freeways had 22.7 micrograms. Traffic police had higher concentrations.

13. The external costs of future users of inner-city dwellings may be capitalized, negatively, in the value of inner-city dwellings, making it difficult for the inner-city dwelling owner to escape these costs by selling the house.

14. These studies might suggest fare increases were not a problem at all. Historically, however, fare increases may have had an effect that could not now be reversed by decreases. As fares rose, people bought cars or moved away from transit lines. Once they had done so, lower fares could no longer attract them back, although increasing fares could drive still more riders away.

15. Meyer, J. R., J. F. Kain, and M. Wohl, The Urban Transportation Problem. Cambridge: Harvard University Press, 1966, p. 205.

16. Keeler, Theodore, "The Economics of Passenger Trains," Journal of Business, 44 (April 1971):148–74.

The Politics of Urban Education

The American elementary and secondary educational system has been marked by three distinctive and in many ways salutary features. First, in contrast to European school systems, which provided high-quality education to a fee-paying middle class while offering only limited educational opportunities to the working-class masses, Americans at an early point developed a common school serving a broader range of children in their communities. Secondly, rather than being administered and financed by a centralized government agency, the control of local schools was left in the hands of locally elected school boards. Thirdly, the professionalization of American schools came early, as teachers, principals, and superintendents were expected to have specialized training in the theory and practice of teaching and educational administration.

THE EARLY AMERICAN SCHOOL

These characteristics of late nineteenth- and early twentieth-century school systems were in many ways appropriate to a rural, frontier society undergoing rapid industrial development. When America was dotted by small towns and medium-sized cities, most neighborhood schools were in fact "common" schools, catering to the educational needs of a fairly wide range of social groups. Rich and poor, Protestants and Catholics, sons of plumbers and doctors, able and slow, all usually attended the same school.

Of course, educational institutions far from obliterated all social distinctions. Many (but not all) Catholics preferred their own parochial schools. In larger cities, neighborhood schools in ethnic and religious enclaves reinforced these divisions in the community. Above all, the educational opportunities for Southern blacks were scandalously limited: Either they had no schooling at all or they were segregated in small, dilapidated buildings with poorly prepared teachers and inadequate supplies.

201

But even with these important exceptions, the common school was nonetheless a great innovation that expanded educational opportunities for young Americans far beyond what their counterparts in Europe enjoyed. As Heidenheimer reports, the proportion of adolescents in secondary schools passed the "10–12-percent mark about 1910" in the United States, while in Europe this was generally not reached until after 1945; "the 30-percent mark was passed by the U.S. in the early 1920's, in Europe not until the 1960's."[1]

Local control of this educational system was also an appropriate arrangement for nineteenth-century American conditions. Although local control had its drawbacks—particularly in the poor treatment that blacks received at the hands of Southern whites—it was clearly the most feasible system of school governance. Because towns and cities were spread out over a vast geographical landscape that could be traversed only with great time and effort, more centralized administration would have been difficult. Moreover, cities and towns at that time were social and economic as well as political units. Children born in the community expected to spend their productive years in the same area. Because the impact of the schools was thus primarily local, it was reasonable that decisions concerning the schools also be made locally. Then, too, America was so diverse a nation, with so many regional, ethnic, and religious groups, that it could forestall conflict over sensitive educational policies only by permitting each community to decide curricular matters and school religious practices in ways consistent with that community's values. All in all, only a locally controlled school board could in those days have won the taxpayer support necessary to finance the rapidly expanding educational system.

Thirdly, the effort to establish high, professional standards was important for schools in a rough, crude society only a few years past its frontier days. Although Americans approved of the practical, economic value of schooling, they lacked much appreciation for the life of the intellectual. Even though schools were felt to be necessary, schoolmen were not held in particularly high esteem. In the words of the familiar cliché, "Those who can, do; those who can't, teach." Such views expressed the American belief that anyone who could read and write should be able to teach others how to do the same. More than in most countries, the job was regarded as "women's work," rather beneath the dignity of an ambitious, forceful male. Because only modest educational accomplishments were expected, teachers were poorly paid and schools were at times staffed by the relatives and friends of board members rather than the most qualified personnel available.

Concerned educators sought to reform these defects by encouraging the professionalization of teaching and educational administration. They established teachers' colleges, programs in educational administration, and agencies of accreditation. They worked in state legislatures for laws that required of teachers a specific number and variety of educational courses and practical teaching experiences. Principals and superintendents were expected to have studied the "science of administration" that was developing in the early 1900s. And these reform efforts were rewarded by more highly educated teachers, tidier administration, gradually improved salaries, and a strict separation of the workings of political parties from the conduct of educational affairs. Indeed, for many Americans, the belief that education and politics should not mix became an unquestioned truth.

THE MODERN AMERICAN SCHOOL

The characteristic features of the nineteenth- and early twentieth-century educational system have since gathered behind them the weight of historical tradition, making their alteration difficult, if not impossible. Yet, however appropriate they once were for an agrarian, postfrontier, newly developing society, these same institutional characteristics are much less adequate for the metropolitan, mobile, highly interdependent, postindustrial society that America has, in recent decades, come to be.

The common neighborhood school no longer serves a wide range of social and intellectual groups in the community. In metropolitan areas, it has become, instead, a highly stratified institution that serves distinctive student populations. The growth of cities and suburbs, together with the class, racial, and ethnic segregation of their neighborhoods, has created neighborhood schools that serve highly selective student populations. The racial segregation in our urban schools is well known. But if blacks attend their own schools, so do working-class whites, middle-class whites, the upper middle class, and, to a lesser extent, Poles, Jews, and Italians. If big-city schools always tended to be more homogeneous than those in rural areas, the recent rapid growth of metropolitan areas, with their one-class suburbs, has only accentuated and aggravated this tendency. Today, it can hardly be said that most young Americans are being educated in a "common" school.

With the change in the composition of the neighborhood school, local control has taken on a new significance. Locally elected boards of education have traditionally depended heavily on local property taxes to finance their schools. This tax falls very unevenly on citizens within the metropolitan area. In some communities, a local industrial plant or valuable residential property provides the school board with ample resources to finance local schools at an almost luxurious level. In other, sometimes adjacent communities, the presence of only modest homes, together with a large school-age population, may require that citizens make a considerable financial sacrifice in order to provide just moderately well-financed schools. Two adjacent cities in Michigan illustrate dramatically a more general pattern described by Campbell and Meranto in their article in this section. In Dearborn, property owners paid in 1970–71 a tax rate of only 25.90 mills per $100 of the assessed value of their property, but the school system was able to spend $1,297 per pupil for current expenditures.[2] In Dearborn Heights, taxpayers in that same year paid a millage rate of 27.90, which yielded enough to allow only $684 per pupil in current expenditures. The Dearborn Heights taxpayers would have had nearly to triple their tax rate to provide the same financial support for their schools that Dearborn already enjoyed at an already *lower* tax rate. The difference between the two cities is due to the large automobile plant in Dearborn; many workers employed by that plant live in Dearborn Heights, a town without industry. Such are the modern inequities of our historical legacy of local control.

Local financing of the educational system has been supplemented by state and federal assistance. But, although state aid has partially modified the inequities caused by variations in the tax base among local communities, it has hardly equalized matters.[3] For example, the Dearborn-Dearborn Heights figures take into account the state aid received by these communities. And federal aid to education, which still accounts for less than 15 percent of the total amount spent on elementary and secondary education, has had at best only a slight equalizing impact on school district expenditures.

Local control of education in metropolitan areas has had another less obvious though no less pernicious consequence as well. With every locally controlled school district competing against other school districts for preferred types of teachers, administrators, *and pupils*, most are constrained by market forces from pursuing innovative programs, especially those with egalitarian consequences. This tendency is most evident in the politics of school desegregation. Although many communities might welcome a limited number of minority group pupils into their schools, most fear that any show of tolerance on the part of their community alone would lead to major minority-group in-migrations. As central cities have lost their competitive advantage vis-à-vis outlying suburban areas, they, too, have considered carefully the impact of any desegregation plans on patterns of racial in- and out-migration. In his study of school politics in Chicago, Peterson shows that school-board desegregation plans were carefully constructed in order to stabilize the white population of that city. But if every community's school board tries to keep or expand its white population, and to dissuade minorities from entering its territory, then the city's school policies will explicitly or implicitly be biased to favor already advantaged pupils.

The professionalization of American education has also had its adverse consequences in urban America. Although it helped to modernize the country school, the very success of this reform has bred new difficulties. Nowhere is this problem more extreme than in New York City. In order to prevent patronage in the city's schools, every promotion within that organization was based on length of time in lower-level positions and performance on written and oral examinations. As a result, individuals from outside of the New York system, who may have new orientations and approaches, cannot be attracted to high-level positions. And performance on these examinations may have little to do with one's ability to act as a good principal or district superintendent. Moreover, the desire to have uniformity in operations in all schools (so as to avoid accusations of favoritism) has stifled individual creativity in a morass of bureaucratic rules, routines, and regulations. For example, the New York City supplies office once refused to issue order forms because the request itself was not filled out on an order form.[4]

THE POWER OF PROFESSIONALISM

The significance of the professionalization of American education is even greater in the political sphere. Because of their successful reform efforts to eliminate patronage politics from the schools, educational professionals have established themselves as the dominant voice in shaping educational policy. Professionally trained superintendents, with large supporting administrative staffs, control access to much of the information upon which a school board must make a decision. Nor can school boards easily dismiss school superintendents and/or their assistants, for this easily leads to charges of political interference in the educational process. Indeed, in most big city school systems, all employees, save only the superintendent, hold tenured positions, from which they cannot be removed unless malpractice or extreme incompetence is proven.

In recent years, teachers, too, have become an increasingly important political force. Previously, the National Education Association (NEA) and its state affiliates had sought to raise teacher salaries indirectly by campaigning for additional state and federal aid to education. In large cities, today, however, teachers are more directly influencing school-board policies affecting their salaries and working conditions. Both the more militant American Federation of Teachers and the previously less-aggressive NEA affiliates have demanded collective-bargaining agreements and carried out successful strikes when these agreements were not satisfactory. Not only have salaries in large city school systems dramatically improved, but teacher organizations are able to influence other policy questions as well. In Chicago, the teachers' union for a long time blocked all federal efforts to integrate the teaching faculty, and, in New York City, it substantially modified plans to introduce a decentralized system of administration and control.

Community organizations active in the educational arena have generally been neither very powerful nor very critical of the professional educators. The Parent-Teacher Association has local affiliates in most communities. Since these are neighborhood-oriented organizations closely associated with specific schools, they have generally had a limited impact on overall school policy. In big cities, there is usually a city-wide organization (in New York, it is known as the Public Education Association; in Chicago, the Citizens Schools Committee) that focuses its attention on broader issues. Its membership consists largely of upper-middle-class Protestant and Jewish liberals interested in protecting the schools from political interference. Typically it has had considerable influence over the selection of school-board members. But once selected to serve, board members seldom feel very beholden to these organizations, which have too small a membership and too few financial resources to press for alternatives to plans developed by professionals within the school system itself.

Few other influential organizations sustain an active interest in the direction of school affairs. Labor unions may be interested in maintaining contact with the vocational programs, the Taxpayers

Association may periodically object to increases in the tax rate for education, and the Chamber of Commerce or some other group of prominent businessmen may offer some public expression of general support for the schools in crisis situations. But, once the educational reformers chased the political parties out of education, they secured a good deal of autonomy over policy-making for themselves. No wonder David Tyack now says (in the article that follows) that a new reform politicizing the educational system is needed to undo the reforms of the past.

The one exception to this pattern has to do with racial issues. Although once again the educational professionals have played a major role in settling the issues of school desegregation, compensatory education, and community participation and control, they have not been able to pursue their goals free of outside pressure. Civil-rights groups, such as the NAACP, CORE, and, more frequently, *ad hoc* collections of black community organizations, have vigorously campaigned for racial integration. School professionals have not responded to these demands with great enthusiasm, and, as a result, little in the way of school integration has taken place in northern American cities.[5] But, when civil-rights groups have seen some hope of winning support from the educators, desegregation plans have aroused such intense opposition from white parents' associations and neighborhood groups that they have failed to be realized.[6] Blacks more recently have promoted the notion of community control as an alternative mechanism for improving the educational opportunities of black children. Here, they have met strong resistance from administrators and teachers, who fear this encroachment on their position of power. But with this demand, blacks may find it easier to form alliances with white neighborhood organizations, who also are demanding more community involvement.[7]

The structure of power within the educational arena is not perfectly stable; educational professionals are coming under increasing attack. The demands for community control are only one sign. The rapidly spreading "free school" idea, where parents pay money to send their children to a school that specializes in maintaining close teacher-parent contacts, is another. The increasing prestige of and state financial support for parochial schools indicate a decline in the pre-eminent position of the public school. Both liberal and conservative economists have suggested that parents be given educational vouchers that could be used to buy their children's education wherever they please. The Office of Economic Opportunity has, in fact, tried a number of experimental "tuition voucher" plans in selected cities. Elsewhere, some urban school boards are contracting particular schools to private firms, promising them extra payment if they can demonstrate that students are performing up to the level expected of them. The power of the professionals is rooted in their monopoly of control over educational opportunities. Should one or more of these various proposals for change be adopted on a widespread scale, the professionals' dominant position in the educational arena would be seriously endangered.

The traditional system is under attack, but one should not expect it to change all that quickly. Many interests in strong political positions are well served by a locally controlled, professionally directed neighborhood school system. Educational administrators have great influence in state capitols, and teachers are better organized than ever before. Politicians are still reluctant to entrap themselves in school controversies. The federal government's attempts at educational reform have made only a minor dent in local bureaucratic behavior.[8] The professionals are not the only beneficiaries, however. Local control of the public schools means that the upper middle class can have luxurious public schools for their children without providing the same, expensive education for all. Neighborhood schools also protect working- and middle-class whites from contact with the poor blacks whom they fear and distrust. The legacy of an outdated educational past will probably continue to contribute to the urban crisis.

NOTES

1. Arnold J. Heidenheimer, "The Politics of Public Education, Health and Welfare in the U.S. and Western Europe: How Growth and Reform Potentials Have Differed" (paper presented at the 1972 Annual Meeting of the American Political Science Association, Washington, D.C., September 5–9, 1972), p. 5.
2. These figures are compiled from data presented in Michigan Department of Education, *Ranking of Michigan Public High School Districts by Selected Financial Data, 1970–71*, Bulletin 1012: December, 1971. The figures were compiled by Alan Thomas, Department of Education, University of Chicago, and we are indebted to Professor Thomas for his permission to use this information.
3. John E. Coons, William H. Clune III, and Stephen D. Sugarman, *Private Wealth and Public Education* (Cambridge, Mass.: Harvard University Press, 1970).
4. The example is taken from David Rogers, *110 Livingston Street* (New York: Random House, 1968), p. 274.
5. See *ibid.*, pp. 305–23; and Robert Crain, *The Politics of Desegregation* (Chicago: Aldine Press, 1968), pp. 115–24.

6. See Rogers, *op. cit.*, Chapter 3; Bert Swanson, *The Struggle for Equality* (New York: Hobbs, Dorman, 1966); and Paul E. Peterson, "The School Busing Controversy: Redistributive or Pluralist Politics," *Administrator's Notebook* XX (May, 1972), pp. 1–4.
7. A good discussion of the issues involved can be found in Henry M. Levin (ed.), *Community Control of Schools* (Washington, D.C.: The Brookings Institution, 1970).
8. The federal government has had a substantial impact on integration policies in the South, however. An excellent analysis of this effort can be found in Gary Orfield, *The Reconstruction of Southern Education* (New York: John Wiley and Sons, 1964).

BIBLIOGRAPHY

CRAIN, ROBERT. *The Politics of Desegregation.* Chicago: Aldine Press, 1968.

CRONIN, JOSEPH M. *The Control of Urban Schools.* New York: Free Press, 1973.

HERRICK, MARY. *The Chicago Schools: A Social and Political History.* Beverly Hills, Calif.: Sage Publications, 1971.

LaNOUE, GEORGE R. and BRUCE L. R. SMITH. *The Politics of School Decentralization.* Lexington, Mass.: Heath, 1973.

MASOTTI, LOUIS H. *Education and Politics in Suburbia.* Cleveland: The Press of Case Western Reserve, 1967.

ORFIELD, GARY. *The Reconstruction of Southern Education.* New York: John Wiley and Sons, 1964.

PETERSON, PAUL E. *School Politics: Chicago Model* (Chicago: University of Chicago Press, 1976).

RAVITCH, DIANE. *The Great School Wars: New York City, 1805–1973.* New York: Basic Books, 1974.

ROGERS, DAVID, *110 Livingston Street.* New York: Random House, 1968.

ROSENTHAL, ALAN, ed. *Governing Education.* Garden City, N.Y.: Doubleday, 1969.

SILBERMAN, CHARLES E. *Crisis in the Classroom.* New York: Random House, 1970.

ZEIGLER, HARMON and KENT JENNINGS. *Governing American Schools.* North Scituate, Mass.: Duxbury, 1974.

THE METROPOLITAN EDUCATION DILEMMA: MATCHING RESOURCES TO NEEDS*

ALAN K. CAMPBELL AND PHILIP MERANTO

The metropolitanization of American society has gained widespread attention in recent years from a notable variety of scholars, popular writers, and public officials. Some scholars have preoccupied themselves with tracing the historical roots of metropolitanism, while others have attempted to demonstrate empirical relationships between metropolitanism and the social, economic, and political dimensions of society. Popular writers have interpreted some of these findings for the general public, and they have usually stressed the so-called "decay" of large American cities and the multitude of problems plaguing these urban centers. While journalists and scholars have been describing and analyzing the metropolitan phenomenon, public officials have been struggling with its policy implications. For these officials, the fact of metropolitanism, however dimly perceived, complicates many of the problems with which they must deal and influences many of the decisions they make.

The extent of this concern with one of the major forces of change in postwar America has been beneficial but, on occasion, misleading. On the one hand, it has stimulated popular interest and knowledge of the changing character of American culture. Further, it has prompted a wide assortment of research efforts about the causes and consequences of metropolitanism. On the other hand, there has been a tendency to see nearly all of the changes and problems which characterize contemporary America

* This article is based, in part, on a Carnegie Corporation-supported larger study of *Policies and Policy-Making in Large City Education Systems* being done at the Metropolitan Studies Center, Maxwell Graduate School, Syracuse University.

From Alan K. Campbell and Philip Meranto, "The Metropolitan Education Dilemma: Matching Resources to Needs," in Marilyn Gittell (ed.), *Educating an Urban Population* (1967), pp. 15–36. Reprinted by permission of the authors and the publisher, Sage Publications, Inc.

as consequences of the metropolitan process. Too often the inter-relationships between substantive problems and metropolitanism have been blurred rather than clarified by this kind of perception. Similarly, there has been a tendency to assume that the problems involved in the provision of any public service (education, welfare, health, transportation, and so forth) are all related to or result from metropolitanism. This is not the case. With every function there are problems that would exist even if the country had not become metropolitan. Further, the fact of metropolitanism is not a problem in itself, but the dynamics which underpin it and the patterns which accompany it may be perceived by individuals and groups within the society as creating problems, and in many instances the problems thus perceived can be solved only by public action.

The tendency to equate both social change and functional concerns with metropolitanism is evident in the field of education. Much of the literature which purports to discuss the implications of metropolitanism or urbanism for education is, instead, simply a catalog of the substantive issues which characterize the education function. The metropolitan component of the problems is often assumed to be self-evident, and no effort is made to demonstrate the relationship between metropolitanism and the substantive issues.

It is the primary purpose of this article to delineate those aspects of metropolitanism which produce important consequences for the performance of the education function in large urban centers. Such an analysis necessitates, first, an investigation of basic population trends and an examination of the distributional results of these trends on income, educational attainment, race, and the nature of school population. Second, the relationships between these population attributes and the provision of educational services are analyzed, as are the relationships between education needs and the quantity and quality of resources available in the various parts of the metropolis. And finally, the public policy alternatives are examined in terms of their ability to meet the demonstrated needs.

CHARACTERISTICS OF METROPOLITAN AMERICA

The most often cited statistic about metropolitanism is the growing proportion of the American population which lives in metropolitan areas.[1] By 1964 this proportion had reached 65 percent, and projections indicate that it will approach 70 percent by 1970. A simultaneous phenomenon, perhaps of even greater significance for the education function, is the redistribution of people between the central city and its suburbs. There has been a gradual but consistent decrease in the proportion of total metropolitan population which lives within central cities. In 1900 over 60 percent of the metropolitan population lived within central cities; by 1965 this share had declined to under 50 percent. . . .

The significance of these shifts for the education function would be substantial even if the population redistribution between central city and suburbs was random relative to the socioeconomic characteristics of the people involved. But this is not the case. The shifting is not only a matter of numbers of people; it also involves a sorting-out process. In general, it is the poor, less educated, nonwhite Americans who are staying in the central city and the higher income, better educated, whites who are moving out, although this description must be qualified somewhat in terms of the size of the metropolitan area and region of the country in which it is located. The larger the metropolitan area, however, the more accurate is this description.[2]

This sorting-out process has resulted in a median family income for central city residents in 1959 which was 88.5 percent of outside central city income; $5,940 for central cities, compared to $6,707 for the suburbs. Although median family income for both central city and outside central city residents has grown since 1959, the gap is widening, with central city median family income in 1964 at $6,697, while for outside central city areas it was $7,772, a proportionate relationship of 86.2 percent.[3] . . .

The explanation for the income and education differences between central city and suburb rests in part on differences in the distribution of nonwhite population within metropolitan areas.[4] Although the nonwhite component of the American population has now distributed itself between metropolitan and nonmetropolitan areas in approximately the same proportion as the white population, the distribution within metropolitan areas follows a quite different pattern. It is well known that the proportion of nonwhites in central cities has been increasing, while the proportion in the suburban areas has been declining. This larger proportion of Negro population in central cities helps to account in part for the differences in educational achievement and income between central cities and suburbs. Due to a history of discrim-

TABLE 1.—Nonwhite Population Contrasted with Nonwhite
School Enrollment for 15 Largest Cities: 1960

City	Percent Nonwhite of Total Population	Percent Nonwhite of School Population	Difference in Proportions of Nonwhite School Enrollment and Nonwhite Population
New York	14.0	22.0	8.0
Chicago	22.9	39.8	16.9
Los Angeles	12.2	20.5	8.3
Philadelphia	26.4	46.7	20.3
Detroit	28.9	42.9	14.0
Baltimore	34.7	50.1	15.4
Houston	22.9	30.2	8.7
Cleveland	28.6	46.1	17.5
Washington	53.9	77.5	23.6
St. Louis	28.6	48.8	20.2
Milwaukee	8.4	16.2	7.8
San Francisco	14.3	30.5	16.2
Boston	9.1	16.4	7.3
Dallas	19.0	26.0	7.0
New Orleans	37.2	55.4	18.2

SOURCE: U.S. Bureau of the Census, U.S. Census of Population: 1960,
Selected Area Reports, Standard Metropolitan Statistical Areas and General
Social and Economic Characteristics, 1960.

ination in all aspects of life, the Negro has a lower income and
less education than does his white neighbor. In central cities, for
example, the 1964 median family income for Negroes was $4,463,
while for whites it was $7,212. In 1964 the percentage of all
Negroes twenty-five years old and over having completed four
years of high school was 17.1; the comparable percentage for
whites was 31.3.

The impact of the growing proportion of nonwhite population
in central cities is intensified for the schools by the even higher
proportion of public school enrollment which is nonwhite. This
difference in population and enrollment proportions is a result
of age distribution, family composition, and the greater tendency
of white parents to send their children to private and parochial
schools. Table [1] shows, for 1960, the proportion of the total
population of the largest cities which was nonwhite and the pro-

portion of public school enrollment which was nonwhite. The ratio of nonwhites to whites is considerably higher in the school population than in the total population, and indications are that this is becoming increasingly the case.

The sorting-out process which produces significant differences in socioeconomic characteristics between central city and suburban populations is the chief background factor against which the educational implications of metropolitanism must be examined. To the extent that these differences in characteristics produce different kinds of educational problems, the fact of metropolitanism is important to the provision of educational services.

POPULATION COMPOSITION AND EDUCATIONAL PROBLEMS

The redistribution process described in the preceding section has left the central city school system with a disproportionate segment of pupils who are referred to as "disadvantaged," and this appears to be a trend that is continually increasing. These students are disadvantaged in terms of the income level and educational background of their parents, their family composition, and their general home environment. To the extent that education of the disadvantaged is a more complex phenomenon than the education of middle-income pupils, the central city school systems face a different and more serious set of problems than do suburban education systems.[5]

In the immediate postwar period, the most striking phenomenon in education related to the metropolitanization of the country was the impact on suburban areas of a rapidly increasing population. The suburbs, however, responded well to the challenge and rapidly met the new requirements in building the necessary physical facilities and the provisions of a teaching staff. The significance of the suburban expansion for the central city schools, however, was only dimly, if at all, perceived. It is now clear that the suburbanization of the country, by draining the higher income families and much economic activity from the central cities, produced greater problems for education in central cities than it did for the suburbs.

As the proportion of disadvantaged students in the central cities has increased, there has been a simultaneous increase in what are known in the community as "undesirable" schools, schools to which parents would prefer not to send their children. Many of these schools are so characterized because of the large proportion (in many cases, nearly 100 percent) of the students who are Negro. Because of population trends and the residential pattern of most of our cities, it is increasingly difficult to rearrange district lines to achieve what is referred to as "racial balance" among schools. As a result, more and more central city schools are being designated as "undesirable."

The underlying cause for the undesirable label in educational terms, however, is low income, not race. Several studies have now substantiated that the single most important determinant of educational achievement is family income.[6] In the high correlation between income and test scores, income undoubtedly is a proxy, and a fairly accurate one, for a combination of factors—family characteristics, educational attainment of parents, home environment. When white parents resist sending their children to undesirable schools, this is not necessarily a racial issue, although it is often difficult to separate the racial and educational questions which currently surround controversies over central city schools.

The undesirable schools are unattractive not only to parents but also to first-rate teachers. Teachers seek to be assigned to the "better" schools within the city system, and many abandon central city districts entirely for more attractive suburban districts. Furthermore, central city systems find it increasingly difficult to attract choice graduates of the universities as new teachers.

The resource needs for central cities relate not only to teachers but to other educational needs as well. Cities have much older school plants than do suburbs, and the site costs for building new schools within central cities are substantially higher than those for the suburbs. In addition, there is greater competition within the cities for resources for such noneducation functions as police protection, street maintenance, and welfare than is true in the suburban areas. These noneducation needs compete for the same resources which the central city schools need to meet their pressing educational problems.

This set of central city education problems exists in a society which is in need of a continuous improvement in its educational output. The very fact of metropolitanization implies extended specialization in a society which is increasingly complex. The need, therefore, is for a better and better educated work force. To some extent, the suburban areas have responded to this need through the gradual improvement and sophistication of its curricula and teaching. Curriculum improvement in central cities, however, is much less discernible and is particularly lacking in the education of the disadvantaged.[7]

The answer to this problem does not rest with providing education with a different purpose for disadvantaged pupils. A suggestion by James Conant that disadvantaged pupils should be concentrated in vocational education hardly seems appropriate.[8] Improvement in the quality of vocational education is needed, but it should not be made especially for the disadvantaged. Among the disadvantaged, there are those who are capable of achieving high educational accomplishment in a great variety of fields and options, and in terms of equity the opportunities should be the same for them as for other pupils. Further, it is apparent that the greatest employment growth of the future will be in the white-collar occupations, not in vocational fields offered by most of today's vocational schools.

One of the central issues confronting large city schools, therefore, becomes the allocation of sufficiently massive resources to the field of education for the disadvantaged to help them overcome their present handicaps. To what extent are large central cities capable of providing the resources needed to meet these problems and where are these resources to come from if the central cities cannot provide them from local assets?

THE AVAILABILITY OF RESOURCES

The educational problems confronting large cities would not be nearly as critical if cities had at their disposal an ample supply of resources to deal with these difficulties. But this is not the case. The metropolitan process has not only redistributed the population in a way that presents the central cities with a population having special educational difficulties; the process has simultaneously operated to weaken the local resource base which must be used to meet their needs.

It has already been noted that the central city component of the metropolitan area population has lower income levels than the population outside the central city. This pattern is particularly significant because it has become increasingly apparent that income is the single most important variable in explaining the expenditure levels of a community for both educational and non-educational services.[9] To a large extent, it is the income available which influences the ability of a governmental unit to meet the service requirements of its population. Central cities are simply losing ground in this respect, while their functional needs are simultaneously increasing.

Metropolitanism is characterized by the decentralization of economic activities from the core city to the surrounding areas, as well as by decentralization of population. Evidence of this trend can be found by examining the distribution of economic activity within specific metropolitan areas over time. For example, an investigation of the proportion of manufacturing carried on in the central city portion of twelve large metropolitan areas demonstrates that the central city percentage has clearly declined over the past three decades, particularly in the post–World War II period. Whereas the twelve cities accounted, on the average, for 66.1 percent of manufacturing employment in 1929, this proportion decreased to 60.8 percent by 1947 and then declined to less than half (48.9 percent) by 1958.[10]

A similar decentralizing trend for retail activity can be demonstrated by examining the growth of retail store sales in the metropolitan area as a whole, in the central city, and in the central business district of the core city for the period 1948 to 1958. Such a comparison was made for a sample of twenty-two large cities. It was found that with the exception of one (Birmingham, Alabama), the entire metropolitan area had increased its retail sales more than had the central city and far more than the central business district. This evidence illustrates that the historical dominance of the central city and its business district over regional retail activity is on the decline.[11] The patterns for manufacturing employment and retail sales reflect the fact that economic activity, like population, has migrated from the central city outward. This push for dispersal is related to a number of factors, including the need for physical space, the introduction of new industrial processes, the ascendance of the automobile and truck as means of transportation and shipping, the building of vast highway systems, and the spreading of the population throughout the metropolis.[12]

The consequences of this economic migration for the tax base of the central city have been widely discussed. As industries continue to move outward, taxable assessed valuation, the source of local property taxes, has barely held its own in many cities and has actually declined in several large cities. For example, in a recent five-year period, the percent changes in taxable assessed valuation for seven cities were as follows: Baltimore, −10.5 percent; Boston, −1.2 percent; Buffalo, −1.0 percent; Detroit, −2.0 percent; St. Louis, + 1.1 percent; Philadelphia, +2.8 percent; and Cleveland −3.4 percent.[13] These changes in taxable valuation do not yield the necessary resources to deal with the problems facing these urban centers.

Translated into educational terms, the recent performance of the tax base in large cities has not kept pace with the growth or nature of the school population in these cities. Indeed, an examination of the per pupil taxable valuation over a five-year period shows that ten large cities out of fourteen experienced a decrease in this source of revenue. Since local property taxes are the most important source of local educational revenues, large city schools can barely meet ordinary education needs let alone resolve the problems resulting from the shifting population distribution.

There is an additional factor which weighs against the capacity of central cities to meet their pressing educational needs. The postwar intensification of urbanization and metropolitanization has resulted in a demand for a wider range and higher quality of public services than at any other time in the nation's history. These demands are particularly great in the largest cities, where the necessity for providing a wide variety of welfare, public safety, sanitation, traffic control, and street maintenance services has been most pressing. An investigation of the fiscal patterns in

TABLE 2.—Five-Year Changes in per Pupil Taxable Assessed Valuation

	Percent of Change over a Five-Year Period*	
	City	State (minus cities listed)
Baltimore	−19.3	10.2
Boston	− 5.3	not available
Buffalo	− 8.6	26.1
Chicago	− 6.0	− 0.2
Cleveland	− 9.9	4.2
Detroit	− 5.7	3.4
Houston	− 2.8	18.9
Los Angeles	5.1	5.6
Milwaukee	− 9.6	− 1.1
New York City	32.4	26.1
Philadelphia	− 0.6	13.6
Pittsburgh	2.2	13.6
St. Louis	−10.6	3.1
San Francisco	5.9	5.6

* Change is for the most recent five-year period for which data are available.
SOURCE: Research Council of the Great Cities Program for School Improvement, The Challenge of Financing Public Schools in Great Cities, Chicago, 1964.

thirty-six Standard Metropolitan Statistical Areas revealed that for the year 1957, the central cities in these areas were spending $25.66 more per capita in total expenditures than the communities in the outlying areas. Unfortunately for education systems, this difference was not due to higher educational expenditures in the central cities. In fact, their education expenditures were $27.82 per capita less than what was spent on education in the corresponding suburban areas. It was in the noneducational category that the central city exceeded the outside central city area in expenditures. In this sample, central cities spent about $53.00 more per capita on noneducation services than their surrounding communities. Further, this difference is largely due to the "all other" classification, which includes the traditional municipal services that cities, unlike suburban communities, must provide. The cost and number of noneducational governmental services tend to increase with the size and density of a district and to consume a larger proportion of the budget in major cities where many services are provided for nonresidents as well as for residents. It is reasonable to suggest that this "municipal overburden" is supported at the expense of the education function.[14]

The central cities were supporting these expenditure levels by taxes that were $23.39 per capita higher than in areas outside the cities. In contrast, the cities received about $5.00 per capita less in total intergovernmental aid and, most importantly, $12.31 less per capita in education aid than did suburban areas, where income was higher. In other words, not only are central cities pressed to support a large array of services by a relatively shrinking tax base, but they tax themselves more heavily to do so and they receive less intergovernmental aid than the more wealthy communities in their metropolitan area. This fiscal pattern borders on the ironic when it is realized that central city education systems must compete for educational resources with suburban school districts which have higher income levels and receive a greater amount of state aid. In fact, the state aid system actually works to intensify rather than to resolve the educational crises facing large city school systems.

The multitude of fiscal difficulties faced by the central cities results in a lower per student expenditure in the cities than in surrounding suburbs. Specifically, an examination of the thirty-seven largest metropolitan areas in the country indicated that the central city school districts in 1962 were spending an average of $144.96 less per pupil than their suburban counterparts.[15] This considerable difference in expenditures per student between central city and suburb would be serious even if the educational problems were the same for the two type areas; but, as has already been demonstrated, such is not the case.

It is not known what amount of additional resources per student would be necessary to provide an adequate education for the culturally disadvantaged. On the basis of studies yet to be published, it is clear that the present small amounts of additional resources being used in some cities for what is generally referred to as "compensatory education" are accomplishing very little.[16] The additional resources currently being allocated to these programs are simply not sufficient. . . .

This analysis of the resources available for central city education demonstrates the disparity between needs and resources. There is little indication that present trends will substantially alter these circumstances; in fact, there is good reason to believe that the situation is becoming more serious. If these trends are to be modified, imaginative public policy decisions must be identified and pursued. What public policy alternatives exist and to what extent are they politically feasible?

PUBLIC POLICY IMPLICATIONS

A variety of means exists for attacking the lack of fit between educational needs and resources. Some of these are politically more feasible than others.

Perhaps the most obvious solution would be to redistribute the population so as to reduce the concentration of disadvantaged pupils in cities. The demand for racial integration within public education points in this direction. There are, however, both physical and political obstacles to this course of action which, at the moment, appear to be insurmountable. First, the disadvantaged are concentrated in wide geographic areas within many cities. To redistribute these pupils throughout the city and throughout the metropolitan area, which would be necessary to achieve integration in the future, would require a transportation network so extensive and costly that it is both physically and politically impractical.

Obviously, there are neighborhood school districts where the redrawing of attendance areas within cities and perhaps the redrawing of district lines between cities and suburbs would substantially alter the present student balance in the schools. Where this is the case, however, political resistance is likely to be stiff.

The recently discovered attachment of many people to the neighborhood school has produced powerful political support for present district lines and attendance areas. To assume that such
changes could be accomplished on a metropolitan-wide basis is
unrealistic.

There is, in fact, an inverse relationship between the intensity
of political opposition to accomplishing some redistribution of
pupils and the size of the area and proportion of the population
involved. In cities where the proportion of disadvantaged students,
particularly the proportion of Negro students, is relatively low
(thereby making the redrawing of attendance area lines a meaningful alternative), the political resistance seems capable of preventing any substantial changes. Boston is a good example of
this situation: On the other hand, where the political strength
of the disadvantaged is great enough to initiate some change, the
high proportion of students and large areas involved present a
practical limitation on how much can be accomplished in this
manner.

An alternative to the decentralization of disadvantaged students
is the much-discussed creation of education parks or campuses
which would contain many more pupils than the present single-
building schools. By drawing on a larger enrollment area, school
campuses would be able to concentrate services and would contain
a more heterogeneous population, thereby, presumably, providing
a higher quality of education for all students.

The concentration of disadvantaged students also would be
lessened by the return of middle-income families to cities from
the suburbs. It had been anticipated by some students of urban
affairs that urban renewal would contribute to such a return. This
reversal of the outward flow of people would have been beneficial
in two ways: The mix of students in the schools would be improved and the tax base for supporting education would be
strengthened. However, the contribution of urban renewal to re-
vitalizing the central city has not been great. Much of the current
disappointment over urban renewal has resulted from the lack of
recognition of the importance of low-quality education as one of
the primary factors motivating the move out of the city. It seems
apparent that physical redevelopment, unless it is accompanied
and closely interrelated with a variety of social improvements,
particularly improvements in public education, will not attract
the suburbanite back to the city.

Whatever the possibility of pupil redistribution, the central
need is and will remain additional resources for the education of

the disadvantaged. Whether educated where they are presently located or elsewhere, the disadvantaged have special education needs. To meet these needs, which is the only way of guaranteeing equality of educational opportunity, additional resources are required.

The present allocation pattern of state aid does little to accomplish this. In fact, the aid pattern runs exactly counter to the need pattern. It is possible that as reapportionment is accomplished and as the nature of the problem becomes more evident, state aid formulas will be revised to correspond more closely with needs. It is important to note, however, that reapportionment will result in a much greater gain in representation for the suburbs than it will for central cities.[17] It may be that the suburban representatives will recognize their stake in an improved central city education system; but if they do not, the present pattern of higher aid to the suburbs may well be accentuated rather than reversed by reapportionment.

Perhaps the single most significant policy response to the set of problems described here has been the response of the Federal government as reflected in the Elementary and Secondary Education Act of 1965.[18] This program, combined with the antipoverty program, has given recognition for the first time to the problem of allocating more resources to education for the disadvantaged. However, although the concept underpinning the legislation is sound, the amount of aid provided for large cities is relatively small in relation to the need. In the case of New York City, for instance, the new Federal aid amounts to only 6.2 percent of total 1962 education expenditures. For Chicago, the figure is 2.9 percent, for Los Angeles 2.6 percent, with the highest figure among the fifteen largest cities being for New Orleans, where the new aid will amount to 17.5 percent of 1962 school expenditures. This program is clearly moving in the right direction; the task is to fortify it with enough money so that it can have a substantial impact.

Whatever means are used to provide the resources for the provision of adequate education services, they will have to come, in large part, from the middle- and higher-income suburbanites. If, therefore, the suburbanites resist a redistribution of population or a redrawing of school district lines to create a more equitable balance in the present pupil ability distribution, the alternative—if the problem is to be met—is greater Federal and state taxes paid by persons of middle and high income.

The fundamental issue, therefore, really revolves around the ability and willingness of Federal and state governments to raise revenue and redistribute the resources according to need. If this is not done, no major improvement in the situation confronting central city school systems can be expected.

There remains, of course, the issue of the ability of school systems to make good use of additional resources. This question, which is discussed elsewhere in this issue, relates to the kinds of changes needed in both curriculum and teaching techniques if the educational disadvantages of many young people are to be overcome.

However that question is answered, the fact remains that quality education for all will not be accomplished until the resources are found to do the job.

NOTES

1. The Census Bureau definition of the metropolitan area and of its component parts is followed throughout this article. That definition is as follows: "Except in New England, a standard metropolitan statistical area (an SMAS) is a county or group of contiguous counties which contain at least one city of 50,000. In addition to the county, or counties, containing such a city or cities, contiguous counties are included in an SMAS if, according to certain criteria, they are essentially metropolitan in character and are socially and economically integrated with the central city." In New England, towns are used instead of counties.
2. For a complete discussion of these differences relative to size and region, see Advisory Commission on Intergovernmental Relations. *Metropolitan Social and Economic Disparities: Implications for Intergovernmental Relations in Central Cities and Suburbs*, Washington D.C.: U.S. Government Printing Office, 1965.
3. U.S. Bureau of the Census, *Consumer Income*, Series P-60, No. 48, April 25, 1966.
4. The terms nonwhite and Negro are used interchangeably in this article since Negroes constitute 92 percent of the nonwhite classification as defined by the Census Bureau.
5. For a sampling of the literature which deals with this topic see Frank Riessman, *The Culturally Deprived Child*, New York: Harper and Row Publishers, Incorporated, 1962; Judith R. Kramer and Seymour Leventman, *Children of the Gilded Ghetto*, New Haven, Yale University Press, 1961; A. Harry Passow (Ed.), *Education in Depressed Areas*, New York: Teachers College, Columbia University, 1963; and C. W. Hunnicutt (Ed.), *Urban Education and Cultural Deprivation*, Syracuse, N.Y.: Syracuse University Press, 1964.
6. Patricia Sexton, *Education and Income: Inequalities in Our Public Schools*, New York: The Viking Press, 1962; H. Thomas James, J. Alan Thomas, and Harold J. Dyck, *Wealth, Expenditures and Decision-Making for Education*, Stanford, Calif.: Stanford University Press, 1963; Fels

Institute of Local and States Government, University of Pennsylvania, *Special Education and Fiscal Requirements of Urban School Districts in Pensylvania,* 1964; and Jesse Burkhead, *Cost and Performance in Large City School Systems,* publication of Metropolitan Studies Center, Syracuse University, as part of the Carnegie supported study of Large City Education Systems, 1967.

7. William W. Wayson, *Curriculum Development in Large City Schools,* publication of Metropolitan Studies Center, Syracuse University, as part of the Carnegie supported study of Large City Education System, 1967.

8. James B. Conant, *Slums and Suburbs,* New York: The New American Library, 1964, pp. 33–49.

9. Alan K. Campbell and Seymour Sacks, *Metropolitan America: Fiscal Patterns and Governmental Systems,* Metropolitan Studies Center, Syracuse University, 1966.

10. See Raymond Vernon, *The Changing Economic Function of the Central City,* New York: Committee for Economic Development, 1960; and U.S. Bureau of the Census, *Census of Manufacturing, 1958.* The cities include: Baltimore, Boston, Chicago, Cincinnati, Cleveland, Detroit, Los Angeles-Long Beach, New York, Philadelphia, Pittsburgh, St. Louis, and San Francisco-Oakland.

11. See U.S. Bureau of the Census, *Census of Business, 1958* for the twenty-two cities which reported all three figures.

12. Edger M. Hoover and Raymond Vernon, *Anatomy of a Metropolis,* Garden City, N.Y.: Doubleday and Company, Inc., 1962.

13. The Research Council of the Great Cities Program for School Improvement, *The Challenge of Financing Public Schools in Great Cities,* Chicago, 1964.

14. David C. Ranney, *School Government and the Determinants of the Fiscal Support for Large City Education Systems,* unpublished doctoral dissertation, Syracuse University, 1966.

15. For a breakdown by individual city, see Seymour Sacks and David C. Ranney, "Suburban Education: A Fiscal Analysis," in Marilyn Gittell (Ed.), *Education and Urban Population* (New York: Sage, 1967), pp. 60–76.

16. Jesse Burkhead, *op. cit.*

17. Robert S. Friedman, "The Reapportionment Myth," *National Civic Review,* April, 1960, pp. 184–188.

18. Title I of this law, which accounts for about $1.06 billion of the approximately $1.3 billion authorized, provides for grants to be made to local school districts on the basis of 50 percent of the average per pupil expenditures made in their state for the school year 1963–1964 multiplied by the number of five- to seventeen-year-old children in the local school district from families with an annual income below $2,000, or with a higher income resulting from aid to dependent children relief payments. Local districts receive their proportion of the funds under this formula only after plans they have submitted indicating how they will meet the special educational needs of disadvantaged students are approved by their state education department. The politics surrounding the enactment of this legislation are analyzed in Philip Meranto, *The Politics of Federal Aid to Education in 1965: A Study in Political Innovation,* unpublished doctoral dissertation, Syracuse University, 1966.

NEEDED: THE REFORM OF A REFORM

DAVID B. TYACK

In 1936, Jodie Foote, a black school board member in Myrtle, Mississippi, wrote this letter to President Franklin D. Roosevelt:

> I am writen you concerning our school at was burn down some time ago we tried to get ade from the state. The state supt said it was not any funds on hand for that purpos. We tried the C.W.A. and failed. Then we tried the W.P.A. but we was the forgoten man. We have been teaching in a old out house. We have the boteing, got the foundation laid we are asking ade to get a cover flowing windows. We would like to seal it over head. Some of white friends have hpe us. Please send us a little ade for the Mc-Dowell school. We are going to have the names printed in our country paper all who help so we will never forget you for ading.[1]

In increasing numbers today, the poor refuse to be forgotten, the black to be invisible, the dispossessed to be powerless. Amid affluence for the majority undreamed of in the depths of the great depression, we now face a social upheaval which threatens to tear the nation apart.[2] Thus I would like to discuss the relations between school boards and the urban poor, the non-white, and the dispossessed.

In this group of forward-looking colleagues, I suppose that I am the only person paid each month for looking backwards. When the world changes as fast as it has in our lifetime, people naturally wonder how pertinent history can be to our present choices of policy. Yet short memories trap us all, and to me one of the values of examining the past is to regain a sense of surprise, to avoid taking our present attitudes and institutions for granted. We are often unwitting captives of history. We retain ingrained values past the time when they are appropriate. Norms relevant

From William E. Dickinson, ed. *New Dimensions in School Board Leadership* (1969), pp. 29–51. Reprinted by permission of the publisher, National School Boards Association, Evanston, Illinois.

to one situation may no longer be functional, yet we find it hard to abandon them. Accordingly, I should like to trace the historical development of such values as professionalization, bureaucratization, and a-political control of schools.[3] Then I should like to examine some alternatives which may hold promise for our troubled cities.

Reform Ideology at the Turn of the Century

Imagine, if you will, a gathering of people concerned about urban education during the period from 1890–1910. I shall take the liberty of putting questions to this panel of experts. Their answers are direct quotations from their speeches and printed works.[4]

D.T. Mr. Jones, you have had a great deal of practical experience as a teacher and as a superintendent in Indianapolis and Cleveland. What do you see as the major problem today in urban education?

L. H. Jones. The unscrupulous politician is the greatest enemy that we now have to contend with in public education. His highest conception of the public school is that its revenues offer him the opportunity of public plunder. Did he accomplish his end without other injury to the cause of education than the depletion of its revenues, he might be ranked merely with the common thief. However, he pushes his corrupting presence into the school itself.[5]

D.T. I believe that you have with you a number of letters from school administrators across the country which refer to this problem of political corruption. Would you kindly share some of these with us?

Jones. A superintendent in one of the Eastern States writes: "Nearly all the teachers in our schools get their positions by political 'pull.' If they secure a place and are not backed by political influence, they are likely to be turned out. Our drawing teacher recently lost her position for this reason." One writes from the South: "Most places depend on politics. The lowest motives are frequently used to influence ends." A faint wail comes from the far West: "Positions are secured and held by the lowest principles of corrupt politicians." "Politicians wage a war of extermination against all teachers who are not their vassals," comes from the Rocky Mountains.[6]

D.T. Mr. Wetmore, you have been a school committeeman in Boston. Have you had similar experience?

S. A. WETMORE. The teachership is still a spoil of office. It is more difficult, at the present time, for a Catholic than for a Protestant young woman to get a place, but nevertheless, some Catholics secure appointments, for "trading" may always be done, while each side has a wholesome fear of the other assailing it in the open board. A member said one day, in my hearing: "I must have my quota of teachers."[7]

D.T. Mr. Cubberley, from your vantage point as a professor at Stanford, how does San Francisco fare?

ELLWOOD P. CUBBERLEY. The worst kind of boss rule has prevailed in San Francisco, and the board of education gradually became a place sought by those who wished to use the position for political preferment or for personal ends. Once every six or eight years there would be an effort at reform, and a few good men were elected; but they were usually in a minority, and the majority, held together by "the cohesive force of plunder," ruled things with a high hand.[8]

D.T. Probably most of you could tell similar stories of corruption. How do you explain this problem?

CUBBERLEY. These Southern and Eastern Europeans (in our cities are) of a very different type from the North and West Europeans who preceded them. Largely illiterate, docile, often lacking in initiative, and almost wholly without the Anglo-Saxon conceptions of righteousness, liberty, law, order, public decency, and government, their coming has served to dilute tremendously our national stock and to weaken and corrupt our political life.[9]

D.T. Mr. Draper, as you know, is superintendent of schools in Cleveland. What were you about to say?

ANDREW S. DRAPER. It is a suggestive fact, that the only real progress in the direction of municipal reform has been made through the imposition of limitations upon the common suffrage.[10]

D.T. As I understand what you gentlemen are saying, the caliber of American citizens has been declining, and this helps to account for the corruption we see in school politics. But why haven't the conscientious citizens taken control? Mr. Ernst, what has been your experience in Boston?

GEORGE A. O. ERNST. For some years there had been a growing

dissatisfaction at the character of party nominations for the School Board. This was not wholly the fault of the party managers. All sorts of charges of dishonesty and incompetence were made against members, and it became rather discreditable than otherwise to accept what ought to be one of the most honorable positions within the gift of the people. One of the most distinguished members has said: "For five years, I served on the Boston Board with a gentleman of high character, a graduate of Harvard University, who sacrificed time and money in order that he might fulfill the sacred duty that had been committed to him; and yet he told me that often when he met his friends they would sneer at him for his sacrifices and throw contempt upon what they were pleased to call his being in politics."[11]

D.T. I don't quite understand how it is possible for laymen to extort such graft from schools. Is there something defective with the plan of organization of school boards? Mr. Boykin, in your work at the U.S. Bureau of Education you have studied this matter. Would you tell us how school boards are selected?

JAMES C. BOYKIN. The possible variations are as great in number as the combinations on the chessboard. The New York board controls the schools of over a million and a half of people, yet it numbers only 21 members, while Pittsburgh, with a population of about a quarter of a million, has 37 members in a central board and 222 in local boards. There are 7 members of the Minneapolis board, while Hartford, with only a third as many inhabitants, has 39 school visitors and committeemen. The first boards were chosen at popular elections and the members were ward representatives. This has not always worked well. The local feeling in members has often prevented them from appreciating any interests other than those of their own districts; and local politicians of small caliber have crept in from out-of-the-way wards, and have made things very unpleasant in various ways. To avoid these things, in many cities the board is elected from the city at large and not as representatives of any particular locality. In other places the mayor appoints the board, often with the advice and consent of the council. But alas, for human devices! instances have often occurred in which both methods of selection have proved to be as objectionable as ward elections, for there are big politicians as well as little ones.[12]

D.T. Mr. Ernst, you have seen how the Boston school committee worked prior to the attempted reforms in 1897. Would you tell us about it?

GEORGE A. O. ERNST. The superintendent and the supervisors had very few executive duties. The schools were governed by the inherently vicious system of sub-committees. There were no less than thirty of these sub-committees, with a total membership of 142. The city was divided into nine geographic divisions, and for each division a "committee in charge" was appointed. Each locality had its old-time traditions and rights which were asserted freely. Thus for years the "second division" had its own text-book on geography, absolutely distinct from that used anywhere else in Boston. The schools were burdened with provincialism in its most extreme and flagrant form. The committees were petty despots, jealously guarding their prerogatives.[13]

D.T. We have heard a lot about the evils of the old system. What can we do about it? As a newspaperman, Mr. Deweese, what is your perspective?

TRUMAN A. DEWEESE. The perfect system of school administration has not yet been devised. The schools belong to the people and the people belong to the politicians; therefore, the complete divorcement of the schools from politics would seem to be well-nigh impossible in this country. The problem that confronts the schoolman then is, how to get the control of the purely educational department of school management as far away from the politician as possible. Obviously this can be done only by a centralization of authority in the superintendent of schools.[14]

D.T. Dr. Rice, as a pediatrician and journalist, you have been outspoken on school reform for some time now—and have scars to prove it. Do you accept complete centralization of control of city schools?

DR. JOSEPH M. RICE. A superintendent cannot well care for more than one hundred and fifty, or at most two hundred teachers; in other words, he cannot properly care, without assistance, for a city of more than seventy-five thousand inhabitants at the utmost. As New York has twenty times two hundred teachers, twenty times seventy-five thousand inhabitants, its schools should be divided into at least twenty independent districts, each one of which should be placed in charge of a superintendent having all the powers and responsibilities of a city superintendent.[15]

D.T. How optimistic are you, Mr. Eliot, about changing the composition and procedures of city school boards? As President of Harvard and as a school reformer you have seen many educational movements come and go.

CHARLES W. ELIOT. I want to point out that a few disinterested and active men may sometimes get good legislation out of an American legislature. It was an extraordinarily small group of men acting under a single leader that obtained from the Massachusetts legislature the act which established the Boston School Committee of five members. The name of that leader was James J. Storrow. I am happy to believe that the group were all Harvard men. I have been much interested during the last year in studying both municipal evils and the chances of municipal reform; and I find the greatest encouragement for the ultimate success of that cause in the fact that many school committees in American cities have been redeemed, and made efficient, far-seeing, and thoroughly trustworthy.[16]

D.T. Mr. Draper, you were one of the first to advocate changes in the governing of urban schools and were mainly responsible for an NEA statement of policy on that matter. Would you care to summarize the reforms you see as essential?

ANDREW S. DRAPER. First. The affairs of the school should not be mixed up with partisan contests or municipal business. Second. There should be a sharp distinction between legislative functions and executive duties. Third. Legislative functions should be clearly fixed by statute and be exercised by a comparatively small board, each member of which is representative of the whole city. Fourth. Administration should be separated into two great independent departments, one of which manages the business interests and the other of which supervises the instruction. The chief executive of the department of instruction should be given a long term and may be appointed by the board. Once appointed he should be independent. He should appoint all authorized assistants and teachers. He should assign to duties and discontinue services for cause, at his discretion. He should determine all matters relating to instruction. The trouble has been that the boards were independent and the machine so ponderous and the prerogatives and responsibilities so confused that people could not get a hearing or could not secure redress, perhaps for the reason that no one official had the power to redress.[17]

THE PROCESS OF CENTRALIZATION

You have heard the views of these reformers. How successful were they? In 1894, when the movement to centralize control of city schools was just gaining momentum, Draper found little agreement among schoolmen on the specifics of urban school reform despite a general belief in smaller and less political school boards.[18] A generation later, a survey of 50 prominent city superintendents showed a remarkable degree of consensus on how urban schools should be run. The years from 1890 to 1910 had produced a set of values which became conventional educational wisdom. Of the 50 superintendents, 45 favored small school boards; 40 preferred election of boards from the city at large rather than by the older ward pattern; 46 thought it better to appoint rather than to elect superintendents; and 43 believed that superintendents were gaining the greater power and independence that befit their professional status.[19]

The watchwords of the reform movement in the city schools became centralization, expertise, professionalization, non-political control, efficiency. The most attractive models of organization were the large-scale industrial bureaucracies rapidly emerging in that age of consolidation. In city after city—Cleveland, New York, Boston, St. Louis, Baltimore, and others—leading business and professional men spearheaded the reforms. As Eliot reported, it was sometimes a very small group of patricians who secured new charters from state legislatures and thereby reorganized the urban schools without a popular vote in the cities. University presidents and leading school superintendents and education professors sometimes collaborated with the elite municipal reformers (Nicholas Murray Butler of Columbia, for example, saw an analogy in function between university trustees and city school boards since both should delegate administration to professional officers and both should be composed of "the best people.")[20] A major forum for the new conceptions of centralized and professionalized urban education became the National Education Association.[21] Often small cities and towns emulated the bureaucratic structures pioneered in the large cities. Professionally-directed urban school surveys helped to spread the gospel of bureaucratic efficiency in the years after 1910. Superintendents of great school systems saw parallels between their work and that of captains of industry. They promoted close ties between school systems and the business community.[22] Underlying much of the reform movement was an elitist assumption that prosperous, native-born Protestant Anglo-Saxons were superior to other groups and thus should determine the curriculum and the allocation of jobs. It was the mission of the schools to imbue children of the immigrants and the poor with uniformly WASP ideals.[23]

As was the case with other progressive urban reforms, the program to centralize and professionalize the schools sometimes failed to win enough votes in the state legislature. Often teachers saw bureaucratization not as a welcome relief from "politicians" but as a new form of autocracy. In Baltimore, for example, large numbers of teachers sabotaged the reform administration of Superintendent Van Sickle.[24]

The debate over centralization in New York City in 1896 illustrated the forces opposing the reformers. In his perceptive study of this battle, David Hammack finds that "in addition to a majority of the School Commissioners, nearly all of the city's school Inspectors, Trustees, principals and teachers opposed centralization." The New York central board of education had been relatively weak. In each of the twenty-four local wards, five trustees of the schools hired teachers and supervised the schools within their jurisdiction. Opponents of centralization argued that these local trustees were valuable mediators between school and community:

> The varied character of our population, and the concentration of special classes of our people in certain districts, makes it desirable that these people be represented in school matters, and this will only be possible by the appointment of local officials with the necessary powers of actions, who are acquainted with the distinctive characteristics . . . of the several neighborhoods.[25]

The editor of *School* Magazine concurred, saying that the active interest of these local officials stimulated public support of the schools. In addition, as Hammack observes, "the local trustee system allowed for a flexible school policy, since diverse community groups could modify basic policies in accordance with local preferences, increasing public confidence in the schools and enabling the trustees to 'harmonize' intergroup conflicts at the local level." Teachers and laymen alike worried about what might happen should the superintendent become "a kind of educational Pooh-Bah."[26] Reflecting this concern the President of the New York Board of Education later forbade the Superintendent to attend meetings of the National Education Association, a central gathering place of the captains of education.[27]

Here and there were powerful school officials who also worried about the effects of centralization of urban schools. One of the pioneers of professional school administration, Burke A. Hinsdale, wrote that

> In all cities, and most of all in large ones, the tendency toward machinery and bureaucracy is very strong in all kinds of work. It is

hard for the individual to assert his personal force. The superintendent's temptation to busy himself with manipulation is great. . . .
These considerations impel me to the conclusion that in the large
cities the superintendent will, as a rule, more and more tend to
machinery and administration; that he will become even more an
office man than he now is; that he will be less known in the form
of educational thought than he is at present—which is certainly
saying a great deal.[28]

Ella Flagg Young, who served as teacher, principal, and superintendent in the Chicago Schools, became concerned that teachers
would feel powerless and isolated in the vast city systems.[29]

Urban school reform in the period from 1890 to 1910 clearly
fits the pattern of elite municipal change described by the his-
torian Samuel P. Hays. Probing beneath the surface rhetoric
which pitted "the corrupt politician" v. "the good citizen," Hays
finds that most of the prominent urban "progressives" were leaders
in the financial and professional life of their cities. Their motives
were more complicated than simple abhorrence of graft. They
deplored the fact that under the decentralized ward system political power belonged mostly to lower- and middle-class groups
(many of them first or second generation immigrants). They
wished to apply to urban government the same process of centralization and bureaucratization, the same delegation of power
to professional experts, as they had developed in their own businesses and associations. Reformers wanted, says Hays, "not simply to replace bad men with good; they proposed to change the
occupational and class origins of decision-makers." When these
innovators talked of selecting "the best people" as school board
members, they, like many schoolmen, tended to disqualify the
working class:

Employment as ordinary laborer and in the lowest class of mill work
would naturally lead to the conclusion that such men did not have
sufficient education or business training to act as school directors.
. . . Objection might also be made to small shopkeepers, clerks,
workmen at many trades, who by lack of educational advantages and
business training, could not, no matter how honest, be expected to
administer properly the affairs of an educational system requiring
special knowledge, and where millions are spent each year.[30]

Underlying the ideology of the "non-political" urban school
board, then, was an actual realignment of power among economic
classes.[31] Behind the doctrine of professional control of instruction, of the bureaucratization of schooling, was a profound shift

of opinion about who should actually determine the goals and processes of education.[32] We live today with some of the unforeseen consequences of these reforms.

WILL PUBLIC EDUCATION SURVIVE IN THE GREAT CITIES?

"Even a cursory glance at the current writing on the state of urban education makes it clear that the first question to ask is whether public schools will survive the next decade in the great cities."[33] This statement by George LaNoue of Teachers College, Columbia, would have sounded apocalyptic in 1960. When he published it, in March, 1968, after riots in the streets and the dismal story told by the Kerner Commission, it sounded pessimistic, but plausible. By the summer of 1969, after the disastrous teachers' strike in New York and turmoil in city schools almost everywhere, the question has new urgency. In any case, urban public education *as we know it today* seems destined to change.[34] How it will change will depend in no small measure on the responses of city school boards.

The achievements of the generation of school reformers at the turn of the century have become the targets of critics today. Centralization of control of schools has produced vast bureaucracies whose red tape and resistance to change have been satirized by Bel Kaufman and analyzed in detail by scholars like Daniel V. Levine, Marilyn Gittell, and David Rogers. Policymaking often has seemed a closed system in which school boards, ostensibly a-political and relying on professionals, simply legitimize the recommendations of the school staff. Board members are often unable to acquire information on which to base independent decisions.[35] The "merit system" has also become a target. Elaborate credential and examination requirements, originally designed to frustrate the spoils system, now seem to exclude members of minority groups who make up an ever-increasing proportion of the population of central cities. They also prevent school boards from employing experts who do not possess proper certificates. In recent years teachers' organizations have also fought changes in the seniority and personnel systems. Unable to make new policies through established channels, disaffected citizens have increasingly pressured the system from outside.[36] In growing numbers the clients—students and their parents—have lost faith in the professionals.

By no means has all criticism come from outside the ranks of schoolmen. Hear Mark R. Shedd, superintendent of the Philadelphia Schools, on the subject of decentralization:

Urban bureaucracies have tended generally to codify and enforce systemic values which divert attention from the presumed focus of education—the classroom. Symbolically, children and teachers rarely appear on the tables of organization. Centrally dictated curriculum and personnel assignments; central office monopoly on status positions; centrally formulated rules and procedures, which gain the force of moral dicta; these are the identifying marks of large school systems . . . those at the bottom of the bureaucratic pyramid—principals and teachers—become clerks. And children, who bear the total weight of the structure, are not so much educated as processed. Ironically, as one principal put it, "We'd have a great school system if it weren't for the kids." . . . One inevitable conclusion is that the bureaucracies of big city schools must either transform themselves or be dismantled by assault from the outside. This means decentralization. . . .[37]

Former U.S. Commissioner of Education Harold Howe, II, called for a system of checks and balances between laymen and schoolmen, asserting that "left unchecked, the professional is liable to become a dictator; a school superintendent is no more exempt from becoming a hometown Hitler than the most pompous and arrogant Babbitt who ever headed a school board." He also said that "we should . . . get rid of some of the prickly requirements for school system employment so that we can have the advantage of special talents that we are now denied."[38]

A Crisis of Authority

At the base of the current conflicts lies a crisis of authority which will probably lead to a restructuring of the control of urban public education. Joe L. Rempson, who has worked with local school boards in Harlem, has argued that "the crucial point is that *the community has the right to elect the members of the local school board.* Having become so accustomed to the status quo, some forget that local control of education is a fundamental right . . . people in a democracy have a right to have a voice in that which importantly affects their life."[39] At a meeting of professionals and Harlem residents, Queen Mother Moore expressed the deep sense of alienation felt by many black people: "Now, this is *your* system! . . . I was sorry not to stand up when you sang the Star Spangled Banner. It has no meaning for me, but *you'd* never understand this. It *has* no meaning for me!"[40]

Whence comes this crisis of authority? In large part it stems from three inter-related, and sometimes conflicting, forces: the quests for black power, teacher power, and student power. A decade ago few observers predicted how important these movements would become in the politics of educational decision-making.[41] Today city boards and superintendents can ignore them only at their peril, although of the three groups, only teachers have as yet attained much real power. The demographic revolution since 1940—displacing whites in the inner city with black and Puerto Rican migrants, accelerating the flight to the suburbs of middle-class whites and business and industry—has profoundly altered the traditional relationship of urban schools to their environments. Today, most of the largest cities have school populations which are 40 percent or more non-white. Blacks are becoming determined to achieve power in a white-dominated system.[42] At the same time, teachers have shown a new militance in strikes and collective bargaining over issues which go well beyond the traditional matters of salaries and fringe benefits. In some cities, as former superintendent Sidney Marland of Pittsburgh has observed, "teachers demand control of all aspects of school policy." This has sometimes brought them into collision with militant blacks, as in New York.[43] And increasingly evident is a student power movement—demonstrated this past year in the Chicago boycotts, unrest in Los Angeles, and the student march on the Philadelphia Board of Education—which in some ways poses the sharpest threat to authority since it is a rebellion of those at the bottom of the educational pyramid.[44]

No doubt there is a mixture of hooliganism, blind self-interest, and mindless militance in some of these protests. If that were all there were to this crisis of authority, one might easily justify a policy of repression and maintenance of the status quo (though that might radicalize the moderates). Indeed, there is already evidence of a backlash of groups that have traditionally influenced the schools. But deeper ideological and practical issues underlie the surface protest. The fact is that urban schools today belie the historic ideals of the American common school, which was to be free, under close public control, inclusive of all social groups, of such high quality that parents would want no other, and offering real equality of opportunity to all children. The ghetto parent can clearly see that his child's school is segregated; that he has little voice in important school policies; and that the graduates of ghetto schools are woefully ill-prepared.[45] Poor schooling might have been unfortunate for the immigrant child in 1900, but not disastrous. Today, the second industrial revolution has destroyed millions of blue-collar jobs, and our society often requires educational credentials for entry into even low-level white-collar positions.[46] Blacks now speak feelingly of "educational genocide," of schooling which not only fails to prepare children to succeed in white society but also denies the validity of Afro-American experience.[47]

Muckraking journalism helped to produce the urban school reforms at the turn of the century, as writers exposed the machinations of school politicians. Today a literature of exposure and protest, coupled with studies by social scientists, is fueling the current reform movement. Only recently have school districts released to the public the bad news on the academic achievement of children in ghetto schools. National studies like the Coleman Report and the U.S. Civil Rights Commission study have corroborated that black children regularly fall behind the national norms farther and farther the longer they remain in school.[48] The titles of two popular books on city schools—*Our Children Are Dying* and *Death at an Early Age*—drive home the writers' conclusions.[49] Whether in 1892 in Joseph Rice's articles or in 1967 in Jonathan Kozol's book, muckraking may not be balanced and judicious, but it powerfully undermines faith in the schools.

RESPONSES TO THE CRISIS

How might urban school boards and schoolmen respond to these upheavals? Like musk oxen in closed ranks with horns lowered, they might repel the attackers. This makes sense only if the current order is best. I would maintain that centralized, professionalized bureaucracies no longer fit the needs of urban society, if indeed they ever did, and that we need massive structural changes in city schools to make them responsive to the people they serve. This does not imply that school board members should give up under fire and abandon their principles, but rather that they should re-examine their principles to see if they still fit. Like Huck Finn, who disregarded his "yellow dog conscience" about slavery to help Jim escape, we need to respond to human needs as we understand them in our time.

In most cities there is still time for planned rather than cataclysmic change. Plans should be as diverse as our pluralistic metropolitan society. I need not remind you that what would be appropriate for Denver might well be wrong for Detroit. Contrary to some Manhattan dwellers, American urban life is not New York writ small. But there are some features of reform which might be generalized:

1. In most large cities integration has ceased to be a major goal of civil rights activists. Despite persistent agitation, they have seen segregation increase. Growing percentages of blacks in restricted ghettos, lethargy of boards and schoolmen in carrying out desegregation, and hostility of whites have often made their efforts futile. Yet in my opinion, it would be poor social policy to abandon the goal of integration. It may be impossible today to desegregate schools in most large cities, at least without crossing city boundaries, but in many small and medium sized cities integration is still possible and desirable. It is just as important for whites as for blacks to learn first-hand how to live together peaceably in a multiracial society.[50]

2. Despite high hopes, compensatory education has produced disappointing results in practice. It is true that many compensatory projects have been funded too sparsely and too briefly for a definitive test. But rapidly accumulating evidence suggests that simply giving pupils an intensified or remedial version of the standard curriculum while retaining the same bureaucratic structure is not likely to break the cycle of failure in urban education for the children who need it most. Often such projects have in effect compensated teachers or added new administrative positions without producing observable gains for the students.[51]

3. I believe the basic need in urban education today is schools which are more responsive and responsible to the populations they serve—and this implies some form of decentralization of control. Social scientists are documenting the common sense notion that if parents and students have a sense of control over their own destinies, and if teachers have high expectations of pupils and are held accountable for results, marked gains in achievement of "disadvantaged" students are possible.[52] The National Academy of Education has observed that "school districts with a pupil population larger than 150,000 are prone to bureaucratic rigidities and impersonalities, and are likely to produce an unhealthy tension between concerned parents on the one hand and top school officials and board members on the other."[53] As we have seen, a major purpose of bureaucratization was originally to fix responsibility, yet legion are the stories of buck-passing and "that's not my department." Centralized control was supposed to give power to the superintendent to adapt the schools to new conditions, yet in large systems he can often be sabotaged and rendered ineffective by subordinates (indeed, some say that real power in many big cities is not bureaucratic but baronial—each

assistant superintendent or section head mutually bound by ties of feudal loyalty to his followers).[54]

Today a tide is turning against centralized solutions to organizational and social problems. Many large business concerns have decentralized and have found delegated responsibility to be efficient. Liberal reformers no longer turn automatically to Washington to solve intractable problems with yet another bureau.[55] And many classical liberals still agree with Toulmin Smith, who wrote in 1851 that "centralization is that system of government under which the smallest number of minds, and those knowing the least, and having the smallest opportunities of knowing it, about the special matter in hand, and having the smallest interest in its well-working, have the management of it, or control over it."[56] The hitch, of course, is that it is most prominently black people who are calling for community control in the central cities. This is hard for a society tainted by centuries of racism to accept, and difficult to get rural-dominated state legislatures to enact into law. But the time has come when the underclasses of the great cities will take matters illegally into their own hands unless those in control find ways to restructure urban schools so that residents may have more voice in the education of their children.

There are dangers in such decentralization, of course. It might fragment the political base education needs. It will doubtless threaten teachers and administrators who have long been insulated from the community by bureaucratic buffers (in Chicago, for example, telephone numbers of elementary schools formerly were not listed in the telephone book). It might increase parochialism and racial and economic segregation. Local control might make teachers easy prey for extremists of all stripes. Decentralization might increase provincialism and bigotry. But controls can be built into a system of community control to deter unwarranted interference with teachers' rights while increasing professional accountability and responsiveness. Also today the mass media and other unifying influences of a corporate society push toward conformity, and it may be time to encourage in our schools a vigorous pluralism and sense of local community. The crucial goal today is to create an open society, not a uniform society.[57]

4. There are many possible models of "decentralization," each with its own assets and liabilities. The New York experience of ambiguous delegation of responsibility to "demonstration districts" hardly seems one to emulate. It did not build on existing

strong community organizations and produced bitter conflict between the staff of the "demonstration districts" and the professional organizations, notably the teachers' union.[58]

The Woodlawn Developmental Project, a collaboration of the Chicago Public Schools, The Woodlawn Organization (a black action association), and the University of Chicago, seems to be a better route to decentralization, resting as it does on agreements hammered out in advance by a strong community group and its partners (although there are few results shown as yet). The President of The Woodlawn Organization made it clear that what his group was seeking was influence and consultation, not total control: "I don't feel the Woodlawn Community Board should have the final authority and responsibility for running the schools . . . but isn't there some way to make sure that the Director of the Experimental District must deal with the Woodlawn Community Board prior to bringing matters to the General Superintendent or to the Board of Education . . . to seek its concurrence . . . ?[59]

Under the leadership of Mark Shedd the Philadelphia Schools have involved parents and students in designing a citywide Afro-American history curriculum, in changing the vocational program, and in a variety of other ways. In addition, like other cities, Philadelphia has attempted administrative decentralization by granting principals and teachers more autonomy to adapt instruction to the pupils. "A basic goal . . . is to make the central office a service agency, instead of a controlling agency . . ." The central staff emulates a foundation in giving grants to individual teachers and schools for innovative projects. Indeed, as Elliott Shapiro demonstrated in Harlem, one way in which a school principal can become effective in the ghetto is by allying as a maverick bureaucrat with the people he serves rather than with his superiors. If schools reward this sort of behavior, it will go far to make education more decentralized and relevant.[60]

5. An essential part of a successful plan of decentralized schools is the indigenous development of community leaders. Nineteenth-century advocates of the ward system of school control argued that local trustees knew their people, stimulated public interest in education, and resolved local conflicts, but such political substructures have often become ineffectual and fragmented in the twentieth century. Accordingly, new political-educational leadership may need to be shaped deliberately. Joe L. Rempson has sketched one such program which promises to educate both community and school board members through the process of election and policy making. He explodes the easy alibi of parents that their

children don't learn because of negative attitudes of teachers, and of teachers that students don't learn because parents are irresponsible. Both share responsibility, he says: "While I do believe that the chief source of the motivation to learn is usually the home, there is no question that . . . the school can—and often does— kill the motivation that the child does bring from home. . . ." Elections should be well publicized and should educate the community about the goals, problems, and achievements of the schools:

> The candidates would not just announce that they would be at certain places and then wait for everyone to show up. Quite literally, the candidates would instead go to the people. An effort should be made to reach the people through every available and conceivable method: house-to-house contact, street corner forums, closed-circuit television, printed bulletins, and automobile loudspeakers.

Because of the importance of this campaign in informing and involving the people, the campaign expenses should be subsidized by the central board, Rempson believes, and consultants available on request to help candidates refine and express their views. Candidates and elected representatives would also attend training workshops to learn more about the operation of schools. The purpose would be not only to create a more sophisticated and effective leadership in the ghetto but also to encourage the residents to regard the school system as *we*, not *they*.[61]

6. The revival of interest in a genuine community school promises to recreate education on a more human scale. What really counts in the daily lives of people is their daily lives—what they see and hear and think and do. Too often residents have regarded the ghetto school as an outpost of a foreign power, a place where the child and his parents are subjects, not citizens. To alter this relationship is a goal of many people today—some of them, like Charles Hamilton, black power exponents—who desire to change the school into a community center. They argue that many services for people of all ages could be located there: legal aid, health and recreation programs, welfare offices, and employment bureaus and training centers.[62] To rebuild schools on a human scale would require changes not only in how schools are run but also in how they are constructed. It is hard for parents not to feel like intruders when they go to see the principal if they are forced to wait in an austere and busy outer office, sitting on a hard bench next to children waiting to be disciplined. Consider how different would be their experience if each school had a parents' room with

carpet and comfortable chairs, where they might drink coffee and talk with the principal or teachers informally. And why should not a school cafeteria be a place where parents as well as children eat?

7. Obviously the sorts of changes I have been suggesting would cost a great deal of money, even if many presently fragmented social services were to contribute to the budgets of the community school. It is obvious that the funds available now are grotesquely inadequate. Christopher Jencks observed in 1967 that "the schools" performance is evaluated not so much in terms of long-term results as in terms of short-term costs. The result is underlined by contrasting the education programs of the city of Philadelphia and the U.S. Armed Forces. At any one time, both are educating between 250,000 and 300,000 students. For this, Philadelphia spends about $100 million a year, while the Armed Forces spend $3 billion—or $400 per pupil compared to $10,000.)"[63] As H. Thomas James has said, "local taxpaying ability is the most important determinant of social policy in education for American cities. Until we find the means to reverse that equation, and let social policy determine the resources to be allocated to education, we face a rising sea of troubles in our cities."[64] Finding these funds is a matter of the utmost importance for central and community school boards and for officials at all levels of government.

THE FUTURE ROLE OF CENTRAL SCHOOL BOARDS

Even if the actual operation of schools should become decentralized, I believe that central school boards will continue into the next decade in large cities and that their job will become increasingly conflict-ridden—that is, politicized. George LaNoue maintains that mayors will increasingly be held responsible for the welfare of public education: "it is clear that education cannot be treated separately from problems of housing, welfare and unemployment. Any political leader who wants to save or even to improve his city is going to have to make public education a priority matter."[65] Whatever the degree of political involvement of the mayor, whatever the amount of decentralization, school board members will need to develop great skill at resolving and mediating conflicts. Freed of the myth that education can be "nonpolitical," they should seek new institutions of accommodation, such as ombudsmen, new means of due process at a time when normal professional channels will be under attack. They will need new sources of information about the schools, and sophistication about the social context within which schooling takes place. A healthy scepticism about the relative importance of schooling in the total education of a child will broaden the scope of their responsibility. For instance, much current research points to the crucial influence of the family on the educational achievement of the child. Thus school board members might protest the educational consequences of taking welfare mothers away from their children while training them for jobs.[66]

But whatever new channels of accommodation they develop, or new roles they acquire, an important measure of urban school board members will still be their personal qualities. And essential in their qualifications, in my view, is an ability to understand the point of view of the boy in Harlem who identified with the worm, not the early bird. Beyond the quarrels of adults, children must still be the central concern. They were for Horace Mann, who declared: "let the next generation be my client."[67]

NOTES

1. Jodie Foote to President Franklin D. Roosevelt, Myrtle, Mississippi, December 22, 1936, in Alfred D. Smith collection of W.P.A. papers, Moorland Collection, Howard University Library.
2. Daniel P. Moynihan has said, "Given the mounting extremism of American politics, to fail to deliver on the promises made to Negro Americans in the first half of this decade would be to trifle with the stability of the American republic." *Harvard Today*, (Autumn, 1967), 19.
3. Very little historical work has been done on the development of bureaucratic norms. Two beginnings are Michael Katz, "The Emergence of Bureaucracy in Urban Education: The Boston Case," *History of Education Quarterly*, VIII (Summer, 1968), 155–88; and VIII (Fall, 1968), 319–57; and David Tyack, "Bureaucracy and the Common School: The Example of Portland, Oregon, 1851–1913," *American Quarterly*, XIX (Fall, 1967), 475–98.
4. To make the text more readable in this interview format I have omitted quotation marks and have occasionally condensed the authors' remarks (without, of course, changing the order or the sense).
5. L. H. Jones, "The Politician and the Public School, Indianapolis and Cleveland," *Atlantic Monthly*, LXXVII (June, 1896), 810.
6. Jones, "Politician," 814–15.
7. S. A. Wetmore, "Boston School Administration," *Educational Review*, XIV (September, 1897), 112.
8. Ellwood P. Cubberley, "The School Situation in San Francisco," *Educational Review*, XXI (April, 1901), 368.
9. Ellwood P. Cubberley, *Changing Conceptions of Education* (Boston: Houghton Mifflin Co., 1909), 15; see also Cubberley, *Public School Administration* (Boston: Houghton Mifflin Co., 1922).

10. Andrew S. Draper, "Plans of Organization for School Purposes in Large Cities," National Educational Association, *Addresses and Proceedings,* XXVIII (December, 1904), 438.
11. George A. O. Ernst, "The Movement for School Reform in Boston," *Educational Review,* XXVIII (December, 1904), 438.
12. James C. Boykin "Organization of City School Boards," *Educational Review,* XIII (March, 1897), 233–34.
13. Ernst, "School Reform," 433–44.
14. Truman A. Deweese, "Better School Administration," *Educational Review,* XX (June, 1900), 62.
15. Joseph M. Rice, *The Public School System of the United States* (New York: The Century Company, 1893), 50.
16. Charles W. Eliot, "Educational Reform and the Social Order," *The School Review,* XVII (April, 1909), 220.
17. Andrew S. Draper, "Educational Organization and Administration," in Nicholas M. Butler, ed., *Education in the United States* (Albany, N.Y.: J. B. Lyon Company, 1900), 14–17.
18. Draper, "Plan of Organization," 302.
19. Arthur H. Chamberlain, "The Growth and Power of the City School Superintendent," University of California *Publications,* III (May 15, 1913), 398–412; see also the consensus expressed by Theodore L. Reller, *The Development of the City Superintendent of Schools in the United States* (Philadelphia: Published by the Author, 1935).
20. Correspondence between Nicholas M. Butler and Mayor William Gaynor of New York, *Educational Review,* XLII (September, 1911), 204–10; Edward C. Eliot, "A Non-partisan School Law," National Education Association, *Addresses and Proceedings,* XLIV (1905), 223–31; William T. Harris, "City School Supervision, V," *Educational Review,* III (February, 1892), 167–72.
21. Chamberlain, "City School Superintendent," 394.
22. Raymond Callahan, *Education and the Cult of Efficiency* (Chicago: University of Chicago Press, 1962).
23. David C. Hammack, "The Centralization of New York's Public School System, 1896: A Social Analysis of a Decision," unpublished M.A. thesis, Columbia University, 1969, ch. 1; Sol Cohen, *Progressives and Urban School Reform: The Public Education Association of New York City 1895–1954* (New York: Teachers College Bureau of Publications, 1964), ch. 1; David Tyack, *Turning Points in American Educational History* (Waltham, Mass.: Blaisdell Publishing Company, 1967), parts 7, 9.
24. George D. Strayer, "The Baltimore School Situation," *Educational Review,* XLII (November, 1911), 329–35.
25. Hammack, "Centralization," 114.
26. Hammack, "Centralization," 115, 117, 121.
27. W. S. Sutton, "The School Board as a Factor in Educational Efficiency," *Educational Review,* XLIX (March, 1915), 261.
28. Burke A. Hinsdale, "The American School Superintendent," *Educational Review,* VII (January, 1894), 50–51.
29. Ella Flagg Young, *Isolation in the Schools* (Chicago: University of Chicago Press, 1906). The superintendent of schools in Rochester, New York, spoke at the N.E.A. about "cities in which supervisors go about from schoolroom to schoolroom, notebook and pencil in hand, sitting for a while in each room like malignant sphinxes, eyeing the terrified teacher,

who in her terror does everything wrong, and then marking her in that little doomsday book"—Charles B. Gilbert, "The Freedom of the Teacher," National Education Association, *Proceedings and Addresses,* XLIII (1903), 167.

30. Samuel P. Hays, "The Politics of Reform in Municipal Government in the Progressive Era," *Pacific Northwest Quarterly,* LV (October, 1964), 163.

31. In addition to the Hays and Hammack studies cited, which give precise information on this shift of social and economic status of political influentials, another useful source is the unpublished essay of Elinor M. Gersman, "Progressive Reform of the St. Louis School Board, 1897" (portions of which will appear in her forthcoming doctoral dissertation at Washington University, St. Louis).

32. A useful general study of changing structures is Joseph M. Cronin, "The Board of Education in the 'Great Cities,' 1890–1964," unpublished Ed.D. dissertation, School of Education, Stanford University, 1965.

33. George R. LaNoue, "Political Questions in the Next Decade of Urban Education," *The Record,* LXIX (May, 1968), 517.

34. Marilyn Gittell, "Urban School Reform in the 1970's," *Education and Urban Society,* I (November, 1968), 9–20.

35. Daniel U. Levine, "Organizing for Reform in Big City Schools," *Phi Delta Kappan,* XLVIII (March, 1967), 311–15; Joseph Pois, *The School Board Crisis: A Chicago Case Study* (Chicago: Educational Methods, 1964); Marilyn Gittell, *Participants and Participation: A Study of School Policy in New York City* (New York: Center for Urban Education, 1967); David Rogers, *110 Livingston Street* (New York: Random House, 1968); Norman D. Kerr, "The School Board as an Agency of Legitimation," *Sociology of Education,* XXXVIII (Fall, 1964), 34–59.

36. Marilyn Gittell and T. Edward Hollander, *Six Urban School Districts: A Comparative Study of Institutional Response* (New York: Frederick Praeger, 1968).

37. Mark R. Shedd, "Decentralization and Urban Schools," *Educational Leadership,* XXV (October, 1967), 32–33.

38. Harold Howe II, "Should Educators Or Boards Control Our Public Schools?" *Nation's Schools,* VII (December, 1966), 31–32.

39. Joe L. Rempson, "Community Control of Local School Boards," *Teachers College Record,* LXVIII (April, 1967), 573; Arthur E. Salz points out some inherent conflicts in "Local Control v. Professionalism," *Phi Delta Kappan,* L (February, 1969), 332–34.

40. Queen Mother Moore, "A Band-Aid for a Cancer," Harvard Graduate School of Education Association, *Bulletin,* XII (Fall, 1967).

41. See Carl F. Hansen, "When Courts Try to Run the Public Schools," *U. S. News and World Reports,* April 21, 1969, 94–96.

42. LaNoue, "Political Questions," 517–18.

43. Donald W. Robinson, "Superintendent Marland of the Pittsburgh Schools," *Phi Delta Kappan,* XLIX (June, 1968), 562. This issue of the *Kappan* contains other articles on teacher militance.

44. Daniel U. Levine, "Black Power: Implications for the Urban Educator," *Education and Urban Society,* I (February, 1969), 150–53; Mark R. Shedd and S. L. Halleck, "Hypothesis of Student Unrest," *Phi Delta Kappan,* XL (September, 1968), 2–8.

45. Peter Schrag, "Why Our Schools Have Failed," *Commentary*, XLV (March, 1968), 31–38; Paul Lauter and Florence Howe, "The School Mess," *New York Review of Books*, February 1, 1968, 16–21.

46. Ivar Berg, "Rich Men's Qualifications for Poor Men's Jobs," *IRCD Bulletin*, V (March, 1969), 1, 9–12.

47. Kenneth Clark, *Dark Ghetto: Dilemmas of Social Power* (New York: Harper Torchbooks, 1967), ch. 6; Alvin Poussaint, "Education and Black Self-Image," *Freedomways*, VIII (Fall, 1968), 334–39.

48. James S. Coleman *et al.*, *Equality of Educational Opportunity* (Washington: U.S. Government Printing Office, 1966); U.S. Civil Rights Commission, *Racial Isolation in the Public Schools* (Washington: U.S. Government Printing Office, 1967); for expert, but differing, interpretations of the meanings of these massive studies, see the special issue of the *Harvard Educational Review* XXXVIII (Winter, 1968), on "Equal Opportunity."

49. Nat Hentoff, *Our Children Are Dying* (New York: The Viking Press, 1966); Jonathan Kozol, *Death at an Early Age* (Boston: Houghton Mifflin Company, 1968); Edgar Z. Fridenberg, "Requiem for the Urban School," *Saturday Review*, November 18, 1967, 77–79, 92–94. The *Saturday Review* has also published several critical journalistic accounts of urban school systems. For a critical look at the critics, see Robert Havighurst, "Requirements for a Valid 'New Criticism,' " *Phi Delta Kappan*, XL (September, 1968), 20–26.

50. Thomas Pettigrew, "School Integration in Current Perspective," *The Urban Review*, III (January, 1969), 4–8; Robert Crain and David Street, "School Desegregation and School Decision-Making," *Urban Affairs Quarterly*, II (September, 1967), 64–82; Robert Dentler *et al*, *The Urban R's: Race Relations as the Problem in Urban Education* (New York: Frederick Praeger, 1967).

51. For a critical review of the assumptions underlying much compensatory education, see Doxey A. Wilkerson, "Blame the Negro Child" and Edward K. Weaver, "The New Literature on the Education of the Black Child," in *Freedomways*, VIII (Fall, 1968), 340–46, 367–76.

52. Wilkerson, "Blame the Negro Child," 343–46; Clark, *Dark Ghetto*, ch. 6; Robert Rosenthal and Lenore Jacobsen, *Pygmalion in the Classroom* (New York: Holt, Rinehart and Winston, 1968). The last study has been both praised and severely faulted by reviewers.

53. National Academy of Education, *Policy Making for American Public Schools* (n.p.: National Academy of Education, 1969), 7–8; Roald Campbell, "Is the School Superintendent Obsolete?" *Phi Delta Kappan*, XLVIII (October, 1966), 50–58, deals with new demands on school administrators.

54. Gittell, *Participants*, 7–10.

55. It is instructive to note how few of the reformers who wrote essays for the brilliant collection *The Schoolhouse in the City* (Alvin Toffler, ed., New York: Frederick Praeger, 1968) advocated turning to the national or state governments for solutions to local problems in education.

56. Toulmin Smith, *Local Self-Government and Centralization* (London: J. Chapman, 1851), 12.

57. Marilyn Gittell and Alan Halvesi, eds., *The Politics of Urban Education* (New York: Frederick Praeger, 1969), part V.

58. Martin Mayer, *The Teachers' Strike New York, 1968* (New York: Perennial Library, 1969); Gittell and Halvesi, *Politics*, 261–377.
59. Willard J. Congreve, "Collaborating for Urban Education in Chicago: The Woodlawn Development Project," *Education and Urban Society*, I (February, 1969), 177–92.
60. Mark R. Shedd, "Recreating the City Schools," Harvard Graduate School of Education Association, *Bulletin*, XII (Spring, 1969), 2–6; Wallace Roberts, "Can Urban Schools Be Reformed?" *Saturday Review*, May 17, 1969, 70–72, 87–91; Henry S. Resnik, "The Shedd Revolution—A Philadelphia Story," *The Urban Review*, III (January, 1969), 20–26; Hentoff, *Our Children*.
61. Rempson, "Community Control," 572–75; Dentler, *Urban R's*, part 3.
62. Charles Hamilton, "Education in the Black Community: An Examination of the Realities," *Freedomways*, VIII (Fall, 1968), 319–24. One of the most successful earlier practitioners of the community school idea, Leonard Covello, has a fascinating interview in *The Urban Review*, III (January, 1969), 13–19. See also Mario Fantini and Gerald Weinstein, *Making Urban Schools Work: Social Realities and the Urban School* (New York: Holt, Rinehart and Winston, 1968), 52–61.
63. Christopher Jencks, "Private Management for Public Schools," *Education Memorandum #4*, October 26, 1965, Institute for Policy Studies, Washington, D.C., 2.
64. H. Thomas James *et al.*, *Determinants of Educational Expenditures in Large Cities of the United States* (Cooperative Research Project No. 2389, Stanford, California: School of Education, Stanford University, 1966), 17.
65. LaNoue, "Political Questions," 527; Robert H. Salisbury, "Schools and Politics in the Big City," *Harvard Educational Review*, XXXVII (Summer, 1967), 408–24; Bernard Mackler and Nancy Bord, "The Role of the Urban Mayor in Education," *The Record*, LXIX (March, 1968), 531–42.
66. H. Thomas James, "School Board Conflict Is Inevitable," *The American School Board Journal*, CLIV (March, 1967), 5–9.
67. Stephen Joseph, ed., *The Me Nobody Knows* (New York: Avon Books, 1969), 113; Peter Binzen, "How to Pick a School Board," *Saturday Review*, April 17, 1965, 72–73, 83–84.

SCHOOL DESEGREGATION AND RACIAL STABILIZATION

PAUL E. PETERSON

School desegregation once again became a lively political issue in Chicago in the fall and winter of 1967–68. After School Superintendent Benjamin Willis, a strong defender of neighborhood schools, had retired as superintendent one year previously, black and white Chicagoans had been waiting quietly but expectantly to see what new moves the new superintendent, James Redmond, would make in this conflictual policy area. Finally, in August, 1967, Redmond unveiled a number of highly regarded, if rather expensive, desegregation proposals, including "magnet schools," so attractive they would draw students—white and black—from all over the city; educational parks around the edges of the city, including the shores of Lake Michigan; financial incentives to teachers working with black children in the inner city; and pupil busing. In keeping with a new spirit of racial comity that had arisen since Willis' departure, the school board unanimously approved "in principle" this document, which rapidly became known as the "Redmond Plan." Encouraged by this response, the superintendent recommended the following December that the plan be initially implemented by busing pupils from a few schools in two Chicago neighborhoods—South Shore and Austin—to schools in South Chicago and Belmont-Cragin. It was proposed that over one thousand black children be bused some distance from their homes.

This proposal encountered bitter opposition from white parents and neighborhood groups, and the board delayed reaching a decision on the superintendent's recommendations in order to give citizens a chance to express their views at public hearings. After the controversy steadily increased, the board considerably altered the superintendent's recommendations. It rejected the South

Shore-South Chicago proposal altogether, asking Redmond to develop an alternative one instead, and it decided that busing in Austin-Belmont-Cragin should be limited to those children whose parents consented to the arrangement. Compulsory busing, it determined, was not feasible.

The significance of substituting voluntary for compulsory busing can scarcely be exaggerated. If school desegregation on as large a scale as that envisioned by the Redmond Plan were to be achieved, the board could not leave decisions concerning school attendance to parents. This would only perpetuate the neighborhood school pattern to which parents, teachers, and administrators were deeply wedded. By announcing that it would not compel attendance of children to any school outside their neighborhood, the board effectively forestalled any effort to desegregate pupils on a massive scale. Moreover, the controversy itself dulled further efforts to implement the large and comprehensive Redmond Plan. As late as 1975—eight years after the plan had been announced— scarcely any detectable progress had been made toward implementing it. The significance of the controversy thus was far greater than its impact on the 1,035 black children who were originally to be sent to predominantly white schools or on the same 10,000 white children who attended those schools.

Why was the initial effort to implement the Redmond Plan rejected by a board that had unanimously approved it only a few months previously? Although a complete explanation cannot be given here,[1] of critical importance was the Chicago school board's commitment to *stabilizing the racial composition of the city of Chicago*. Put more harshly, the board wanted to discourage blacks from entering and whites from leaving Chicago as a place of residence. Redmond's plan was unanimously approved because it was conceived with this goal in mind. At the same time, the board later withheld implementation of this same plan out of this same concern for racial stability. Let us see if we can account for such a strange paradox.

RACIAL STABILITY THROUGH INTEGRATION

As early as 1964 the school board asserted that its "policy [was] to seek and take any possible steps which may help to preserve and stabilize the integration of schools in neighborhoods which already have an interracial composition." Since the major threat to the resegregation of interracial schools was the flight of whites from a spreading ghetto, the policy statement clearly implied a commitment on the part of the board to the preservation of whites in the interracial community. What was implicit in the 1964 policy statement became explicit in the Redmond Plan. Indeed, the plan's elaborations on this point are so sharply spelled out that its line of reasoning is worth quoting in detail:

> Unless the current exodus of whites from the city is quickly arrested, the question of school integration may become academic. Chicago will become a predominantly Negro city unless dramatic action is taken soon. Anyone who carefully analyzes the block-by-block neighborhood patterns of Negro in-migration and white flight cannot help but see the handwriting on the wall for Chicago as well as other large cities. The immediate short range goal must be to anchor the whites that still reside in the city. To do this requires that school authorities quickly achieve and maintain stable racial attendance proportions in changing fringe areas. If this is not done, transitional neighborhood schools will quickly become predominately Negro as whites will continue to flee. One does not have to be a sage to predict this result. This has happened to dozens and dozens of schools in Chicago and other urban areas.
>
> In Chicago the pressure to integrate often has been placed on those elements of the white population that are least prepared. Working class whites who are often just one step ahead . . . of the rolling ghetto are less secure economically and socially than their middle class counterparts. The Negro is perceived as a threat and appears to jeopardize their tenuous economic security and social status. We . . . propose . . . that Negro enrollments in the schools in these changing sections of the city be limited and fixed immediately. If this is not done by the Board of Education . . . , long range planning for racial integration of schools within the City of Chicago's boundaries will be a futile exercise.

Although the Redmond Plan affirmed other values and goals as well, these were stated in such generalized terms they gave little policy guidance. Specifically, the plan declared that "integration is desirable for white and Negro children alike." But it no-where defended this claim in any way whatsoever; moreover, it expressly indicated that the goal could not be maximized and therefore the system would concentrate on improving education "particularly in ghetto schools" that were a concomitant of "the present housing segregation pattern in this city [which] will probably continue for some time." Given the acceptance of these all-black ghetto schools, the plan's vague commitment to integration for its own sake provided no criteria for determining which children and how many children would experience an integrated education.

The racial stabilization objective, on the other hand, provided guidelines for action throughout the entire document. In making pupil assignments, the plan insisted "that every effort should be made to retain the white population and promote stabilization in integrated school situations." In order to maximize this goal, "responsibility for integration should be shared by all of the white community by maintaining fixed racial proportions in all schools," a strategy which must include, among other things, "transporting of students by the school system."

Many details followed from these general guidelines. According to the Redmond Plan, it was necessary to "limit the Negro or other minority percentage in the fringe area schools" so whites would not flee. The board would select out black children in the neighborhood who were threatening school stability and "bus" them some distance away. Moreover, the board would insure that schools to which students are bused never become more than 15 percent black. Finally, in anticipation of what was regarded as necessary in South Shore, the plan provided that in one area of the city the system might even transport white students so as "to equalize the minority percentages in the selected schools." Of course, this had to be an experimental program, because there was considerable danger that parents of transported white children would leave the city.

Racial stabilization was not simply the foundation for Redmond's overall plan as submitted to the board in August, 1967. It was also the explicit justification given by board members for adopting the plan "in principle." For example, board member Cyrus Adams, a downtown department store executive, asserted:

> The principles that are involved in this report, which are noncontiguous attendance areas, the transportation that is involved, the problem of quotas . . . in my mind is the only way that we can prevent the exodus from the city. . . .

Another board member, Louise Malis, in explaining her enthusiasm for Redmond's report, said that she would like to "inject a note of urgency. Three years from now or two years from now will be too late to do anything, maybe, for [stabilizing whites in] Austin or Lincoln Park or South Shore." Labor leader John Carey also observed: "I don't know whether the busing is going to help stabilize Chicago or not, but we have to try something."

Even board members concerned about protecting neighborhood schools, and therefore more skeptical of Redmond's integration schemes, admitted that stabilization was a major concern. Although labor leader Thomas Murray seemed to regret the board was "going to have to depart from the neighborhood school policy," he agreed that the plans, "if they are ever put into effect immediately, [will] solve the problems. If you wait, I'm afraid it is going to be too late [to stabilize whites]." And, some months later, confronted with busing proposals for the first time, Marge Wild, herself a resident of South Shore, said, "I'm for anything that will stabilize our community."

INTERESTS SERVED BY RACIAL STABILIZATION

This overwhelming commitment to racial stabilization by members of the school board is to be expected, given the array of interests dependent upon preserving racial balance in Chicago. To begin with, many of the already integrated neighborhoods along Chicago's lake-shore and on other edges of the expanding black community hoped to halt any further movement into at least their area. For any Chicago neighborhood, the costs of racial transition to the indigenous white population are high. People are uprooted from their homes, property values are at least temporarily jeopardized, racial conflict increases, community institutions decay, businesses falter and go bankrupt, churches and synagogues lose their members, and local political leaders lose office.

What is true for a neighborhood can prove to be the case for cities as a whole, when the extent of racial change citywide reaches a high enough level. Property values throughout the city as a whole can decline to the point where city property taxes become a severe burden on citizens. At the same time the cost of city services may increase either because poorer citizens are more dependent on governmental services than more affluent ones or because civil service employees expect higher levels of compensation in return for servicing a racially differentiated clientele.[2] As significant as racial transition is for city government, its impact on central business institutions is probably greater. As the central city becomes black, fewer people shop downtown, firms and office headquarters migrate to suburban locations, and cities develop a hollow core. As a result, advertising revenues of leading metropolitan dailies decline, sustenance of art museums, symphony, orchestras, variegated restaurants, and other cultural institutions becomes difficult, and United Fund drives that support a host of private welfare activities of the city are less successful. Last but not least, substantial racial change threatens the dominance of Irish and other ethnic group leaders within the urban Democratic party. As diverse as these interests were, they and many others had a common stake in racial stability. For Chicagoans, Newark, Gary, Washington, and Detroit were potent negative images.

Given these interests, racial-stability objectives governed policy formation in an array of policy spheres. City leaders vigorously supported statewide open occupancy laws in order to facilitate black migration into the suburbs; opposed desegregated public housing within the central city lest such housing endanger additional white neighborhoods; promoted urban renewal in transition neighborhoods in order to attract white families to these parts of the community; apparently permitted (encouraged?) a higher quality of public services, including park maintenance, street cleaning, and fire protection, in white than in black portions of the city; and pushed the development of regional shopping centers within the black community in order to reduce rapidly increasing black usage of the central business district (that threatened to drive white customers away).

As widespread as the policy ramifications of the concern for racial stabilization were, school policy remained the area in which the commitment was most dramatically clear. The reasons for this are fairly obvious. Schools are compulsory institutions that force individuals to interact with one another in close proximity. The individuals affected are children and adolescents who cannot be expected to exercise the same self-discipline and self-control adults usually can take for granted. Parents are quite naturally more concerned about the character of the schools their children attend than about the operation of most urban institutions. If parks, playgrounds, or beaches are thought to be dirty, disreputable, or dangerous, they can be avoided, even if this means a deprivation in public amenities that are enjoyed. Only by incurring the substantial cost of sending one's child to a parochial or other private school can parents similarly avoid the public school.

Since many white parents have even been willing to incur these costs in order to more directly control their children's educational experiences, the problem of racial transition in schools is further complicated. With much larger percentages of white than black children attending nonpublic schools, and with the younger age structure of Chicago's black community, racial change in public schools has been much more rapid than the rate of change in the city's overall population. By 1970 Chicago was still only 32 percent black, but when the public schools took their first racial headcount in 1963, school officials discovered that black pupils already accounted for 46.5 percent of the school-age population. By the

time of the school-busing conflict in 1967 this had increased to
52.3 percent, and by 1970 blacks amounted to 55 percent of all
pupils.

If this pattern was evident citywide, it was even more clear in
the two communities for which busing was planned. In both areas,
schools were virtually the first community institutions to become
black-dominated, forecasting and *apparently causing* racial transition in the area as a whole. The racial composition of Austin's
high school district changed from virtually all-white in 1960 to 48
percent black in 1970; South Shore's high school district changed
from no more than .2 percent black in 1960 to 62 percent in 1970.
As dramatic as were these rates of racial transition in the community at large, the racial changes in schools were even greater.
Austin High increased from 15 percent black in 1965 to 75 percent
black by 1968, and by 1970 it had become more than 90 percent
black—even while Austin, as a community, remained nearly 50
percent white. South Shore High increased from 25 percent black
in 1965 to 90 percent black in 1968 and became virtually all-black
in 1970—even while South Shore, as a community, continued to
be only marginally more black than white.

Quite clearly, public schools change before community populations as a whole do. Although these changes are obviously influenced by differing age structures and propensities to use nonpublic
schools of the black and white communities, it is clear that residents can at least *perceive* the *cause* of racial transition in their
area as school-related. Consequently, they ask school officials to
act to stabilize their schools in order to "save" their community.

Racial Stabilization and Busing

The school system's December, 1967, busing proposals were consistent with Redmond's overall plan for halting these processes of
racial transition. In choosing Austin and South Shore as the initial sites for implementing the plan, Redmond was cognizant that
he had selected the areas in which the "biggest racial shifts during the [preceding] year" had occurred.

In South Shore an early two-way busing plan was designed to
preserve a substantial white majority in all of the affected schools;
hopefully, this would keep any school from "tipping" towards
becoming an all-black school. In Austin, schools close to the area
of racial transition were deliberately eliminated as receiving
schools so as not to jeopardize community stability. Instead, black
students at May and Spencer were bused to schools in Belmont-

Cragin, which was thought to be far enough away from the black community so that white stability could be safely assumed. Moreover, the plan for Austin insured that no receiving school would have a black population greater than 15 percent. When the board approved an allocation of funds for busing, they were approving "in principle" early, tentative plans that the staff assured them were designed with racial stabilization foremost in mind.

In January and February, however, the board received information from residents of the affected communities which indicated that white stabilization might not be enhanced by school desegregation. Residents in South Chicago and Belmont-Cragin insisted that even though they were not on the immediate edge of the black belt, they nonetheless felt their property values and neighborhood stability threatened. They argued that even if only 10 to 15 percent of the student body were black, it would mean "an exodus of whites to the suburbs." The school system, far from slowing down the rate of racial transition, would be only speeding it, for even communities not on the edge of the black community would suffer a weakening in the real estate market. As long as parents have all-white suburbs into which they can move, it was argued, the school system could not maintain white stability simply by limiting the percentage black to less than 15 to 20 percent. As the *Chicago Tribune* editorialized, "The current busing program, which was put forward partly to arrest the flight of white families to the suburbs, has had only the opposite effect."

These criticisms of the plan by neighborhood groups had an impact on board members. When the administrative staff substituted a one-way busing plan for the original two-way busing proposal for South Shore, the board rejected the compromise because it did little for racial stability. Indeed, the compromise plan only marginally reduced black percentages in schools undergoing racial transition. The impact this had on the board is indicated by Bernard Friedman's comment in an interview:

> Those who were for busing in South Shore, but not for that particular plan was what impressed me, and that is if you are going to use busing as a way to help an integrated community stay integrated . . . then you had better have at least the acceptance of the pupils to be sent and their parents. The people involved and the other important leaders in the community [felt] that it did not accomplish [enough] to warrant the busing plan. . . .

Since the consequences for Austin were not so clear, board members divided on the advisability of busing pupils there. But once again the intensity of community opposition to busing gave at least one key board member—Cyrus Adams—grave doubts about the success of the scheme: "If plans intended to retain middle-class people in the city are going to drive a larger number of middle-class people out of the city, they don't make sense." Board actions with respect to Austin, taken as a whole, indicate that it, as a group, shared Adams's judgment. Redmond's plan was carefully enough designed so that if busing from the overcrowded May and Spencer schools was made voluntary, the board decided by a 9–1 vote that it could alleviate the pressure on Austin without adversely affecting Belmont-Cragin. But the board also found it necessary to reject (if only by a close vote) compulsory busing—even of black children—in order to demonstrate to all parents, and especially to white ones, that transference from one's neighborhood school would only be done on a voluntary basis. Significantly, the next year, when elementary schools in Austin became overcrowded once again, no more children were bused to Belmont-Cragin; the overcrowded schools were instead placed on a double-shift schedule. All the conflict over busing demonstrated to the school board and school system as a whole that busing was not a viable means of achieving racial stability.

In sum, the school board shared a common objective that shaped its general approach to school desegregation and gave coherence to what at times seemed to be a wandering, inconsistent set of decisions. The board could approve the Redmond Plan "principles" because it agreed racial stabilization was necessary. When first proposed, it could accept as conducive to that end a limited busing program in two transition communities. But when the compromise plan for South Shore was rejected by the leading South Shore organization concerned about racial stabilization, the board also turned it down. When white neighborhood groups in Belmont-Cragin, South Chicago, and throughout the city attacked the proposals, the board decided to make the plan for Austin voluntary to demonstrate that busing would not be used in a generalized manner. It was willing to accept a modest, voluntary busing plan in one area because busing there might possibly help stabilize Austin without adversely affecting all-white neighborhoods receiving the black children.

Generalizing from the Chicago Case

Chicago school board's concern for racial stability is by no means unique. Crain found in eight northern cities that "one of the major forces operating to integrate schools is the need to maintain racially stable neighborhoods."[3] He also discovered that when community groups "wanted to maintain a sufficiently high percentage of whites (or sufficiently low percentage of Negroes) to prevent whites from moving out," such groups were more "successful in achieving their [integrationist] goals" than were "traditional civil rights groups" such as the NAACP.[4] In a study of New York, racial stabilization seemed to have been a major concern of the New York board; for example, the board dropped sixteen of twenty schools out of a two-way busing or "pairing" plan because parents' associations convinced the board the "white schools in each pairing . . . had already started to tip."[5] Vitullo-Martin's analysis of successful desegregation in Teaneck, New Jersey, shows that the leading concern of integrationists in that prestige community was to keep a neighborhood school from becoming so black that whites would no longer move into that part of the city.[6] And LaNoue and Smith found that the Detroit board altered attendance zones "to preserve predominantly white schools to keep neighborhoods from tipping."[7] Significantly, they add, "Every issue is examined by both blacks and whites for its effect on the city's delicate racial balance."[8]

CONCLUSIONS

These examples are too few and too fleeting to conclude that concern for racial stabilization determines desegregation policies in most American cities. But at least in Chicago, racial stability was such an overriding concern that no integration plan, unless ordered by a court, would have been taken seriously by board members had it not been formulated with this goal foremost in mind. For this reason, the Redmond Plan flatly asserted that there would remain in Chicago many all-black ghetto schools where improved educational services would have to compensate for their segregated character. At the same time, Redmond's desegregation plans contained within themselves what seems in retrospect to have been a fatal flaw. As much as they were based on the proposition that maintaining low levels of black children in transition-area schools would stabilize these areas, there was little empirical evidence offered to support this basic assumption. Neighborhood-school groups could persuasively argue that no matter what happened in the schools, Austin and South Shore could not be "saved." Continuing racial prejudices, an enlarging black community, lack of housing opportunities for blacks in suburban areas, and white preferences for suburban living might well combine to insure that Chicago, as well as other large American cities, would continue to have neighborhoods in various stages of racial transition. Far more comprehensive social planning than what could be proposed by any school superintendent seemed to be needed in order to control these forces. Because the theory upon which Redmond's integration plan based itself was at least dubious from the beginning, Chicago's school board, committed to racial stabilization, found many persuasive arguments against school desegregation. In short, much in this case is consistent with Carmichael and Hamilton's charge that the

> middle class manifests a sense of superior group position in regard to race. This class wants "good government" *for themselves*; it wants good schools *for its children*. . . . They will fight off the handful of more affluent black people who seek to move in; when they approve or even seek token integration, it applies only to black people like themselves—as "white" as possible.[9]

At the very least, much that central cities must do, in order to survive socioeconomically, can only appear as institutionalized racism.

NOTES

1. A full account is given in Paul E. Peterson, *Chicago School Politics* (Chicago: University of Chicago Press, 1976), ch. VII.
2. Compare Frances Piven, "The Urban Crisis: Who Got What, and Why," in Robert Paul Wolff (ed.), *1984 Revisited* (New York: Random House, 1974).
3. Robert Crain, *The Politics of School Desegregation* (Chicago: Aldine, 1968), p. 106.
4. *Ibid.*, pp. 107, 131.
5. David Rogers, *110 Livingston Street: Politics and Bureaucracy in the New York City School System* (New York: Random House, 1968), p. 398.
6. Thomas Vitullo-Martin, "Community Conflict and Policy Theory: Implications of Four Communities' Changes in Integration, Development and Pollution Control Policies," (Ph.D. dissertation, Department of Political Science, University of Chicago, 1972).
7. George LaNoue and Bruce Smith, *The Politics of School Decentralization* (Lexington, Mass.: Heath, 1973), p. 116.
8. *Ibid.*, p. 117.
9. Stokely Carmichael and Charles V. Hamilton, *Black Power: The Politics of Liberation in America* (New York: Vintage, 1967), p. 41.

Urban Politics and the Police

As central cities have declined socioeconomically, their crime rates have dramatically increased. In the United States, as a whole, reported major crimes more than doubled in the decade from 1960 to 1969, and even if one adjusts for the increasing numbers of crime-prone adolescents during those years, the net increase was still close to 14 percent per year. To be sure, these increasing crime rates have been affecting central city and suburban areas alike, but it was nonetheless the case that in 1971 major "index" crimes reported by police departments to the FBI occurred in central cities at an average rate of 53 for every 1,000 inhabitants, while in suburbs the rate was less than half this level, averaging only 22 per 1,000 inhabitants. Accordingly, cities, with considerable federal assistance, have greatly expanded personnel, equipment, and facilities of their police departments. But these efforts, however necessary, require the increased exercise of a power so potent that it needs to be carefully circumscribed in order to safeguard the rights and liberties of citizens.

For this reason, the original formation of a special cadre to "police" the activities of urban communities was a step not taken until well into the middle years of the nineteenth century. Earlier, as James Wilson points out in one of the following essays, apprehension of criminals was left to private agencies hired by the victims of crimes. Only gradually did the problems of maintaining public order in the city become so significant that a public police force was established. Even then, police were regarded more as night watchmen expected to keep order than as law enforcers who would apprehend criminals whenever infractions of the law occurred.

Although today we can hardly imagine maintaining order in a complex, urban society without a professional cadre hired by the community to enforce the law, establishing a police force brings with it several potential dangers that have surfaced at one time or another in American cities. Aside from the potential threat of armed patrolmen to the liberties of the community, a police force can exacerbate value conflicts in the community, can itself become a corrupt arm of criminal forces, and can use its great powers for the benefit of one or another political faction in the community. Various police reforms have been proposed to remedy these difficulties, but each reform seems to have only aggravated another separate but closely related problem.

THE NIGHT WATCHMAN

The police in the nineteenth century (and in some communities even today) seemed to be particularly sensitive to the first of these potential dangers, for they were quite adept at mediating among the value conflicts that divided various social and ethnic groups in the population. The need to do so was particularly obvious in those cases where government had legislated on matters affecting the personal moral conduct of individuals. These laws gave rise to what have become known as "victimless" crimes, illegal actions that do no direct harm to anyone, except perhaps to the perpetrators of the crimes themselves. Public drunkenness, pauperism, vagrancy, and loitering are misdemeanors in most American communities. Gambling, prostitution, homosexuality, use of both marijuana and hard drugs, and, at one time, the sale of alcoholic beverages have been regarded as more serious crimes. Far from being minor matters, these crimes are a major police preoccupation; the offense of public drunkenness alone accounts for one of every three arrests.[1]

When large groups of people engage in behaviors legally declared to be deviant, the police may find themselves in conflict with a significant segment of the community. In order to mitigate this possibility, police traditionally arrested individuals for committing victimless crimes only when the illegal actions threatened the peace and order of the community. Acting as night watchmen concerned about the public peace rather than as guardians of private morality, they tolerated, in certain parts of the community, practices that, if detected elsewhere, might be harshly punished.[2] Prostitution was permitted along the "strip"; public drunkenness in "skid row"; gambling in private clubs and in certain ethnic communities; and vagrancy in underutilized portions of public parks. During the Prohibition era, whole cities were "wet," and their police openly tolerated bootlegging, speakeasies, and rumrunners. More recently, police have become increasingly tolerant of homosexual behavior in "gay bars" and "pot smoking" in university communities.

By defining their responsibilities as maintaining public order rather than rigorously enforcing all laws, night-watchmanlike police departments eased their relationships with minority groups, the poor, and other factions of the community whose values differed from those of its lawmakers. The recruitment of policemen from low-income and immigrant families further softened conflicts between police and those "dangerous classes" in the community that the more affluent expected police to control. Policemen developed close ties to the communities in which their beats were located; after some years of patrolling the streets, they became local figures of some importance. Indeed, ties between police and community could become so close that bribery and corruption often pervaded the operations of police departments.

The potential for corruption is, after all, inherent in certain activities expected of law-enforcement agencies. Because the police are supposed to apprehend criminals and secure the evidence necessary for their conviction, policemen are brought into regular, perhaps daily, contact with individuals operating on the edges of the law. These individuals are often the best "informants" about the whereabouts of stolen goods, the sources of supply for a "dope ring," or an important clue in a "big case." Such information comes at a price, and police usually have limited budgets to spend on such confidential purposes. They thus find it convenient to create informants by arresting (or threatening to arrest) prostitutes, drug users, and other petty criminals on minor charges, offering to drop or reduce the charges if the criminals assist in the solution of bigger cases.[3] This kind of bargaining is routine in detective work, and few police officials regard it as an unacceptable practice.

The line between maintaining contacts among criminals and out-right corruption is a slim one, however. If minor, especially victimless, crimes are overlooked in order to create "informants," they also can be ignored for a fee. More generally, just as other governmental agencies are frequently co-opted by the better organized of their clientele (for example, the tendency of highway departments to come under the influence of the trucking industry), so police departments have to guard themselves against too close an association with the better organized of forces outside the law, who are among the "clients" of the police.

This basic susceptibility of police departments to corrupting influences, especially in cases involving victimless crimes, was hardly discouraged by the political machines that at one time dominated American cities. Indeed, the night-watchmanlike department, which concentrated on maintaining public order rather than enforcing all laws, was well suited to nineteenth-century machine-style politics.[4] Party organizations that maintained their strength in low-income, immigrant neighborhoods by doing favors for particular individuals found it helpful to have policemen who did not take the letter of the law too seriously. Poor immigrants valued their precinct captain's ability to drop charges being brought against their son (placing him instead in the hands of the parish priest), to protect numbers and crap games, and to bail them out of jail, if necessary. More organized racketeers provided some of the "boodle" that helped "oil" the machine, in return for which the party insured police protection for their illegal, but usually "victimless," activities. Moreover, selective enforcement of laws could be of service in more directly political activities. Police could harass political opponents and ignore abuses of election laws by party workers. Not surprisingly, the police and the courts generally were among the last bastions of power that party machines conceded to reform pressures.[5]

POLICE REFORMS

The night-watchmanlike police department may have established a tolerable, even friendly relationship with the poor as it tried to maintain order in the inner city. But, the attendant corruption and undue partisan influences over police behavior that were typically a concomitant of this type of law enforcement aroused the ire of middle-class reformers at the turn of the century. Consequently, most cities witnessed persistent and increasingly successful efforts to change the character of police departments.

Before examining the actual reforms implemented, it might be instructive to consider one sweeping proposal for change that the reformers themselves never considered: revision of the law so that "victimless" crimes were no longer illegal. Norval Morris and Gordon Hawkins have argued that victimless crimes are not properly a subject for legal action.[6] However immoral, improper, or indecent public drunkenness, gambling, drug abuse, prostitution, or homosexuality may be, these actions do not disturb the public order or directly injure an innocent party. The state should consequently absolve itself of the responsibility of trying to regulate private morality. They stress that the police resources now used to detect such crimes could then be freed to combat crimes against persons and property. Equally important, we might add, the abolishment of such laws would remove many of the incentives that maintain the debilitating system of informers, bribery, and corruption that are so particularly a part of the world of victimless crimes.

Reformers did not consider this approach to resolving the problems of selective law enforcement and police corruption. Very likely, such proposals would have been too controversial to win much public support but, significantly, the reformers themselves made no effort to repeal laws regulating personal conduct. They were too interested in creating better citizens in a better community, too oriented toward creating the good "City on a Hill," and too concerned with the moral improvement of others to encourage permissive legislation.[7] In a sense, the reformers' very strength was their weakness. They were appropriately concerned about dishonesty in government, unfair police practices, and the close association between politicians and special interests. Morally outraged, they campaigned for reform when most people were only apathetic about public affairs. Yet, their very moral fervor made it difficult for them to tolerate differences in values that were so much a part of the pluralistic life of American cities.

The police reforms that they proposed were far different. Rather than changing the law, reform concentrated on a variety of normative and structural changes that together were intended to bring police practice into conformity with the existing law. According to reformers, police officers should be paid more, have more education, and have more extensive pre-service and in-service training. In this way, reformers hoped to recruit a better class of policemen, who would be carefully trained in the norms of behavior that reformers felt properly governed police activities. Reformers also sought more centralized direction of the police force in order to insure more uniform enforcement of the law and less opportunity for corruption by low-ranking patrolmen. Accordingly, they sought to eliminate neighborhood offices and establish a system of rotation whereby no officer would remain in one neighborhood for too long a period. Centralization could also be furthered by requiring detailed reports concerning all incidents that patrolmen encountered. A more extensive division of labor was proposed in order to permit specialization within the police force, closer supervision of sensitive tasks, and the recruitment of especially qualified men for high-level positions. As a result, more "advanced" departments established vice squads, traffic details, and aggressive patrolling task forces. Over the years, new technological innovations, including police cars with elaborate communications equipment, were introduced not only to speed police reaction time to reported incidents but also to bring police under still more centralized direction. All these and other changes reduced the opportunities for low-ranking patrolmen to develop, in their communities, the personal contacts that might lead to corruption.[8]

Early reformers also sought to separate the police force from partisan influences. Recruitments to and promotions within the force came to be governed by performance on examinations. Civil-service coverage was extended to policemen, which precluded removal of officers from the force unless corruption or extreme incompetence could be clearly established. Eventually, all appointments to high-ranking positions, save perhaps only that of police commissioner, had to be made from within the existing ranks of the organization—a rule designed to eliminate the appointment of party favorites to key positions.

With the decline of the political machine, many of these reform measures have been widely adopted. The old connections between police officers and party precinct captains have all but disappeared. The improved training of police officers has very likely reduced police brutality and differential enforcement of the law among various social and racial groups. Police interference with balloting on election day, once quite prevalent in inner-city areas, now rarely occurs. It also seems that police relationships with organized crime are less extensive than they were during the Prohibition era. (On the other hand, the recent widespread use of illegal drugs is creating an atmosphere that encourages police collaboration with "pushers" quite comparable to their collaboration with "bootleggers" in the 1930s).

Yet these police reforms have not come without costs. Although law enforcement is more uniform, it thereby loses sensitivity to variations in the cultures and life-styles of differing groups in the community. Teen-age rowdyism, which policemen once brought under control with a bit of manhandling on the spot, now leads to arrests and juvenile court proceedings. Family squabbles, once ended by the mere presence of policemen, now more frequently lead to indictments based on the reports officers are expected to file. Rigid, universalistic enforcement of the law has increased tensions between police and those relatively powerless groups (such as blacks and young people) whose moral code differs from that dominant in the larger society. The extensive, almost exclusive use of patrol cars in big cities has sharply limited informal contacts between police and community. Rotation of police officers among beats and districts has further made the police officer more of a soldier in an army of occupation and less of a neighborhood leader. Civil-service examinations have made it difficult to recruit and promote blacks, Puerto Ricans, and Chicanos in numbers proportionate to their share of the urban population, and efforts of politicians to achieve increased minority recruitment have been attacked as undue political interference.

Nor have the elaborate technological innovations, complex administrative structures, and specialized departments typical of big-city police departments markedly improved the levels of law enforcement. In a careful comparative study of two black suburbs with three inner-city black neighborhoods in Chicago, Ostrom and Whitaker found little difference in the quality of police services, as reported by a random sample of citizens in these five communities.[9] What differences they did find indicated somewhat higher levels of satisfaction in the suburban communities, even though the Chicago police were better paid, had more extensive training, and were assisted by a more elaborate set of supporting services. Although Chicago was spending fourteen times as much on a per-capita basis as were the suburban communities, the quality of service was much the same.

Finally, the reform of the police has not taken police out of politics. If most departments no longer have close ties with a political machine, they have become more active as an independent force in city affairs.[10] In recent years, police have used such tactics as "blue" sickness, excessive ticket-writing for minor infractions, and even outright strikes in order to secure salary increases and other desired changes. Through their patrolmen's associations, they have openly campaigned against civilian review boards, "lenient" judges, and mayoral candidates thought to be insufficiently strong supporters of "law and order." In Philadelphia, in fact, police enthusiastically helped elect their own commissioner, Frank Rizzo, as mayor.

POLICE AND THE BLACK COMMUNITY

These developments are not unrelated to the changing racial composition of the central cities of the North. The estrangement between police and urban blacks has made law enforcement a major issue in the contemporary urban crisis. White citizens are afraid to walk the streets at night, flee to suburban "fortresses"

that guard against black penetration, and support overt, even pro-
vocative political activities by law-enforcement officials that previously would have been strongly condemned. At the same time,
blacks have become increasingly hostile to the officers in charge of
maintaining order in their communities. Nearly all the major riots
in the late 1960s were sparked by an incident between police and
a black suspect. Black leaders have demanded civilian review
boards that would have the power to investigate allegations of
police brutality. And, out of concern for their own safety, officers
have insisted that they patrol black communities (both in cars
and on foot) in pairs rather than singly. For many blacks, police
have become an army of occupation within their territory, a grim
realization of the possibility that opponents of any police force
feared over a century ago.

There is little solid evidence that black suspicion of the police
is due to discriminatory behavior by white policemen against
blacks in particular. It is true that policemen make racial slurs
when referring to blacks behind their backs and, sometimes, to
their faces.[11] But if police call blacks "niggers" and "coons," that
seems little different than their references to Italians as "wops"
and to people of Polish descent as "Polacks." Street language is
not invariably polite; it hardly seems the root of the problem.
More significantly, it is difficult to find conclusive evidence in
modern departments that policemen treat blacks in a discriminatory fashion. For example, Skolnick found little evidence that
policemen collecting fines for cumulative traffic and parking vio-
lations called the paddy wagon any more frequently for blacks
than for whites (once social class and permanence of residence
had been taken into account).[12] Reiss found a high incidence of
police brutality directed especially against those who question
the officer's authority, but he found no higher incidence of brutal
treatment of black than white suspects.[13] And Wilson found that
modernized, reformed departments arrested far fewer blacks on
the vague charge of public drunkenness than did more traditional,
night-watchmanlike departments.[14] Police are far from color-blind,
but there is some evidence that they find characteristics other
than race more useful in making routine decisions on patrol.

The tensions between police and the black community are nonetheless very real. A variety of interpretations of this fact exist, and
the evidence for any one is skimpy at best. Still, the changes in the
structure of urban police departments seem to be at least one important factor. The reforms that have modernized the police have
perhaps made them more honest, efficient (in a narrow sense of

the word), and equitable. Yet the centralization of control has so divorced the patrolmen from the communities for which they have responsibility that it has made vastly more difficult the development of a sense of trust between police and community. Ironically, the very steps taken to improve the police have added to the mutual distrust that has typically characterized relations between police and a city's poorer minority groups. If reform is to succeed in the future, it must focus not so much on increasing police efficiency as on creating the conditions of trust between police and the law-abiding community, upon which effective law enforcement ultimately depends.

In this context, proposals for community control of the police have some merit. Although the unforeseen consequences of previous reforms caution against suggesting that any panacea is available, community-controlled police would offset many of the tendencies of today's modernized, reformed police departments. Officers would be more likely to live in the neighborhoods they patrolled and to share the communities' racial, ethnic, and class characteristics. If directed by representatives of their local community, they would enforce the laws selectively whenever such was necessary for maintaining peace and trust with community residents.

Some have argued that community control of police would mean conflict among armed racial groups within the central city. Others seem to fear that in black areas law and order would totally break down. Such criticisms ignore the fact that community control of police is prevalent in the mostly white suburban areas; it is not easy to see the justification for accepting such a governing structure there but opposing it for the central city. The claim that blacks could not or would not enforce order in their own community, aside from bordering on the most blatant racism, ignores the fact that blacks, more often victims than any other group, are concerned about "crime in the streets." Admittedly, coordinating police work among competing jurisdictions would require cooperative mechanisms among community-controlled departments, but establishing once again a respect for law officers, as well as for the law, seems to be a higher priority.

NOTES

1. Norval Morris and Gordon Hawkins, *The Honest Politician's Guide to Crime Control* (Chicago: University of Chicago Press, 1970), p. 6.
2. James Q. Wilson, *Varieties of Police Behavior* (Cambridge, Mass.:

Harvard University Press, 1968), Ch. 5. Wilson argues that police traditionally used these laws more to maintain public order than to regulate
personal conduct. On the other hand, these laws do permit police abuse
of "drunks," vagrants, and other outcasts of society. See Albert J. Reiss,
"How Much 'Police Brutality' Is There?" *TRANS-action*, IV, 8 (July/
August, 1967), pp. 10–19.

3. Jerome Skolnick, *Justice Without Trial* (New York: John Wiley and
   Sons, 1967), Ch. 6.
4. John Gardiner, "The Politics of Corruption," in Task Force on Organized Crime, The President's Commission on Law Enforcement and
   Administration of Justice, *Task Force Report: Organized Crime* (Washington: U.S. Government Printing Office, 1963), pp. 61–79.
5. Wallace Sayre and Herbert Kaufman, *Governing New York City* (New
   York: Norton, 1965), pp. 538–48.
6. Morris and Hawkins, *op. cit.*, Ch. 1.
7. On the moralistic flavor of the reform movement, see Richard Hof-
   stadter, *The Age of Reform* (New York: Random House, 1955); see
   also Daniel Elazar, *Cities of the Prairie* (New York: Basic Books, 1968).
8. Together, these reforms have been the basis for the "legalistic" style of
   law enforcement, which Wilson contrasts with the "nightwatchman"
   style of an early period. See Wilson, *Varieties of Police Behavior*, Ch. 6.
9. Elinor Ostrom and Gordon Whitaker, "Black Citizens and the Police:
   Some Effects of Community Control." Paper presented before the
   Annual Meeting of the American Political Science Association, Chicago,
   Illinois, September, 1971.
10. This problem is discussed in some detail in Jerome Skolnick, *The Politics
    of Protest* (New York: Ballantine, 1969), pp. 286–89.
11. Skolnick, *Justice Without Trial*, pp. 80–83.
12. *Ibid.*, pp. 83–90.
13. Reiss, *op. cit.*, pp. 15–17.
14. Wilson, *op. cit.*, pp. 188–89.

BIBLIOGRAPHY

MORRIS, NORVAL, and GORDON HAWKINS. *The Honest Politician's Guide to
   Crime Control*. Chicago: University of Chicago: Press, 1970.
NIEDERHOFER, ARTHUR. *Behind the Shield: The Police in Urban Society*.
   Garden City, N.Y.: Doubleday, 1967, p. 60.
President's Commission on Law Enforcement and Administration of Justice.
   The Challenge of Crime in a Free Society. Washington, D.C.: U.S.
   Government Printing Office, 1967. See also various staff reports to this
   Presidential commission.
REISS, ALBERT J., JR. *The Police and the Public*. New Haven: Yale University
   Press, 1971.
SKOLNICK, JEROME H. *Justice Without Trial: Law Enforcement in Demo-
   cratic Society*. New York: John Wiley and Sons, 1967.
———. *The Politics of Protest*. New York: Ballantine, 1969.
WILSON, JAMES Q. *Varieties of Police Behavior: The Management of Law
   and Order in Eight Communities*. Cambridge, Mass.: Harvard University
   Press, 1970.
———. *Thinking about Crime*. New York: Basic Books, 1975.

THE POLICE DEPARTMENT

WALLACE SAYRE AND HERBERT KAUFMAN

The Police Commissioner [of New York City] heads the most visible, the most publicized, the most dramatic and controversial of the city's line agencies. His Department is also one of the city's largest, its staff numbering over 26,000 at the end of 1957, of which more than 25,000 were members of the uniformed force.* Representing one of the oldest of the city government's functions, but confronted with constantly changing problems and pressures in its assignments, the Department presents to the Police Commissioner and his deputies complexities and dilemmas not often matched in difficulty in the city's other line agencies.

The Police Department has the broadest regulatory assignment among all the regulatory activities of the city government. From the charter alone, the Department derives a sweeping obligation and power to "preserve the public peace, prevent crime, detect and arrest offenders, . . . preserve order . . . , enforce and prevent the violation of all laws and ordinances . . . ," accompanied by a series of more specific assignments. But the greater body of the Department's assignments comes from state laws and local ordinances and codes containing extensive regulatory and law enforcement provisions which the Department is expected to apply to all violators. Still other provisions of charter and statute make the Police Commissioner the licensing, inspecting, or supervising authority over certain trades (for example, public dance halls, cabarets, taxicabs and taxi drivers, pawnbrokers, cartmen, and others). To all these regulatory assignments of the Department there must also be added the traditional and widespread expectations that the police force is a service agency, obliged to at-

---

* Although the department expanded in size in subsequent years, numbering over 31,000 at one point, by 1975, budgetary constraints had reduced its personnel approximately to the 1957 figures.—Eds.

From Wallace S. Sayre and Herbert Kaufman, *Governing New York City*. © 1960 by the Russell Sage Foundation, New York. Reprinted with permission.

tend to the countless necessities and conveniences of an urban population for whom the police are a visible and available resource. The Commissioner can find few boundaries to his responsibilities; he has less difficulty in discovering the limits of his opportunities and resources.

The Police Commissioner's hopes for the exercise of personal leadership and initiative as the responsible head of his Department revolve around his capacity to secure internal control over his agency, his relations with the Mayor, with other city officials and the party leaders, and with the Department's complex constituency. These basic conditions of his leadership and initiative are rarely fully mastered by the Police Commissioner. Resolute outsiders and insiders, in their turn as Commissioners, have each expended great energies and varied strategies upon this dilemma without triumphant results. Other Commissioners have accepted the prevailing arrangements, expressing satisfaction in quite marginal increments of change; still others have moved quickly on to more responsible or less taxing environments.

Securing internal control of the Department is the insurmountable barrier to leadership, initiative, and innovation by Police Commissioners. The Commissioner is not lacking in formal power for this purpose. The charter declares that he "shall have cognizance and control of the government, administration, disposition and discipline of the department, and control of the police force of the department" and, further, that he "shall be the chief executive officer of the police force." But these formal powers must in reality be exercised in the context of a personnel system which blunts their use, in the face of the close-knit organized police bureaucracies determined to limit the Commissioner's initiative and discretion, and through an organization structure designed to preserve the traditions of the force and its settled patterns of operation. The Commissioner has few "civilian" helpers; they are mainly clerical and custodial. The personnel system dictates that every member of the uniformed police force must be first recruited and inducted as a patrolman, a "rookie" without special skills or knowledge who enters upon a long apprenticeship in the tradition-centered doctrines and practices of the force, rising slowly rank by rank through examinations which also emphasize seniority and mastery of the Department's established codes of police practice.

The police captains who emerge from this process of advancement by apprenticeship, indoctrination, and seniority constitute the pool of talent from which the Commissioner must select his officers for the command posts and the managerial tasks of the Department—the deputy inspectors, the inspectors, the deputy chief inspectors, the assistant chief inspectors, and the Chief Inspector who is the head of the uniformed force. In recent decades, Police Commissioners have increasingly chosen, or have been persuaded, to select their deputy commissioners from this group also. Thus the Commissioner is enclosed within (or ostracized by, if he does not conform) a personnel system which limits his choices of key personnel and provides him but rarely with fellow champions of innovation, or with experts and specialists in fields of knowledge (technological and sociological) which might transform police administration under his leadership, or even with that modicum of competition in ideas among different segments of his staff which might give him limited opportunities for catalytic action as Commissioner.

If the personnel system confronts the Commissioner with a tradition-centered top command—"the top brass," composed of approximately 100 inspectors at various grades and of not quite 200 captains—the organized police bureaucracies (lieutenants, sergeants, patrolmen) bring additional restrictive pressures to bear upon him. Mayor McClellan observed long ago that the Police Department was "run by the inspectors," not by the Commissioner; for the past several decades, he would have needed to add "and by the police bureaucracies." They have power inside the Department to mold the behavior of their members in such ways as will reduce the impact of any change in policy or procedure sponsored by the Commissioner. They have secured special protections for their members in both state statutes and city rules, which preserve their capacity to resist without much risk of reprisal or severe discipline. They have power in the more general political arena, where officials and party leaders have learned to listen to them and to act sympathetically. Police Commissioners may bristle at bureaucratic boldness and evoke the symbols of command and discipline, but the organized police groups are confident and persistent; they are on familiar ground and have often waited out these storms before. Their goal is self-direction in their accustomed ways, not an eager responsiveness to either the "top brass" or the current Commissioner.

The twin forces of the Department's closed personnel system and the organized police bureaucracies help to preserve a third barrier to leadership by the Commissioner—an organization structure awkwardly suited to the Commissioner's purposes of leadership and innovation. The basic structure is traditional and does not yield much to the requirements of changes in policies and in assignments, or of advances in police technology developed elsewhere. Organizationally, the Department is wedded to performing its work through geographical units—precincts, districts and divisions, borough commands—at the expense of greater specialization and mobility of its resources. The major concessions to specialization which have been made (the detective, traffic, and emergency service patrol groups) are themselves each organized geographically. In this and other ways specialized personnel is almost invariably squeezed into the geographical chains-of-command. Methods and procedures must also conform to the mold of geography, affecting adversely the attraction and feasibility of almost every proposed change in technology or police. Police Commissioners are only occasionally aware of this tyranny of geography as an organizational vise; they have no managerial staff to develop for them the alternatives in police organization and procedures which might give them unsuspected opportunities for breaking the crust of custom and habits in police administration. For example, the Police Commissioner was forced in 1949 to yield the traffic planning assignment to a new city agency because his personnel system and his organizational arrangements could produce neither the specialized personnel (the traffic planners, traffic engineers, and statistical analysts) nor the specialized methods necessary to handle the traffic problem at a high level of experiment and innovation.

The closed personnel system, the power of the police bureaucracies, and the inflexible organization structure of the Department have an additional by-product for the Commissioner: he must expend a great part of his energies in attempts at "policing the police." His problems are concentrated in two phenomena: police corruption and police violence. However aggressively the Commissioner pursues the goal of police integrity by the use of special squads to investigate the force, by shake-ups and transfers of command, by swift suspensions and other forms of discipline, he accepts ultimately that police corruption is endemic to his organization, and that he is fortunate if he can prevent its reaching epidemic proportions. He lacks the resources to do more. On the score of police violence, he is compelled to yield in a different fashion: he must almost invariably take a tough line in justification of the use of force by the police, whether it be rationalizing the promiscuous use of the club, the gun, or the "third degree." His organization (and his own training, if he is a career Commissioner) does not permit him to depart from this doctrine.

Police Commissioners thus exercise formal but essential peripheral control over the Police Department. They can dramatize the role of the Department in the life of the city; they can urge forcefully and often successfully the expansion of the Department in numbers and budget and thus win some internal support; they can lead crusades against selected targets ("round-ups" of alleged vagrants; raids on gamblers, narcotic "rings," houses of prostitution; arrests of alleged subversives); and they can be stern disciplinarians in dealing with individual members of the force who violate overtly the regulations of the Department. But these are the outer boundaries of their control. The more positive measures of leadership are beyond their reach.

Police Commissioners in New York City have long sought an autonomous status for their Department with freedom from supervision by the Mayor, from interventions by party leaders, and from jurisdictional invasions by other governmental agencies. "No outside interference" has been their uniform motto for several decades, and all external influences have usually been condemned as "politics." In seeking to maximize the self-directing capacity of the Department, Commissioners have presumably sought also to maximize their own opportunities for leadership and direction of the police agency. But autonomy for the Department has also meant isolation for the Commissioner from sources which might help him in his difficult task of securing internal control. The police bureaucracy seems to be the main beneficiary of the autonomy which the Police Commissioners have secured.

Freedom from supervision by the Mayor has been a special target of the drive for police autonomy. Mayoral interest in police policy and police administration has been consistently rebuffed by equating it with the interests of party leaders or, more ambiguously, with politics. In their acceptance of this formula for ostracizing Mayors from any opportunities to assume general responsibility for leadership in law enforcement, the Police Commissioners have had the support of the police bureaucracy, the civic groups, the communication media, and others. There is a general consensus that Mayors merit only the blame for police failures. The assistance which Mayors might give Police Commissioners in their efforts to acquire leadership within the Department has been forfeited in preference for the ambiguous formula of autonomy.

Removal of the influence of party leaders from police administration has also been a goal of most Police Commissioners, supported by the police bureaucracy and by almost all the articulate voices in the city. Several Commissioners have given this problem high priority, and the long-term trend in the Department has been to reduce steadily the opportunities of party leaders to intervene overtly either in the personnel system or in police policy. The most striking example is the neutralization of the police role in election administration. The upper limits of the trend are to be found, however, in the disposition of individual members of the force to build mutually useful relationships with party leaders. It party leaders have been largely excluded at headquarters, they are not yet ignored in the precincts or other local commands. One consequence of this development may be that the Commissioner is isolated from the party leaders in a way in which his lieutenants, detectives, captains, and inspectors are not.

Other governmental agencies give Police Commissioners less difficulty. The Police Commissioners are especially able to escape some of the tight controls of the overhead agencies—Budget, Personnel, Law, Investigation, and others—which so often burden the discretion of other department heads. With other line agencies, the relations are often more complex and sometimes characterized by jurisdictional friction, for example, with District Attorneys, and the Departments of Education, Fire, Health, Sanitation, Traffic, Welfare, the Youth Board, and the special authorities. In the main, however, the Police Department tends more often to have its own way, the other agencies yielding to its power, its autonomy, and its cohesiveness. The other side of the medal is the Police Commissioner's limited opportunities to offer firm cooperation with other agencies even when he wishes to do so. His control over his own Department is not sufficient for him to pledge its affirmative participation in programs involving important innovations in police attitudes or methods.

The Police Department has one of the most complex constituencies among the city's line agencies. It is the object of relatively constant attention from a wider range of nongovernmental groups than any other single agency. With such extensive attention directed at them, Police Commissioners have great difficulty in deciding to which voices they must listen most receptively, and on what subjects. The most relevant constituency elements are difficult to identify. Fragmentation in organization and ambivalence in attitudes toward the Department are their most distinctive characteristics. Police Commissioners never quite succeed in identifying the hard core either of their supporting groups or of the opposition groups with whom they must come to terms. The formations and their attitudes tend to be fluid and unpredictable.

There are a few certainties upon which the Police Commissioner can reasonably depend in his dealings with the Department's constituency, but the sum total of these several certainties is likely to confront him with as many inconsistencies as clarifications. He can usually expect more support than opposition for proposals to expand the size of the police force; the economy groups have a traditional tolerance for police budgets, and most other groups are regularly demanding more police services. He can count upon the groups licensed or inspected by the Department to attempt to capture the licensing and inspection units of his organization, thus threatening his control over policy and exposing him to the risks of unfavorable exposés. He can reasonably anticipate that the communication media, especially the press, will be ambivalent in their attitudes toward him and his agency, publicizing with equal zeal and emphasis the dramatic accomplishments of the police and the sordid chapters of police corruption and violence. He will note, too, that the merchant and automobile associations urging more effective traffic control are also inclined to condemn "arbitrary" or "rigid" enforcement techniques. Each religious group presses for its doctrines of law enforcement. Employer groups urge strict supervision of picketing; labor unions emphasize their hard-won standards of strict neutrality by the police in labor disputes. Some groups demand a hard line by police toward juvenile delinquents; others insist upon a subordinate role for the police in such matters. Some voices advocate wide use of the nightstick and the dragnet against gangsters, punks, and gamblers; others, such as bar associations, civil liberties groups, and some communication media, remind the Police Commissioner of the due process of law. There are no "peak associations" tying these groups together, either as support or opposition. The prime difficulty for the Police Commissioner is that, while his highly fragmented constituency can cause him much trouble, he cannot expect much help from it; he cannot, in fact, find even a stable and significant center of opposition with which he might reach long-term accommodations. Nor does his constituency furnish him with a lever which he might use to move the police bureaucracy toward greater responsiveness to his leadership.

The Police Commissioner—isolated from the Mayor and other

elected officials, from the party leaders, and from other agencies, and confronted by an unstructured, fragmented constituency—is thus cut off from effective external alliances and thrust back upon his own limited resources in attempting to lead and direct the police bureaucracy. Autonomy for the Department spells isolation for the Commissioner. With energy and resolution, and some public relations skill, he may create a favorable public image of himself as an omnipresent, incorruptible, and determined administrator. He may exploit the competitive relation between the 300 members of "the brass" and the 24,000 members of the rank and file, in ways that may increase somewhat his influence with both; he may emphatically invoke the semimilitary command structure and vocabulary of the Department to make his purposes unambiguous. He may find tangible and intangible rewards to bestow as incentives for innovation and for responsiveness to his leadership, and he may exhort his officers and men to aspire to the status of a profession, to embrace the trends toward modernization, to take the lead among police systems. All these efforts will help him in his leadership, but their combined long-range increment is not strikingly large. In the end, whatever the dash and determination at the beginning, the Commissioners yield to the necessity of being more the spokesman and the advocate than the leader and the innovator.

WHAT MAKES A BETTER POLICEMAN?

JAMES Q. WILSON

Current discussions of the problems of the American police seem fraught with paradox. While everyone seems to agree about remedies, criticisms of the police arise out of radically different conceptions of the police function. Some people see the police as the chief means of ending or reducing "crime in the streets"; others see them as an agency by which white society confines and suppresses black ghettos; still others view them as an organization caught on the grinding edge of a class conflict among competing standards of order and propriety. Yet despite these utterly disparate diagnoses, the prescribed treatment tends to be quite conventional and generally endorsed—higher salaries, better training, clearer policies, more modern equipment. And a further paradox: despite this apparent agreement on what should be done, little, in fact, happens. In some places, voters and politicians appear to be universally sympathetic to the needs of the police, but they are unwilling to appropriate more money to meet those needs. In other places, the extra funds have been spent but the criticisms remain—little, apparently, has changed.

One reason for this confusion or inaction lies, I believe, in the fact that the police perform a number of quite different functions. The controversies in which the police are embroiled reveal this as various disputants emphasize crime prevention, or law enforcement, or the maintenance of order, or political power. Liberty, order, legitimacy—important and fundamental values are in conflict. The adherents of various points of view take refuge in a common (and perhaps peculiarly American) set of proposals: spend money, hire better men, buy more things. I suspect that spending more money and hiring better men *are* essential to police improvement, but I also suspect that one reason so little extra money is spent and so few men are hired is that beneath our

From James Q. Wilson, "What Makes a Better Policeman?" in *The Atlantic Monthly* (March, 1969), pp. 129–34. Copyright © 1969 by the Atlantic Monthly Company, Boston, Massachusetts. Reprinted with permission.

agreement on means, we remain in deep disagreement on ends. Spend the money on *what*, and *why*? What *is* a "better" policeman, anyway?

This is not a new issue. The history of the American municipal police is in great part a history of struggles to define their role in our society. What makes the controversy so intense today is only partly that it is linked to the question of race; indeed, in the past the police have repeatedly been in conflict with new urban migrants of whatever color. The reason for the heat generated by the police question is probably the same as the reason for the emotions aroused by the crime issue: we compare present circumstances with an earlier period when we thought we had solved the problem. Police behavior, like crime, was not a major issue in the 1940s and 1950s. When the police did become an issue, it was usually because a department was found to be corrupt, and that discovery produced a standard response—bring in a reform chief, reorganize the force, and get back to work.

CROOK CATCHERS

That work was law enforcement, or so it was thought. The job of the police was to prevent crime and catch crooks. Corruption was a serious problem because it seemed to mean that crime was not being prevented and crooks were not being caught. Organized criminals were buying protection, or petty thieves were putting in a "fix," or the police themselves were stealing on the side. Reforming a department not only meant ending corruption and alliances with criminals; it also meant improving training and developing new methods—more courses on crime detection, tighter departmental discipline to prevent misconduct, better equipment to facilitate getting to the scene of a crime and analyzing clues. When the public was invited to inspect a refurbished department, it was shown the new patrol cars, the new crime laboratory, the new communications center, and perhaps the new pistol range. The policeman was portrayed as a "crime fighter," and to an important degree, of course, he was.

But that was not all or even the most important thing he was. Given the nature of the crime problem, it was impossible for him to be simply a crime fighter. Most crime is not prevented and most criminals are not caught, even in the best-run, best-manned departments. Murder, for example, is a "private" crime, occurring chiefly off the streets and among "friends" or relatives. No police methods can prevent it, and only general domestic disarmament, an unlikely event, might reduce it. Many, if not most, assaults are similarly immune from police deterrence. Most crimes against property—burglary, auto theft, larceny—are also crimes of stealth, and though the police might, by various means, cut the rate somewhat, they cannot cut it greatly because they cannot be everywhere at once. Street crimes—robberies, muggings, purse snatches—are more susceptible to police deterrence than any other kind, though so far few, if any, departments have had the resources or the community support to carry out a really significant strategy to prevent street crime.

The result of this state of affairs is that though some police departments are regarded as "backward" and others as "modern" and "professional," neither kind seems able to bring about a substantial, enduring reduction of the crime rate. If this is true, then the characterization of the police as primarily crime fighters places them in a potentially embarrassing position, that of *being judged by a goal they cannot attain*. In the 1950s, when crime rates were either stabilized or ignored, this awkward situation and the police response to it were not apparent.

What most policemen were doing even when they were being thought of as crime fighters was not so much enforcing the law as maintaining order. In a recent study, I have tried to show what makes up the routine work-load of patrolmen, the police rank which has the largest number of men. The vast majority of police actions taken in response to citizen calls involve either providing a service (getting a cat out of a tree or taking a person to a hospital) or managing real or alleged conditions of disorder (quarreling families, public drunks, bothersome teen-agers, noisy cars, and tavern fights). Only a small fraction of these calls involve matters of law enforcement, such as checking on a prowler, catching a burglar in the act, or preventing a street robbery. The disorders to which the police routinely respond are not large-scale. Riots and civil commotions are, in any given city, rare occurrences and when they happen, the police act en masse, under central leadership. Rather, the maintenance of order involves handling disputes in which only two or three people participate and which arise out of personal misconduct, not racial or class grievances.

The difference between order maintenance and law enforcement is not simply the difference between "little stuff" and "real crime" or between misdemeanors and felonies. The distinction is fundamental to the police role, for the two functions involve quite dissimilar police actions and judgments. Order maintenance arises out of a dispute among citizens who accuse each other of being at fault; law enforcement arises out of the victimization of an innocent party by a person whose guilt must be proved. Handling a disorderly situation requires the officer to make a judgment about what constitutes an appropriate standard of behavior; law enforcement requires him only to compare a person's behavior with a clear legal standard. Murder or theft is defined, unambiguously, by statutes; public peace is not. Order maintenance rarely leads to an arrest; law enforcement (if the suspect can be found) typically does. Citizens quarreling usually want the officer to "do something," but they rarely want him to make an arrest (after all, the disputants are usually known or related to each other). Furthermore, whatever law is broken in a quarrel is usually a misdemeanor, and in most states, an officer cannot make a misdemeanor arrest unless he saw the infraction (which is rare) or unless one party or the other will swear out a formal complaint (which is even rarer).

Because an arrest cannot be made in most disorderly cases, the officer is expected to handle the situation by other means and on the spot, but the law gives him almost no guidance on how he is to do this; indeed, the law often denies him the right to do anything at all *other* than make an arrest. No judge will ever see the case, and thus no judge can decide the case for the officer. Alone, unsupervised, with no policies to guide him and little sympathy from onlookers to support him, the officer must "administer justice" on the curbstone.

Early Patterns

In the nineteenth century, it was widely recognized that the maintenance of order was the chief function of the police. Roger Lane's informative history, *Policing the City: Boston, 1822–1885* (Cambridge: Harvard University Press, 1967), recounts how that department, the oldest in the United States, was first organized as a night watch to keep the peace in the streets. Beginning in 1834, men drafted from the citizenry were required to take their turns in seeing (as the governing statute required) "that all disturbances and disorders in the night shall be prevented and suppressed." Wild creatures, human and animal alike, were to be kept off the street, and a hue and cry was to be set up should fire or riot threaten.

The job of law enforcement—that is, of apprehending criminals who had robbed or burgled the citizenry—was not among the duties of the watchmen; indeed, it was not even among the duties of the government. A victim was obliged to find the guilty party himself. Once a suspect was found, the citizen could, for a fee, hire a constable who, acting on a warrant, would take the suspect into custody. Even after detectives—that is, men charged with law enforcement rather than the maintenance of order—were added to the force in the nineteenth century, they continued to serve essentially private interests. The chief concern of the victim was restitution, and to that end, the detectives would seek to recover loot in exchange for a percentage of the take. Detectives functioned then as personal-injury lawyers operate today, on a contingency basis, hoping to get a large part, perhaps half, of the proceeds.

Since in those days there was no law against compounding a felony, the detectives were free to employ any methods they wanted to recover stolen property. And with this as their mission, it is not surprising, as Lane notes, that the best detectives were those who by background and experience were most familiar with the haunts and methods of thieves.

The emergence of a municipal police force out of its watchmen antecedents was not so much the result of mounting crime rates as of growing levels of civil disorder. In time, and with the growth of the cities to a size and heterogeneity too great to permit the operation of informal social controls, the problem of order maintenance became too severe to make reliance on part-time or volunteer watchmen feasible. The Boston Police Department was created to deal with riots, as was the Department in Philadelphia. The Boston police first acquired firearms in the aftermath of the Draft Riot of 1863, though they were not fully armed at public expense until 1884.

The Philadelphia case is illustrative of many. Like Boston, that city relied on watchmen rather than an organized, quasimilitary constabulary. But a series of riots among youthful gangs (the Rats, the Bouncers, the Schuylkill Rangers, and the Blood Tubs, among several) persuaded the city fathers that stronger measures were necessary. To a degree, the riots were under semiofficial auspices, thus magnifying the embarrassment the politicians faced. It seems that volunteer fire companies were organized to handle conflagrations. The young toughs who sat about waiting for fires to happen found this boring and, worse, unrewarding, whereupon some hit upon the idea of starting a fire and racing other companies to the scene to see who could put the blaze out more quickly, and just as important, who could pick up the most loot from the building. Though this competitive zeal may have been a commendable aid to training, it led to frequent collisions between companies speeding to the same fire, with the encounter often leading to a riot. It is only a slight exaggeration to say that the Philadelphia policemen were created in part to control the Philadelphia firemen.

Sometimes on Sunday

The growth and formal organization of the police department did not, in themselves, lead to changes in function. The maintenance of order was still the principal objective. What did lead to a change was twofold: the bureaucratization of the detectives (putting them on salary and ending the fee system), and the use of the police to enforce unpopular laws governing the sale and use of liquor. The former change led to the beginning of the popular confusion as to what the police do. The detective became the hero of the dime novel and the cynosure of the public's romantic imagination; he, and not his patrolman colleague, was the "real" police officer doing "real" police work. Enforcing liquor laws caused the police to initiate prosecutions on their own authority rather than on citizen complaint, particularly in cases where the public was deeply divided regarding the wisdom of the law. In Philadelphia, enforcing the Sunday closing laws, especially with regard to saloons, was widely resented, and when the mayor ordered the police to do it, he was, according to a contemporary account, "caricatured, ridiculed, and denounced." In Boston Mayor Jonathan Chapman was led to remark that police enforcement of temperance laws had created a situation in which "the passions of men are aroused and the community is kept in a constant state of ferment."

What kept the police from being utterly destroyed by the liquor controversy was their determination to do no more than was absolutely necessary, given whatever regime was in power. Edward Savage, the able chief of the Boston force in the 1870s and 1880s, was a man of modest but much exercised literary talents, and in one of his better-known essays, entitled "Advice to a Young Policeman," he set forth the essential role of good police work: "In ordinary cases, if you find yourself in a position of not knowing exactly what to do, better to do too little than too much; it is easier to excuse a moderate course than an overt act."

In addition, the police provided on a large scale a number of services to citizens, especially to those who, because of drink, indolence, or circumstance, were likely to become sources of public disorder. Roger Lane calculates that in 1856 the Boston police provided "lodgings" to over nine thousand persons, not including those who had been arrested for drunkenness. By 1860 the total exceeded seventeen thousand. Perhaps because the police were the principal city agency to witness the lot of the poor, perhaps because one of the original collateral duties of the police chief was superintendent of public health, the officers provided a wide range of services in addition to lodgings—coal for needy families, soup kitchens for the hungry, and jobs as domestics for girls they thought could be lured away from a life of prostitution.

In time, this service policy, which probably did much to mitigate the hostility between police and public occasioned by the enforcement of liquor laws, was curtailed on the complaint of the leaders of the organized charities who objected, apparently, to unfair competition. The advocates of "scientific charity," it seems, did not believe the police were competent to distinguish between the deserving and the undeserving poor.

The relations between police and public even during the period of free soup were not consistently amicable. One issue was the appointment of Irish police officers. For political purposes, the Boston Whigs demanded that, as we would say today, "representatives of indigenous and culturally-deprived groups" be added to the force. Then as now, the "culturally deprived" were responsible for a disproportionate share of those arrested for crimes. Then as now, the police objected to the appointment of an Irishman on the grounds that the man selected by the politicians was not qualified and had himself been arrested for a crime a few years earlier—it seems he had participated in a riot. The police, of course, denied that they were prejudiced but claimed that appointing a person on grounds of ethnicity would be destructive of morale on the force. The mayor insisted that the appointment take place. On November 3, 1851, the new man reported for work, announcing himself loudly and proudly as "Barney McGinniskin, fresh from the bogs of Ireland!"

THE CHIEF EVIL

By the end of the nineteenth century, the groundwork had been laid for the modern municipal police force, and for the modern problems of the police. The bureaucratization of the detectives and the police enforcement of liquor laws had not as yet overshadowed the order-maintenance function of the police, but two events of the twentieth century ensured that they would—Prohibition and the Depression. The former required the police everywhere to choose between being corrupted and making a nuisance of themselves; the latter focused public attention on the escapades of bank robbers and other desperadoes such as John Dillinger, Baby Face Nelson, and Bonnie and Clyde. Police venality and rising crime rates coincided in the public mind, though in fact they had somewhat different causes. The watchman function of the police was lost sight of; their law enforcement function, and their apparent failure to exercise it, were emphasized.

President Herbert Hoover did what most Presidents do when faced with a major political issue for which the solution is neither obvious nor popular—he appointed a commission. In 1931 the National Commission on Law Observance and Law Enforcement —generally known, after its chairman, as the Wickersham Commission—made its report in a series of volumes prepared by some of the ablest academic and police experts of the day. Though many subjects were covered (especially the question of whether immigrants were more criminal than native-born Americans), the volume on the police was of special importance. On page one, the first paragraph stated a twentieth-century conception of the police function and a new standard by which policemen were to be judged:

> The general failure of the police to detect and arrest criminals guilty of the many murders, spectacular bank, payroll, and other hold-ups, and sensational robberies with guns, frequently resulting in the death of the robbed victim, has caused a loss of public confidence in the police of our country. For a condition so general there must be some universal underlying causes to account for it.

Now, of course there may have been some "universal underlying causes," but the ones that come readily to mind—Prohibition, post-war readjustment, and the economic cycle—were not ones about which a presidential commission could at that time speak very candidly. Besides, it was far from clear what could be done about at least the second and third of these causes. What was necessary was to find a "universal cause" about which something could be done. Needless to say, two groups on whom we have long felt free to cast blame for everything from slums to hoof-and-mouth disease—the police and the politicians—seemed appropriate targets. Accordingly, the Commission wrote:

> The chief evil, in our opinion, lies in the insecure, short term of service of the chief or executive head of the police force and in his being subject while in office to the control of politicians in the discharge of his duties.

Some Proposals

Following on this analysis, the Commission detailed a number of specific proposals—putting the police on civil service, buying modern equipment ("the wireless"), and of course, hiring better men and giving them better training. In truth, there probably was a need for some police reforms; many departments had become dumping grounds for the fat relatives of second-rate politicians, and modern bank robbers were in many cases more mobile and efficient than the police chasing them. But the "professional" view of the police went further than merely proposing changes in equipment and manpower; it argued in addition that since the police *can* prevent crime, if the crime rate gets out of hand, it is in good measure because the police are incompetent as a result of political influence.

Now, some members of the Commission were no doubt perfectly aware that the police do not cause crime, but, like many commissions anxious to make a strong public impression and generate support for desirable changes, they inevitably overstated the case in their report. A report that said that many improvements in police practice were necessary but that these improvements, if adopted, would have only a slight effect on the crime rate would not generate many headlines. (Thirty-seven years later, the Kerner Commission had not forgotten this lesson; what made the newspapers was not its proposals for action but its charge of "white racism.")

The consequences of assigning to the police a law-enforcement, crime-prevention function to the exclusion of anything else were profound. If the job of the police is to catch crooks, then the police have a technical, ministerial responsibility in which discretion plays little part. Since no one is likely to disagree on the value of the objective, then there is little reason to expose the police to the decision-making processes of city government. *Ergo,* take the police "out of politics." So powerful (or so useful) did this slogan become that within a few decades whenever a big-city mayor tried to pick his own police chief or take charge of his department for the purpose of giving it a new direction, *the police themselves* objected on the grounds that this was an effort to exercise "political influence" over the force.

Furthermore, if the technical objective of law enforcement was primary, then non-law-enforcement duties should be taken away from the police: no more soup kitchens; no more giving lodging to drunks; no more ambulance driving. These things are not "real police work." Let the police see the public only in their role as law enforcers. Let the public, alas, see the police only as adversaries. Of course, these changes were more in the public's mind than in everyday reality. If politics was taken out of the police, the police were not taken out of politics. They continued—in fact, with the decline of party machines, they increased—their involvement in electoral politics, city hall intrigue, and legislative lobbying. And whatever professional police leadership may have said, the patrolman on the beat knew that his job was not primarily law enforcement—he was still handling as many family fights and rowdy teen-agers as ever. But lacking support in the performance of these duties, he came also to believe that his job "wasn't real police work," and accordingly that it was peripheral, if not demeaning.

But perhaps the most important consequence was the police response to the public expectation that they could prevent crime. Their response was perfectly rational and to be encountered in any organization that is judged by a standard it cannot meet— they lied. If police activity (given the level of resources and public support available) could not produce a significant decline in crime rates, police record-keeping would be "adjusted" to keep the rates in line. Departments judged by professional standards but not controlled by professional leaders were at pains to show progress by either understating the number of crimes or overstating the number of crimes "cleared" by arrest. Often this was not the policy of the chief, but the result of judging officers by crime and arrest records.

In the public's eye, the "hero cop" was the man who made the "good pinch." For a while (until the mass media abandoned the standards of the middle-aged and the conservative in favor of the standards of the young and the radical), the ideal cop was the "G Man." FBI agents, of course, are different from municipal police forces precisely because their task *is* law enforcement, and often enforcing important laws against quite serious criminals. Few special agents need to wade into a skid-row brawl. But within city departments, the emphasis on the "good pinch" grew. This was only partly because the newspapers, and thus the public, rewarded such accomplishments; it was also because the departments rewarded it. The patrolman could look forward, in the typical case, to remaining a patrolman all his life *unless* he could get promoted or be made a detective. Promotion increasingly came to require the passing of a written examination in which college men would usually do better than less articulate but perhaps more competent "street men." Appointment as a detective, however, was in many departments available to men with a good arrest record (or a strategically placed friend in headquarters). If you want to get away from drunks, kids, and shrews, then make a pinch that will put you in line for becoming a dick. Though there is in principle nothing wrong with rewarding men for having a good arrest record, one frequent result of this system has been to take the best patrolmen off the street and put them into a headquarters unit.

POLICE REFORM: THE CHOICES AHEAD

Today, the conception of the police role underlying the foregoing arrangements is being questioned. Perhaps the landmark event was the 1967 report of the President's Commission on Law Enforcement and Administration of Justice, the executive director of which was James Vorenberg of the Harvard Law School. Unlike the Wickersham or Kerner Commission reports, this document made relatively few headlines, and the reason, I think, was that it did not provide the reporters with a catchy slogan. The nine volumes of the Vorenberg report insisted that the problems of crime and police work are complicated matters for which few, if any, easy solutions are available. There were no dramatic scandals to uncover; the police "third degree" (on which the Wickersham Commission, in the report drafted by Zechariah Chafee, lavished much attention) had declined in occurrence and significance. Most police departments had been taken out of the control of party machines (in some cases, it would appear, only to be placed under the influence of organized crime). Instead, the Commission devoted considerable attention to the order-maintenance function of the police:

A great majority of the situations in which policemen intervene are not, or are not interpreted by the police to be, criminal situations in the sense that they call for arrest. . . . A common kind of situation . . . is the matrimonial dispute, which police experts estimate consumes as much time as any other single kind of situation.

The riots in Watts and elsewhere had, by the time the report appeared, already called the attention of the public to the importance (and fragility) of public order. The rise of demands for "community control" of various public services, including the police and the schools, has placed the problem of order on the political agenda. Whether the problems of managing disorder can best be handled by turning city government over to neighborhood groups is a complicated question. (Provisionally, I would argue that war becomes more, not less, likely when a political system is balkanized.) In any case, we have come full circle in our thinking about the function of the police.

Or almost full circle. The current anxiety about crime in the streets continues to lead some to define the police task as wholly or chiefly one of crime deterrence, and thus any discussion of redefining the police role or reorganizing police departments to facilitate performing their other functions tends to get lost in the din of charges and countercharges about whether or not the police have been "handcuffed." This is unfortunate, not because crime in the streets is a false issue (the rates of street crime, I am convinced, *are* increasing in an alarming manner), but because handling this problem cannot be left solely or even primarily to the police; acting as if it could raises false hopes among the citizens and places unfair and distorting demands on the police. At least as much attention to the courts and correctional systems will be necessary if much progress is to be shown in reducing street crime.

The simultaneous emergence of a popular concern for both crime and order does put in focus the choices that will have to be made in the next generation of police reforms. In effect, municipal police departments are two organizations in one serving two related but not identical functions. The strategy appropriate for strengthening their ability to serve one role tends to weaken their ability to serve the other. Crime deterrence and law enforcement require, or are facilitated by, specialization, strong hierarchical authority, improved mobility and communications, clarity in legal codes and arrest procedures, close surveillance of the community, high standards of integrity, and the avoidance of entangling alliances with politicians. The maintenance of order, on the other hand, is aided by departmental procedures that include decentralization, neighborhood involvement, foot patrol, wide discretion, the provision of services, an absence of arrest quotas, and some tolerance for minor forms of favoritism and even corruption.

There is no magic formula—no prepackaged "reform"—that can tell a community or a police chief how to organize a force to serve, with appropriate balance, these competing objectives. Just as slogans demanding "taking the police out of politics" or "putting the police in cars" have proved inadequate guides to action in the past, so also slogans demanding "foot patrolmen" or "community control" are likely to prove inadequate in the future. One would like to think that since both points of view now have ardent advocates, the debate has at last been joined. But I suspect that the two sides are talking at, or past, each other, and not *to* each other, and thus the issue, far from being joined, is still lost in rhetoric.

HOW MUCH "POLICE BRUTALITY" IS THERE?

ALBERT J. REISS

"For three years, there has been through the courts and the streets a dreary procession of citizens with broken heads and bruised bodies against few of whom was violence needed to effect an arrest. Many of them had done nothing to deserve an arrest. In a majority of such cases, no complaint was made. If the victim complains, his charge is generally dismissed. The police are practically above the law."

This statement was published in 1903, and its author was the Hon. Frank Moss, a former police commissioner of New York City. Clearly, today's charges of police brutality and mistreatment of citizens have a precedent in American history—but never before has the issue of police brutality assumed the public urgency it has today. In Newark, in Detroit, in Watts, in Harlem, and, in fact, in practically every city that has had a civil disturbance, "deep hostility between police and ghetto" was, reports the Kerner Commission, "a primary cause of the riots."

Whether or not the police accept the words "police brutality," the public now wants some plain answers to some plain questions. How widespread is police mistreatment of citizens? Is it on the increase? Why do policemen mistreat citizens? Do the police mistreat Negroes more than whites?

To find some answers, 36 people working for the Center of Research on Social Organization observed police-citizen encounters in the cities of Boston, Chicago, and Washington, D.C. For seven days a week, for seven weeks during the summer of 1966, these observers, with police permission, sat in patrol cars and monitored booking and lockup procedures in high-crime precincts.

Obtaining information about police mistreatment of citizens is no simple matter. National and state civil-rights commissions receive hundreds of complaints charging mistreatment—but proving these allegations is difficult. The few local civilian-review boards, such as the one in Philadelphia, have not produced any significant volume of complaints leading to the dismissal or disciplining of policemen for alleged brutality. Generally, police chiefs are silent on the matter, or answer charges of brutality with vague statements that they will investigate any complaints brought to their attention. Rank-and-file policemen are usually more outspoken: They often insinuate that charges of brutality are part of a conspiracy against them, and against law and order.

THE MEANING OF BRUTALITY

What citizens mean by police brutality covers the full range of police practices. These practices, contrary to the impression of many civil-rights activists, are not newly devised to deal with Negroes in our urban ghettos. They are ways in which the police have traditionally behaved in dealing with certain citizens, particularly those in the lower classes. The most common of these practices are:

the use of profane and abusive language,
commands to move on or get home,
stopping and questioning people on the street or searching them and their cars,
threats to use force if not obeyed,
prodding with a nightstick or approaching with a pistol, and
the actual use of physical force or violence itself.

Citizens and the police do not always agree on what constitutes proper police practice. What is "proper," or what is "brutal," it need hardly be pointed out, is more a matter of judgment about what someone did than a description of what police do. What is important is not the practice itself but what it means to the citizen. What citizens object to and call "police brutality" is really the judgment that they have not been treated with the full rights and dignity owing citizens in a democratic society. Any practice that degrades their status, that restricts their freedom, that annoys or harasses them, or that uses physical force is frequently seen as unnecessary and unwarranted. More often than not, they are probably right.

Many police practices serve only to degrade the citizen's sense of himself and his status. This is particularly true with regard to the way the police use language. Most citizens who have contact with the police object less to their use of four-letter words than to *how* the policeman talks to them. Particularly objectionable is the habit policemen have of "talking down" to citizens, of calling them names that deprecate them in their own eyes and those of others. More than one Negro citizen has complained: "They talk down to me as if I had no name—like 'boy' or 'man' or whatever, or they call me 'Jack' or by my first name. They don't show me no respect."

Members of minority groups and those seen as nonconformists, for whatever reason, are the most likely targets of status degradation. Someone who has been drinking may be told he is a "bum" or a "shitty wino." A woman walking alone may be called a "whore." And a man who doesn't happen to meet a policeman's standard of how one should look or dress may be met with the remark, "What's the matter, you a queer?" A white migrant from the South may be called a "hillbilly" or "shitkicker"; a Puerto Rican, a "pork chop"; a young boy, a "punk kid." When the policeman does not use words of status degradation, his manner may be degrading. Citizens want to be treated as people, not as "nonpersons" who are talked about as if they were not present.

That many Negroes believe that the police have degraded their status is clear from surveys in Watts, Newark, and Detroit. One out of every five Negroes in our center's post-riot survey in Detroit reports that the police have "talked down to him." More than one in ten says a policeman has "called me a bad name."

To be treated as "suspicious" is not only degrading, but is also a form of harassment and a restriction on the right to move freely. The harassing tactics of the police—dispersing social street-gatherings, the indiscriminate stopping of Negroes on foot or in cars, and commands to move on or go home—are particularly common in ghetto areas.

Young people are the most likely targets of harassing orders to disperse or move on. Particularly in summer, ghetto youths are likely to spend lots of time in public places. Given the inadequacy of their housing and the absence of community facilities, the street corner is often their social center. As the police cruise the busy streets of the ghetto, they frequently shout at groups of teenagers to "get going" or "get home." Our observations of police practices show that *whites as well as Negro youths* are often harassed in this way.

Frequently the policeman may leave the car and threaten or force youths to move on. For example, one summer evening as the scout car cruised a busy street of a white slum, the patrolmen observed three white boys and a girl on a corner. When told to move on, they mumbled and grumbled in undertones, angering the police by their failure to comply. As they slowly moved off, the officers pushed them along the street. Suddenly one of the white patrolmen took a lighted cigarette from a 15-year-old boy and stuck it in his face, pushing him forward as he did so. When the youngsters did move on, one policeman remarked to the observer that the girl was "nothing but a whore." Such tactics can only intensify resentment toward the police.

Police harassment is not confined to youth. One in every four adult Negroes in Detroit claims he has been stopped and questioned by the police without good reason. The same proportion claim they have been stopped in their cars. One in five says he has been searched unnecessarily; and one in six says that his car was searched for no good reason. The members of an interracial couple, particularly a Negro man accompanying a white woman, are perhaps the most vulnerable to harassment.

What citizens regard as police brutality many policemen consider necessary for law enforcement. While degrading epithets and abusive language may no longer be considered proper by either police commanders or citizens, they often disagree about other practices related to law enforcement. For example, although many citizens see "stop and question" or "stop and frisk" procedures as harassment, police commanders usually regard them merely as "aggressive prevention" to curb crime.

PHYSICAL FORCE—OR SELF-DEFENSE

The nub of the police-brutality issue seems to lie in police use of physical force. By law, the police have the right to use such force if necessary to make an arrest, to keep the peace, or to maintain public order. But just how much force is necessary or proper?

This was the crucial problem we attempted to answer by placing observers in the patrol cars and in the precincts. Our 36 observers, divided equally between Chicago, Boston, and Washington, were responsible for reporting the details of all situations where police used physical force against a citizen. To ensure the observation of a large number of encounters, two high-crime police precincts were monitored in Boston and Chicago; four in Washington. At least one precinct was composed of primarily Negro residents, another primarily of whites. Where possible, we also tried to select precincts with considerable variation in social-class composition. Given the criterion of a high-crime rate, however, people of low socio-economic status predominated in most of the areas surveyed.

The law fails to provide simple rules about what—and how much—force that policemen can properly use. The American Bar Foundation's study *Arrest*, by Wayne La Fave, put the matter rather well, stating that the courts of all states would undoubtedly agree that in making an arrest a policeman should use only that amount of force he reasonably believes necessary. But La Fave also pointed out that there is no agreement on the question of when it is better to let the suspect escape than to employ "deadly" force.

Even in those states where the use of deadly force is limited by law, the kinds of physical force a policeman may use are not clearly defined. No kind of force is categorically denied a policeman, since he is always permitted to use deadly force in self-defense.

This right to protect himself often leads the policeman to argue self-defense whenever he uses force. We found that many policemen, whether or not the facts justify it, regularly follow their use of force with the charge that the citizen was assaulting a policeman or resisting arrest. Our observers also found that some policemen even carry pistols and knives that they have confiscated while searching citizens; they carry them so they may be placed at a scene should it be necessary to establish a case of self-defense.

Of course, not all cases of force involve the use of *unnecessary* force. Each instance of force reported by our observers was examined and judged to be either necessary or unnecessary. Cases involving simple restraint—holding a man by the arm—were deliberately excluded from consideration, even though a policeman's right to do so can, in many instances, be challenged. In judging when police force is "unwarranted," "unreasonable," or "undue," we rather deliberately selected only those cases in which a policeman struck the citizen with his hands, fist, feet, or body, or where he used a weapon of some kind—such as a nightstick or a pistol. In these cases, had the policeman been found to have used physical force improperly, he could have been arrested on complaint and, like any other citizen, charged with a simple or aggravated assault. A physical assault on a citizen was judged to be "improper" or "unnecessary" only if force was used in one or more of the following ways:

If a policeman physically assaulted a citizen and then failed to make an arrest; proper use involves an arrest.

If the citizen being arrested did not, by word or deed, resist the policeman; force should be used only if it is necessary to make the arrest.

If the policeman, even though there was resistance to the arrest, could easily have restrained the citizen in other ways.

If a large number of policemen were present and could have assisted in subduing the citizen in the station, in lockup, and in the interrogation rooms.

If an offender was handcuffed and made no attempt to flee or offer violent resistance.

If the citizen resisted arrest, but the use of force continued even after the citizen was subdued.

In the seven-week period, we found 37 cases in which force was used improperly. In all, 44 citizens had been assaulted. In 15 of these cases, no one was arrested. Of these, 8 had offered no verbal or physical resistance whatsoever, while 7 had.

An arrest was made in 22 of the cases. In 13, force was exercised in the station house when at least four other policemen were present. In two cases, there was no verbal or physical resistance to the arrest, but force was still applied. In two other cases, the police applied force to a handcuffed offender in a field setting. And in five situations, the offender did resist arrest, but the policeman continued to use force even after he had been subdued.

Just how serious was the improper use of force in these 44 cases? Naturally there were differences in degree of injury. In about one-half of the cases, the citizen appeared little more than physically bruised; in three cases, the amount of force was so great that the citizen had to be hospitalized. Despite the fact that cases can easily be selected for their dramatic rather than their representative quality, I want to present a few to give a sense of what the observers saw and reported as undue use of force.

OBSERVING ON PATROL

In the following two cases, the citizens offered no physical or verbal resistance, and the two white policemen made no arrest. It is the only instance in which the observers saw the same two policemen using force improperly more than once.

The police precinct in which these incidents occurred is typical of those found in some of our larger cities, where the patrolmen move routinely from gold coast to slum. There are little islands of the rich and poor, of old Americans and new, of recent migrants and old settlers. One moves from high-rise areas of middle- and upper-income whites through an area of the really old Americans—Indians—to an enclave of the recently arrived. The recently arrived are primarily those the policemen call "hillbillies" (migrants from Kentucky and Tennessee) and "porkchops" (Puerto Ricans). There are ethnic islands of Germans and Swedes. Although there is a small area where Negroes live, it is principally a precinct of whites. The police in the district are, with one exception, white.

On a Friday in the middle of July, the observer arrived for the 4 to 12 midnight watch. The beat car that had been randomly chosen carried two white patrolmen—one with 14 years of experience in the precinct, the other with three.

The watch began rather routinely as the policemen cruised the district. Their first radio dispatch came at about 5:30 P.M. They were told to investigate two drunks in a cemetery. On arriving they found two white men "sleeping one off." Without questioning the men, the older policeman began to search one of them, ripping his shirt and hitting him in the groin with a nightstick. The younger policeman, as he searched the second, ripped away the seat of his trousers, exposing his buttocks. The policemen then prodded the men toward the cemetery fence and forced them to climb it, laughing at the plight of the drunk with the exposed buttocks. As the drunks went over the fence, one policeman shouted, "I ought to run you fuckers in!" The other remarked to the observer, "Those assholes won't be back; a bunch of shitty winos."

Not long after they returned to their car, the policemen stopped a woman who had made a left turn improperly. She was treated very politely, and the younger policeman, who wrote the ticket, later commented to the observer, "Nice lady." At 7:30 they were dispatched to check a suspicious auto. After a quick check, the car was marked abandoned.

Shortly after a 30-minute break for a 7:30 "lunch," the two policemen received a dispatch to take a burglary report. Arriving at a slum walkup, the police entered a room where an obviously drunk white man in his late 40s insisted that someone had entered and stolen his food and liquor. He kept insisting that it had been taken and that he had been forced to borrow money to buy beer. The younger policeman, who took the report, kept harassing the man, alternating between mocking and badgering him with rhetorical questions. "You say your name is Half-A-Wit [for Hathaway]? Do you sleep with niggers? How did you vote on the bond

issue? Are you sure that's all that's missing? Are you a virgin yet?"
The man responded to all of this with the seeming vagueness and joviality of the intoxicated, expressing gratitude for the policemen's help as they left. The older policeman remarked to the observer as they left, "Ain't drunks funny?"

For the next hour little happened, but as the two were moving across the precinct shortly after 10 P.M., a white man and a woman in their 50s flagged them down. Since they were obviously "substantial" middle-class citizens of the district, the policemen listened to their complaints that a Negro man was causing trouble inside the public-transport station from which they had just emerged. The woman said that he had sworn at her. The older policeman remarked, "What's a nigger doing up here? He should be down on Franklin Road!"

With that, they ran into the station and grabbed the Negro man who was inside. Without questioning him, they shoved him into a phone booth and began beating him with their fists and a flashlight. They also hit him in the groin. Then they dragged him out and kept him on his knees. He pleaded that he had just been released from a mental hospital that day and, begging not to be hit again, asked them to let him return to the hospital. One policeman said: "Don't you like us, nigger? I like to beat niggers and rip out their eyes." They took him outside to their patrol car. Then they decided to put him on a bus, telling him that he was returning to the hospital; they deliberately put him on a bus going in the opposite direction. Just before the Negro boarded the bus, he said, "You police just like to shoot and beat people." The first policeman replied, "Get moving, nigger, or I'll shoot you." The man was crying and bleeding as he was put on the bus. Leaving the scene, the younger policeman commented, "He won't be back."

For the rest of the evening, the two policemen kept looking for drunks and harassing any they found. They concluded the evening by being dispatched to an address where, they were told, a man was being held for the police. No one answered their knock. They left.

The station house has long been suspected of harboring questionable police practices. Interrogation-room procedures have been attacked, particularly because of the methods the police have used to get confessions. The drama of the confession in the interrogation room has been complete with bright lights and physical torture. Whether or not such practices have ever existed on the scale suggested by popular accounts, confessions in recent years, even by accounts of offenders, have rarely been accompanied by such high drama. But recently the interrogation room has come under fire again for its failure to protect the constitutional rights of the suspect to remain silent and to have legal counsel.

Backstage at the Station

The police station, however, is more than just a series of cubicles called interrogation rooms. There are other rooms and usually a lockup as well. Many of these are also hidden from public view. It is not surprising, then, that one-third of all the observations of the undue use of force occurred within the station.

In any station there normally are several policemen present who should be able to deal with almost any situation requiring force that arises. In many of the situations that were observed, as many as seven and eight policemen were present, most of whom simply stood by and watched force being used. The custom among policemen, it appeared, is that you intervene only if a fellow policeman needs help, or if you have been personally offended or affronted by those involved.

Force is used unnecessarily at many different points and places in the station. The citizen who is not cooperative during the booking process may be pushed or shoved, have his handcuffs twisted with a nightstick, have his foot stomped, or be pulled by the hair. All of these practices were reported by policemen as ways of obtaining "cooperation." But it was clear that the booking could have been completed without any of this harassment.

The lockup was the scene of some of the most severe applications of force. Two of the three cases requiring hospitalization came about when an offender was "worked over" in the lockup. To be sure, the arrested are not always cooperative when they get in the lockup, and force may be necessary to place them in a cell. But the amount of force observed hardly seemed necessary.

One evening an observer was present in the lockup when two white policemen came in with a white man. The suspect had been handcuffed and brought to the station because he had proved obstreperous after being arrested for a traffic violation. Apparently he had been drinking. While waiting in the lockup, the man began to urinate on the floor. In response, the policemen began to beat the man. They jumped him, knocked him down, and beat his head against the concrete floor. He required emergency treatment at a nearby hospital.

At times a policeman may be involved in a kind of escalation of force. Using force appropriately for an arrest in the field seemingly sets the stage for its later use, improperly, in the station. The following case illustrates how such a situation may develop.

Within a large city's high-crime rate precinct, occupied mostly by Negroes, the police responded to an "officer in trouble" call. It is difficult to imagine a call that brings a more immediate response, so a large number of police cars immediately converged at an intersection of a busy public street where a bus had been stopped. Near the bus, a white policeman was holding two young Negroes at gun point. The policeman reported that he had responded to a summons from the white bus-driver complaining that the boys had refused to pay their fares and had used obscene language. The policeman also reported that the boys swore at him, and one swung at him while the other drew a screwdriver and started toward him. At that point, he said, he drew his pistol.

The policemen placed one of the offenders in handcuffs and began to transport both of them to the station. While driving to the station, the driver of one car noted that the other policeman, transporting the other boy, was struggling with him. The first policeman stopped and entered the other patrol car. The observer reported that he kept hitting the boy who was handcuffed until the boy appeared completely subdued. The boy kept saying, "You don't have any right to beat me. I don't care if you kill me."

After the policemen got the offenders to the station, although the boys no longer resisted them, the police began to beat them while they were handcuffed in an interrogation room. One of the boys hollered: "You can't beat me like this! I'm only a kid, and my hands are tied." Later one of the policemen commented to the observer: "On the street you can't beat them. But when you get to the station, you can instill some respect in them."

Cases where the offender resists an arrest provide perhaps the most difficulty in judging the legitimacy of the force applied. An encounter that began as a dispatch to a disturbance at a private residence was one case about which there could be honest difference in judgment. On arrival, the policemen—one white, the other Negro—met a white woman who claimed that her husband, who was in the back yard and drunk, had beaten her. She asked the policemen to "take him in." The observer reported that the police found the man in the house. When they attempted to take him, he resisted by placing his hands between the door jamb. Both policemen then grabbed him. The Negro policeman said, "We're going to have trouble, so let's finish it right here." He grabbed the offender and knocked him down. Both policemen then wrestled with the man, handcuffed him, and took him to the station. As they did so, one of the policemen remarked, "These sons of bitches want to fight, so you have to break them quick."

A MINIMAL PICTURE?

The reader, as well as most police administrators, may be skeptical about reports that policemen used force in the presence of observers. Indeed, one police administrator, indignant over reports of undue use of force in his department, seemed more concerned that the policemen had permitted themselves to be observed behaving improperly than he was about their improper behavior. When demanding to know the names of the policemen who had used force improperly so he could discharge them—a demand we could not meet, since we were bound to protect our sources of information—he remarked, "Any officer who is stupid enough to behave that way in the presence of outsiders deserves to be fired."

There were and are a number of reasons why our observers were able to see policemen behaving improperly. We entered each department with the full cooperation of the top administrators. So far as the men in the line were concerned, our chief interest was in how citizens behave toward the police, a main object of our study. Many policemen, given their strong feelings against citizens, fail to see that their own behavior is equally open to observation. Furthermore, our observers are trained to fit into a role of trust—one that is genuine, since most observers are actually sympathetic to the plight of the policeman, if not to his behavior.

Finally, and this is a fact all too easily forgotten, people cannot change their behavior in the presence of others as easily as many think. This is particularly true when people become deeply involved in certain situations. The policeman not only comes to "trust" the observer in the law-enforcement situation—regarding him as a source of additional help if necessary—but, when he becomes involved in a dispute with a citizen, he easily forgets that an observer is present. Partly because he does not know what else to do, in such situations the policeman behaves "normally." But should one cling to the notion that most policemen modify their behavior in the presence of outsiders, one is left with the uncomfortable conclusion that our cases represent a minimal picture of actual misbehavior.

Superficially it might seem that the use of an excessive amount of force against citizens is low. In only 37 of 3826 encounters observed did the police use undue force. Of the 4604 white citizens in these encounters, 27 experienced an excessive amount of force —a rate of 5.9 for every 1000 citizens involved. The comparable rate for 5960 Negroes, of whom 17 experienced an excessive amount of force, is 2.8. Thus, whether one considers these rates high or low, the fact is that the *rate of excessive force for all white citizens in encounters with the police is twice that for Negro citizens.*

A rate depends, however, upon selecting a population that is logically the target of force. What we have just given is a rate for *all* citizens involved in encounters with the police. But many of these citizens are not logical targets of force. Many, for example, simply call the police to complain about crimes against themselves or their property. And others are merely witnesses to crimes.

The more logical target population consists of citizens whom the police allege to be offenders—a population of suspects. In our study, there were 643 white suspects, 27 of whom experienced undue use of force. This yields an abuse rate of 41.9 per 1000 white suspects. The comparable rate for 751 Negro suspects, of whom 17 experienced undue use of force, is 22.6 per 1000. If one accepts these rates as reasonably reliable estimates of the undue force against suspects, then there should be little doubt that in major metropolitan areas the sort of behavior commonly called "police brutality" is far from rare.

Popular impression casts police brutality as a racial matter— white police mistreating Negro citizens. The fact is that white suspects are more liable to being treated improperly by the police than Negro suspects are. This, however, should not be confused with the chances a citizen takes of being mistreated. In two of the cities we studied, Negroes are a minority. The chances, then, that any Negro has of being treated improperly are, perhaps, more nearly comparable to that for whites. If the rates are comparable, then one might say that the application of force unnecessarily by the police operates without respect to the race of an offender.

Many people believe that the race of the policeman must affect his use of force, particularly since many white policemen express prejudice against Negroes. Our own work shows that in the police precincts made up largely of Negro citizens, over three-fourths of the policemen express prejudice against Negroes. Only 1 percent express sympathetic attitudes. But as sociologists and social psychologists have often shown, prejudice and attitudes do not necessarily carry over into discriminatory actions.

Our findings show that there is little difference between the rate of force used by white and by Negro policemen. Of the 54 policemen observed using too much force, 45 were white and 9 were Negro. For every 100 white policemen, 8.7 will use force; for every 100 Negro policemen, 9.8 will. What this really means, though, is that about one in every 10 policemen in high-crime rate areas of cities sometimes uses force unnecessarily.

Yet, one may ask, doesn't prejudice enter into the use of force? Didn't some of the policemen who were observed utter prejudiced statements toward Negroes and other minority-group members? Of course they did. But the question of whether it was their prejudice or some other factor that motivated them to mistreat Negroes is not so easily answered.

Still, even though our figures show that a white suspect is more liable to encounter violence, one may ask whether white policemen victimize Negroes more than whites. We found, for the most part, that they do not. Policemen, both Negro and white, are most likely to exercise force against members of their *own* race:

67 percent of the citizens victimized by white policemen were white.

71 percent of the citizens victimized by Negro policemen were Negro.

To interpret these statistics correctly, however, one should take into account the differences in opportunity policemen have to use force against members of their own and other races. Negro policemen, in the three cities we studied, were far *less* likely to police white citizens than white policemen were to police Negroes. Negro policemen usually policed other Negroes, while white policemen policed both whites and Negroes about equally. In total numbers, then, more white policemen than Negro policemen used force against Negroes. But this is explained by the fact that whites make up 85 percent of the police force, and more than 50 percent of all policemen policing Negroes.

Though no precise estimates are possible, the facts just given suggest that white policemen, even though they are prejudiced toward Negroes, do not discriminate against Negroes in the excessive use of force. The use of force by the police is more readily explained by police culture than it is by the policeman's race. Indeed, in the few cases where we observed a Negro policeman using unnecessary force against white citizens, there was no evidence that he did so because of his race.

The disparity between our findings and the public's sense that Negroes are the main victims of police brutality can easily be resolved if one asks how the public becomes aware of the police misusing force.

The Victims and the Turf

Fifty years ago, the immigrants to our cities—Eastern and Southern Europeans such as the Poles and the Italians—complained about police brutality. Today the new immigrants to our cities—mostly Negroes from the rural South—raise their voices through the civil-rights movement, through black-nationalist and other race-conscious organizations. There is no comparable voice for white citizens since, except for the Puerto Ricans, they now lack the nationality organizations that were once formed to promote and protect the interests of their immigrant forbears.

Although policemen do not seem to select their victims according to race, two facts stand out. All victims were offenders, and all were from the lower class. Concentrating as we did on high-crime rate areas of cities, we do not have a representative sample of residents in any city. Nonetheless, we observed a sizable minority of middle- and upper-status citizens, some of whom were offenders. But since no middle- or upper-class offender, white or Negro, was the victim of an excessive amount of force, it appears that the lower class bears the brunt of victimization by the police.

The most likely victim of excessive force is a lower-class man of either race. No white woman and only two Negro women were victimized. The difference between the risk assumed by white and by Negro women can be accounted for by the fact that far more Negro women are processed as suspects or offenders.

Whether or not a policeman uses force unnecessarily depends upon the social setting in which the encounter takes place. Of the 37 instances of excessive force, 37 percent took place in police-controlled settings, such as the patrol car or the precinct station. Public places, usually streets, accounted for 41 percent, and 16 percent took place in a private residence. The remaining 6 percent occurred in commercial settings. This is not, of course, a random sample of settings where the police encounter suspects.

What is most obvious, and most disturbing, is that the police are very likely to use force in settings that they control. Although only 18 percent of all situations involving suspects ever ended up at the station house, 32 percent of all situations where an excessive amount of force was used took place in the police station.

No one who accepts the fact that the police sometimes use an excessive amount of force should be surprised by our finding that they often select their own turf. What should be apparent to the nation's police administrators, however, is that these settings are under their command and control. Controlling the police in the field, where the policeman is away from direct supervision, is understandably difficult. But the station house is the police administrator's domain. The fact that one in three instances of excessive force took place in settings that can be directly controlled should cause concern among police officials.

The presence of citizens who might serve as witnesses against a policeman should deter him from undue use of force. Indeed, procedures for the review of police conduct are based on the presumption that one can get this kind of testimony. Otherwise, one is left simply with a citizen complaint and contrary testimony by the policeman—a situation in which it is very difficult to prove the citizen's allegation.

In most situations involving the use of excessive force, there were witnesses. In our 37 cases, there were bystanders present three-fourths of the time. But in only one situation did the group present sympathize with the citizen and threaten to report the policeman. A complaint was filed on that incident—the only one of the 37 observed instances of undue force in which a formal complaint was filed.

All in all, the situations where excessive force was used were devoid of bystanders who did not have a stake in being "against" the offender. Generally, they were fellow policemen, or fellow offenders whose truthfulness could be easily challenged. When a policeman uses undue force, then, he usually does not risk a complaint against himself or testimony from witnesses who favor the complainant against the policeman. This, as much as anything, probably accounts for the low rate of formal complaints against policemen who use force unnecessarily.

A striking fact is that in more than one-half of all instances of undue coercion, at least one other policeman was present who did not participate in the use of force. This shows that, for the most part, the police do not restrain their fellow policemen. On the contrary, there were times when their very presence encouraged the use of force. One man brought into the lockup for threatening a policeman with a pistol was so severely beaten by this policeman that he required hospitalization. During the beating, some fellow policemen propped the man up, while others shouted encouragement. Though the official police code does not legitimate this practice, police culture does.

VICTIMS—DEFIANT OR DEVIANT

Now, are there characteristics of the offender or his behavior that precipitate the use of excessive force by the police? Superficially, yes. Almost one-half of the cases involved open defiance of police authority (39 percent) or resisting arrest (9 percent). Open defiance of police authority, however, is what the policeman defines as *his* authority, not necessarily "official" authority. Indeed in 40 percent of the cases that the police considered open defiance, the policeman never executed an arrest—a somewhat surprising fact for those who assume that policemen generally "cover" improper use of force with a "bona-fide" arrest and a charge of resisting arrest.

But it is still of interest to know what a policeman *sees* as defiance. Often he seems threatened by a simple refusal to acquiesce to his own authority. A policeman beat a handcuffed offender because, when told to sit, the offender did not sit down. One Negro woman was soundly slapped for her refusal to approach the police car and identify herself.

Important as a threat to his authority may appear to the policeman, there were many more of these instances in which the policeman did *not* respond with the use of force. The important issue seems to be whether the policeman manages to assert his authority despite the threat to it. I suspect that policemen are more likely to respond with excessive force when they define the situation as one in which there remains a question as to who is "in charge."

Similarly, some evidence indicates that harassment of deviants plays a role in the undue use of force. Incidents involving drunks made up 27 percent of all incidents of improper use of force; an additional 5 percent involved homosexuals or narcotics users. Since deviants generally remain silent victims to avoid public exposure of their deviance, they are particularly susceptible to the use of excessive force.

It is clear, though, that the police encounter many situations involving deviants where no force is used. Generally they respond to them routinely. What is surprising, then, is that the police do not mistreat deviants more than they do. The explanation may lie in the kind of relationships the police have with deviants. Many are valuable to the police because they serve as informers. To mistreat them severely would be to cut off a major source of police intelligence. At the same time, deviants are easily controlled by harassment.

Clearly, we have seen that police mistreatment of citizens exist. Is it, however, on the increase?

Citizen complaints against the police are common and allegations that the police use force improperly are frequent. There is evidence that physical brutality exists today. But there is also evidence, from the history of our cities, that the police have long engaged in the use of unnecessary physical force. No one can say with confidence whether there is more or less of it today than there was at the turn of the century.

What we lack is evidence that would permit us to calculate comparative rates of police misuse of force for different periods of American history. Only recently have we begun to count and report the volume of complaints against the police. And the research reported in this article represents the only attempt to estimate the amount of police mistreatment by actual observation of what the police do to citizens.

Lack of Information

Police chiefs are notoriously reluctant to disclose information that would allow us to assess the nature and volume of complaints against the police. Only a few departments have begun to report something about citizen complaints. And these give us very little information.

Consider, for example, the 1966 Annual Report released by the New Orleans Police Department. It tells us that there were 208 cases of "alleged police misconduct on which action was taken." It fails to tell us whether there were any allegations that are *not* included among these cases. Are these all the allegations that came to the attention of the department? Or are they only those the department chose to review as "police disciplinary matters"? Of the 208 cases the department considered "disciplinary matters," the report tells us that no disciplinary action was taken in 106 cases. There were 11 cases that resulted in 14 dismissals; 56 cases that resulted in 72 suspensions, fines, or loss of days; and 35 cases involving 52 written or verbal "reprimands" or "cautionings."

The failure of the report to tell us the charge against the policeman is a significant omission. We cannot tell how many of these allegations involved improper use of force, how many involved verbal abuse or harassment, how many involved police felonies or misdemeanors, and so on. In such reports, the defensive posture of the nation's police departments is all too apparent. Although the 1966 report of the New Orleans Police Department tells us much about what the police allege were the felonies and misdemeanors by citizens of New Orleans, it tells us nothing about what citizens allege was misconduct by the police!

Many responsible people believe that the use of physical brutality by the police is on the wane. They point to the fact that, at least outside the South, there are more reports of other forms of police mistreatment of citizens than reports of undue physical coercion. They also suggest that third-degree interrogations and curbstone justice with the nightstick are less common. It does not seem unreasonable, then, to assume that police practices that degrade a citizen's status or that harass him and restrict his freedom are more common than police misuse of force. But that may have always been so.

Whether or not the policeman's "sense of justice" and his use of unnecessary force have changed remains an open question. Forms may change while practices go on. To move misuse from the street to the station house, or from the interrogation room to the lockup, changes the place but not the practice itself.

Our ignorance of just what goes on between police and citizens poses one of the central issues in policing today: How can we make the police accountable to the citizenry in a democratic society and yet not hamstring them in their legitimate pursuit of law and order? There are no simple answers.

Police departments are organizations that process people. All people-processing organizations face certain common problems. But the police administrator faces a problem in controlling practice with clients that is not found in most other organizations. The problem is that police contact with citizens occurs in the community, where direct supervision is not possible. Assuming our unwillingness to spend resources for almost one-to-one supervision, the problem for the police commander is to make policemen behave properly when they are not under direct supervision. He also faces the problem of making them behave properly in the station house as well.

Historically, we have found but one way—apart from supervision—that deals with this problem. That solution is professionalization of workers. Perhaps only through the professionalization of the police can we hope to solve the problem of police malpractice.

But lest anyone optimistically assume that professionalization will eliminate police malpractice altogether, we should keep in mind that problems of malpractice also occur regularly in both law and medicine.

III
Can the Political System Respond
to the Urban Crisis?

III

Can the Political System Respond to the Urban Crisis?

The American city is now experiencing a period of sustained economic and social decline. By the last quarter of the twentieth century, it appears that decentralization, or suburbanization, is a predominant characteristic of metropolitan areas. According to the 1970 census, more of the American population lived in suburban areas than in the core cities.[1] Moreover, the recent population growth has been overwhelmingly located in these fringe areas. During the decade of the sixties, suburban population growth was more than four times that of the central cities (whose population expansion was limited to newer cities located in the South and Southwest). And as recent surveys undertaken by the Census Bureau as late as 1975 reveal, these trends are continuing.[2]

Characteristics of the population living in central cities and suburbs differ considerably. While central cities contain higher proportions of low- and moderate-income households, suburbs have higher proportions of upper-income groups. Besides these class differentials, the racial composition of the metropolitan area has its own geographical shape. While in the sixteen largest central cities the percentage of blacks in the population increased from 11 percent in 1940 to 27 percent in 1970, in suburban areas it has never risen above 5 percent. As these population contrasts continue to intensify, neighborhoods in central cities experience transitions during which low-income minority groups displace better-off white residents, who are moving outward to the suburbs.

Economic growth has accompanied this population movement. The suburbs are now the area of economic expansion, as industrial concerns and service establishments formed to meet the needs and conveniences of an affluent population provide vast new employment opportunities. The central-city economy, on the other hand, is now increasingly dependent on office jobs in the private and public sectors, an economic base increasingly threatened by

311

the movement of large corporate headquarters to suburban locations. As Sternlieb concluded in his essay in the first section, this leaves government jobs, for an increasing number of the core cities' inhabitants, as almost "the only game in town."

By the 1960s, these trends had transformed themselves into what was widely understood as an urban crisis of major proportions. Particularly after civil violence broke out not only in Watts, Newark, Detroit, Cleveland, and Chicago but also in virtually every major metropolitan center with dense aggregations of low-income blacks, policy-makers realized that our society, for all its affluence, was endangered by a potentially explosive discontent at its very center. At the peak of these racial conflicts, President Lyndon Johnson appointed a National Advisory Commission on Civil Disorders, which was to investigate the causes of and solutions for this massive upheaval. Its report, issued in 1968, surveyed a vast range of urban-centered problems, not the least of which was the polarization of a central city filled with poor minorities surrounded by affluent white suburbs. Simultaneously, the federal government sponsored a host of new programs aimed primarily at low-income urban minorities: the war on poverty, elementary and secondary education act, model cities program, manpower development and training act, revised FHA mortgage guidelines facilitating central city investments, headstart, medicaid, and stricter enforcement of equal opportunity legislation.

In part these programs were aimed at reducing the social and economic disadvantages of racial minorities. But as the Fainsteins and Francis Fox Piven discuss in the articles in this section, many of these policies also attempted to rectify the political under-representation of blacks and other minorities in central cities. Indeed, it was this political objective that they achieved most successfully. Not only did these programs provide new opportunities for government service at a time when minorities were most vigorously demanding them, but, by placing minority personnel in professional positions within those bureaucratic agencies serving minority neighborhoods, the appearance of white "colonial" domination which had been all too visible in the past was minimized. Moreover, by providing organizing resources to new community groups, these federal programs provided blacks and other minorities with much greater capability for participating in the electoral process. Black mayors, almost nonexistent in 1964, were elected in Newark, Detroit, Cleveland, Los Angeles, and in 105 other cities ten years later.

The very success of these efforts to incorporate blacks into the political life of our nation's biggest cities has had some secondary consequences, however. Because black leaders now have opportunities to participate within the officially sanctioned political process, they no longer provide the leadership and organization for mass civil disobedience. As a result, affluent whites and political leaders, comforted that political stability has been restored, have turned their attention in other directions. Not only has the Ford Administration made it known that it views the "urban crisis" of the 1960s as over,[3] but even a leading Democratic presidential candidate, appealing to a liberal constituency, has defined the issues of the seventies as "energy, economy, and the environment," forgetful that racial "equality" was once a pressing concern of his prospective supporters.

Although the racial riots and protest activity of blacks and other minority groups have diminished, the conditions of the central city and its inhabitants have not improved. In fact, according to the Census Bureau, the socioeconomic gap between the central core and suburbia has continued to grow between 1970 and 1974. If one defines the crisis from the vantage point of the urban poor rather than from that of political leaders concerned about social disorder, then little has changed. That racial minorities suffer in decaying central cities is no less a crisis simply because they now do so more quietly.

Even though more representative, central cities are still unable to reverse their continuing decline. The fragmentation and dispersion of governmental authority sharply limits the direction and leadership that urban elites can provide. Indeed, leaders seem to be losing whatever power strong party organizations once provided to increasingly aggressive service-delivery bureaucracies and their employee associations. Frances Fox Piven, in the concluding essay to this volume, attacks the popular notion that the central cities' money problems are due to the expanding service needs of their poor inhabitants. Instead, she argues that mayors, in the past decade, have been forced to grant generous salary increases to municipal employees to maintain political support from organized elements within the middle-class white community. These provider groups have extracted this money, not as a response to the growing service needs of their clients, but as a response to the changing political context within central cities. Piven concludes that whatever gains minority groups made, producer interests have done much better.

This inability of mayors to resist the demands of provider groups has aided the growth of suburbia and hastened the core city's decline. Increases in local taxes to meet these increased expenditures have driven businesses and productive residents to the suburbs. In the face of declining revenues, cities have become more dependent upon state and federal levels of government which no longer are as concerned about urban problems.

In addition to the fiscal problems posed by the central cities' own bureaucracies, the division of public authority among hundreds of local governmental units has abetted the private market forces dispersing population and industry. The sheer number of these governmental units has made it all but impossible for metropolitan elites to undertake a unified, integrated approach to the area's problems. Intergovernmental cooperation has been minimal and generally limited to technical matters (such as the purchase of services by one government from another). Suburban governments have resisted regional attempts to coordinate policies affecting the life styles and socioeconomic interests of their residents. Instead, to the extent that public authority is being exercised by the numerous suburban units, it typically takes the form of zoning laws and tax policies that intensify the divisions and differentiations that mark our metropolitan areas.

As much as these political arrangements have augmented the decline of central cities, it must be concluded that even without problems of fragmentation and inadequate representation, metropolitan areas would still be unable to arrest the decay at their core. This is due to the vulnerability of American localities to national economic and social developments, including such national trends as the movement of rural poor into urban locales and dispersion of industry into areas more accessible by truck and automobile.

This vulnerability of central cities stems from our federal structure, which places local governments in competitive relationships with one another. In more centralized, European systems, the national government either finances and directs policy on such crucial matters as welfare, health, transportation, and education, or else it gives strong financial support to local governments. In contrast, American local governments have traditionally been expected to be the major domestic service providers without major reimbursements from other governmental levels. The result has been to place all localities in a position where they compete with one another for productive uses of their territorial space so that adequate tax revenues will be available for the financing of public services. The pressures upon local governments are therefore intense. They must constantly find an appropriate "balance" between their service levels and tax rates—i.e., attain the most favorable ratio between revenue sources and service responsibilities.

This competition places governments in declining communities in a very difficult position. They are unable to prevent other communities from attracting their business and industry, and they soon find their most productive labor following close behind. Within metropolitan areas, as suburbs induce industries and homeowners to their communities to strengthen their tax base, the core city lacks the sanctions to prevent these losses from occurring.

At most, central cities can attempt to persuade citizens and businesses to remain. There are two possible sets of events or scenarios which might enable the core city to succeed. One such scenario depends upon a reversal of the current workings of the private market. Presently, the only foreseeable factor which might reverse the suburbanizing impact of private market factors is the energy shortage. Any sustained shortage of fuels or massive increases in their prices could retard decentralization of metropolitan areas. Concentrated land use results in far less energy usage and costs than low-density development. However, this possibility must be regarded as remote, at best. An energy problem of this magnitude would not merely affect metropolitan development patterns; it would slow our economic growth and lower our standard of living. Major national policy efforts will try to forestall such eventualities.

The other scenario to aid the central city involves the intervention of the state and federal governments. There are a number of policies these higher levels of government could support which would retard, if not reverse, the present trend. Limiting ourselves to the four policy areas covered in this reader, federal and state governments could in each of them pursue a purposeful and coordinated attempt to shape the metropolis. In the area of housing and land use, state governments could restrict the zoning powers of localities, one of the prime tools used by suburban governments for exclusionary purposes. The federal government could again make urban renewal a high priority while curtailing its programs which promote low-density suburban housing (e.g., FHA home loan guarantees). The transportation arena would also require a coordinated and consistent response from the federal government. Federal mass-transit programs could be expanded while federal funding for roads could be curtailed. In education, a state takeover of financing would lower the differentials in educational spending between suburban communities and the central city. Increased federal funds in the areas of education and police might improve services and expand job opportunities for city residents (especially if central cities enact residency requirements for all new job holders). While the impact of these policies is impossible to predict with certainty, they would (as part of a package intended to aid the central city) probably work to somewhat "balance" the centrifugal forces present in metropolitan areas.

The political feasibility of such a program is another matter. Both Piven and the Fainsteins are pessimistic about the impact of state and federal intervention. Piven emphasizes the increasing importance of the suburbs in state and national politics. Their enormous population growth has made them pivotal in winning statewide elections. Even Democratic Party presidential candidates, who depend upon big-city and minority support, must run well in suburban areas in order to win the electoral votes of the large industrial states. The Fainsteins do not believe that any influential nationwide alliance, which would include the urban poor, can be formed in the foreseeable future. The Democratic Party has suffered nationally because of its affiliation with minority groups. For a variety of reasons, white working-class groups have often opposed the demands of minority groups; their conflicting racial interests, rather than their similar class interests, have proved to be of more import in determining their political behavior. Moreover, the organized representatives of working-class interests, the trade union movement, has given a higher priority to the particularistic interests of their organizations than to the broader interests of the have-not members of the population. Finally, a potential alliance with urban bureaucracies, who share with their clients a similar interest in obtaining more funds for the central cities from the state and federal governments, has been hampered by the conflicts between these two groups at the local level.

There appears little reason to expect that the development of our urban areas will be changed, that the trend toward continuing suburbanization will be reversed. Our local governments are too fragmented to cope with this problem. The increased representation achieved by minority groups at the local level has not led to governmental action to prevent the core cities from becoming a dumping ground. The state and federal governments have become increasingly less responsive to the central cities' plight. The prediction of the Kerner Commission, made in 1968, has become all too true. Our urban areas do contain two separate and unequal societies. Our metropolitan areas can increasingly be characterized with the label "Black cities; white suburbs."

NOTES

1. Residents of suburbia are defined by the U.S. Bureau of the Census as living in the outlying portions of "Standard Metropolitan Statistical Areas."
2. *New York Times,* June 16, 1975, p. 1; July 20, 1975, p. 52.
3. *Ibid.,* March 23, 1975, p. 1.

THE URBAN CRISIS: WHO GOT
WHAT, AND WHY

FRANCES FOX PIVEN

For quite a while, complaints about the urban fiscal crisis have
been droning on, becoming as familiar as complaints about big
government, or big bureaucracy, or high taxes—and almost as boring as well. Now suddenly the crisis seems indeed to be upon us:
school closings are threatened, library services are curtailed, subway trains go unrepaired, welfare grants are cut, all because big
city costs have escalated to the point where local governments can
no longer foot the bill. Yet for all the talk, and all the complaints,
there has been no convincing explanation of just how it happened
that, quite suddenly in the 1960s, the whole municipal housekeeping system seemed to become virtually unmanageable. This is especially odd because, not long ago, the study of city politics and
city services was a favorite among American political scientists,
and one subject they had gone far to illuminate. Now, with
everything knocked askew, they seem to have very little to say
that could stand as political analysis.

To be sure, there is a widely accepted explanation. The big
cities are said to be in trouble because of the "needs" of blacks for
services—a view given authority by the professionals who man the
service agencies and echoed by the politicians who depend upon
these agencies. Service "needs," the argument goes, have been
increasing at a much faster rate than local revenues. The alleged
reason is demographic: The large number of impoverished black
Southern migrants to the cities presumably requires far greater
investments in services, including more elaborate educational programs, more frequent garbage collection, more intensive policing,
if the city is to be maintained at accustomed levels of civil decency

and order. Thus, city agencies have been forced to expand and elaborate their activities. However, the necessary expansion is presumably constricted for lack of local revenues, particularly since the better off taxpaying residents and businesses have been leaving the city (hastened on their way by the black migration). To this standard explanation of the crisis, there is also a standard remedy: namely, to increase municipal revenues, whether by enlarging federal and state aid to the cities or by redrawing jurisdictional boundaries to recapture suburban taxpayers.

It is true, of course, that black children who receive little in the way of skills or motivation at home may require more effort from the schools; that densely packed slums require more garbage collection; that disorganized neighborhoods require more policing. For instance, the New York City Fire Department reports a 300 percent increase in fires the last twenty years. But fires and similar calamities that threaten a wide public are one thing; welfare, education, and health services, which account for by far the largest portion of big city budgets, quite another. And while by any objective measure the new residents of the city have greater needs for such services, there are several reasons to doubt that the urban crisis is the simple result of rising needs and declining revenues.

For one thing, the trend in service budgets suggests otherwise. Blacks began to pour into the cities in very large numbers after World War II, but costs did not rise precipitously until the mid-1960s. *In other words, the needs of the black poor were not recognized for two decades.* For another, any scrutiny of agency budgets shows that, except for public welfare, *the expansion of services to the poor, as such, does not account for a very large proportion of increased expenditures.* It was other groups, *mainly organized provider groups,* who reaped the lion's share of the swollen budgets. The notion that services are being strained to respond to the needs of the new urban poor, in short, takes little account either of when the strains occurred or of the groups who actually benefited from increased expenditures.

These two facts should lead us to look beyond the "rising needs—declining revenues" theory for an explanation of urban troubles. And once we do, perhaps some political common sense can emerge. School administrators and sanitation commissioners may describe their agencies as ruled by professional standards and as shaped by disinterested commitments to the public good, and thus define rising costs as a direct and proper response to the needs of people. But schools and sanitation departments are, after all, agencies of local government, substructures of the local political apparatus, and are managed in response to local political forces. The mere fact that people are poor or that the poor need special services has never led government to respond. Service agencies are political agencies, administered to deal with political problems, not service problems.

Now this view is not especially novel. Indeed, if there is any aspect of the American political system that was persuasively analyzed in the past, it was the political uses of municipal services in promoting allegiance and muting conflict. Public jobs, contracts, and services were dispensed by city bosses to maintain loyal cadres and loyal followers among the heterogeneous groups of the city. Somehow political analysts have forgotten this in their accounts of the contemporary urban crisis, testimony perhaps to the extent to which the doublethink of professional bureaucrats has befogged the common sense of us all. That is, we are confused by changes in the style of urban service politics, failing to see that although the style has changed, the function has not. In the era of the big city machine, municipal authorities managed to maintain a degree of consensus and allegiance among diverse groups by distributing public goods in the form of private favors. Today public goods are distributed through the service bureaucracies. With that change, the process of dispensing public goods has become more formalized, the struggles between groups more public, and the language of city politics more professional. As I will try to explain a little later, these changes were in some ways crucial in the development of what we call the urban crisis. My main point for now, however, is that while we may refer to the schools or the sanitation department as if they are politically neutral, these agencies yield up a whole variety of benefits, and it is by distributing, redistributing, and adapting these payoffs of the city agencies that urban political leaders manage to keep peace and build allegiances among the diverse groups in the city. In other words, the jobs, contracts, perquisites, as well as the actual services of the municipal housekeeping agencies, are just as much the grist of urban politics as they ever were.

All of which is to say that when there is a severe disturbance in the administration and financing of municipal services, the underlying cause is likely to be a fundamental disturbance in political relations. To account for the service "crisis," we should look at the changing relationship between political forces—at rising group conflict and weakening allegiances—and the way in which these disturbances set off an avalanche of new demands. To cope with these strains, political leaders expanded and proliferated the benefits of the city agencies. What I shall argue, in sum, is that the urban crisis is not a crisis of rising needs, but a crisis of rising demands.

Any number of circumstances may disturb existing political relationships, with the result that political leaders are less capable of restraining the demands of various groups. Severe economic dislocations may activate groups that previously asked little of government, as in the 1930s. Or groups may rise in the economic structure, acquiring political force and pressing new demands as a result. Or large scale migrations may alter the balance between groups. Any of these situations may generate sharp antagonism among groups, and, as some new groups acquire a measure of influence, they may undermine established political relationships. In the period of uncertainty that ensues, discontent is likely to spread, political alignments may shift, and allegiances to a political leadership may become insecure. In the context of this general unrest, political leaders, unsure of their footing, are far more likely to respond to the specific demands of specific groups for enlarged benefits or new "rights." Periods of political instability, in other words, nurture new claims and claimants. This is what happened in the cities in the 1960s, and it happened at a time when the urban political system was uniquely ill-equipped to curb the spiral of rising demands that resulted.

THE POLITICAL DISTURBANCES THAT LED TO RISING DEMANDS

If the service needs of the black poor do not account for the troubles in the cities, the political impact of the black migration probably does. Massive shifts of population are almost always disturbing to a political system, for new relations have to be formed between a political leadership and constituent groups. The migration of large numbers of blacks from the rural South to a few core cities during and after World War II, leading many middle-class white constituents to leave for the suburbs, posed just this challenge to the existing political organization of the cities. But for a long time, local governments resisted responding to the newcomers with the services, symbols, and benefits that might have won the allegiance of these newcomers, just as the allegiance of other groups had previously been won.

The task of political integration was made difficult by at least four circumstances. One was the very magnitude of the influx. Between 1940 and 1960, nearly 4 million blacks left the land and, for the most part, settled in big Northern cities. Consequently, by

1960, at least one in five residents of our fifty largest cities was a black, and in the biggest cities the proportions were much greater. It is no exaggeration to say that the cities were inundated by sheer numbers.

Second, these large numbers were mainly lower-class blacks, whose presence aroused ferocious race and class hatreds, especially among the white ethnics who lived in neighborhoods bordering the ghettos and who felt their homes and schools endangered. As ghetto numbers enlarged, race and class polarities worsened, and political leaders, still firmly tied to the traditional inhabitants of the cities, were in no position to give concessions to the black poor.

Not only was race pitted against race, class against class, but the changing style of urban politics made concessions to conflicting groups a very treacherous matter. Just because the jobs, services, and contracts that fueled the urban political organization were no longer dispensed covertly, in the form of private favors, but rather as matters of public policy, each concession was destined to become a subject of open political conflict. As a result, mayors found it very difficult to finesse their traditional constituents: New public housing for blacks, for example, could not be concealed, and every project threatened to arouse a storm of controversy. Despite their growing numbers and their obvious needs, therefore, blacks got very little in the way of municipal benefits throughout the 1940s and 1950s. Chicago, where the machine style was still entrenched, gave a little more; the Cook County AFDC rolls, for example, rose by 80 percent in the 1950s, and blacks were given some political jobs. But in most cities, the local service agencies resisted the newcomers. In New York City and Los Angeles, for example, the AFDC rolls remained virtually unchanged in the 1950s. In many places public housing was brought to a halt; urban renewal generally became the instrument of black removal; and half the major Southern cities (which also received large numbers of black migrants from rural areas) actually managed to reduce their welfare rolls, often by as much as half.

Finally, when blacks entered the cities, they were confronted by a relatively new development in city politics: namely, the existence of large associations of public employees, whether teachers, policemen, sanitation men, or the like. The provider groups not only had a very large stake in the design and operation of public programs—for there is hardly any aspect of public policy that does not impinge on matters of working conditions, job security, or fringe benefits—but they had become numerous enough, organized enough and independent enough to wield substantial influence in matters affecting their interests.

The development of large, well-organized, and independent provider groups has been going on for many years, probably beginning with the emergence of the civil service merit system at the turn of the century (a development usually credited to the efforts of reformers who sought to improve the quality of municipal services, to eliminate graft, and to dislodge machine leaders). But although the civil service originated in the struggle between party leaders and reformers, it launched municipal employees as an independent force. As city services expanded, the enlarging numbers of public employees began to form associations. Often these originated as benevolent societies, such as New York City's Patrolmen's Benevolent Association, which formed in the 1890s. Protected by the merit system, these associations gradually gained some influence in their own right, and they exerted that influence at both the municipal and the state level to shape legislation and to monitor personnel policies so as to protect and advance their occupational interests.

The result was that, over time, many groups of public employees managed to win substantial control over numerous matters affecting their jobs and their agencies: entrance requirements, tenure guarantees, working conditions, job prerogatives, promotion criteria, retirement benefits. Except where wages were concerned, other groups in the cities rarely became sufficiently aroused to block efforts by public employees to advance their interests. But all of this also meant that when blacks arrived in the cities, local political leaders did not control the jobs—and in cases where job prerogatives had been precisely specified by regulation, did not even control the services—that might have been given as concessions to the black newcomers.

Under the best of circumstances, of course, the task of integrating a new and uprooted rural population into local political structures would have taken time and would have been difficult. But for all of the reasons given, local government was showing little taste for the task. As a result, a large population that had been set loose from Southern feudal institutions was not absorbed into the regulating political institutions (or economic institutions, for they were also resisted there) of the city. Eventually that dislocated population became volatile, both in the streets and at the polls. And by 1960, that volatility was beginning to disrupt national political alignments, forcing the federal government to take an unprecedented role in urban politics.

By 1960 the swelling urban black population had a key role in national politics, especially presidential politics. With migration North, blacks became at least nominal participants in the electoral system, and their participation was concentrated in the states with the largest number of electoral votes. By 1960, 90 percent of all Northern blacks were living in the ten most populous states: California, New York, Pennsylvania, Ohio, Illinois, New Jersey, Michigan, Massachusetts, Indiana, and Missouri. It was the heavy Democratic vote in the big cities of these states, and especially the black Democratic vote in these cities, that gave Kennedy his slim margin. That narrow victory helped mark the importance of troubles in the cities, especially the troubles with blacks in the cities.

Urban blacks, who had been loyal Democrats for almost three decades, had begun to defect even as their numbers grew, signaling the failure of the municipal political machinery. In 1952, 79 percent voted Democratic; by 1956, the black vote slipped to 61 percent. Kennedy worked to win back some of these votes (69 percent in 1960) by taking a strong stand on civil rights in the campaign. But once in office, his administration backed off from supporting civil rights legislation, for that was sure to jeopardize Southern support. Other ways to reach and reward the urban black voter were needed.

Accordingly, administration analysts began to explore strategies to cement the allegiance of the urban black vote to the national party. What emerged, not all at once, but gropingly, was a series of federal service programs directed to the ghetto. The first appropriations were small, as with the Juvenile Delinquency and Youth Offenses Control Act of 1961, but each program enlarged upon the other, up until the Model Cities legislation of 1966. Some of the new programs—in manpower development, in education, in health—were relatively straightforward. All they did was give new funds to local agencies to be used to provide jobs or services for the poor. Thus, funds appropriated under Title 1 of the Elementary and Secondary Education Act of 1965 were earmarked for educational facilities for poor children: the medicaid program enacted in 1965 reimbursed health agencies and physicians for treating the poor; and manpower agencies were funded specifically to provide jobs or job training for the poor.

Other of the new federal programs were neither so simple nor so straightforward, and these were the ones that became the hallmark of the Great Society. The federal memoranda describing them were studded with terms like "inner city," "institutional change," and "maximum feasible participation." But if this language was often confusing, the programs themselves ought not to have been. The "inner city," after all, was a euphemism for the ghetto, and activities funded under such titles as delinquency prevention, mental health, antipoverty, or model cities turned out, in the streets of the cities, to look very much alike. What they looked like was nothing less than the old political machine.

Federal funds were used to create new storefront-style agencies in the ghettos, staffed with professionals who helped local people find jobs, obtain welfare, or deal with school officials. Neighborhood leaders were also hired, named community workers, neighborhood aides, or whatever, but in fact close kin to the old ward heelers, for they drew larger numbers of people into the new programs, spreading the federal spoils.

But federal spoils were not enough, for there were not many of them. What the new ghetto agencies had to offer was small and impermanent compared to ongoing municipal programs in education, housing, or health. If blacks were to be wrapped into the political organization of the cities, the traditional agencies of local government, which controlled the bulk of federal, state, and local appropriations, had to be reoriented. Municipal agencies had to be made to respond to blacks.

Various tactics to produce such reform were tried, at first under the guise of experiments in "institutional change." This meant that the Washington officials who administered the juvenile delinquency program (under Robert Kennedy's direction) required as a condition of granting funds that local governments submit "comprehensive plans" for their own reform (that is, for giving blacks something). But the mere existence of such paper plans did not turn out to be very compelling to the local bureaucrats who implemented programs. Therefore, as turbulence spread in the Northern ghettos, the federal officials began to try another way to promote institutional change—"maximum feasible participation of residents of the areas and members of the groups served." Under that slogan, the Great Society programs gave money to ghetto organizations, which then used the money to harass city agencies. Community workers were hired to badger housing inspectors and to pry loose welfare payments. Lawyers on the federal payroll took municipal agencies to court on behalf of ghetto clients. Later the new programs helped organize the ghetto poor to picket the welfare department or to boycott the school system.

In these various ways, then, the federal government intervened in local politics, and forced local governments to do what it had earlier failed to do. Federal dollars and federal authority were used to resuscitate the functions of the political machine, on the one hand *by spurring local service agencies to respond to the black newcomers*, and on the other *by spurring blacks to make demands upon city services.*

As it turned out, blacks made their largest tangible gains from this process through the public welfare system. Total national welfare costs rose from about $4 billion in 1960 to nearly $15 billion in 1970. Big cities that received the largest numbers of black and Spanish-speaking migrants and that were most shaken by the political reverberations of that migration also experienced the largest welfare budget rises. In New York, Los Angeles, and Baltimore, for example, the AFDC rolls quadrupled, and costs rose even faster. In some cities, moreover, welfare costs were absorbing an ever-larger share of the local budget, a bigger piece of the public pie. In New York City, for example, welfare costs absorbed about 12 percent of the city's budget in the 1950s; but by 1970 the share going to welfare had grown to about 25 percent (of a much larger budget), mainly because the proportion of the city's population on Aid to Families of Dependent Children increased from 2.6 percent in 1960 to 11.0 percent in 1970. In other words, the blacks who triggered the disturbances received their biggest payoffs from welfare, mainly because other groups were not competing within the welfare system for a share of relief benefits.

But if blacks got welfare, that was just about all they got. Less obvious than the emergence of black demands—but much more important in accounting for increasing service costs—was the reaction of organized whites to these political developments, particularly the groups who had direct material stakes in the running of the local services. If the new upthrust of black claims threatened and jostled many groups in the city, none were so alert or so shrill as those who had traditionally gotten the main benefits of the municipal services. These were the people who depended, directly or indirectly, on the city treasury for their livelihood: They worked in the municipal agencies, in agencies that were publicly funded (e.g., voluntary hospitals), in professional services that were publicly reimbursed (e.g., doctors), or in businesses that depended on city contracts (e.g., contractors and construction workers). Partly they were incited by black claims that seemed to threaten their traditional preserves. Partly they were no longer held in check by stable relationships with political leaders, for these relations had weakened or become uncertain or even turned to enmity: Indeed, in some cases, the leaders themselves had been toppled, shaken loose by the conflict and instability of the times. In effect, the groups who worked for or profited from city government had become unleashed, at the same time that newcomers were snapping at their heels.

The result was that the provider groups reacted with a rush of new demands. And these groups had considerable muscle to back up their claims. Not only were they unusually numerous and well organized, but they were allied to broader constituencies by their class and ethnic ties and by their union affiliations. Moreover, their demands for increased benefits, whether higher salaries or lower work load or greater autonomy, were always couched in terms of protecting the professional standards of the city services, a posture that helped win them broad public support. As a result, even when the organized providers backed up their demands by closing the schools, or stopping the subways, or letting the garbage pile up, many people were ready to blame the inconveniences on political officials.

Local political leaders, their ties to their constituencies undermined by population shifts and spreading discontent, were in a poor position to resist or temper these escalating demands, especially the demands of groups with the power to halt the services on which a broader constituency depended. Instead, to maintain their position, they tried to expand and elaborate the benefits —the payrolls, the contracts, the perquisites, and the services— of the municipal agencies.

Nor, as had been true in the era of the machine, was it easy to use these concessions to restore stable relationships. Where once political leaders had been able to anticipate or allay the claims of various groups, dealing with them one by one, now each concession was public, precipitating rival claims from other groups, each demand ricocheting against the other in an upward spiral. Not only did public concessions excite rivalry, but political officials lost the ability to hold groups in check in another way as well; unlike their machine predecessors, they could attach few conditions to the concessions they made. Each job offered, each wage increase conceded, each job prerogative granted, was now ensconced in civil service regulations or union contracts and, thus firmly secured, could not be withdrawn. Political leaders had lost any leverage in their dealings; each concession simply became the launching pad for higher demands. Instead of regular exchange relationships, open conflict and uncertainty became the rule. The result was a virtual run upon the city treasury by a host of organized groups in the city, each competing with the other for a larger share of municipal benefits. Benefits multiplied and budgets soared—and so did the discontent of various groups with the schools, or police, or housing, or welfare, or health. To illustrate, we need to examine the fiscal impact of mounting political claims in greater detail.

RISING DEMANDS AND THE FISCAL CRISIS

Education is a good example, for it is the single largest service run by localities, accounting for 40 percent of the outlays of state and local government in 1968, up from 30 percent in 1948. The huge expenditures involved in running the schools are also potential benefits—jobs for teachers, contracts for maintenance and construction, and educational services for children—all things to be gained by different groups in the local community. Accordingly, the educational system became a leading target of black demands, at first mainly in the form of the struggle for integrated schools. Later, worn down by local resistance to integration and guided by the Great Society programs that provided staff, meeting rooms, mimeograph machines, and lawyers to ghetto groups, the difficult demands for integration were transformed into demands for "citizen participation," which meant a share of the jobs, contracts, and status positions that the school system yields up.

Blacks made some gains. Boards of education began hiring more black teachers, and some cities instituted schemes for "community control" that ensconced local black leaders in the lower echelons of the school hierarchy. But the organized producer groups, whose salaries account for an estimated 80 percent of rising school costs, made far larger gains. Incited by black claims that seemed to challenge their traditional preserves and emboldened by a weak and conciliatory city government, the groups who depend on school budgets began rapidly to enlarge and entrench their stakes. Most evident in the scramble were teaching and supervisory personnel, who were numerous and well organized and became ever more strident—so much so that the opening of each school year is now signaled by news of teacher strikes in cities throughout the country. And threatened city officials strained to respond by expanding the salaries, jobs, programs, and privileges they had to offer. One result was that average salaries in New York City, Chicago, Los Angeles, Philadelphia, Washington, D.C., and San Francisco topped the $10,000 mark by 1969, *in most instances having doubled* in the decade. Nationally, teachers' salaries have risen about 8 percent each year since 1965. Not only did the teachers win rapid increases in salaries but, often prompted by new black demands, they exploited contract negotiations and intensive lobbying to win new guarantees of job security, increased pensions, and "improvements" in educational policy that have had the effect of increasing their own ranks—all of which drove up school budgets, especially in the big cities where blacks were concentrated. In Baltimore, where the black population has reached 47 percent, the school budget increased from $57 million in 1961 to $184 million in 1971; in New Orleans from $28.5 million to $73.9 million in 1971; in Boston, school costs rose from $35.4 million in 1961 to $95.7 million in 1971. Total national educational costs, which in 1957 amounted to $12 billion, topped $40 billion by 1968, and the U.S. Office of Education expects costs to continue to rise, by at least 37 percent by 1975. In this process, blacks may have triggered the flood of new demands on the schools, but organized whites turned out to be the main beneficiaries.

What happened in education happened in other services as well. Costs rose precipitously across the board as mayors tried to extend the benefits of the service agencies to quiet the discordant and clamoring groups in the city. One way was to expand the number of jobs, often by creating new agencies, so that there was more to go around. Hence, in New York City, the municipal payroll expanded by over 145,000 jobs in the 1960s, and the rate of increase doubled after Mayor John V. Lindsay took office in 1965. By 1971, 381,000 people were on the municipal payroll. Some 34,000 of these new employees were black and Puerto Rican "paraprofessionals," according to the city's personnel director. Others were Lindsay supporters, put on the payroll as part of his effort to build a new political organization out of the turmoil. Most of the rest were new teachers, policemen, and social workers, some hired to compensate for reduced work loads won by existing employees (teachers won reduced class sizes, patrolmen the right to work in pairs), others hired to staff an actual expansion that had taken place in some services to appease claimant groups who were demanding more welfare, safer streets, or better snow removal. As a result, total state and local governmental employment in the city rose from 8.2 percent of the total labor force in 1960 to 14 percent in 1970. A similar trend of expanded public employment took place in other big cities. In Detroit state and local employment rose from 9 percent of the labor force in 1960 to 12.2 percent in 1970; in Philadelphia from 6.9 percent to 9.8 percent; in Los Angeles from 9.8 percent to 12.0 percent; in San Francisco, from 12.2 percent in 1960 to 15.2 percent in 1970.

Another way to try to deal with the clamor was to concede larger and larger salaries and more liberal pensions to existing employees who were pressing new demands, and pressing hard, with transit, or garbage, or police strikes (or sick-outs or slowdowns) that paralyzed whole cities. In Detroit, garbage collectors allowed refuse to accumulate in the streets when the city offered them only a 6 percent wage increase, after the police won an 11 percent increase. In Cincinnati, municipal laborers and garbage collectors threatened a "massive civil disobedience campaign" when they were offered less than the $945 annual raise won by policemen and firemen. In Philadelphia garbage collectors engaged in a slowdown when a policeman was appointed to head their department. A San Francisco strike by 7,500 city workers shut down the schools and the transit system and disrupted several other services simultaneously. An unprecedented wildcat strike by New York City's policemen, already the highest paid police force in the world, would have cost the city an estimated $56,936 a year for every policeman (and $56,214 for every fireman), if demands for salaries, pensions, fringe benefits, and reduced work time had been conceded. If these demands were perhaps a bit theatrical, the pay raises for city employees in New York City did average 12 percent each year in 1967, 1968, and 1969. Meanwhile, the U.S. Bureau of Labor Statistics reported that the earnings of health professionals in the city rose by 80 percent in the decade, at least double the increase in factory wages. In other cities across the country similar groups were making similar gains; municipal salaries rose by 7–10 percent in both 1968 and 1969, or about twice as fast as the Consumer Price Index.

The pattern of crazily rising municipal budgets is the direct result of these diverse and pyramiding claims on city services, claims triggered by political instability. Accordingly, budget trends followed political trends. New York City, for example, received about 1.25 million blacks and Puerto Ricans in the years between 1950 and 1965, while about 1.5 million whites left the city. The political reverberations of these shifts weakened the Democratic party organization and resulted in the Lindsay victory on a fusion ticket in 1965. But the Lindsay government was extremely unstable, without ties to established constituents, virtually without a political organization, and extremely vulnerable to the demands of the different groups, including the ghetto groups whose support it was trying to cultivate. New York also had very strong and staunch provider groups, as everyone knows from the transit, garbage, teacher, and police strikes, each of which in turn threatened municipal calamity. The subsequent escalation of demands by blacks and Puerto Ricans on the one hand, and municipal provider groups on the other, produced the much publicized turmoil and conflict that racked the city.

To deal with these troubles, city officials made concessions, with the result that the municipal budget almost quadrupled in the last decade. And as the turmoil rose, so did city costs: an annual budget rise of 6 percent in the 1950s and 8.5 percent in the early 1960s became an annual rise of 15 percent after 1965. New York now spends half again as much per capita as other cities over a million (excluding educational costs), twice as much per capita as cities between 500 thousand and a million, and three times as much as the other 288 cities.

A few cities where the existing political organization was firmly entrenched and machine-style politics still strong were spared. Chicago is the notable example, and Chicago's political organization shows in lower welfare costs, in per pupil expenditures that are half that of New York City, in garbage collection costs of $22 a ton compared to $49 in New York City. Mayor Daley never lost his grip. With the white wards firmly in tow, he made modest concessions to blacks earlier and without fear of setting off a chain reaction of demands by other groups. And so he never gave as much, either to blacks or to organized whites. But most other large cities show a pattern of escalating discontent and escalating service budgets more like New York City than Chicago. By 1970, the total costs of local government had risen about 350 percent over 1950.

The cities are unable to raise revenues commensurate with these expenditures; and they are unable to resist the claims that underlie rising expenditures. And that is what the fiscal crisis is all about. Cities exist only by state decree, and depend entirely on the state governments for their taxing powers. Concretely this has meant that the states have taken for themselves the preferred taxes leaving the localities to depend primarily on the property tax (which accounts for 70 percent of revenues raised by local governments), supplemented by a local sales tax in many places, user charges (e.g., sewer and water fees), and, in some places, a local income tax. The big cities have had little choice but to drive up these local taxes to which they are limited, but at serious costs. New York City, for example, taxes property at rates twice the national average, yielding a property tax roll three times as large as any other city. New York City also has an income tax, which is rising rapidly. Newark, plagued by racial conflict, ranks second in the nation in its rate of property tax.

The exploitation of any of these taxes is fraught with dilemmas for localities. By raising either property or sale taxes excessively, they risk driving out the business and industry on which their tax rolls eventually depend, and risk also the political ire of their constituents. For instance, it was estimated that a 1 percent increase in the New York City sales tax had the effect of driving 6 percent of all clothing and household furnishing sales out beyond the city line, along with thousands of jobs. A New York property tax rate of 4 percent of true value on new improvements is thought by many to have acted as a brake on most new construction, excepting the very high yielding office buildings and luxury apartments. Boston's 6 percent of true value property tax brought private construction to a halt until the law was changed so that new improvements were taxed only half as heavily as existing buildings. Increases in either sales or property tax rates thus entail the serious danger of diminishing revenues by eroding the tax base. To make matters worse, with the beginning of recession in 1969, revenues from sales and income taxes began to fall off, while the interest the cities had to pay for borrowing rose, at a time that local governments were going more and more into hock.

FISCAL CONSTRAINTS AND POLITICAL TURMOIL

In the face of fiscal constraints, demands on city halls do not simply stop. Indeed, a number of frustrated claimants seem ready for rebellion. When pension concessions to some employees in New York City were thwarted by the state legislature, the enraged municipal unions closed the bridges to the city and allowed untreated sewage to flow into the city's waterways, while the president of Local 237 intoned that "Governor Rockefeller needs to be reminded that the teamsters are made of sterner stuff than the people of Czechoslovakia and Austria who caved in so easily to Hitler three decades ago." If most groups were less dramatic in pressing their demands, it is probably because they were more quickly conciliated than these workers, many of whom were black and Puerto Rican. The political instability, which escalating demands both signify and exacerbate, rocked one city government after another.

The mayors speak of the twin troubles of scarce revenues and racial confrontation. And it is no accident that the troubles occur together and are most severe in the biggest cities. It was the biggest cities that experienced the most serious disturbance of traditional political relations as a result of the influx of blacks and the outflux of many whites. In this context, demands by black newcomers triggered a rush of new demands by whites, especially the large and well-organized provider groups that flourished in the big cities. The weakened and vulnerable mayors responded; they gave more and more of the jobs, salaries, contracts, and services that had always worked to win and hold the allegiance of diverse groups. The eventual inability of the cities to garner the vastly increased revenues needed to fuel this process helped bring the urban political process to a point of crisis. The fiscal crisis is indeed real—not because of mounting "needs" for services, but because of mounting demands for the benefits associated with the municipal bureaucracies. To block the responses of the bureaucracies to these demands for lack of revenues is to block a process of political accommodation in the largest population centers of the nation. The defection of the mayors was another sign of how deep the disturbances were, not in health agencies or welfare agencies, but in the urban political structure.

Federalism as a Constraining Influence

If mayors cannot resist the demands of contending groups in the cities, there are signs that the state and federal governments can, and will. The fiscal interrelations that undergird the federal system and leave the cities dependent on state and federal grants for an increasing portion of their funds are also a mechanism by which state and federal politics come to intervene in and control city politics. This is happening most clearly and directly through changes in state expenditures for the cities.

With their own taxing powers constricted from the outset, the mayors had little recourse but to turn to the states for enlarged grants-in-aid, trying to pass upward the political pressures they felt, usually summoning the press and the urban pressure groups for help. Since governors and legislators were not entirely immune to pressures from the city constituencies, the urban states increased their aid to the big cities. Metropolises like New York City and Los Angeles now get roughly a quarter of their revenues from the state.

Accordingly, state budgets also escalated, and state taxes rose. All in all, at least twenty-one states imposed new taxes or increased old taxes in 1968, and thirty-seven states in 1969, usually as a result of protracted struggle. North Carolina enacted the largest program of new or increased taxes in its history; Illinois and Maine introduced an income tax, bringing to thirty-eight the number of states imposing some form of income tax; South Carolina passed its first major tax increase in a decade. Even Ohio moved to change its tradition of low tax and low service policies that had forced thirteen school districts in the state to close. Overall, state and local taxes rose from 5 percent of the Gross National Product in 1946 to more than 8 percent of the GNP in 1969. Americans paid an average of $380 in state and local taxes in the fiscal year 1969, $42 more per person than the previous year, and more than double the fiscal year 1967. The rate tended to be highest in urban states: In New York the per person tax burden was $576; in California, $540; in Massachusetts, $453. The low was in Arkansas, with a tax rate of $221.

But raising taxes in Albany or Sacramento to pay for politics in New York City or Los Angeles is no simple matter, for the state capitals are not nearly as vulnerable as city halls to urban pressure groups, but are very vulnerable indeed to the suburbs and small towns that are antagonized by both higher taxes and city troubles. Besides, the mass of urban voters also resent taxes, especially when taxes are used to pay off the organized interests in the service systems, without yielding visibly better services. Accordingly, even while taxes are raised, state grants to the cities are cut anyway. Thus, the New York State legislature reduced grant-in-aid formulas in welfare and medicaid (programs that go mainly to the central cities and mainly to blacks in those cities) in 1969 and again in 1971 (1970 was an election year and so the governor proposed increased aid to the cities without tax increases). Each time, the cuts were effected in all-night marathon sessions of the legislature, replete with dramatic denouncements by Democratic legislators from the cities and cries of betrayal from the mayors. Despite the cuts, anticipated state spending still rose by $878 million in 1969, the highest for any single year excepting the previous fiscal year in which the rise had been $890 million. By 1970 when the proposed budget had reached $8.45 billion, requiring $1.1 billion in new taxes, the outcry was so terrific that the governor reversed his proposals and led the legislature in a budget-slashing session, with welfare and medicaid programs the main targets.

When Governor Ronald Reagan, a self-proclaimed fiscal conservative, nevertheless submitted a record-breaking $6.37 billion budget for the 1969–1970 fiscal year, he met a storm of political protest that threatened a legislative impasse, leaving California without a budget. The next year Reagan proposed to solve the state's "fiscal crisis" by cutting welfare and medicaid expenditures by $800 million; even so, he submitted another record budget of $6.7 billion. When the long legislative battle that ensued was over, the governor signed an unbalanced budget of $7.3 billion, with substantial cuts in welfare and medicaid nevertheless.

Other state governments are locked in similar fiscal and political battles. Michigan began the 1972 fiscal year without authorization to spend money after the legislature had been virtually paralyzed by a six-month struggle over the $2 billion budget, which the governor had proposed to finance with a 38 percent increase in the state income tax. Wisconsin cut welfare and urban aid expenditures over Governor Ody J. Fish's protest and, having enacted a new and broadened sales tax, precipitated a march on the capital by Milwaukee poor. Not long afterward, Governor Fish resigned, imperiling the Wisconsin Republican party. In Rhode Island, Democratic Governor Frank E. Licht promised no new taxes in his reelection campaign in 1970 and two months later recommended an income tax, amidst loud voter protest. When Texas, having passed the largest tax bill in its history in 1969, faced a deficit of $400 million in 1971. Governor Preston E. Smith vetoed the entire second year of a two-year budget, which totaled $7.1 billion.

In brief, pressures from the big cities were channeled upward to the state capitals, with some response. At least in the big urbanized states, governors and legislatures moved toward bailing out the cities, with the result that state expenditures and state taxes skyrocketed. But the reaction is setting in; the taxpayers' revolt is being felt in state legislatures across the country. And as raucous legislative battles continue, a trend is emerging: The states are turning out to be a restraining influence on city politics, and especially on ghetto politics.

While in the main, grants-in-aid were not actually reduced, they were not increased enough to cover rising city costs either, and the toll is being taken. Some municipalities began to cut payroll and services. By 1971, vacancies were going unfilled in New York City, Baltimore, Denver, and Kansas City. San Diego and Cleveland reduced rubbish collection; Dallas cut capital improvements; Kansas City let its elm trees die. Detroit started closing park toilets. And some city employees were actually being dismissed in Los Angeles, Cleveland, Detroit, Kansas City, Cincinnati, Indianapolis, Pittsburgh, and New York City. "This is the first time since the

Depression that I have participated in this kind of cutback of education," said Cincinnati's Superintendent of Schools. "You run as far as you can, but when you run out of gas you've got to stop," said Baltimore's Mayor Thomas J. D'Alesandro.

But the biggest cuts imposed by the states were in the programs from which blacks had gained the most as a result of their emergence as a force in the cities. Special state appropriations for health and education in ghetto districts were being cut; nine states cut back their medicaid programs; and most important, at least nineteen states reduced welfare benefits by mid-1971, according to a *New York Times* survey. Moreover, new state measures to root out "welfare fraud," or to reinstitute residence restrictions, or to force recipients into work programs threatened far more drastic erosion of black gains in the near future.

There are signs that the federal government has also become a restraining influence on city politics. In the early 1960s, the national Democratic administration had used its grants to the cities to intervene in city politics, encouraging ghetto groups to demand more from city halls and forcing recalcitrant mayors to be more responsive to the enlarging and volatile ghettos, whose allegiance had become critical to the national Democratic party. But a Republican administration was not nearly so oriented to the big cities, least of all to the ghettos of the big cities. Accordingly, the directions of the Great Society programs that the Nixon administration had inherited were shifted; bit by bit the new federal poverty agencies were scattered among the old-line federal bureaucracies, and the local agencies that had been set up in the ghettos were given to understand that confrontation tactics had to be halted. By now the Great Society looks much like traditional grant-in-aid programs; the federal fuel for ghetto agitation has been cut off. And new administration proposals for revenue sharing would give state and local governments firm control of the use of federal grants, unhampered by the "maximum feasible participation" provisions that helped to stir ghetto demands in the 1960s.

There are other signs as well. The wage freeze stopped, at least temporarily, the escalation of municipal salaries, and this despite the outcry of teachers across the country. Finally, and perhaps most portentous for blacks, the administration's proposal for "welfare reform" would give the federal government a much larger role in welfare policy, lifting the struggle for who gets what outside of the arena of city politics where blacks had developed some power and had gotten some welfare.

Nor is it likely, were the Democrats to regain the presidency and thus regain the initiative in federal legislation, that the pattern of federal restraint would be entirely reversed. The conditions that made the ghettos a political force for a brief space of time seem to have changed. For one thing, there is not much action, either in the streets or in the voting booths. The protests and marches and riots have subsided, at least partly because the most aggressive people in the black population were absorbed; it was they who got the jobs and honorary positions yielded to blacks during the turmoil. These concessions, together with the Great Society programs that helped produce them, seem to have done their work, not only in restoring a degree of order to the streets, but in restoring ghetto voters to Democratic columns.

In any case, it was not ghetto insurgency of itself that gave blacks some political force in the 1960s. Rather it was that the insurgents were concentrated in the big cities, and the big cities played a very large role in Democratic politics. That also is changing; the cities are losing ground to the suburbs, even in Democratic calculations, and trouble in the cities is not likely to carry the same weight with Democratic presidents that it once did.

To be sure, a Democratic administration might be readier than a Republican one to refuel local services, to fund a grand new cornucopia of social programs. The pressures are mounting, and they come from several sources. One is the cities themselves, for to say that the cities are no longer as important as they once were is not to say Democratic leaders will want the cities to go under. Moreover, the inflated costs of the city are spreading to the suburbs and beyond, and these communities are also pressing for federal aid. Finally there is the force of the organized producers themselves, who have become very significant indeed in national politics; the education lobby and the health lobby already wield substantial influence in Washington, and they are growing rapidly. But while these pressures suggest that new federal funds will be forthcoming, the rise of the suburbs and the parallel rise of the professional lobbies indicate that it is these groups who are likely to be the main beneficiaries.

The future expansion of the federal role in local services has another, perhaps more profound, significance. It means that the decline of the local political unit in the American political structure, already far advanced, will continue. No matter how much talk we may hear about a "new American revolution," through which the federal government will return revenues and power to the people, enlarged federal grants mean enlarged federal power, for grants are a means of influencing local political developments, not only by benefiting some groups and not others, but through federally imposed conditions that come with the new monies. These conditions, by curbing the discretion of local political leaders, also erode the power of local pressure groups. As localities lose their political autonomy, the forces that remain viable will be those capable of exerting national political influence. Some may view this change as an advance, for in the past local communities have been notoriously oligarchical. But for blacks it is not an advance; it is in the local politics of the big cities that they have gained what influence they have.

The general truths to be drawn from this tale of the cities seem clear enough and familiar enough, for what happened in the 1960s has happened before in history. The lower classes made the trouble, and other groups made the gains. In the United States in the 1960s, it was urban blacks who made the trouble, and it was the organized producer groups in the cities who made the largest gains. Those of the working and middle classes who were not among the organized producers got little enough themselves, and they were made to pay with their tax monies for gains granted to others. Their resentments grew. Now, to appease them, the small gains that blacks did make in the course of the disturbances are being whittled away.

There is, I think, an even more important truth, though one perhaps not so quickly recognized. These were the events of a political struggle, of groups pitted against each other and against officialdom. But every stage of that struggle was shaped and limited by the structures in which these groups were enmeshed. A local service apparatus, which at the outset benefited some and not others, set the stage for group struggle. Service structures that offered only certain kinds of benefits determined the agenda of group struggle. And a fiscal structure that limited the contest mainly to benefits paid for by state and local taxes largely succeeded in keeping the struggle confined within the lower and middle strata of American society. School teachers turned against the ghetto, taxpayers against both, but no one turned against the concentrations of individual and corporate wealth in America. Local government, in short, is important, less for the issues it decides, than for the issues it keeps submerged. Of the issues submerged by the events of the urban crisis, not the least is the more equitable distribution of wealth in America.

URBAN POLITICAL MOVEMENTS

NORMAN I. FAINSTEIN AND SUSAN S. FAINSTEIN

Urban political movements are vehicles by which minority groups have attempted to address their social problems through collective political action. Movements have sought to act as agents of political socialization, as interest articulators, and as means of creating and utilizing power. Each of these functions is also performed by routine or normal institutions in a liberal-democratic society—by political parties, electoral competition, and legislative bodies. The existence of urban movements and the reasons given by members for participation, however, attest to the inadequacy of routine political institutions for serving the needs of urban minority groups. Urban movements have constituted an attempt by minority group activists to perform functions which other institutional forms have served inadequately.

The rise of urban movements should not be interpreted as necessary or inevitable. While all lasting structural forms are maintained in part because they are functional for at least some set of actors, many needs are unfulfilled or performed badly by available social and political structures. The political needs of urban minority groups were not well served prior to the rise of movements in the 1960s. The appearance of movements was not only a result of minority group perception that new forms had to be created; it also resulted from forces outside the control of movement leaders. Thus, the interpretation that movements fulfill functions not being served by other institutions should be freed from any teleological implications.

In addition, the identification of the functions which movement structures perform for minority groups does not tell us how well movements actually do fulfill these functions. Urban movements

From Norman I. Fainstein and Susan S. Fainstein, *Urban Political Movements: The Search for Power by Minority Groups in American Cities* (Englewood Cliffs, N.J.: Prentice-Hall, 1974), pp. 215–18, 227–31, 233–36. © 1974 by Prentice-Hall, Inc. Reprinted by permission.

are limited in their effectiveness because of their own character-istics and because of the larger political situation within which they must operate. Indeed, under present circumstances no politi-cal structures are likely to serve the needs of urban minorities very well since these collectivities are triply plagued by low income and class standing, by being racially outcast, and not least, by consti-tuting an electoral minority in a democratic system.

A basic institutional vehicle for linking the activities of govern-ment with the needs, demands, and interests of particular collec-tivities is, according to modern democratic theory, the political party. The party is the instrument which rationalizes the process of elections in large societies by recruiting candidates, defining policy positions, and orchestrating the activities of elected repre-sentatives both within the legislature and between it and the executive. The importance of the party is especially great for col-lectivities whose members are relatively powerless as individuals, since the party is the institutionalized means for converting num-bers into power. The mere existence of parties does not, however, mean that they in fact perform the functions which, in theory, they might. *The failure of the American political parties and the choices they make available at times of election to reflect the needs of urban minority groups is one of the functional voids which urban movements have sought to occupy.*

Since urban minority groups are, as the name implies, national minorities, we might expect their needs to be advanced by a national party in which they were united with a larger group on the basis of class interest. This party would attempt to minimize racial and ethnic differences, reconcile conflicting interests among its various constituencies, and direct national governmental policy in an egalitarian and welfare-state direction. Of course, this is an idealization of how the party would function, especially in the face of considerable ethnic and racial divisions within the lower strata. But we should not forget that the absence of an effective socialist party in the American experience has, itself, eliminated an institu-tional source of propaganda and leadership which might have changed the major polarities in the direction of class division. [However,] the present American party system includes no socialist alternative of more than trivial strength:

> Nothing, indeed, is clearer than that the two major American parties are and always have been overwhelmingly middle-class in organization, values, and goals. From a European point of view, they can hardly fail to appear exquisitely old-fashioned, as nineteenth-century anachronisms.[1]

America had the first developed democratic party system in the world. By about 1840 the national parties had assumed their current form. But the American parties did not move in the direction of the mass-membership, programmatic parties which evolved in Europe toward the end of the nineteenth century. This, in effect, is equivalent to saying that a powerful socialist party never emerged here, for the left-wing European parties had a considerable influence in making center and right-wing parties more popularly rooted and programmatic. The course of historical evolution of the American parties has led a number of analysts to speak of their "arrested development" and their failure to function as a regularized mechanism of linkage between ordinary citizens and their government. In particular, the parties have not offered policy alternatives addressing the problems which have arisen as a result of the major social trends of this century—industrialization, urbanization, the emergence of an estranged nonwhite minority, and the decline in significance of legislative bodies in the face of growing bureaucracies, both public and private. Lowi makes the case—perhaps a bit too strongly—when he concludes:

> It is as though parties, having no institutional involvement with public policy, were under no pressure to alter the system in ways which each new public problem might require. In fact, the existing system can be presumed to be a vested interest of party leaders.[2]

The limited ability of the major American parties to represent the interests of the lower classes in the national government is replicated at the local level. Here it might be more appropriate to speak of retrogression and not merely arrested development. The political machine did provide linkages between the urban masses and city hall, even though machine structures were incapable of advancing programs or of acting in the collective interest of the people whose votes were a source of machine power. The institutional reforms of the first decades of the century destroyed the party infrastructure which integrated city neighborhoods into the decisionmaking process. The machines which functioned so as to deter the mobilization of the lower classes were largely replaced by Progressive institutions which altogether proscribed any mass input into local government. The social composition of urban political elites shifted in favor of the educated and professional classes. This was the case in city councils, school boards and the management of various service bureaucracies. The dual concomitants of Progressive reform were thus the insulation of the governmental center from the neighborhoods and the hegemony over the center by the middle class. As Samuel Hays puts it, "One observes a gradual exclusion of local community leaders from the decisionmaking process which, in turn, involved a gradual exclusion of direct representatives of lower socio-economic groups."[3] The rise of Progressive institutions meant that "a functional system of representation in a cosmopolitan upper-middle-class context had replaced a geographical system of representation which had involved leaders from all segments of the . . . socio-economic structure."[4]

In many cities Progressive reform eliminated the electoral functions of the political parties by instituting nonpartisan elections. But even where elections continued to be partisan, the parties did not integrate the new urban masses into the local political system. Urban minority groups in particular tend to be underrepresented both as individuals in the party leadership and as collectivities in party programs.[5] Those who benefit most directly from the party organizations are the cadres of those organizations and other already powerful groups.

The failure of urban minorities to find their interests represented in government is aggravated by the atrophy of the legislative branch of government in relation to the executive. The rise of great, centralized bureaucracies accountable in only remote ways to elected representatives means that party and electoral institutions cannot control the emergent centers of power. There is an absence of representative institutional forms which operate directly on the behavior of urban bureaucracies. Bureaucratic structures have tended to be controlled internally rather than by the mayor's office or city council. What we see in American cities is not only a partisan politics which is not functional for urban minorities but one which is increasingly irrelevant to the actual sources of power. The universalistic bureaucracies which the Progressives hoped would put an end to undemocratic, personalistic politics have themselves moved beyond the control of normal political structures. *Representation of the interests of bureaucratic clients directly within urban agencies (not just indirectly through influence on elected officials) constitutes a second function which has not been adequately performed for urban minority groups and which movements have attempted to serve.*

Urban political movements, however, constitute a remedy with significant drawbacks. These hinge upon the use of a conflict strategy and the choice of public service bureaucracies as primary targets. In the first place, because bureaucratic reform depends upon elite innovation, too much pressure from below may be counterproductive—it discredits would-be professional reformers instead of providing an external constituency for internal reform; its outcome is frequently immobilization rather than innovation. In the second place, attacks against the agencies which service the ghetto and their politicization jeopardize the routine provision of public services. Once the professional hegemony over the granting of public services is undermined, other (white) collectivities may begin to question the allocation of benefits, and relative group power instead of group needs may become the sole criterion for determining who gets what. In such a situation, minority groups may be at a serious disadvantage. Finally, by embroiling service bureaucracies in conflict and undermining their legitimacy, movements may also be destroying the resources available to the agencies most concerned with the condition of the ghetto. Minority groups share a common interest with welfare bureaucracies in an expansion of public revenues allocated to social welfare. Bureaucracies under attack from below cease to be effective advocates in the state legislature and federal government. Since resources for the poor must come from the public fisc, a strategy of antagonizing public officials can be extremely costly.

Thus, to conclude that urban political movements do, in fact, articulate the interests of their constituents requires that we accept their costs as unavoidable. We do so primarily because we see no alternative structural form which can function more effectively in the interest of urban minority groups, given the larger context of American politics. Within this larger context, however, we must now ask the question of whether the interests articulated by urban political movements can be aggregated so as to create a force for change beyond the most local level.

URBAN MOVEMENTS AND NATIONAL INTERESTS

The structure of urban movements protects them from succumbing to the tendencies toward rigidity and oligarchy that afflict large, stable organizations.[5] But the virtues of responsiveness and representativeness are mainly produced by the small size and instability which constitute the chief weakness of these movements in their efforts to achieve external goals. Low organizational capacity, the risks of participation, orientation toward narrow issues, and the decreasing incentives to individual activity caused by increasing group size[6] all limit the magnitude of these bodies. Yet even movements which have succeeded in sparking mass revolutions have consisted mainly of collections of small disconnected groups. Oberschall observes that:

> In revolutionary situations there is a tremendous outpouring of words, pamphlets, posters, and meetings, but communication and influence take place in small groups of neighbors, coworkers, associates, and so on. . . . Contemporary research has discovered the great importance of small groups and local influentials in routine mass communication processes. Their importance is perhaps even greater in the period of mobilization for collective behavior episodes.[7]

Our case studies, Eisinger's findings on the level of participation in protest activities,[8] and impressions gathered from newspaper accounts and discussions with activists all suggest that the size of contemporary urban movements, except in rare instances of peak mobilization, does not exceed a few hundred, and that the stable core of activists seldom goes beyond fifty. Groups of this size cannot, except in the most unusual circumstances, hope to have more than a highly specific and localized impact.

Our analysis of urban movements leads us to hypothesize that they will not become much larger. In major cities with a high level of radical consciousness there will be more groups rather than larger ones. Once groups go beyond the number that can participate directly in an open meeting, they require an elaborate infrastructure to maintain communications, allocate tasks, and dispense individual rewards. The level of financial support and organizational ability required for operations of this scope is considerable, and their source is at the moment nowhere apparent. Aggregation of the interests embodied in the variety of small-scale movements is not the result of links which they have created with each other. Most of them work in isolation, rooted in their neighborhoods and engaging individuals with few outside ties. To the extent that all the various small movements for community control and improved social services add up to a single force for institutional change, their consolidation rests in the perception of outsiders, who see the common goals of a multitude of efforts despite their origins in a variety of sources.

There are two conceivable modes through which the demands of minority groups might be concerted at citywide or national levels. The first is through a mass movement of the urban poor, and the second is through the development of a national coalition which would unite the interests of minority groups with those of other collectivities. The possibility of the former is impeded by the organizational obstacles we have described, but might nonetheless arise under the leadership of a charismatic individual. Marcus Garvey and Martin Luther King managed to inspire thousands of people to activity, although not long-term participation. Whether another such person may appear and maintain mobilization long enough to gain major concessions from the national government, or have sufficient organizational abilities to develop a coherent, stable framework for ongoing participation, is an unanswerable question at this time.

The second possibility, that of a national coalition, is less dependent on fortuitous events and thus more open to systematic analysis. The forging of such a coalition depends only partly on the minority groups that would participate in it. It would be largely the result of the attitudes and strategies of potential partners, even though these would in some measure be determined by the stance of minorities toward them. Efforts to achieve working-class unity across racial divisions have so far borne little fruit. The "natural" alliance of the poor with the working class is severely limited by racial antagonism. This hostility is created partly by prejudice. It is also rooted in the manipulation of the lower strata to exploit divisions among them by those who profit from such divisions; and in the real threat which, given the current distribution of resources and capitalist structure, the aggressiveness of minority groups presents to those who occupy the rungs just above them on the social ladder. While the racial prejudice of the working class has been mitigated in this century in association with rising levels of education, tensions over jobs and "turf" continue to be exacerbated by thrusts toward minority job quotas, integrated housing, and school desegregation. The ideology of movement leaders further militates against coalition by emphasizing the racial rather than class basis of solidarity among urban minority groups. Cross burning and other overt acts of racial hostility have diminished, yet the essential vision of minorities as competitors rather than allies has not been abandoned by the white working class.

Divisions among the lower strata could be overcome through the acceptance of a unifying, class-based ideology. Such an ideology, however, has never taken firm root in the United States, and short of economic collapse there is little reason to predict it now. In our discussion of the political machine we asserted that it confined the development of a socialist party through providing an alternate institution representing lower-class interests in a manner stifling to the growth of class bonds. The interests of workers are now aggregated largely through the trade unions, which function similarly to frame working-class demands in narrow terms. We see, for example, little pressure from unions for a national health care plan or for income redistribution. Instead, they prefer to bargain for health care and wage increments within industry contracts, thus delivering benefits to their own workers and no one else. Except for the protection of trade union rights, organized labor pursues a political program only halfheartedly and rarely frames its desires in ideological language. Union officials see little advantage to themselves in a mobilized working class, and besides leaders of the few unions such as the United Farmworkers which represent primarily minority workers and have a leadership drawn from the ranks, they do little to elicit mass enthusiasm for general causes. The refusal of union elites to devote themselves to raising working-class consciousness and propounding broad political demands means that the only significant social structure which could provide an institutionalized basis for class action abstains from doing so. As in the case of the machine, the role of unions can be explained by general factors in American social development. But similarly the fact of union behavior restricts future possibilities and reinforces the tradition of nonideological politics.

The absence of a labor-based mass party has meant that urban minorities have had few alternatives at the local level besides movement-type organizations through which to press their demands. Urban political movements in their redistributive goals (although less so in their antibureaucratic aims) resemble socialist parties. The expression of these goals in structures outside the realm of routine politics results from the absence of more suitable structures of interest aggregation. At the national level urban minorities have not been able to develop alternative political structures. They form a component of the Democratic Party, but the substantial role played by organized labor in that body and the continued importance of Southern Democrats in Congress inhibit that party's capacity to express the interests of nonwhites.

The forces dividing minority groups from whites with whom they share a similar class situation have caused them to find their chief national allies among Progressive idealists drawn from the upper middle class. This alliance began during the New Deal, but its implications did not become fully apparent until the 1960s when foundation and federally sponsored efforts directed specifically at the urban poor commenced. Then the incompatibility of interests between upper class reformers and the deprived lower class began to reveal itself within both the Democratic Party and the government.

The attempt by the modern Progressives to build a constituency among urban minorities backfired. Reform of the Democratic Party, led by the McGovern forces, produced in 1972 a far larger representation of urban blacks in the National Convention than ever before. But the alliance between inner-city blacks and suburban liberals was uneasy. Blacks were distrustful of the personal style of the McGovern people and felt that the issues of the Vietnamese War, the environment, and women's rights, which were the primary concerns of the suburbanites, were of secondary importance to them. The subsequent election showed that while those blacks who voted, voted overwhelmingly Democratic, most blacks found the two candidates insufficiently attractive to vote at all.[9] The triumph of the Democratic left wing in 1972 caused a considerable desertion of the white working class from its traditional political allegiance; the Nixon landslide victory indicated that this was a price the Democrats could not afford to pay.

Urban movements were only one, and not the most important, of many factors contributing to the Republican victories of 1968 and 1972. The War in Vietnam and the riots of the mid-sixties both weighed more heavily in creating distrust of the Democratic regime. Minority groups seeking to use the movement structure to force concessions to themselves were the victims of historical forces which they did not control. But unquestionably black disquiet in the 1960s, as expressed in civil disorders and street crime, demands for school and neighborhood integration, conflicts over control of new federal programs and old urban bureaucracies, and refusal to accept the legitimacy of established authority became lumped together in general public attitudes. Opposition politicians exploited this sentiment, while oldtime liberal supporters began to back away from the tide they had at least in part created.

By linking themselves with minority groups, Democratic liberals became associated in the minds of many with street crime and ghetto riots. Even though the radicalism associated with some of the federal programs would probably have ultimately been absorbed through a combination of institutional response and individual co-optation, it provoked counter-mobilization and feelings that minority groups were being given too much. The popular reaction to urban disorder was not to buy off the lower classes but to repress them. Whatever truth there might or might not be in the connection frequently made between ghetto lawlessness and the rising expectations stimulated by antipoverty programs, many people became determined to prevent future encouragement of such expectations. President Nixon's dismantling of the Office of Economic Opportunity, the community mental health centers, and other programs involving participation of the poor meant the end of institutions which had provided at least an arena for mobilization if not a direct incentive to it. The 1969 revision of the Internal Revenue Code, which effectively stopped foundations from financing community groups, further suppressed the liberal-minority alliance by jeopardizing the tax-free status of foundations and threatening their officials with criminal penalties if funds were determined to be supporting political action. As assertion of the needs of minority groups became increasingly risky for politicians and foundations, the lack of shared material interests between minorities and their upper class allies meant that there was little basis beyond moral appeal for continued ties.

Urban political movements developed in response to a perception that only pressure tactics could force changes in ongoing institutional structures. These movements have frequently resorted to direct action, and the threat of violence has been implicit in their activities. A sustained campaign of actual violence might have forced greater responsiveness—although greater repression seems the more likely outcome. The left-wing argument, however, that the effort to achieve local organization meant a diversion of militant leaders from their best strategy misses the point that the effective employment of violence requires organization and the delineation of goals, both to attract supporters and coerce the opposition. The development of guerrilla organization confronts many of the same problems as does that of nonviolent movements; and to the degree that the risks of violent action are greater, the possibility of attracting participants other than to sporadic outbursts of rage is less.

The conclusion that the mobilization of urban minority groups into nonviolent movements provoked reaction and the loss of outside support does not imply that minorities would have been better off quiescent, or that they would have profited more from concentrating exclusively on the electoral process. The winning of political office by candidates drawn from minority groups will not change the overall position of those groups unless they also can mount enough pressure to change the policy alternatives presented in elections. The experience of the immigrant lower class with the machine demonstrates that descriptive representation does not assure the substantive representation of broad constituency interests.

We have explained the nature of contemporary urban movements in terms of the urban dialectic: The structure of the political machine partly created and partly reinforced a system of representation whereby the urban poor did not have their interests articulated on a class basis. The antithesis to the machine—Progression reform—both destroyed the political infrastructure of most cities and contributed to the growth of the large impersonal bureaucracies which the minority poor presently find unresponsive to their needs. Urban political movements arose in opposition to Progressive reform and have tried to recreate a political structure through which the lower classes can press their demands. These movements resemble the machine in their localism and some of their procedural aims, but they differ from the machine in their substantive goals. They have adopted from Progressivism an emphasis on widespread community participation in politics and on the public service role of government. Many of the public interest norms of Progressivism have been retained even while their application has been challenged. Urban political movements are an attempt to move outside the machine-progressivism dichotomy that has dominated urban politics in this century so as to obtain a form of government and set of social policies more representative, in all the senses described [here], of urban minority groups.

These movements cannot be called a success. Many of them have not been able to withstand internal disaffection or diversion from their stated goals. Externally they have largely not managed to exploit local issues for broader purposes. The political and numerical weakness of urban minorities has caused them to concentrate their demands on local targets. Here the need to appeal to followers on the basis of narrowly defined issues has resulted in movements oriented toward highly specific goals. Within the limits of this arena, however, they have made some gains. Most important, they have assisted in forcing local governmental institutions to consider constituencies which they had previously ignored, and this consideration has resulted in an improvement in public services in some instances and, at the least, the halting of such policies as indiscriminate urban renewal. At the national level the advances are more doubtful. While urban minorities have achieved greater representation within the Democratic Party, they have lost ground in the government itself. The Republican Administration in Washington constitutes a swing of the pendulum away from concern with the deprived, both ideologically and in the actual substance of policy. It has also produced a decline in the strength of urban political movements, as national policies have been implemented on the local level. The replacement of federal programs categorically directed at the poor by revenue sharing terminates policies that stimulated the growth of political agitation by minorities.

We do not, however, consider urban political movements to be purely a historical phenomenon. The situational factors and consciousness which produced them in the 1960s have not disappeared, and we expect their resurgence in the presence of a more sympathetic national government. A Democratic victory would not result in the attainment of the demands of minority groups. Democrats have been burned by their association with urban radicals, and the increased power of minorities within the party will be balanced by wariness among white professional politicians. But a different atmosphere in Washington would provide a new incentive to radical movements among the poor. While urban movements have constituted a possible synthesis of earlier political forms, they are not a final synthesis, and in white counter-mobilization their own antithesis has appeared. Just as the earlier forms of the machine and Progressivism have lingered on, we may expect that urban movements and also white antagonism to them will continue as important factors contributing to an enduring state of tension in American cities.

NOTES

1. Walter Dean Burnham, "Party Systems and the Political Process," in *The American Party Systems*, eds. William Nisbet Chambers and Walter Dean Burnham (New York: Oxford University Press, 1967), pp. 280–81.
2. Theodore J. Lowi, "Party, Policy, and Constitution in America," in *The American Party Systems*, eds. Chambers and Burnham, p. 275. Internal reference is to Samuel P. Huntington, "Political Modernization: America versus Europe," Paper presented at the Annual Meeting of the American Political Science Association, Washington, D.C., 1965.
3. Samuel P. Hays, "Political Parties and the Community-Society Continuum," in *The American Party Systems*, eds. Chambers and Burnham, p. 180. Also see Hays' article, "The Politics of Reform in Municipal Government in the Progressive Era," *Pacific Northwest Quarterly*, LV, (1964), 157–69.
4. Hays, "Political Parties," p. 181.
5. S. M. Lipset, when studying the Typographical Union, found that the iron law of oligarchy prevailed most strongly in the largest (national) unit. He concluded: "The monopoly which an incumbent administration has over

the channels of intraunion communication is lessened considerably in most union locals. There, a small group of individuals with relatively few resources may reach entire memberships with their propaganda." S. M. Lipset, Martin A. Trow, and James S. Coleman, *Union Democracy* (New York: Doubleday, 1956), p. 397.

6. Mancur Olson's analysis shows that it becomes less rational for individuals to participate in organizations producing public goods when they are large than when they are small. Mancur Olson, *The Logic of Collective Action*, rev. ed., (New York: Schocken, 1971), chap. 2.

7. Anthony Oberschall, *Social Conflict and Social Movements* (Englewood Cliffs, N.J.: Prentice-Hall, 1973), p. 174. Brinton makes a similar comment concerning the role of small groups before the French and American Revolutions. Crane Brinton, *The Anatomy of Revolution* (New York: Random House, 1958), pp. 87–89.

8. Eisinger, "The Conditions of Protest Behavior in American Cities," *American Political Science Review*, LXVII (March, 1973), p. 17.

9. According to a Joint Center for Political Studies (JCPS) survey of predominantly black inner-city precincts and wards in 24 major cities, 87 percent of the voters in those areas voted for McGovern. JCPS, however, calculated that nationwide only 41 percent of blacks of voting age voted in the 1972 presidential election. *Focus*, publication of JCPS, Washington, D.C., I, December, 1972, 7–8.